Backpacking
Beyond
Boundaries

Backpacking Beyond Boundaries

A South African's Travels

TIM RAMSDEN

Order this book online at www.trafford.com
or email orders@trafford.com

Most Trafford titles are also available at major online book retailers.

Printed in the United States of America.

ISBN: 978-1-4269-8233-0 (sc)
ISBN: 978-1-4269-8234-7 (e)

Trafford rev. 07/21/2011

 www.trafford.com

North America & International
toll-free: 1 888 232 4444 (USA & Canada)
phone: 250 383 6864 ♦ fax: 812 355 4082

Dedicated to my amazing son Shaun,
and those fellow backpackers who I crossed paths with.

'Backpacking travel is like a drug to an addict, one yearns for more
with the desire to keep pushing beyond the boundaries.'
Tim Ramsden

… the earth serves me to walk upon, the sun to light me …
Montaigne

Contents

FOREWORD

I need to say a word of thanks to my parents who never once in five years told me to stop travelling and return home, even though I bet they wanted to. I had left behind in South Africa a well paid job with a company car and a career with a great future in order to realise my dream of one day seeing the Berlin Wall and travelling through Communist East Germany.

I had a return ticket for six months to a year, but that soon lapsed and from then on my ambition was to see as much as I could before one day returning to my homeland. I worked in Holland, Germany, England, Italy and Hong Kong earning money to keep me going and saving desperately for my next destination. The jobs were not glamorous, in fact back in South Africa they would be considered unskilled labour fit for a Black man, but I didn't care what I did as long as I earned enough to keep moving on to the next place.

I was a waiter, an apple sorter on a conveyor belt, a labourer on a construction site, a worker for a cable television company digging trenches and laying cables, a garbage collector, a textile worker folding and pressing T-shirts, a dish washer in restaurants, a tree planter in a nursery, and a leaflet distributer on the roadside. Many nights had been slept on the floor or a mattress if I was lucky, on a beach, in a toilet stall, a train station, at airports and in some cases in dirty small rooms with cockroaches and bedbugs.

I always appreciated what each new country presented to me. I was often asked which my favourite country was – I never had one because all 35 were unique in their own way. I had better experiences in some, and a few tough lessons in others, like being robbed in Holland and again in Thailand, and yet those two countries hold the most amazing memories for me while I regrouped and worked on Plan B. I have to thank my Dad for helping me through those tough times, wiring money until my Travellers Cheques were refunded and I had a new crimson British passport in my hands ready for the next border crossing.

I often thought that one day I would tell people what I did and how I lived for such a long time with hardly any money to my name. With only my backpack I travelled on foot, by train, plane, bus, taxi, thumb, my loyal Bulldog van, boat and ferry, a land-rover through the desert in Morocco and a camel in Rajasthan. I used what I could to get me where I needed to go. I felt that I had in fact Backpacked Beyond Boundaries into remote areas off the beaten track in my quest to see foreign lands. In Asia there could not be more of a stark contrast between beauty and squalor, and in the Eastern Bloc there were people uncertain of their future after the collapse of communism. Back in Africa after two years I saw a land that was more Middle Eastern than African; Morocco brought my soul back home.

Backpacking certainly isn't easy but it makes one really appreciate what one has after struggling through foreign countries to see, to try and understand and learn about their cultures.

I feel privileged and proud to have had so many enriching experiences during my life-changing journey of self-discovery.

Tim Ramsden

SOUTH AFRICA (Pre 1990)

MY SOUTH AFRICAN ROOTS

The Nationalist government, in power since 1948 had done a good job of educating its white citizens to look down upon their fellow African, even though for the most part people were not aware of their actions and judgments. It just seemed normal and commonplace to feel better as a white person and be worth more to society than a black person.

The whites were known as the Europeans and the blacks were the Natives or Non-Europeans. The Europeans had originated from Holland, Germany, France and England and had established themselves as the governing body over the land, the police, the military and the workplace. The Natives filled in where the donkey work was needed. Many were cut off from their families as work steered them faraway across the country to earn a living. For some it was the gold mines, or labourers on farms, menial jobs or as servants and garden boys to their white masters and madams.

Thanks to my Dad for leaving England, I would be born South African, a fact that makes me so proud in spite of the injustices that my country has had to deal with.

Dad was born in Fisherton-de-la-Mere in Wiltshire, at his grandmother's home. After WWI Dad's parents moved to Italy and later to the south of France to avoid the high English taxes, but his mother Winifred (nee' Cowan), returned to England for the birth of each of their six children, thus giving them British status. All except David, the youngest, who was born three months prematurely in France.

In 1931 the family returned to England for good and after settled in Bourne End near Marlowe and Maidenhead, which was along the Thames in Buckinghamshire.

From here Dad was packed off to boarding school in Shropshire, at the tender age of six.

With my Dads mother having said 'Africa needs you,' My Dad left England as a 29 year old bachelor on 1 February 1956 sailing from London to Durban aboard the Bloemfontein Castle. This ship was given the familiar Union Castle profile of a well-raked rounded stem, cruiser stern, a low streamlined funnel and a single mast behind the stern, giving a well balanced appearance. The Bloemfontein Castle was built to cater for an expected emigrant boom after World War II and to alleviate pressure for accommodation at lower range fares. For £99, Dad left England for Rotterdam in icy conditions where the ship was cracking a path through the ice before docking at the harbour as more passengers were taken on board. Through the Bay of Biscay the ship pitched from side to side allowing the propellers to lift out of the water leaving those aboard to heave and hold down the nausea that the ocean was meting out.

The ship then called at the Canary Islands and Las Palmas before heading for the African continent down the West coast on the Atlantic Ocean. Eventually land loomed as the ship docked in at Lobito Bay in Angola. This was my Dad's first glimpse of Africa and wow was it beautiful. The beach was untouched, cleaned by the swell of the crystal blue ocean as it ran up the fine sand like a carpet being unrolled. Majestic tall palm trees stood like look outs along the shore and it was every bit like a tropical paradise.

Excited passengers were allowed ashore and for most set their first foot print on the African continent, a step that would change and mould their lives forever.

Dad saw an African policeman decked out in a white uniform standing on a box directing traffic coming at him from five roads. Frantically his arms waved back and forth as the cars either halted or streamed past. For some unknown reason he lowered his arms and all the traffic stopped in the centre around his box creating a nightmarish traffic jam. Calmly he stepped off the box and simply walked away from the havoc, never to be seen again.

Then there was a man selling watches from his shop. Dad looked at one and was told it was £20, and so he walked away back to the ship.

The man chased him dropping the price with every stride, until it was down to £3 when he boarded the ship.

This was Dad's first real glimpse of Africa and its third world way of functioning, but it left an impression never to be forgotten.

From Lobito Bay the ship docked at Walvis Bay and then headed to Cape Town where the unmistakable Table Mountain loomed from the mist as the backdrop to this ever so important shipping route. After a quick visit through the Kirstenbosch Botanical Gardens it was back on the ship and up the east coast to Port Elizabeth and finally after a three week voyage the Bloemfontein Castle docked at the Durban Harbour.

Dad's mother had travelled through parts of Africa so he had some sort of idea what to expect, and the heat was a welcome relief from the cold and dampness of England, now so far away. His life in Africa had begun.

Mum's parents, Francis Barry Smith and Denise Tyzack, on the other hand had been born in South Africa, and had struggled through the great depression living on a farm in Mooi River. Her grandparents had been born in England binding them to the British Empire that had spread its colonial influence so prominently across the globe.

On the Barry Smith side, my great great grandfather, Alex Smith sailed from England in February 1849 in a three-decker East Indiaman and settled in Pinetown. Later he moved to Congella, and was one of the first growers of sugar cane on Springfield Flats.

My great great grandparents on the Tyzack side had been stained-glass makers in France until they fled to England in 1685 during the feud between the Catholic and Protestants.

In May 1850, after 112 days at sea, Richard Webber Tyzack arrived in Port Natal, South Africa.

The Great War of 1914 left its mark on my Dad's father, Arthur Geoffrey Francis Ramsden, a Major losing a lung in the trenches in the Battle of the Somme in 1916, as the poisonous mustard gas ate it away.

My Dad told me how the Germans and the English would play soccer with each other at Christmas, and then the very next day, continue killing each other. Soldiers would whistle and sing in the trenches with the quiet and stillness drifting the melody across enemy territory.

My grandfather Francis Barry Smith served in a British regiment as a Captain, with his rank allowing him to ride a horse. He spent his time in World War I in Mesopotamia, now Iraq and was stationed in the desert and in Bagdad.

My grandmother Denise Tyzack lost her first love to the Germans in the war to end all wars, and with her soul shattered she wrote the following poems.

Lest we forget

If you could walk the sodden, death-filled trenches,
With the lurid star-shells' weird fantastic gleams,
The thunderous shells, the whistling of the shrapnel,
The awful pauses with the strangled screams-
If you could hear the ranks before the battle,
Passing the hour with merry jest and quip,
Laughing to calm the wildly-beating pulses,
Stilling the passionate prayer on every lip!

Could you but see those men an hour after,
When the flaming, maddened rush is past and o'er,
Still twisting tortured lips into a smile,
Though torn with all the agony of War!
Could you but see their patient, anguished eyes
Grow dim with yearning for the face loved best,
Passing alone, unaided down the Trail
That runs for ever to the boundless West.

Could you but see those little wooden crosses,
With slim white arms outstretched beneath the sky,
Guarding the simple resting-place of heroes
Of those we knew and loved-so young to die!
But, oh the pathos of those humble flowers,
All parched and withered on an unmarked grave,
Laid by some weary, war-worn soul in passing-
A man's last tribute to the deathless brave.

All that they had they gave so freely,
And never paused to reckon up the price,
Strong in the greater love that reckons nothing-
The symbol of the Glorious Sacrifice!
So when the shattered ranks come limping home,
Forget not, but with tender love and pride
Remember those who, smiling, charged for Britain,
Who fell unflinching and unconquered died!

Denise W. Tyzack

To The Men of To-day

Men of the mighty Empire! Sons of a glorious line!
List to the words of a nation's dead echoing down through time.
They fought for your land, they bled for your land, and they made her
    queen of all,
Now, which of you is it who dares stand back at the sound of the
    country's call.

We have travelled north in the tracts of ice, and south in the gleaming
    snows,
And we've swept the seas from east to west with every wind that blows.
Some of us fell on foreign strands and we stiffened side by side;
And some of us pushed where no man had dared, and our bones in the
    jungle dried.
But at every place we left a mark in the strength of our racial pride.

We gave our all in the glow of youth on Afghan hill and plain,
And we hacked our way through Delhi's gates with Lawrence and
    Nicholson.
We stood to our posts on the 'Birkenhead'; we charged with the Light
    Brigade,
And e'en as we passed to the Never Land we were smiling and unafraid.
And every time we held our own by our birth and a dripping blade.

When Nelson called, we leapt to obey like a sweeping, human tide,
For the honour of England lay in our hands and all that is England's
   pride.
We had followed where Drake and Raleigh led to lands of the bold and
   free,
But on every voyage we left our dead in the blue of some nameless
   sea.
And these lives were given ungrudgingly for you men of the yet to be.

All this have we done for your England! Land of eternal flame!
Purged with the tears of broken hearts, and the life-blood of the slain.
Men of this glorious Empire, borne on this sacred mould!
Follow on in the steps we have made and die like the Sons of Old.

Denise W. Tyzack

War is a terrible curse and it harms everyone in its wake.
Unfortunately the war to end all wars was not lesson enough for leaders
to heed.

In World War II Peter Large, a cousin on my mother's side was
killed. He was in the Natal Mounted Rifles, but was seconded into a
British regiment for the invasion of Normandy. Ironically he survived
the landing on 6 June 1944, but was killed by a sniper a week later.
He is buried in the Military Cemetery at Caen near Bayeaux, with a
Springbok on his headstone, standing out as the only South African in
the cemetery.

His brother, Tony Large was torpedoed and survived 39 days at sea
in a life boat. He was one of only four survivors and was taken to Free
Town in Sierra Leone where he was nursed back to health and then
finally shipped back to South Africa receiving a hero's welcome in his
hometown of Durban. The newspaper captured the story and with
pictures that tell a thousand words, his ordeal was printed showing the
rejoicing times in war.

John Incledon, another cousin of my mother's was killed when his
submarine was torpedoed.

My Dad's sister's husband Dick Leggott, was torpedoed and sunk
twice, but he survived.

Tim Ramsden

My Dad's favourite aunt, Joan Baring-Gould lost two sons, one in the airforce and the other in a tank regiment in North Africa. She was always bitter that her two sons were taken and my Dad's family of four brothers remained intact.

Although my Dad's father Major Arthur Geoffrey Francis Ramsden had lost a lung in WWI, he played an important part in WWII. He was flown over Germany in the early stages to report on the anti-aircraft flak, to assist the RAF in plotting their bombing routes.

My uncle Dennis Cowley was in the Merchant Navy and in 1942 accompanied the convoys of ships ferrying ammunition and food across the Atlantic from the United States to the United Kingdom. There was a one in three chance of getting torpedoed when the German U-Boat wolf packs would hunt down stragglers and destroy them.

Stanley Bowley-Smith, another of my mother's cousins, was in the Natal Carbineers. He served in North Africa and was taken prisoner when Tobruk fell to the German Army led by Rommel, in 1941.

He was in an Italian POW camp at first and then moved to Germany where he spent the remainder of the war.

My Dad as a child would sit with the family and listen to the radio as Churchill's voice instilled confidence and courage as he spoke slowly and deliberately allowing the full meaning of his words to sink in.

It must have been an eerie feeling listening to the man who was the fighting heart behind Great Britain.

'We shall fight them on the beaches, we shall fight them on the landing grounds, we shall fight them in the fields and in the streets, we shall fight them in the hills; we shall never surrender.'

In 1943 when Dad was at school in Shropshire, he saw two US planes collide, one pilot managed to bail out but unfortunately he roman-candled with the school children watching it.

When London was being bombed during the Blitz, Dads family could see it burning from 36 miles away.

For three years during the war Winifred, Dads mother, worked in a munitions factory.

South Africa was not excluded from the war even though its proximity to the battlefront was on the other side of the globe.

Simons Town at the southern tip of Africa was a British naval base that was of great strategic importance in keeping the shipping lanes open for the troopships.

South African Blacks who heroically volunteered to fight for Britain entered the war but were prohibited from carrying rifles. These were people who did not walk on the pavement (sidewalk), and if by chance they did, they had to step into the gutter to allow a white person clear passage on the pavement.

With my family linked to the Empire, white men had no choice but to serve for Crown and Country.

After the war, when the Nationalist Party took over the government of South Africa, my Grandmother Denise Barry Smith became a member of the Black Sash, which was a non-violent white women's resistance organization founded in 1955. With courage she stood alongside many other white women in long lines in front of important government buildings with their stark Black Sashes worn as a mark of mourning in silent protest against the severe and unjust pass laws that governed and restricted Blacks' movements. Many members of the Black Sash were vilified in their own white communities with some physically attacked by those hardcore supporters of apartheid.

My parents were married in March 1960 in Hillcrest on the front lawn of Westerford, my Grandfathers six acre property with its gracious 100 year old colonial style iron roofed homestead.

A magnificent feature of the house was its wide pillared verandahs on three sides where the family could enjoy tea while gazing over the green lawns and majestic old trees. The front door was an old oak handmade stable door that opened in its halves into the spacious interior with its beautiful Oregon floor boards and antique furniture that stood out from the white walls. An old Grandfather clock chimed on the hour as servants were busy at work, cleaning and cooking in their sparkling white starched uniforms.

Granny and Grandpa had four servants, two in the garden, Pungula the cook and a house girl or maid who made the beds, dusted, polished the brass, polished shoes and the list went on. The cook also polished the floors, kept the coal stove clean and then waited at the table, offering the food in silver entrée dishes from person to person while dressed immaculately in pearl whites.

Granny always gave the servants and their families a good Christmas which was celebrated in the laundry room situated a little way from the backdoor. Grandpa did not really approve but allowed Granny to go ahead anyway. Roast beef, vegetables and jelly for pudding were cooked in the kitchen and then taken to the laundry room to be served and eaten with grateful and very happy hearts.

It seemed like any other country in the world, where life was being lived and people were working for a livelihood. But when one looked closer it was clear that there was a class system where the whites were set on a pedestal and the blacks rushed around them doing their menial tasks to earn money for their families. My grandparents' servants lived on the premises in a long bungalow style row of four separate rooms with a communal washing area and behind the garages a long drop toilet.

There was an old iron bell that my grandfather would beat with an iron pipe that would reverberate across the property as the signal to the garden boys that it was lunchtime. Never being allowed to eat or drink from their master's crockery they ate their meat and doorsteps of bread from their enamel metal plates and steaming tea from the well used enamel mugs.

It had always been a white joke that if one gave an African something he would either break it or lose it. These enamel plates and mugs could be chipped but not broken and so they were a safe bet in all white households.

The smell that some of the blacks gave off was something else, a combination of wood smoke, and not washing properly creating a very pungent odour that would flare any nostrils.

In 1956 my Dad and his brother Peter shared a house in Winston Park near Hillcrest while they were still bachelors, and they had a servant called 'Zebbalon' who also gave off this awful smell. Zebbalon followed Dad as he looked in each and every cupboard, every drawer and virtually turning the place upside down to locate the smell. After an hour they stopped and with Zebbalon right next to Dad, Dad looked right at him and realized to his horror that he had located the smell. With Zebbalon totally oblivious to the fact that he was the guilty party the search was called off.

To this day the story still raises a laugh.

Apartheid in this time was iron fisted and written as law with land acts and passes acting as restrictions to lives that could only be half lived.

Blacks had to walk for miles to work, with buses and trains often too expensive to catch. Many Blacks would walk for two hours to get to work, and then begin a day of heavy labour with a reward of a two hour walk back into their place of segregation.

Blacks had to enter through different entrances to a post office, butchery, a grocer, bottle store, train station and so the list went on. Trains had 1st, 2nd and 3rd class compartments. The 3rd class was for blacks only and was right at the back of the train fitted with plain wooden seats. They were also not welcome in Department Stores as their skin colour denoted lack of funds and white customers weren't prepared to tolerate them.

Benches at bus stops were for whites only, toilets were labeled 'whites only' or in Afrikaans, *slegs blankes*.

At the holiday town of Durban, there were beaches for whites and beaches for blacks. The best beaches along the Marine Parade were for whites only as we enjoyed the amusement park, aquariums, Snake Park, mini town and all the hotels, bars and restaurants that blacks were not permitted to enter.

Blacks had to have a pass which they carried at all times which restricted them to a certain area. If they were caught without a pass they were arrested by the police and thrown in jail. Lilly our servant in Johannesburg did not have a pass for the Johannesburg area and was arrested and held in jail until my mother paid the fine releasing her.

Blacks working in a kitchen wore a regulation 'Kitchen Boy' suit of white cotton shorts and a loose shirt edged with blue or red binding.

If blacks entered a white bus they had to sit on the upper deck in the back three rows and could only board when all whites had already taken their seats. Later there were stricter regulations and I only knew white buses and black buses where no blacks were permitted at all to ride on a white bus.

If whites needed land where blacks were living a whole community could be forcibly removed, their flimsy tin shacks demolished by bulldozers or re-located in the open *veld*, sometimes in the harshness of winter. Cato Manor settlement on the outskirts of Durban was a good example of this.

Their lives were simple, thanks to a lack of education which helped keep them down where the white government wanted them. Their staple foods were mealie meal which they either ground themselves or bought, and brown bread and brown sugar if they had the money. They also rolled their own cigarettes out of newspaper with Boxer tobacco and drank their Juba and milk stouts that got them thoroughly wasted extremely quickly.

They also drank wood alcohol which was a methyl extract from timber like methylated spirits which eventually caused blindness.

Education of Blacks was at a much lower level than whites and with only a few schools in the rural areas, education was a luxury, definitely not a necessity. In 1976 the government forced blacks to learn the white language of Afrikaans causing black pupils to riot. It became known as the Soweto Riots. The police quelled the uprising killing many and it created a turning point in many white families who chose to emigrate overseas, with many of the Jewish population choosing Canada.

Blacks were not permitted to partake in sport and a classic example of this was Basil D' Oliviera, a coloured cricketer who was forbidden to play in the South African test squad. With his love for the sport so passionate he left South Africa and played for England. When England toured South Africa, the South African government refused to give Basil accommodation in 'whites only' hotels and so the MCC cancelled the tour.

Apartheid ruled everywhere from sport, to work, to leisure, to dwelling, to gravesite, this was the South Africa where the white minority ruled the majority.

My childhood in Johannesburg was a happy time. Our Black servant Sena would look after us when Dad was at work and Mum was out shopping. There were times when she would bundle one of us three children onto her back with a blanket. With us nestled into her back she would continue with her chores as she rocked us to sleep.

She had taught me a childlike rhyme that has stuck with me over the years and which I can still recite today. It is written how I used to say it and is nowhwere near the correct pronounciation in Zulu.

'Moenya, mabeli, matatu. Mama bambeli masenza. Masenza ifili, mama kalili. Moenya, mabeli, matatu.' 'One, two, three. Mummy caught a flea. Flea died. Mummy cried. One, two, three.'

Blacks lived in separate quarters, cooking their own meals and never ate at our table or sat on our chairs let alone use our toilet.

I remember Lily in Johannesburg, living in one room which had her bed raised with a paint tin under each leg to keep the dreaded little green man away while she slept. She, like most Blacks believed in the Tokolosh who she superstitiously thought would come to kill her in the night. With the bed raised from the ground by the paint tins, this is what she trusted would save her from this evil little green monster.

Johannes our garden boy became my soccer opponent as he rushed to finish what his master (my Dad) had asked of him, before being granted time to kick the soccer ball around. Like all Blacks he loved soccer and he relished the time he had to pass the ball back and forth with me.

Pippa our Irish Terrier rushed around while we played on the grass in the back garden with the lemon tree on one side and a huge oak on the other.

Big red double decker trolley buses would pass the front of our house with the two arms running along the electrified wires. Almost every day they would come to a halt after taking a corner too wide and one of the arms would come off the electrified cable.

While John and I waited to go to Ridge, our primary school, a bus driver would always pass us and wave and then he would weave the bus to the right and left as he sped by.

We soon got to know him. His name was Ted and he really made our day along with the rest of the all white passengers on the red double decker.

One day he stopped and met with us and asked if we would like a free trip into the city. With full trust in Ted, Mum allowed him to take us. Our eyes were wide as we went to the fast and furious city all seen from the top of the bus through the huge front and back windows. Ted entrusted the money collection belt to John and with all the excitement it was left on a seat with the days takings in it. Ted was very good about it and it was tracked down and found thanks to the honesty of all those who saw it. What a great day we had when one could still trust a relative stranger with kids less than 10 years of age.

Dad was always working on making our house better and bigger along with moving the garage further back from the road.

Sitting on the wall, watching the activity my sharp eyes caught sight of a glinting object buried in the ground. I went over to pick it up and it kept on coming out of the soil. It was a nail, but not any nail. It was the biggest I had ever seen and much longer than a ruler. I carried it over to where I was sitting on a half demolished wall and cradled it in my hands.

Unthinking, with it clutched in my fist and sticking out like a knife, I charged down the wall in a cavalry charge and raced towards a pile of bags of cement, 15 metres away.

My Dad stopped what he was doing and just watched me, not believing that I would do anything with my prize.

As soon as I reached the cement my arm came down and I stabbed the bag, to my Dad's absolute horror. With air on the cement powder it would harden in no time.

With a shout of disbelief from my Dad, I said: 'Sorry Dad I slipped!' I was lucky to get off the hook without a good beating.

I always seemed to tempt myself to doing things. This time I wanted to see if my tongue would stick to the inside of the freezer. Well it did and with my Dad pulling of my stretched out tongue along with some warm water it was eventually pried free after what felt like an agonizingly long time.

My Granny Barry Smith died in 1971, ironically at the same hospital where my other granny had been admitted in 1958. They both died of cancer at the Mariannhill Hospital. My Grandfather Barry Smith had got too old to maintain his home, Westerford, in Hillcrest and in 1972 he moved in with my great aunt Joy and uncle Gerald in Durban, leaving the house in the hands of uncaring tenants who eventually abandoned it.

In 1975 when I was 10 years old my parents decided to move back to Hillcrest and reoccupy the old family home, where my mother was born and grew up.

Driving up the dirt drive way with the grass as high as the car, I looked from the back seat through the window at the house. It looked as haunted as one could ever get. Windows were broken, the interior was dark, it looked deserted and neglected and not lived in for many years. The garden was filled with looming tall trees and huge bushes that I felt were holding secrets and hiding spooky ghosts.

Driving round to the back my Dad stopped the Volvo between the row of garages and servants quarters and my brother John and I got out with inquisitive wonder what this new home held for us. Mum and my sister Paula got out of the Corsair and we all walked to the backdoor. Spiders had woven their webs undisturbed for a year barricading our entry and as we opened the door so they scurried nimbly across their web into hiding.

We walked into the kitchen and stood for a while as we adjusted to the darkness and this strange place we were standing in. There was a huge old fridge with a fan motor on the top made by Frigidaire back in 1935. It was cast iron on four legs with four doors and wood paneling on the inside of each door which was wide enough to take a body.

'It looks like a morgue to store bodies,' John said as we pulled on the metal handle only to be greeted by stale air. Having to use force we slapped the door shut. This old fridge had been purchased by my grandfather in 1936 for a £100 when fridges were a luxury and had been shipped from the United States.

The house was dusty and dead quiet as we walked over the creaking floor boards, taking in the surroundings with the comfort of family close at hand. The rooms were huge and empty and then venturing out onto the side veranda we saw many more spider webs and a flat yellowish black spider that went by the name of Maude. A row of wild tree ferns grew like stubby straight pillars along the edge of the veranda with a row of Yesterday, Today and Tomorrow bushes lining the boundary fence with the Boyce's property. Azalea bushes were also visible from the veranda which in spring blossomed into beautiful colour along St. Margarets Road, and were all the talk in the village. Flatcrown trees planted in a row by my granny stood steadfast at the bottom of the garden on the shady lawn we named as the meadow. A gigantic jacaranda tree stood at the curve of the driveway and the petals that dropped off would carpet the grass in a beautiful thick bed of lush purple, so soft and soothing to the eye. At ten years old the grass stood up to my chest and we would have to wait to see the beautiful purple carpet. Instead we walked through litter, human feces, newspaper used as toilet paper and tons of discarded beer bottles and Juba cartons all proof that the local Africans were using our property as a toilet and a drinking place. Cars were using the lawn as a parking lot and it seemed as if the inhabitants of Hillcrest had somehow laid claim to this unfenced expanse of parkland in the middle of this little village.

We found an open area and started piling all the litter in a heap along with broken branches and rotten logs from old trees that had toppled over. With a blaze like I had never seen before we had a humongous bonfire that burned for seven days.

As the cars left the property that day we rolled the heavier logs to the edge of the roadside some of which had been chained sawed in half. We had made our own fence and reclaimed the land where my mother was born in 1932.

From walking through the grass and brushing against bushes I came out in a severe rash which we later found out was caused by the beautiful red rues tree that I began to steer well away from.

Mum and Paula cleaned out the inside of the house and found an old German passport, proof that a traveller from far away had been living in the abandoned house.

The first few sleeps were very scary in this big house with a passage that seemed to stretch for miles, and rooms that were dimly lit. Every creak and every branch that scraped against a window had my thoughts running wild.

We all started school at the Hillcrest Primary school in September 1975. I remember walking to school and passing lines of Blacks walking briskly to get to work. Every time one passed me I felt nervous, as though he would come right up and attack me.

'Sawubona, unjani,' I said, greeting the Africans in Zulu. I felt by being polite to them, they would not want to attack me. I realized how scared I actually was of these dark Black people.

At school and amongst ourselves we would always see who would win or go first by a simple but now a deeply racist caption:

'Eanie, meanie, minie, moe. Catch a nigger by his toe, if he hollers let him go. Eanie, meanie, minie, moe.'

Naturally it was said without a single thought of its offensive nature.

1977 was also the year that Dad bought a television set. It was unbelievable to see this box come to life which it did for only two hours a night, from 6pm to 8pm.

We watched Charlie Chaplin and Laurel and Hardy with their slapstick humour that had us glued to the sofa, as we ate our dinner without taking our eyes off the screen. I remember the first adverts that ran and they were Big T burgers and Bata shoes which had us watching every scene with as much wonder as if it was the main show.

Another really entertaining program was The Villagers, a South African television series set on a gold mine in the Johannesburg area, depicting the day to day events with humour and thrill that any South African could relate to.

Those two hours of TV were like no other and at school it was all the talk with anyone that had been lucky enough to view the programs.

It began to replace the radio that was set on the table around which we gathered to listen to the news and certain radio shows, the most listened by us was Squad Cars on a Friday night. This was a radio show about the South African police who patrolled the streets 24 hours out of every 24.

Renting a film meant walking down the garden to Bremm's Building and paying for a projector and a case of film reels at the film store that we lugged back home. A white sheet was stretched across a wall and the film flickered and jumped across the makeshift screen with all of us thrilled to be part of the moment.

Fish and chips wrapped in newspaper from the one and only fish and chip shop in Hillcrest was a treat, and with Dad's first pay cheque in our new home it was celebrated with a huge portion of hake and chips covered in salt.

Lill's Corner was the small shop at the corner of Old Main Road and across from Leslie Grant's Butchery. We often collected beer bottles and then took them down to the Bottle Store for white patrons only, and then with a handsome refund we headed for Lill's. This is where we bought sweets and chips, one of our favorites being round black balls called, 'nigger balls,' and Wilson black toffee squares.

I became an avid stamp collector and it brought the world a lot closer with intrigue and mystique as I handled stamps from worlds away. I started to learn about countries like Basutoland, Bechuanaland,

Nyasaland, Tanganyika, Northern and Southern Rhodesia and the Belgian Congo. I soon learned that the European colonies had or were about to hand over independence and abdicate their rule.

Later I learned stories of how people would go to great lengths to get their money and valuables out of the country. In Mozambique Portuguese families would let their silver go black so no one would confiscate it when they left the country. In Zimbabwe a man filled his spare tyre with wads of cash. Unfortunately he got a puncture at the border post and was forced to put the spare on, which ended up burning the money as he drove away.

In South Africa, people bought boats and sailed them across oceans only to sell them, or gold Kruger Rands to be sold overseas.

There was also a story of a Portuguese man who welded a box filled with money onto the side of some earth removing equipment. Once it reached Portugal he removed the box and the money.

I had a chopper bicycle that I was really proud of and so did my brother John, who was an expert in attending to the mechanical maintenance of these cycles. We toured the village on our bicycles loving the thrill of this backward and yet adventurous place.

Hillcrest had no traffic lights, but instead an African man dressed smartly in uniform and white gloves stood on a box and directed traffic looking as professional as any. The village had progressed from an African man holding a stop/go sign to an African feeling ever so important as he halted and directed traffic at will. Tractors and trailers hauled sugar cane to the Hillcrest train station where it was loaded into open carriages before being transported to Durban to be refined into sugar, a vital commodity for black and white alike as well as being an important export.

At the train station we often picked up a burned piece of cane that had fallen onto the ground. Peeling back some of the burned reed we chewed on the stem and sucked on the sweet sugar that tasted cooked from the burning before it was chopped and harvested.

There was a black trading store that sold kerosene for the lamps, Lifebuoy soap, mealie meal, batteries, Lion matches, enamel mugs, kitchen boy suits and everything that an African would need to buy. Whites on the other hand would shop at Christians and Richdens for their groceries, until Richdens caught fire on the night of 2 June, my birthday and burned to the ground.

That night in 1976 Dad and Mum woke us up, and in our pyjamas we walked to the bottom of the garden in pitch darkness. In the meadow under the flatcrown trees we were suddenly standing in bright light and to our amazement we saw a fire like no other. We stood mesmerized as we watched flames curling high into the night burning and charring the Richdens store and incinerating all the merchandise within.

Hillcrest certainly seemed like an exciting and backward village without robots (traffic lights) and with the most basic amenities and with a climate to die for.

Miriam became our servant, a nice thin old lady who was so respectful of us who had also worked for my grandparents. Miriam always called me *inkosane*, son of the master, in the apartheid days when the white person was boss. One could see in her eyes the pride she felt in watching the three of us grow up. Looking back it was a sad fact that most servants watched the white children they were looking after growing up into adults and deprived of watching their very own go through these same stages of life.

Ephraim became our garden boy, mowing the grass and raking up the fallen leaves for all the trees, two never ending jobs.

When he lost something and we asked where it was it was always met with a dumbfounded look followed with '*Angazi*' or I don't know. This was so typical for most blacks when they lost, forgot or broke something.

Needing firewood Ephraim helped himself to some of my Dad's sapele mahogany that he was using to make furniture with. To my Dad's horror and anger, this really expensive wood had been used to cook a meal and also used as a means to keep warm.

How Dad never strangled him I will never know. Blacks on the whole were uneducated and would never have seen the difference between good wood and firewood.

Every year on 31 May, the day South Africa became a Republic we would walk to the Old Main road and watch the Comrades Marathon as the leaders almost sprinted through with cheering crowds of onlookers lining each side of the roadway cheering each beaten body forward. Hours later the stragglers would come shuffling past still with that desire of beating the gun that would end their hopes of finishing the gruelling 88 kilometres from the city of Petermaritzburg to Durban if they did not cross the line within 11 hours. When the brown and white striped shirts of the Hillcrest Villagers ran through their home town loud shouts erupted, lifting their spirits.

Watching them I hoped that one day I would be able to run this marathon feeling like a king on the road and get a bronze medal for beating the cutoff.

One Sunday in early March 1977, I sat at a table in the living room and listened to the radio. The Formula 1 Grand Prix was being hosted at Kyalami in South Africa. I loved Formula 1 and was glued to the radio listening to the commentator as he painted a colour picture of the action on the track.

Then I heard something about a car on fire and a fire marshal dashing across the track and then death.

I turned to my parents and said: 'A car caught fire and someone died!'

I went cold with the thought that one second earlier someone was alive and well and in the next second he was dead. It was as if the sound from the speaker had just emitted death.

With my ears strained I soon learned that a Welsh racing driver, called Tom Pryce had hit a fire marshal as he hurtled over a blind rise. Jansen van Vuuren, the fire marshal was hurled in the air and cut in two. His fire extinguisher had hit Tom Pryce in the head at 170mph and he too died instantly. The fire extinguisher bounced off his helmet, struck the roll bar and was found in the parking lot.

At school the next day everyone was talking about it. Those with TVs saw the tragedy live without any censorship to dull the gore.

In August of the same year everyone was talking about ELVIS who had suddenly died.

'Who is ELVIS,' I asked as a young 12 year old, expecting the answer to be a person from outer space, after all this was a very peculiar name.

Little did I know that the king of rock had just died?

The radio was a powerful tool and it would bring much humour and comfort to many. There was the Goon Show with its English humour, a joy to many ex-pats, which had my Dad in fits of laughter as Peter Sellers, Spike Milligan and Harry Secombe performed their comical antics. On a more serious note Esme Euvrard read messages and letters every Sunday to the soldiers serving the country.

It left me with an odd feeling that one day I too would be serving my country in uniform.

In 1978 John and I went off to boarding school in Mooi River called Treverton, a good hour and a half drive from Hillcrest. I had not even turned 13 years old and I knew my life would change with the teachers becoming our guardians.

The night before I was to go to boarding school, my Mum came into my room to wish we goodnight. Sitting in the darkness she said: 'Your life is about to change forever.' Petrified I closed my eyes, hardly sleeping a wink, I dreaded the path that had been chosen for me.

I went to the Treverton Preparatory starting in Std 5. There was an Indian bus driver who drove us to soccer and cricket matches in a little E20 minivan. Joking around, I said to him: 'Bow to the King,' as I pointed to myself, and did a half bow.

He took one look at me, frowned in disgust and said: 'I don't bow to no shit.' Craig, a friend from my class, took one look at me and then we just burst out laughing.

Treverton was a good school, it was also an all white school that had just gone co-ed and so we had a handful of girls. Life here quickly taught me how to become independent and do everything from polishing shoes to making my own bed, things that most servants would be doing in the white households. Homework was done without any help besides a friend, meals were nothing to write home about and we made the best out of what had been decided for us, a place that most of us would not have chosen as it was so much harder to live far away from the easy and taken-for-granted life of home and family.

At 15 years old and in Standard 7 our class climbed an area in the Drakensberg Mountains and it was the first time I ever saw and touched snow. We were like big kids in a playground as one snow ball was hurled after the next. We felt on top of the world, and paid the price with snow blindness, bleeding noses from the altitude and not to mention freezing our arses off.

At 16 we filled out papers registering all of the white males for military service that was mandatory.

'You're in the army now. You're in the army now!' Hambly sang to us. He was our Geography teacher who was a member of the Flat Earth Society, but after lengthy debates he taught us that it was round but still professed to believe it was flat.

In 1982 Treverton became multi racial as a handful of Indians, blacks and Coloureds became Trevertonians. Login and Raven were both Indians from Durban and one holiday my brother John and myself decided to meet up with them for a few drinks. We tried a few bars but because of the apartheid laws of segregation in restaurants and bars we were forbidden from bringing them inside for a simple drink or two.

After abandoning the idea we bought a bottle of Mainstay Cane spirits and a bottle of Coke and parked our cars on the roadside. Leaning against the cars with music playing we drank in freedom where no colour of skin could interfere with racial inequalities.

At school we had all sorts of nicknames for the teachers, Moses with his ginger beard, Spring onion for the spring in his step, Whacky for all his caneing, Humbug for Hambly, Rope, because he was thick hairy and twisted.

On a history tour in Zululand learning about the bloody Zulu War of 1879, three of us decided to help ourselves to a couple of beers and some biltong. From our tents we wandered up to the main house under darkness and snuck into the storage area where we took advantage of the good hospitality we had been given by this old boy from Treverton a few years ahead of us.

Once back at school Wacky got to hear of this and one by one we were given a severe caning, of six strokes that left black and blue lines across our buttocks. Very lucky for us we were not suspended or worse expelled.

I enjoyed sport and played cricket for the school as well as rugby which was compulsory for all of us.

In life you make the most of what you are dealt, and I made some good friendships, got a good education and did well in some of the sports, doing the best at cricket.

In December 1983 I matriculated and before I left school I had my army papers in my hand. I was to report to Natal Command on 12 January 1984.

Just before Christmas I went down with a few friends to the Imperial Hotel in Pinetown. Shortly after midnight we staggered out.

There was some commotion in the parking lot and then I saw a car stop and a person get out.

I saw he had a baton in his hand and then he swung it with force hitting someone across the forehead.

I heard the dull thud and through the shadows saw his forehead smashed in. A second later the victim dropped to the ground like a stone.

The attacker fled, and then there were screams as blood spewed. In minutes an ambulance was on the scene.

A week later I learned that the victim was from Hillcrest and his attacker was from Kloof, a rivalry that had been brewing for years.

John, my brother told me it was Bruce Celliers, one of his friends. Unfortunately Bruce never made it out of hospital and I had witnessed a murder from the shadows.

The day before I went into the army I went to the Pinetown Licensing Centre to do my practical for my car licence.

On entering I was met with dozens of graphic blown up photos of black people killed in road accidents. The goriness was enough to make one sick from bloodied bodies of men women and children, severed limbs, decapitated heads and bodies strewn across the tarmac and left uncovered with no dignity or respect. There was not a single white body in any frame.

The message I took away was drive carefully otherwise this is what is in store.

It was a known fact that most road deaths came from the infamous kamikaze African taxis with drivers who drove at break-neck speed, with many drunk at the wheel. Unfortunately there were at least 20 people crammed in a ten seater van.

The newspapers always reported any deaths of Africans as Blacks, whereas the whites were identified with a name. Twenty Africans killed in an accident would never make the front page, but 20 whites certainly would. It was just another black and white injustice on the black and white pages of the newspapers.

I dreaded the day that I was drafted into the army for my mandatory two years of National Service. When 12 January arrived I was sick to my stomach with fear, but I masked it well, for only I knew. My parents thought that going to the army was a good thing and for most they accepted it as part of South African life. Those parents, and there were many that didn't like the idea of sending their kids to army and a bush war on the Angolan border, left the country with their teenagers for a freer life in Canada, England, or Australia. Thinking back to Britain with many young teenagers just milling about with no direction in life, my parents thought it was a way of giving the youth direction, independence with good life lessons.

It would be 20 years later when they really understood what we as teenagers were put through in our two years that shocked them to the core.

As one senior officer put it: 'In my view SWAPO, despite inferior weaponry, was ahead of us in most respects. We took a boy who had just matriculated, gave him a gun, two or three months of basic training and threw him into the middle of a country that he didn't know, people he didn't understand and an enemy he had never seen. No wonder he didn't do very well. Nevertheless, the young conscripts bore a terrible load, for which they received little gratitude.'

It was the call of duty to our country and whatever it took, we gave.

Hatred was instilled in me that grew with each day of army misery. Each and every day we as soldiers were labeled by our rank as being 'lower than black shit,' and we certainly felt like it.

Blacks were branded with some terrible names; *Kaffirs, Firs, Pekkies, Zots, Coons, Boogs, Moents, Moentoo's, Black bastards*, and a waste of skin were just a few that were callously spat from our white racist mouths.

It was so strange, how I as a youth loved to play soccer with our garden boy, Johannes, and now inside I viewed him as a black bastard, and a burden to South African society.

I had buried black people in Angola, mostly women and children that had been massacred and left to rot and stink to high heaven. The smell had me gasping for clean air, and the sight as horrific as it was, was tolerable only because they were black.

'Thank God they are black. If they were white I would have flipped out!' we had commented amongst our fellow platoon of soldiers.

I felt nothing for them, they were black and I was white, they were a burden to society and there were too many of them.

'Twelve less to worry about!' someone said as we dug two big holes, big enough to layer six bodies in each.

On pass from the border Wayne, the gunner from my section and I got totally drunk at the Imperial Hotel in Pinetown. On the way back to his mothers flat we spotted a lone black man walking through an open field on his way back from work. It was dark and misty and we were angry.

'Let's kick the shit out of him!' I said to Wayne.

Walking over to him we punched and kicked him to the ground and to somehow appease our actions I blurted out: 'We have been shitting ourselves on the border because of the likes of you. You fuckin Kaffir!' And with another kick to his head we left lying pathetically in the wet grass clutching his head.

To calm ourselves we drove around the block laughing through heavy breathing, and too our anger we saw him getting up. Again we rushed at him and kicked him down, until the cries of a white woman sent us on our way.

The next morning our feet hurt and I felt the injustice I had done. We never spoke about it ever again. The drink and the fear we experienced on the border, the anger of being in the army and the suffocating hold it had over us along with the freedom of a pass had made us commit this most cowardly act. I have never forgotten it, and cannot explain what provoked it, but it shames me to this day. An action so not part of my character before the army took over my life.

The army had certainly indoctrinated me to hate and despise those very people who were the majority in chains while the minority ruled with brutal force in the strength of the white army and police force.

Two years had been taken from me and in return it was replaced with anger and a feeling of being lost once I had been returned to society. Every experience in life builds character and these years certainly helped build mine. There is no money in the world that would be enough to repeat my army years. For me they remain buried in the back of my mind like a deep hole now covered over, as though the experience was lived in another very distant life.

I embraced the freedom with alcohol and there were many times when it got the better of me from car accidents to fights.

Once I uprooted a traffic light and still managed to get my car from Pinetown to the top of Fields Hill before the twisted fender cut the tyre to shreds.

At the Imperial Hotel I was pushed by a bouncer and being intoxicated I pushed him back and then he hit me. Drunk as I was I connected him well but it wasn't enough. He chased me out of the establishment like a stray dog and then he pushed me down. I fell into the road wedged between a Mini Minor and the curb. He climbed on top of me and rained blows into my face that felt like huge hail stones raining down from the heavens.

The next day I looked as though I had been run over by a bus and I definitely felt as though I had.

Car accidents and fights were a part of growing up and there were many. I had been through a wall with Steven and landed in their garden and if that wasn't bad enough we fled the scene with the owners shaking their fists and screaming murder as they attempted to run after us.

An accident I will never forget was seeing two young drunk teenagers trapped in a car. They had been drinking at Aladdin's Cave in Kloof with a group of us when they went under a barrier as drunk as skunks. I saw for myself the metal barrier that had smashed through the windscreen and was inches away from their heads. They were alive but needed the Jaws of Life to free them. It was a narrow escape and just another example how drink can impair judgment.

After the army I joined the Standard Bank and hated every passing minute feeling like a wild animal trapped behind glass, with the typewriter keys, and ringing of phones chiseling away at my sanity. I had been living in the open bush for four months and now I was behind bullet proof glass and bars and I felt myself starting to crumble as claustrophobia took a stranglehold of me.

Work soon drove me to take up running to escape this new life that was screwing with my mind. I ran up Botha's Hill to Inchanga and the more I ran the more I felt I was liberating myself. It did not take long before I decided to enter the Comrades Marathon, running for the Hillcrest Villagers. Decked out in my white and brown striped vest and brown shorts I set out from Petermaritzburg along with Sean, a friend from Hillcrest in our quest to beat the 11 hour cut off and get a bronze medal for the ordeal which having done the army was an *opfok* of note.

Incredibly Sean and I crossed the line together with 55 minutes to spare and achieved the dream of having a medal hanging around our necks. It was an achievement where the mind willed the beaten legs to keep going as if I was under some sort of hypnosis. What a thrill it was to cross the line after having run through the chilly darkness covered in a plastic rubbish bag to keep warm, into the burning heat with one's body literally rubbed raw and battered to the very core to beat the allotted time.

It was an experience that I shall never forget, an experience made easier by the two years I served in the army. The army had instilled an iron will in me that very little could ever prevent me from achieving what I had set out to do.

After leaving the bank I started work at the OK Bazaars, a retailer in business since the early 1920s. I became a trainee manager at the Pinetown branch and after a couple of years in training with many store openings under my belt, I was sent up to Hillbrow for three months of management training.

Clad in a red blazer our group of around 16 future managers walked to the head office from the hotel, looking more like a circus act all identical with our fiery red jackets.

Hillbrow was a crazy place and a melting pot of all races in spite of apartheid, with many whites begging on the streets, which I had never before seen. I remember one old white man that I stopped and gave bread to. With his mind far gone and his eyes sunken and glazy blue in colour, he told me to get lost. It was common knowledge that most tramps 'rode the blue train,' which was drinking purple methylated spirits through white bread acting as a sieve to somehow help purify the toxin before it entered the bloodstream. I did not have to be a genius to see that he was one of the many.

Often at night we heard screams and sirens only to see blood on the pavement the next day. Hillbrow was the murder capital of South Africa, and one saw police where ever one turned.

One Saturday morning we awoke to pandemonium in our hotel as a body was removed from the pool area. The man had jumped from his balcony and ended his life in a bloody selfish mess.

Hillbrow was a great experience nonetheless and after three months we all graduated as Assistant Managers, reporting to our respective

Branch Manager. In my case I was transferred to Ladysmith, a good two hour drive from Hillcrest, and a place made famous by the Anglo Boer War in 1899.

The store was situated close to a bus rank where the PUTCO buses loaded and off loaded Africans in their hundreds. They would swarm into the store pulling money from their bras if we were lucky or some would rob us blind. A good one was all the trade in's in our footwear department where the old pair of shoes was left behind and a new pair was worn out of the door with the thief grinning from ear to ear. We caught overweight black women waddling through the cashier checkpoints with a 4 litre tin of oil wedged between their thighs. There was also one who tried to steal a chicken under her hat and another who ate a full packet of sausages as he pretended to be working the shelves. The theft was out of control and the Security led by a fierce Hindu called Silver, patrolled the store like flies in search of bloody meat. Silver often caught the thieves and this Indian showed no remorse on the poor black who got a few slaps across the face and an odd shove into a hard wall for his digging into company revenues.

An African man in his mid thirties came walking into the store from the bus stop side, looking every bit like a customer. I was shocked to see he was crying and holding his mouth very tightly with tears streaming down his face and over his fingers.

'Boss help me!' he cried out.

'What's the matter?' I asked, now realizing that something was wrong.

Slowly he moved his hands away from his mouth and I was stunned to see a gaping hole with a mouth of teeth. It took me a second to realize that a huge chunk of his bottom lip had vanished. In tears of pain he told me that another African had bitten the chunk out. Looking at him I can remember thinking, not even an animal would do this. African on African violence was just part of South African life. Nonchalantly I handed him over to Silver to deal with and what became of him I have no idea, as I continued with the day's business.

I felt superior to all blacks with a motto that had been instilled in us: 'You can take the Kaffir out of the bush, but you can never take the bush out of the Kaffir.' In other words we had been made to believe that the African belonged in the bush, and no matter what one did those bush mentalities would remain forever.

The names of some black people were colourful and slightly embarrassing. Some of the best names I came across were Please, Naughty, Precious, Shadwick and Jelly.

A friend once asked his garden boy to clean his records. When he got back he could not believe his eyes when he saw that they had all been scrubbed with a brush.

We were told stories of when the government was building houses for the less privileged. The blacks moved in and almost immediately a fire was burned in the toilet and a crap was taken in the fireplace.

It was stories like this that further amplified the fact that to most white people our blacks were uneducated (thanks to us) and stupid.

It was common knowledge that what they could not break they would lose or break. Two items that we knew were 'Kaffir proof' were the AK47 and the enamel mug and plate set.

The Spionkop dam became the hangout on days off, especially with Alain, who was a member of the district office who had a magnificent speed boat. Water skiing and whisky in the winter months went hand in hand until one day while trying to make a braai, the grass around the fire caught alight and suddenly we had a serious fire on our hands. The wind came up and spread it out of control. Running around like drunken idiots we grabbed what we could to try and put it out. With luck on our side the wind changed direction and fanned the flames back to the area which had already been burned. Beating the flames furiously we finally put them out, leaving a charred area as big as a rugby field, and us blackened and out of breath.

With relieved smiles we headed back to Ladysmith thankful to have not burned the whole of Spionkop to a cinder.

On another occasion, driving totally drunk I veered off the road in my company car. Seeing this Rodney, a trainee manager at the OK Bazzars, took hold of the wheel and corrected the steering. I got a fright and grabbed the wheel resulting in an over correction which had the car lurching completely across the road and up a small hill before rolling a couple of times.

Landing upside down on the roof, we crawled out in the pitch darkness, disorientated and shocked at how quickly this had all happened.

Tim Ramsden

Alain and Silver who were towing the boat ahead of us, wondered where we were and so turned around. They were stunned to see the car in a mangled heap.

With hidden strength and adrenalin working wonders, and on the count of three, we rocked and rolled the car onto its four wheels.

It started, and off we went with broken windows and a spider webbed windscreen, with the car pulling to the side and driving like a crab would scuttle across a beach.

After a long and tiring journey I finally made it back to my flat where I parked the car in the shield of darkness, hoping that by morning the daylight would somehow fix the situation and make it not look as bad.

Seeing it in the sobriety of morning rocked me back into my deepest nightmare. This was my company car, a train smash on four wheels. I had some explaining to do and I knew that after all this settled I would be lucky to be given a company bicycle.

With some help from a couple of friends in the local police station I had a valid police statement; my district manager let me off the hook. A month later I had an even better company car that was driven with care and far less quantities of alcohol in my bloodstream.

One night Alain and I joined our cop friends for a braai in the courtyard of the police station. While the meat was sizzling a beautiful and juicy sound we were invited into the morgue which happened to be right next to us. A drawer was pulled open as if one was opening a filing cabinet, except there were no files but a black body. It was that of a woman, covered in a white sheet with her throat slit. After two more drawers had been pulled open and our inquisitive stares scanned the black bodies we decided we were hungry. Passing by the large ceramic sink where the bodies were cleaned, we exited into the dark night and stood around the braai with a nice cold beer in each of our hands.

Again the apartheid rules of deep rooted indoctrination were ever present in our thoughts and actions where I would rather see a dead black than a dead animal, and I was certainly not going to lose my appetite over it. I knew that if it was a white person I had seen it would have left an impression on me. Eating the steaks and drinking the beer we cursed the dead bastards in the morgue fridge with laughter and the cheers of our bottles ringing into the quiet night.

In Ladysmith I had met a girl called Tracey and along with her sister Penny, we went to the Klip River and parked the car below the tall trees that lined the banks of the river.

There were two people who looked down and out and had been living in a concrete house that barely had a roof. We got talking to these two tramps that were dirty, stinking to high heaven and hadn't got two brass beans to rub together, with their last coins spent on the discarded empty beer bottles around them.

'How did you land up in this situation?' I asked, half expecting a fuck you, it is none of your business.

'We were mercenaries in the Belgian Congo, under Mike Hoare!' one answered.

On hearing this I realized that this must have been the catalyst for their downfall and fallout from society, having been involved in this war where many mercenaries died.

It was always odd to see whites living like blacks when they had all the advantages of a white first-class world with silver spoons in their mouths.

Bearded and dirty and in a different world from ours they relished the interaction and friendship that we offered.

After a few hours we left, grateful to be in our world and far from the filth and squalor of theirs.

At the OK Bazaars there was an Indian woman married to a white Afrikaner man. This was taboo at its worst in our racially divided society, where no non-white was permitted to live in white society. To remain together they had no choice but to live in the Indian area where there was more acceptance of their marriage. Either way they still lived a life of finger pointing and racial sneers.

Also under the Group Areas Act, if a white couple produced a child with crinkly hair, the whole family was reclassified as Coloured and moved to a Coloured area where the children would have to attend a Coloured school.

It did not matter how rich you were or where you worked if your skin colour was anything other than white you had no choice but to live in an Indian, Coloured, Asian, or Black township or location.

Vish, one of my bosses from the District team in Ladysmith was Indian and very professional, wealthy and classier than many whites.

But unfortunately his skin colour denoted his dwelling place and many more injustices by the strict apartheid policies.

Ladysmith was often flooded when the Klip River burst its banks resulting in a nightmare in the store as it flooded in some areas as much as two feet deep. Rubber ducks and row boats cruised the main streets as we battled the water and the turmoil that it left in its wake. Mud, waterlogged and damaged stock and totally exhausted spirits had us working for two days non-stop until we could re-open the store for business.

Many staff were cut off from food and basic essentials as the flood created havoc in the non-white areas. One to always treat his fellow staff member with respect and dignity, we rounded up some supplies and drove them to their flooded houses, where the food items were received with warm smiles and a slight lift in spirits.

Back at home for Christmas, as always we had a spectacular meal cooked so perfectly by my Mum, from an amazing tasting turkey with bread sauce, glazed ham, to Christmas pudding with money in it along with sweet brandy butter and mince pies. It was a feast eaten in the dining room, the room where my mother was born.

After the meal John and I decided to go out for a few drinks to the Hillcrest Hotel, an old colonial building with a wide verandah and a meeting place for all of us young adults.

It just felt normal for only white people to be allowed in, and where the only blacks inside the hotel were the waiters and ones serving behind the bar quenching our thirsts.

After a good night and one too many beers later we returned home and on our last turn we saw that the Standard Bank was on fire. The neon lit Standard Bank sign had flames shooting out of it, and there was no one around except for us. With John's quick thinking we rushed to the Caltex petrol station where John kicked the glass door in, shattering the glass and lacerating his foot in the process.

Grabbing hold of the fire extinguisher we dashed towards the Bank. I helped John onto the ledge and then passed him the fire extinguisher. He crept as close as he dare get, before spraying the powder over the flames, which after a few sprays and an empty cylinder the flames were out. The Standard Bank, which was part of the old Richdens building, with all thanks to my brother could continue to do business in our village.

My time back at Hillcrest was always filled with drunken times and stories of car accidents, drunk at the wheel. There was a time I knocked out a traffic light, that fell to the ground and yet with a smashed up car I still made it to Maytime, before the tyre was cut to shreds by the smashed in wheel arch. I also remember a time in Ant's Anglia with Steve at the wheel, when to my amazement I looked out of the passenger window only to see a tyre come bouncing past us. We both laughed as it sped by before being lost in the bush. Before we had finished laughing the car came to a grinding halt as it dropped to one side. It was only then that we realized that the wheel was in fact ours.

While nursing a hangover Steve and I went to the bottle store in Gillitts and were met with a commotion of shouting, screams and cries. To our disbelief we saw a black man holding a small penknife with the blade covered in blood. And then next to him was a black woman holding her head as blood streamed down her face as she shrieked out in pain. There was no one around except for us.

'Drop the knife!' Steve screamed and after three more unsuccessful shouts Steve dealt the drunken man a flat hand across his face.

As the slap hit him so the knife dropped to the tarmac.

'She stole my beer,' the attacker stuttered in a drunken voice as he pointed to his wife. He staggered to hold his balance as he swayed and slurred totally drunk out of his skull, his eyes as bloodshot as red lines on a roadmap.

An ambulance had been called, but Black ambulances always took forever to reach a black person compared to a white ambulance that would be there in a flash.

We were told there was another woman who had been attacked and so we went looking for her. Eventually we found her propped against the wall clutching her throat with blood soaked into her clothing and her hands covered in the sticky red film.

When the ambulance finally arrived the woman with the stab wound to the head was loaded into the back, but for some unknown reason the woman clinging to life with her throat slit was left behind.

The police arrived on the scene and we left it in their hands, but unfortunately the woman with the slit throat bled to death and I am sure little to nothing ever came of the murder which would have been documented as a drunken domestic dispute.

Blacks were always lining up for everything from a bus ride, a taxi to a simple purchase in a General trading store.

When it was raining and there was a huge puddle many white motorists would veer slightly towards the pool of water and drive through it in the hope of spraying a black person walking to or from work. It was always met with a laugh when one scored a direct hit, with little to no feeling displayed to the soaked human being who could do or say nothing about the unfair treatment.

We would also go for rides on our motorbikes down the Valley of the Thousand Hills, a beautiful area to visit, but a rural home to thousands of Africans. We rode through the river beds, up and down hills and selfishly through people's properties. Thirsty we would stop for a bottle of coke at a small General store, with black faces sizing us up and down.

On one occasion as we were heading out of the location I was trailing the three bikes in front, and struggling with grit in my eyes, I noticed a teenage kid with a brick in his hand.

Seeing this I opened the throttle and lay myself flat over the tank and out of the corner of my eye I saw the brick in slow motion being launched at me. It passed over my back, and even though it did not touch me I could feel it passing over me, as I waited half expecting to feel the pain of it in my back.

We had been in their yard, disrupting the peace and this was his way of saying get out. I was lucky that day.

John was often filled with road rage and once there was an African taxi filled to capacity that cut him off. On his IT 200 he rode up right next to it and like a madman on drugs he began kicking at the side of the van with his heavy steel capped riding boots. Dent after dent he left his mark along with a list of racial slurs directed at the timid driver and his cargo of frightened passengers.

Shongweni Dam was another great place we would venture to for a good braai and many Castle beers. On one occasion I took my XR200 and drove through a good kilometer-long storm drain that ran under the dam. Keeping the tyres on the surface was like getting a grip on a fish, I slipped and slid all the way through the dark, dank and very cold tunnel. On the exit I opened the throttle to give me enough speed to ascend the slight incline that took me out into the fresh open air. As soon as I was up the incline I hit the brakes and it was like braking on ice and I was sliding right towards a solid concrete wall with no crash helmet. Miracously I threw the bike to one side preferring to hit the wall side on rather than head on and with delayed drunken reactions I performed an amazing stop right against the slimy wall thanks to a pile of sand that gave me all the traction I needed. Bennie who was on the back thought his end had come, but thanks to the alcohol in my body it was only afterwards that I realized how very close I had come to smashing my head into the solid dam wall.

John in his brand new Ford Escort XR3 accidentally hit a black woman as she crossed a highway. After a few cartwheels in the air she landed dead on the tar mac. There was no investigation and life continued on as normal.

On another occasion while John was at work at the Spar supermarket in Howick, a shoplifter was caught stealing and brought to the office. While they waited for the police the black thief tried to reach for something which my brother mistook as a weapon, which resulted in John drawing his gun. A shot was fired and the shoplifter was killed instantly.

His mother was given some free groceries to appease the situation which she accepted and the homicide disappeared never to surface again.

Back in the Ladysmith store there was a tall thin Indian called Gorra, who was not employed by the store, but whenever he passed by, he packed groceries for customers at lightning fast speed. He was comical and loved by the rest of the store's employees.

In July 1988 I was called up for a two month army camp and was sent to the border of SWA/Namibia just south of Ruacana. The fear of death and the hatred of the African for the predicament I was in, lived with me daily as we prepared for a major operation against a Cuban mobilized brigade. We had been one step away from rolling over the border into Angola and into full attack as a mechanized division.

In August I returned from my last camp. The tension had been hell and I honestly thought that had we attacked I would be one of the statistics.

On arriving back in Hillcrest, I went to the Hillcrest Hotel for a few beers, feeling very quiet and out of place. Friends of mine commented on my healthy brown tan and how nice it must have been relaxing on the border away from the winter. I nodded my head and turned drinking my beer. How could I explain that I prayed every night to have my life spared in the inevitable attack that loomed like heavy fog through a dark night, bogging my thoughts into complete paranoia. I had lived like this for two months in dugouts, dirty and shit scared.

Unfortunately when I finished the camp there was still that inbred army hatred to those branded so much lower than us.

But with hate in me, I still knew it was wrong to take someone's life, no matter how one thought.

But there was an Afrikaner who thought differently and honestly thought he was doing the country a favour. The newspapers and the SABC were all over this American style shooting that sent a chill through me and the country.

On 15 November 1988, an Afrikaner, Barend Hendrik Strydom, also known as the *Wit Wolf* (White Wolf) and a member of the AWB, (Afrikaner Weerstands Beweging), and an active policeman, went on a shooting spree in Pretoria. He calmly walked to the Strydom Square, specifically chosen for its link to Prime Minister JG Strydom, who had strong apartheid ideals. Then with a 9mm pistol in hand, and pockets bulging with magazines he walked casually and shot any black person that came his way, killing eight and wounding 16.

When it was plastered over every newspaper there were still those staunch right wingers that celebrated while the rest of the country was sickened.

Nic Strydom, Barend's father had confessed proudly in court that he had 'planted the seeds of religion and right wing political views in his son's heart.' He believed blacks were animals, and according to his Bible, blacks were not human beings.

Barend Strydom was sentenced to death, but in 1990 when capital punishment was abolished he was given a life sentence. And in 1992 he was released by President FW de Klerk as one of 150 political prisoners which included Robert McBride, who had planted a bomb at Magoos nightclub in Durban killing and lacerating many whites. In

1994 Strydom was granted amnesty by the Truth and Reconciliation Commission.

On my last day as the Assistant Manager at the store a group of the employees met me, Tracey, Penny and Rodney along the banks of the Klip River for a few beers and some hard spirits.

Gorra was there and he wished me well on my world travels. He placed his hand on my head and said a few words regarding my safety and well being as I stepped into the unknown. As he spoke these words I felt an electric shock pass through my body from my head to my feet. I went cold and felt a shiver pass down my spine as if a hand of protection had been placed over me. It was a great feeling and after more beers and loud music it was time to have my last sleep in Ladysmith before flying overseas into a world only dreamed about.

The day before I was to fly to Johannesburg to begin my overseas adventure, my parents, John and I were asked to go to Pinetown to meet with some executives from the Standard Bank.

After a great speech of thanks dedicated to us for saving their bank from being gutted by fire, we were awarded a gold pen and pencil set with the Standard Bank emblem on it. News reporters from the Highway Mail were there to take the story and along with a photo it was printed with the heading: Bank honours brave brothers. Even though I was there, my brother was the one that deserved all the honouring; it was his fearless approach to anything and everything in life that was a testament to his exceptionally strong willed character.

Sitting at home back in Hillcrest I looked out of the window with Piglet and Wesley, our two Jack Russells, asleep in the sun at my feet.

'My life is going to change,' I said to myself as I projected my thoughts overseas with that tinge of unknown fear sitting in the pit of my stomach. I thought about the recent news footage of the Berlin Wall, and how badly I wanted to see East Germany while it was still governed by the ruthless elements of communism.

It was time; I needed to see the world. Not through news clips and television broadcasts, but to be right in it and see and feel the experience firsthand.

THE WORLD OUTSIDE SOUTH AFRICA (1990) EUROPE AND COMMUNISM IN THE EASTERN BLOC

EAST GERMANY AND CZECHOSLOVAKIA

Never once did I ever consider the idea that I might choose another country in which to live. Having been born in Johannesburg the link to the land was like a mother to a child. Nothing could ever break that bond. I knew travel would change me but I had no idea how it would map out my future.

Before the barriers of apartheid came tumbling down and Nelson Mandela was still incarcerated, I decided to explore the outside world with sharp curiosity, a brainwashed narrow mind and a backpack.

On 6 February 1990 at the age of 24, I left the South Africa that I knew and that was one where the whites were in power and lived an extremely good life. Blacks on the other hand were subjected to being fourth class citizens, Indians and Coloureds ahead of them in the racial line, but all living a terrible life of ruthless segregation.

Along with Bruce, a friend that had called on the OK Bazaars store as a Beecham Representative, we boarded SAA from Louis Botha for Johannesburg. What a feeling it was to board the South African airways flight destined for London and a new world overseas. The excitement was intense and I never for one moment thought, what the hell am I doing leaving behind a career and a well paying one at that, a company car and a secure life.

When the plane took to the air little did I know that I was leaving behind the old South Africa that I had known and accepted as the only and right way to live in our segregated society.

Never once did I bother to think that our blacks were living the lives of slaves without the chains but nevertheless subservient to their white masters. In South Africa there was the freedom in a segregated society without civil war, but there was no freedom of speech for black and white. The government controlled what the public should or shouldn't know. For the blacks it was a life of repression with a helping of food on the table in a simple shack in a location, which was more than in most African countries which had gained independence from their European colonists.

I did not even know what Nelson Mandela looked like, and had never learned about him in school. I was told he was a terrorist that wanted Blacks in power, and with this fact I deemed him as a threat, and totally agreed that he should be imprisoned or even better hanged.

It would be years later that I would respect this man for leading the new South Africa, a man that believed in reconciliation.

Being overseas was like being a big kid in an outside classroom, with adventure, culture and breath taking scenery a total high for me.

As a traveller I was always asked which country I came from and there were many occasions when I replied 'South Africa,' I was given the cold shoulder or even worse humiliated as a racist. I felt myself standing up for my country as some sort of backpacking ambassador with my patriotic pride pouring from my soul as I backed the government in its stance on segregation of races, and the fact that non-whites were not permitted to vote.

In Ireland at a small place called Clifton, which was a very pro IRA area, we met a local who was so friendly towards us. We spoke about rugby and the Springboks who were still considered to be the best in the world in spite of being banned from playing internationally because of apartheid. His friendship seemed to change in mid sentence on hearing that we were South African.

'Yes we are South African. We aren't British,' we said, shocked that he was so anti South African.

'You are all the blood of an Englishman. Get away!' he said sternly, moving away from us as though we carried a deadly disease.

Knowing that there was a strong IRA presence we piled into our rented car and left in a hurry.

We not only had to deal with the act that we were white racists but also that we where blood of the Englishman and considered just as vile.

In Dublin after a long night of Guinness I took a leak behind some parked cars. I was confronted by two stern looking Irish policemen.

'What are you doing?' they shouted.

'I am from South Africa!' I replied not knowing what to say.

'No wonder you have so many fucken problems in your country!' they retaliated and walked away.

I honestly thought that I would be spending the night behind bars in an Irish jail.

After parting ways with my South African friends I caught a ferry alone from Harwich to the Hoek van Holland and then a train to Amsterdam. What a great feeling it was to be in Europe, but unfortunately on the second day I was robbed while I slept. My leather jacket, with my passport, travellers cheques, camera and address book with all my key contacts were taken. I was left feeling ill but I had no choice but to dig deep and get myself on track for travel.

I had always wanted to know what it felt like to be penniless and for two days I slept on the streets below a building in dirt and rubble along with two down and out Englishmen.

I had to find work and along with another South African I became a waiter on the beach, making really good tips and within two months I had another passport and money to my name.

In Holland I was reminded all too often that apartheid was a Dutch word, with the architect of apartheid heralding from the Netherlands, his name Dr. H.W. Verwoed.

Throughout my travels I never lied about where I was from and always welcomed the challenge that my answer would bring. For the most part I was accepted as a traveller in search of worldly experience, and not as a white racist.

After four months of hard work I took a train to Maastricht and then crossed into West Germany passing through Hannover on my way to the Helmstedt-Marienborn border crossing. The train came to a sudden stop at the border crossing and we were all ordered out and ushered towards a row of buildings. I was now at Checkpoint Alpha. Uniformed East German border guards patrolled the area as we entered a building and waited in line as the border guard checked each passport and validated it with a stamp.

With my backpack on my back I sauntered up to the officer who looked at me with cold piercing eyes that intimidated the shit out of me. He took his time as he looked through my passport paging through the pages with numerous stamps and visas. He looked keenly at each and I was waiting for a question on why I had a British passport having been born in South Africa. While he looked I thought about my place of birth, Johannesburg and what that meant to their communist ideals. The East Germans had served in Angola as advisers to the communist MPLA cause and they knew about South Africa and its bush war in Namibia and cross border raids into Angola. With not a word spoken he hammered the stamp into my passport with vile written across his face. I was now officially in East Germany. I followed the line of people and bordered an old East German train that looked very outdated compared to the West German train I had just exited. Sitting on a hard seat next to a window I thumbed through the passport pages and found the stamp from the border guard. It was a rectangular stamp with DDR and the coat of arms of the German Democratic Republic.

I felt eyes watching my every move as I waited for the train to take me to Berlin. It was an uneasy feeling but this was life where everybody watched each other caught up in the states control of its citizens. No one trusted each other with informants everywhere.

I felt as though I was in a dream sitting on the border of East Germany with communism in ruin and yet so prevalent in the buildings and people that poured onto the train.

After a long wait with thoughts running wild the train started moving. It never got to the speed of its neighbor as it chugged along through wide open countryside and cultivated fields with farms and narrow roads and little towns screaming this is the Iron Curtain. I was for the first time in my life behind the Iron Curtain, once impenetrable from the West.

The towns looked drab and depressing as little communist cars drove by oblivious to my stares as I took in my surroundings like a hungry scholar on a school outing.

My excitement was building with each click of the railway track to realize my desire of seeing the Berlin Wall. My dream of getting to

East Berlin had begun when as a young kid I had collected stamps, fascinated with the letters DDR and the communist coat of arms. I soon learned which countries were behind the Iron Curtain propped up by the Soviet Union. I looked at the stamps and knew a hand written letter had crossed the border, but learned in the Eastern Bloc that the people were not permitted to cross it themselves.

East Germany in 1990 was still called East Germany or the DDR (*Deutsche Demokratische Republik*) but one East German Mark was now equivalent to one West Mark and life in the East was still dirt cheap compared to the West. And as a traveller this sounded good.

Still to this day it leaves me yearning to learn more about a country divided from Aug 1961 to Nov 1989 with a 166 kilometre wall encircling Berlin, a life behind the massive divide cut off from the rest of the world, communism and dictatorship, Secret Police called Stasi (the most effective and repressive intelligence agencies in the world), and a border crossing called Checkpoint Charlie.

It was a long slow journey with me trying to work out how I could be in East Germany and soon would be in West Berlin, part of West Germany, was very confusing. Eventually the train pulled into the station in West Berlin. I didn't know where I would stay or where I was going but the drug of travel had kicked in and I was rushing. Here I was at this landlocked island called Berlin in the middle of the German Democratic Republic, close to 170 kilometres from the West German border, and it felt great.

I found a place to stay in Chalottenburg in the British Sector of West Berlin at a bed and breakfast run by a Lebanese man called Hatab. He was in his late forties or early fifties, looked unclean and had dark stubble and hazel nut piercing eyes that stared through me. I was left with a feeling that I did not trust this man one bit, and made sure to lock my backpack.

I sauntered up to the 18th century Brandenburg Gate passing people selling East German soldiers hats still with the East German coat of arms planted like a symbol of total power. I remembered a speech by Roland Reagan in June 1987 in front of the Brandenburg Gate as he challenged the Soviet leader Mikhail Gorbachev to 'tear down this wall.'

The Reichstag stood to the side barely on the west side of the wall. This was the parliament of the German Empire where Hitler met with his party members. On the other side of the Brandenburg Gate in Tiergarten, there was the Soviet War Memorial for the 80 000 soldiers of the Soviet Armed Forces who died during the Battle of Berlin. It was guarded very respectfully by two Russian soldiers standing with rifles at attention. Ironically it was in the British sector.

West Berlin was divided into three sectors, the British, the French and the American. East Berlin was controlled by the Soviets.

In an open area there was a mound of earth which I was told was Hitler's Bunker, supposedly where he ended his life along with Eva Braun. The bunker didn't impress me too much. Firstly because no one seems to know exactly where he died, and secondly because the man was a lunatic and a coward, too scared to face a firing squad.

The Brandenburg Gate was under repair having stood neglected for so many years on the East side of the wall. It still stood magnificently as a symbol of Prussian military might.

Construction workers were hurriedly getting it ready for the unification of Germany. This would be where East and West would finally come together after nearly three decades.

I was about to walk from the west to the east and it felt like walking from a white affluent neighbourhood in South Africa into a far less privileged society that was bleak and depressing like that of our blacks minus the tin shacks.

Our South African blacks were behind their own wall, the colour divide of apartheid which was black and white, townships and pass books and ruthless police. Germany's was East and West, capitalist and communist, rich and poor with the latter being a perfect fit for our divide.

It had always been known in the military circles that East Germany was a training ground for our black freedom fighters fighting for a free South Africa.

When the wall began to tumble and freedom for the East Germans was in the air, it was like a wave that spread to the shores of Africa. Within a couple of months Nelson Mandela was a free man, our South African border war with SWA/Namibia and Angola ended. Gorbachov and Reagan had ended the Cold War and history was changing. Like a never ending Siberian winter that seemed impossible to break, the spring buds of change were appearing through the cracks. The East Germans were giddy with freedom and the blacks in South Africa were now for the first time looked at as equals, free to ride what bus where they chose, swim at which beach they liked and eat at what restaurant they felt appealed to them. The new South Africa had awakened at the same time as the new Germany.

The contrasts of east and west were still as prominent as ever. Sitting in Kurfurstendamm I sipped on a coffee as I watched brand new BMWs and Mercedes racing by with the status of wealth oozing from their shiny paintwork. Neon lights flashed and flickered excitement as women stood in sexy tight jeans and faces beautified with makeup as they plied their trade.

Turks and Lebanese added another dimension to the white faces along with an aroma of kebabs in the air. This was the West that had been rebuilt from the devastation of World War II where the Deutsch-mark was one of the strongest currencies in the world.

Unfortunately the East was completely the opposite. Trabants or Trabis as they were affectionately known, was a fibre glass car running on a two stroke engine and sounded more like a lawn mower. Ladas and Yugo's charged up the depressing streets along with the Trabis putting the communist stamp on the country.

Alexanderplatz of East Berlin was the equivalent of Kurfurstendamm of the West minus the excitement and flashing lights with the communist depressing tone setting the scene. Alexanderplatz was ringed with offices and hotels modern by communist standards, on the edge of a wide open circle with a fountain in the middle. Flags added the only colour to the cold concrete as people hurried; carrying bags and cheap cartons of cigarettes.

Moving away from Alexanderplatz, I noticed there were no billboards or dressed up window displays. The buildings were just as old as the west but were decaying with neglect, blackened with pollution and scarred with shrapnel still from 1945.

People milled around as if they were in a trance half expecting the Berlin Wall to be re erected as suddenly as it had gone up in 1961 with rolls and strands of barbed wire as had been the case decades ago.

My dream of one day touching the wall finally came true on 12 September 1990. It was amazing to see and I even got a chisel and a hammer and whacked out a chunk. I held it in my hand knowing that it represented a cold barrier like our invisible apartheid divide.

I stood in the middle of no man's land with the capitalist west on one side and the communist east on the other. It was called the 'death strip' and was like a barren moat of open sand snaking its way through the city.

The wall was rock solid concrete, high and cold with barbed wire mesh in the middle. This divide had been erected to keep those in at all costs with a no man's land in between the double wall. Street lights and high concrete guard towers ran the length of the wall as further intimidation to those planning an escape to the west. The soldiers armed with rifles manning the towers were gone as were the viscious dogs, the floodlights, the trip alarms and beds of upturned spikes. Once all part of the security zone it was now just nothing other than a huge out of place wall and open land with guard towers and street lamps.

Some stretches on the west side were painted. Pink Floyd 'The Wall' decorated a stretch of the bland wall right next to what I thought was the most impressive painting of a blue Trabby smashing through the wall from the East side. Concrete splintered everywhere under the caption 'Test the Best'. It was sinister and evil as I looked through the wall and walked down no man's land, feeling that a fortress had been erected to keep communism in and the world out.

In no man's land I found the spot marked by a crude looking cross with barbed wire, where in 1962 Peter Fechter, a teenager had been shot by an East German guard as he attempted to flee to the west. His name was painted on the wood. He lay dying next to the Berlin Wall tangled in barbed wire with no one able to help him. After an hour an East German guard removed his body. He had been left to bleed to death.

He was one of the 171 people killed as they tried to escape to the west.

The East Germans had called the wall, 'the antifascist protective barrier.'

Tim Ramsden

Life here was the apartheid back home with the South African townships having the dividing wall built on colour, with squalor and fear keeping whites out and blacks in.

I passed a parked convoy of eight old East German troop carriers painted a dull green with canvas coverings. I treaded carefully past anything military scared that the Secret Police may think I was some sort of spy. I still managed to sneak a picture with one eye on the target and the other for soldiers. Seeing this made me wonder about all the East German advisers that had been shipped over to Angola in support of the ruling MPLA and its communist ideals. They had worked closely with the Soviets and Cubans against our ally, Jonas Savimbi's UNITA.

Surprisingly there didn't seem to be many soldiers around. At the Neue Wache (New Guard House) a pillared building built in 1816 as a monument to fallen soldiers I saw my first East German soldier. He was standing guard, over the remains of the Unknown Soldier and an unknown concentration camp victim from WWII. I took a good picture of him decked out in his soon to be extinct grey East German uniform with his low cut steel helmet, white gloves and belt and long heavy black boots. His rifle with bayonet was held in his left hand and rested against his shoulder. His face stared unflinchingly forward, his body rigidly stiff and I could almost read the uncertainty of what lay ahead for him in his expression. When his guard beat was up he would do the Prussian march and march the goose step.

Young men were drafted into the military and police in the same way as white males were in South Africa.

A demonstration passed me. There were hundreds of people some waving flags. There was one of Mao Tse-tung's face, the Chinese communist leader, and an old East German flag with the black strip cut off. The coat of arms was in the middle of the flag featuring a hammer and a compass, surrounded by a ring of rye. The hammer represented the workers in the factories, the compass the intelligentsia, and the ring of rye the farmers.

For some reason there was a huge albatross made from paper Mache that was propped up with sticks and walked along with the chanting crowd. Someone had an enlarged 100 DM note stuck on his back. I was surprised not to have seen a picture of the bespectacled Erich Honecker the communist leader of the GDR from 1971-1989. The rally definitely had a communist notion to it, watching it with keen interest as it disappeared around some buildings.

I found an old district of East Berlin and asked a woman if I could exchange some West German Marks for some East German Marks. She pulled out an old 5 East German note and I gave her 5 West German Marks. It was a very small note, almost half the size of a West Mark. It had Thomas Muntzer face on it with the words, *Staatsbank Der* DDR, *Deutschen Demokratischen Republik*. The coat of arms of East Germany was on the front and back. It was still crisp and in good condition considering it was dated 1975.

After some interesting walking through the drab surroundings I found Checkpoint Charlie. This was controlled by the Americans and was famous for the sign, 'You are leaving the American sector.' The words were also written in Russian, French and German. It had been erected in 1961 and closed in 1990 with the unification. This was the main passage for East West crossings with extremely tight security.

I found the Checkpoint Charlie museum and spent an hour looking at all the photographs and memorabilia. There were hundreds of pictures of escapes through tunnels, in balloons, in vehicles some successful and others not. It was the most interesting museum I had seen especially with my fascination to anything regarding the Berlin Wall.

I had heard about a Nazi concentration camp about 35 kilometres north of Berlin in East Germany. I caught a train through open country side to Oranienburg. There I found the Sachsenhausen concentration camp which was used primarily for political prisoners from 1936 until 1945. Of the 200 000 people who passed through the gates 30 000 perished, the majority being Soviet prisoners of war. The camp was also used as a training area for SS officers, who would be used to oversee other camps.

Walking around the camp made me feel uneasy and I didn't even bother to take a photograph. Just to think that these Nazis who had committed such atrocities walked on the same earth as I was walking over made my soul cringe. In less than half an hour I was back on the train and on my way to Berlin.

I caught an old yellow and red train from an East Berlin station to Potsdam that looked as though it had been running since the end of

World War II, and certainly felt it. It was slow, the seats were hard and the wheels whined for grease. The ticket was in German and Russian. I sat back in the uncomfortable seat and looked out of the window at a sight that most of the outside world had never seen. The buildings were black and ugly, old East German cars cut through the traffic and life was as dull and colourless as the darkening gloomy sky.

In Potsdam where the Potsdam Conference was held as a wartime meeting with heads of government in July to August 1945, I saw dozens of Russian soldiers. They were smart in their uniforms with the hammer and sickle displayed prominently on their visor hats and their AK47s slung over their shoulders. They looked lost as if waiting for orders as to when they were leaving their old communist satellite state.

I found the Glienicker Bridge with the Soviet flag still flying and manned by Russian soldiers as though nothing had changed. This was where east and west political prisoners were exchanged.

Close to the bridge was the Radio Tower which transmitted messages across East Germany, and like everything else was totally controlled by the state.

In Streckenzuschlag Bahnhoff, East Berlin, I bought a ticket to Dresden for a quarter of the price that the West would charge, it cost me only 6 DMs. I boarded an old East German train with my ticket in German and Russian and sat with people who were looking around with a new set of eyes still with a robotic communist brain that would take a while to change.

I could feel the double life they had lived for so long. They had lived by command and obedience too scared to trust anyone with shadowy informers and secret police everywhere. Each citizen had to carry their identity pamphlet summarizing their public life.

One could see those dreams in their eyes and those invisible shackles removed. This new-found freedom had been embraced, and yet their lives were being lived as though nothing had ever changed. After all, the wall had come down, and people still had to work and live their life the way they knew how. One still needed money to live like a capitalist and most didn't.

In Dresden, the sister city to Prague I saw for myself the destruction left behind from the allied bombing in 1945. A once beautiful cathedral lay in rubble without the funds to restore it, and buildings as black as coal, cut and marked by shrapnel stood out like ugly reminders that communism had everyone equal, but the rest was left to another day with no money in state coffers to fund it.

A statue of Lenin and two comrades stood outside a communist style apartment block looking more out of place than ever before. No one had tried to desecrate it in anger towards a system that hadn't worked. I had always been fascinated by Lenin, a man who stood behind his beliefs. His face was unsmiling, his head was held high and one could see he was looking to the future, and maybe it was this sort of propaganda that drew the people in to believing in the communist ideals.

I met up with some young East German students who knew all about South Africa, the apartheid situation, Nelson Mandela and the South African war on SWAPO in SWA/Namibia and Angola. They told me about news footage that they would watch about communism in Angola and Mozambique with East German and Soviet advisers, weapons from the communist states along with the massive Cuban presence of soldiers in their thousands courtesy of Fidel Castro.

It knocked me backwards what these people knew. Most people I had met in my travels knew little to nothing about South Africa let alone its fight against communism and its geographical position on a world map. These people behind the Iron Curtain had certainly been educated on this part of their cold war history.

They were also very good at sport, especially in the Olympic Games and how many medals the communist countries could tally up. It was like a showing of power to the world that communist countries were strong.

East Germany had always been determined to outdo their German neighbor when it came to medal counts. With strict state run programs they were able to achieve this. Since 1968, West Germany with twice the land and three times as many people had won fewer than half the Olympic medals than East Germany. East Germany took 40 gold medals in the 1976 Montreal games alone.

It would emerge years later that heavy steroid and doping use contributed to these high medal counts, tarnishing the unfair success of these athletes through their dark sided state run programs.

Leaving the city of Dresden I took a train that cut through the countryside of East Germany to the Czechoslovakian border. My passport was stamped at the border with a cold nod from the officer. I looked at the stamp and it had the letters CSSR. I was now in the Czechoslovak Socialist Republic and entering behind the Iron Curtain. On Czechoslovakian soil, uniformed border guards with communist visor hats and communist symbols climbed onto the train. AK 47s were slung over their shoulders as they moved stiffly like Gestapo officers with an aura of power. Hardened unflinching expressions were plastered over their faces as they walked the carriages.

When the train rolled in to the Prague station I had to change a certain amount of money which was written onto a currency form which I could not lose. In turn I was handed wads of worthless currency which I had been told it would be hard to spend.

In Prague, the capital of Czechoslovakia I walked through Wenceslas square where the Velvet Revolution had taken place. I passed a shrine of black and white photos of young teenagers who had paid the ultimate price with their lives to gain freedom through a unified voice that had sent shock waves through the communist leadership in 1989. The faces forever young stared wide eyed forward with candles flickering keeping their memories alive as family members stood at the shrine like mourners at a graveyard. Melted wax lay in hardened pools amongst the photos like a frozen pond of tears.

Also in Prague while sitting in a quaint old beer garden bordering an old Jewish cemetery minding my own business I was called a racist pig by a German girl, on her hearing that I was a South African.

'How can you judge me for my government policies, look at you and what your country did to the Jews!' 'You are a hypocrite!' I shouted back in such rage that my body shook and I could feel my face contorted in anger.

She walked away and left me alone to finish my beer. She had killed the beautiful moment.

Getting lost in the city I found the old historical Charles Bridge which crosses the Vltava River. It was constructed with stone in 1357 under King Charles IV. It is the most spectacular bridge I have ever seen. At 516 metres long and 10 metres wide it rests on 16 arches and is decorated by a continuous alley of 30 statues and statuaries, most of them baroque style. It makes the perfect setting for a post card photograph.

With a few loud Americans and Steve, also an American but far more cultured in a low key way, we went into a small restaurant just off Wenceslas Square for an early breakfast. There was no seating at all in the restaurant, just stainless steel tables high enough to stand and eat from and so we circled one and christened the start of the day with a round of beers. The beers were dirt cheap, just a few Kourona which worked out to about 20 Canadian cents, the only place in the world where I as a traveller could afford to buy a round. It felt great and the beer tasted that much better. A black man from Mozambique joined our table. He stood out like a sore thumb in the sea of white faces.

I told him about the capture of three soldiers from my section back in 1985 and how they were held captive in Maputo for three months. He looked at me with no emotion in his face and yet his eyes gave off a sense of scorn. Right away I wished I had never told the story feeling I had just betrayed the captured three, Paul, Laurence and Sandor. He said he was studying and now I thought, yes studying to be a soldier for FRELIMO. I felt sick and turned away making conversation with the others at the table, wishing I could erase what I had said.

After the meal I went into a department store. It was drab and depressing and one could see true communism at work where everyone had a job and worked for the state. There were three people doing one persons job and also many other redundant positions that gave people an income. People were poor and yet they seemed happy. The window displays facing the cobbled streets were without flair and appeal and lacked vibrant colour, with the merchandise either made in the satellite states or in the Soviet Union.

I met some students who had been involved in the Velvet Revolution in Wenceslas Square. They also spoke of open hatred for the Soviets and what the Russian tanks did in the summer of 1968 to quell the uprising against communism. Leonid Brezhnev, the Soviet Premier had given the order for the Red army to move into Czechoslovakia. They rolled into Prague and blasted buildings and people to rubble and ruin. I saw one of the Soviet tanks still standing in the square as a monument.

Steve and I decided to head to Plzen by train and then our plan was to get to Munich by hitchhiking from the Czechoslovakian border.

Steve had been travelling for three years and had been around the world. He had seen and learned so much and had travelled like me on a shoestring. I looked at him and wondered what I would see before I ventured back to my roots in South Africa. We stayed a night in Plzen and found this small bar with hard drinking Czechs. There was a band playing and when they heard Steve was from America they sang, 'Bye Bye Miss American Pie.' It gave me goosebumps when I realized why they were playing this particular song. America had liberated Czechoslovakia from the Germans in World War II, and they had never forgotten this. It took me back to my army days with patriotism and pride having served for ones country.

After a drunken couple of days at the Munich Beerfest, I made my way into Yugoslavia. I spent a day in Zagreb, waiting for my train. It was another deprived city rich in architecture with little shops and cobbled streets. Old communist cars like Skoda's, Ladas, and Yugo's drove along the clean roads with the screeching of trams which ran down the middle of the road. The station was filled with gypsies who I had been told had come from Albania, which only forced me to hold onto my pack that much tighter.

This was once Marshal Tito's country propped up by the Soviets. He was Secretary General and later President of the League of Communism of Yugoslavia from 1939 until his death in 1980. A few years later on I was to learn firsthand from my mother in law how the Russians had treated the Danube Swabians after the end of the war. In 1948 she and her family were taken and placed in forced labour camps run by the partisans. Many died but because the Germans lost the war, very little is ever known about this dark chapter in Yugoslavia's history.

When the train finally came I readied myself for a very long trip through the country to Athens in Greece. The train was packed and I couldn't get a seat. The only spare spot was outside the toilet. For hours on end I sat on my pack waiting for a precious and comfortable seat. To my horror the toilet overflowed saturating my backpack with water and urine and I hoped that was all. Swearing I pushed myself down the aisle and found another place to sit.

The train took us through the middle of the country stopping at the capital Belgrade. Everyone seemed to be carrying something whether it be a parcel, a big bag of clothing or bags of food. It looked as though this was the hub to come and go from, buying and selling to keep their subsistent lives going. People poured off the train while others pushed their way on fighting for a seat.

After 12 hours I had a seat and still had at least another 12 hours before I arrived in Athens. Seeing the Parthenon, feeling the humidity and experiencing the pollution in Athens, I island-hopped from Ios to Santarini, and then Crete before getting a night ferry from Rhodes to Turkey.

I was now about to set foot in the Middle East, with no idea what I should expect. This was travel, it was like a drug and it felt great.

TURKEY

It was getting late when the ferry docked at Marmaris and we all filed down the gangplank with eager anticipation. A little giddy from the ride we made our way to the passport control booth forming a long line. A bright red Turkish flag fluttered and flapped in the sea breeze with the crescent moon and star reminding me of the Halal symbol. I met two South African's ahead of me who were travelling on South African passports. When they reached the customs office, their passports were looked over by the Turkish authorities with keen interest. And then to my shock, they were waved away and told to go to the back of the line like disobedient school children.

They took one look at my passport, thankfully a British one and stamped it without a single question. I always felt gifted with my crimson British passport. It was like a first class ticket across the world compared with my fellow South African's and their costly visa filled blue passports. It was like reverse apartheid that we whites were linked to in South Africa, which was now being applied in the greater world. No white South African was permitted into India, as well as Morocco along with many other lands, sympathetic to the non-white situation in South Africa. I had entry to where ever I chose and I often said a silent thanks to my Dad for being born British.

Along with an Australian girl who I had met on the ferry, we went in search of accommodation and shared a room. It didn't take long to find one and drop our bags before setting out to a bar where a few of us in the line had decided to meet to christen our arrival in Turkey.

It was getting dark and on the way we passed the two South African's who after a lengthy ordeal with the officials were waved through. They looked relieved and smiled.

'Howzit. Good they let you in!' I smiled back.

'See you at the bar!' which made them move quicker towards their accommodation.

There were lots of Western travellers at the bar which was on the second floor in a very poor looking area. It was open with a few chairs and a rustic looking bar. Tuborg's were being served and I gladly sipped on one, the ice cold beer cooling my system from the sticky humidity.

Before long an American nicknamed 'Eagle,' arrived on the scene in a very loud and obnoxious way. The South African's who joined us said they had met him on the ferry and had tried to get rid of him, but to no avail.

'He is fucken crazy!' one of them commented. He was right.

'I hate all kaffirs. Kill the kaffirs!' he shouted like a madman. He then began naming Generals in the SADF, places and battles in Angola that no one would know about unless having read about it, or actually being there. We soon learned that he had been a mercenary in Angola. He was really drunk and kept on jumping off things from the bar counter to tables and chairs and then progressed to chairs on top of tables. He then crouched on a window ledge and to our horror jumped two storeys down and miracously landed plumb on his feet. This is how he got his name, 'Eagle.'

From the bar we all went to have a kebab which was out of this world. To our relief we had lost Eagle. We planned to meet at the pier in the morning and after a great night we all went our different directions for a good first night's sleep in Turkey.

In the morning the heat had us rising early and as arranged we all met at the pier. It didn't take long for us to get in to the anis flavoured Raki's, which was a Turkish spirit consisting of 45 % alcohol. The drink was made with grapes, figs and plums. We met some Turkish people working in the bar cum fishing hut and they were extremely friendly to all of us. By the afternoon we had decided that the whole group of us were going to go to a beautiful place called Oludeniz. We met by the pier with our backpacks and then 10 of us in crammed a small bus. We were rushing like hell, all wanting to leave Marmaris before 'Eagle' caught wind of our plan.

We wound our way through roads carved into the mountains in the direction of Fethiye. Someone had a cassette player and Tom Petty's Full Moon Fever rocked the bus and put a song to a journey that will forever be imprinted in our minds. After some long hours of driving we eventually came to an open lagoon area with a nice beach called Oludeniz. There was hardly a soul around and we knew why. It was near the end of October 1990 and everyone was talking about war in the Middle East. Just to confirm the threat we saw two warships on their way to the Gulf. It could not have been better to have cheap accommodation and a beach completely to ourselves. The average tourist was really scared to travel at this time with the invasion of Iraq set to take place anytime soon. At our accommodation, a long white bungalow divided into rooms, we met a nice old couple. They were in their late 60s and had been backpacking for a couple of years with no signs of stopping. The woman shared some stories with us that had me thinking enviously of more places that I had to see.

'Look at them and what they have seen. That's remarkable at that age!' I said to our group as we listened intently to their reminiscences. Travel stories were like another language, a language that we could all relate to.

At the end of the journey we all felt as though we had known each other for ages. There were the two English girls from Farnborough, Jo and Phil, who continually smiled and joked with sarcastic wit. Charlie or Chuck shit, and Pat were both from America. Daryl was from Canada out in British Columbia; Melissa was from Australia along with Mike and Jeremy. Nicole and Jane who were travelling together also came from Australia. I was given the nickname Timbavati from Phil who had heard about the White Lions of Timbavati in South Africa, and I called her Philemon. We were all roughly the same age and we felt like a small group of United Nations delegates with our mission to see parts of Turkey and have a blast while exploring it.

We all clambered aboard a sail boat and lazed on the deck. Deep in conversation forming new friendships we were taken around the lagoon to other little islands covered in rocks and bush with remains of old stone walls and houses. We drifted by with the sun warm on our bodies, until we had to dive into the turquoise ocean to cool ourselves down.

After a couple of days we decided we all wanted to head out to the middle of the country. We organized a bus for all of us and set out towards Antalya and then turned off towards Denizli to Pamukkale.

The bus stopped at the bottom and we looked up to what is known as the Cotton Castle. It seemed so out of place, a terraced mountain of brilliant white ledges, water cascading like a small waterfall over the calcium ridges and pooling in hundreds of small sauna sized pools. We walked through the white warm and creamy pools looking like hot milk, each ledge saturated with white dissolved calcium bicarbonate bubbling up from the Cal Dagi Mountains beyond. We stood in the thick water and splashed around all having never seen such a natural phenomenon in our lives. The sun reflected off the calcium like a mirror and had us squinting and fumbling for sun glasses. It reminded me of Namibia and the white sand in the salt pans when I was in the army, and how that drilled into our eyes like piercing daggers.

From here we walked to the Pamukkale Termal and found the sacred pool on the top of the ridge. It was a hot day but we all wanted a therapeutic swim in the springs. The water was 35 degree Celsius as we let the warm water massage our bodies, and sat on the sunken Roman columns, using them as underwater benches. Here I was sitting on history from the Roman Empire absorbing a country and a culture that I knew nothing about. Turkish Delight chocolates were my only recollection as a child linked to the country Turkey.

From Pamukkale we headed for Konya making our way along the coast. In the afternoon under the burning midday heat we stopped 47 kilometres east of Antalya at a place called Aspendos which lay in the middle of nowhere between Antalaya and Alanya. Stretching our legs we walked into Turkeys best preserved ancient theatre built by the Romans in the second century. It was mind blowing to see it still standing with an arc of stone seating perfectly intact with a semi circle being the stage and a backdrop of pillars and statues in half their former glory. It added that old touch of pure artwork and master skill that these Romans had in them. I sat on the stone steps and could almost visualize a performance by a bunch of serious Romans.

From the coast we made our way inland through wide open land with the odd rural village kept alive through subsistence living. We arrived in Konya as it was getting dark and stayed a night in a humble Turkish house. Konya was the midpoint between Antalaya and Neveshir, very close to Goreme. We all rolled our sleeping bags on the floor and slept in two rooms. I found a bed pan in the room and asked

Tim Ramsden

Phil and Jo what I was meant to do with it. I had never seen such a thing in my life, and with my straight face and oozing sarcasm I had them in stitches.

In the early morning we had a light breakfast and still under darkness we made our way towards Cappadocia.

After some long hours of driving with Zombie Zoo and Free Falling cranked up on the cassette player, with loud chatter adding to the noise and hands and feet tapping to the music, we drove into Cappadocia.

The driver stopped and we all got out. I gazed as far as I could see and it felt as though I was on another planet.

'Is this Mars?' I asked, because in my mind this just couldn't be on earth. The scenery was unique and I just couldn't believe what I was looking at. All around us there were pointed rock formations some as white as snow and others brown and hollowed. People actually lived in these rock-cut houses which looked as though a bomb had gone off peppering holes into them. They were all like houses from a fairy tale with cut outs for windows and chimneys to waft the smoke away from the cooking fires. They had been dubbed fairy chimneys by the locals.

I also learned that the ancient Silk Road ran through Cappadocia, the long route being from Turkey to China which allowed trade to flourish between the great empires.

We got out and walked through one of the rock cut outs and followed an underground hollowed out path cut from the rock with stairs and well worn sides where many hands had made the once rough surface as smooth as polished marble. We walked bent over like hunchbacks, laughing and shouting obscenities until we came to an open room that had a slightly higher ceiling. People actually lived underground along with their livestock especially in the freezing temperatures of a treacherous Turkish winter with utter barrenness all around. We sat and got our breath back thinking of life underground and how people had escaped from marauders into these networks of tunnels and rooms.

We continued to Kayseri and then turned off. A sign that read 'Goreme' was our destination and it wasn't too much further. Another village of rock formations popped up looking every bit like a stage set for a science fiction movie. Over centuries a thick layer of volcanic tufa had been eroded into these eerie and odd shapes of all sizes with carved out chambers used as churches, stables and homes.

We chipped at the rock and powder poured like salt from a salt cellar onto the rock surface. Windows looked like sinister eyes peering from the rock formation with others bricked up tightly with rock to shelter against the bone chilling wind that would torment them in winter.

Our bus took us to a small pension in the rocks, where we divided up for sleep in a hollowed out room. Entertainment was in another room with carpets hung like pictures from the walls. Urns and vases decorated the open spaces and candles burned adding ambiance to the setting. Carpets covered the floor from wall to wall and also a long hard bench which was the only seating in the room. Five Turkish men played music; guitars, a small hand drum, a man flicking spoons and clapping resounded through the room. Tuborg beer flowed as we all became so absorbed in the moment with the Turkish culture in full swing. Like being at a concert our eyes never left the stage as these men made music from literally nothing.

Mike being the clown he was picked up a guitar and started strumming it. Totally out of tune and with a face riddled with frowns of fake emotion and a sly smile of sarcasm he joined the band under a barrage of laughter from all of us. It was one of those evenings where a life long bond formed in our group of friends from all corners of the earth, and we clinked bottles of Tuborg until the early hours of morning when all the beer had been drunk. Stumbling back to our hollowed out room we passed out for the night and woke when the sun cooked us out of our sleeping bags with no mercy.

Looking like a bunch of homeless bums we searched for water to hopefully wash our hangovers away. With little luck we faced the day with bloodshot eyes and slowed movements.

In the heat of the day we walked into the rocks and watched Dave a fellow traveller climb up a rock face as white as snow. Half way up he stopped and froze. He was 25 to 30 metres up.

'I can't move! It's too slippery!' he shouted.

He had walked up the rock following the chiselled out footsteps deep enough to hold a foot. The further up he went the harder it got and the shallower the foot holds were. The hard rock was slippery with fine granules flowing down the sides with each step. One wrong movement and he would slide all the way down losing layers of skin and breaking bones in the process. He was scared and we were too. A Spanish traveller found a long stick and held it out to him for support while Mike held his foot in place and Jeremy in turn held Mike's foot from sliding out. After a couple of long agonizing hours Dave made his way down using the stick as an aid. Pale and exhausted he forced a smile of relief to be back on level land and walking once again.

In town we played the Turks a game of soccer on a very sandy surface with a stone wall around it. The Turks egged on their team with loud shouting as we looked more like idiots with our hangovers still very present. It helped sweat the beer out and gave us some well needed exercise.

Donkey carts with car wheels and axles and a bin from a pickup rode by with Muslim women at the reins with white head scarves flapping in the wind. Everything in Turkey had a use and in this case an old car was cannibalized to make a cart. I had seen the same in Africa where the poor will do what it takes to make use of everything to make their lives that much easier.

There was a call to prayer and a wail resounded through the speakers across this little town that looked as though it had been cut off from the rest of the country. Suddenly a Turkish voice shouted through the speaker.

'What did he just say?' I asked a Turkish man next to me.

'He has lost his donkey and if anyone sees it to let him know!' I smiled at how crazy it sounded.

Feeling hungry with the aroma of lamb stewing on the rotisserie, we lined up for a kebab. The Turkish man ran his business from a small portable hut. Picking up a knife he sharpened it as though he was about to kill something. Slowly and meticulously he ran the knife down the spiral of meat allowing small pieces to drop into the open pita bread. Our saliva was almost oozing out of our mouths as he packed the meat in and then added in cut lettuce and tomato. He wrapped it up and gave it to us like a present. We tore it open and devoured it like cavemen eating their kill. It was delicious and tasted even better for the dirt cheap price.

After another night of Turkish music mixed with our Tom Petty we made our way to through Kirikkale to Ankara, the capital of Turkey since 1923, for the night. Tired and exhausted we piled into a few cheap rooms before heading out for Izmir the next morning, a journey we knew was a long one. The heat gnawed at us as the hot breeze rushing past our arms which dangled out of the windows. We passed through Afyon having cut through the middle of the country with Izmir our sleeping destination. In Izmir we made a bee line for a street vendor as if we hadn't seen food in days. The vendor was an old man who casually smoked on his cigarette while boiling his corn, totally unfazed by our stampede.

'Philemon these are *mielies*!' I said making reference to the Afrikaans word for corn.

He layered on the butter and we held it like kids with big popsicles, and then chewed it like chipmunks.

Izmir is home to about 3 million people and was mostly burned down during the Greek-Turkish war of 1922. Today it is a modern and booming cosmopolitan town.

Wandering around we nearly vomited as we walked through a fish market with fish lying in the sun and flies buzzing about like vultures. It shocked me to watch people buying, oblivious to the smell as though it was only in our imagination. Turkish fishmongers hacked off fishes heads on chopping blocks thick with dirt and filleted them in the most appalling conditions while flies feasted on the blood and intestines. Thank God we had eaten, as my appetite had left me on this short but smelly walk.

A man stood on the side of the market looking like a walking shop. He was covered in merchandise from head to toe, front to back with items hanging off him pinned to his clothes. Even his hands were full. He literally was a one stop shop from brushes to beads and cloths to clothes hangers.

In the early morning we took a short drive in the direction of Selcuk and the famous tourist spot Kusadasi to see the famous ruins of Ephesus, once the Roman capital in the province of Asia. Again I felt like I was on another planet with only rock and stone. The structures were amazing as we wandered down what would have been the old main street passing the Temple of Hadrian and Marble Way. Mike, Chuck and I sat in a row and posed for a photo sitting on a slab of marble with six holes, with our pants at our ankles and our faces straining. We were sitting on the public latrines with a high wall behind us and a lower one in front of us for privacy. The ancient fountain of Trajan was next before we came face to face with the reconstructed facade of the monumental library of Celsus. Pillars two storeys high towered over us as we posed beneath it for a photo. Pieces of rock looked as though they could fall at any moment, balanced by time and weathered by the elements. The precision and art work in the rock was a masterpiece adding to the grandeur of this wonder of the world.

We found the old theatre and sat on the stone steps terraced evenly down to the open stage, a semi circle of white hardened sand. We sat as if waiting for the Romans to walk out and begin the show and we also had a splendid view of the surrounding countryside.

After the long hot day we were taken by our bus into Selcuk to a *Hamam* (Turkish bath) where we all stripped down. The men were given a thin red and white chequered cloth and the women a striped grey and white cloth to wear. We all wore brown plastic slip-on shoes in our efforts not to catch foot fungus. Coals were burning and steam poured into the huge ceramic tiled room like a gas chamber. The more we rubbed our skin the more we noticed it peeling off along with our nice Turkish tans. The steam opened up our pores and sweated out all the dirt and pollution from our skin. We emerged feeling as clean as whistles and as light as feathers.

After a very deep and rewarding sleep we left for Cesme on the Aegean Sea. Unfortunately we left without Chuck as he had to head back to America and no persuasion from us could deter him. With waves of farewell and a sad face from Phil we left Chuck to continue to the airport for his flight back to America.

Leaving Selcuk we passed through Kusadasi glad not to be stopping to avoid bus loads of camera frenzied package tourists. We did see an old fort stuck out in the ocean and linked to the shore line by a stone road.

Cesme was a quiet sleepy town right on the water. The sea was as calm as the day and as blue as the sky. Little rowing boats with a bundle of netting bobbed peacefully as the fisherman got ready for their days work. Two wise old Turkish men, the only people on the beach were deep in conversation puffing on cigarettes and frowning with concentration as they contemplated their next words. We had stumbled across another paradise with not a single traveller in sight which made us feel even more special to be here.

With lunch dictating the order of the day, we found a small shop and emerged with loaves of fresh bread, cheese and tomatoes and bottles of water. Sitting on the beach in a circle we used our knives to cut the warm bread and spread the soft cheese over it. Slapping slices of tomatoes into the middle we kicked back and ate with the turquoise blue sea lapping ever so gently at the white sandy shoreline.

'This is the life!' a phrase I had used so often in my escape from the corporate rat race that most of the world was trapped in. With a full and content belly we swam and then moved across to a cluster of rocks which were used as a good fishing spot by the locals. An ugly dog emerged literally out of the rocks and befriended us. To everyone's delight I found a small fish and held it above my head. The dog, a brown spotted mix, that was surprisingly well looked after compared to some of the animals we had seen, stood on its back feet to get at the dried fish. After a few acts of standing and balancing I rewarded it with the fish which it devoured in a flash.

On our walk back into town we got a ride on a tractor and trailer which had returned from the nearby farming fields which grew aniseed, sesame and artichokes along with fig and gum trees which were dotted over the plains. The town was really quiet, almost like a ghost town as it chugged through with diesel spewing in thick black clouds behind us. Phil and Jo rode on the tractor and Nicole and I sat in the trailer with our arses feeling every bump with a curse following each one. I saw a man on a donkey with two wicker baskets strapped to its sides. He was an old Turkish man with an olive brown face, white stubble and a white moustache. He was dressed all in brown oddly enough with a jacket as if he felt the weather may turn ice cold. He was in his seventies and rode the donkey with the agility of a young man. When I aimed my camera at him he waved his hand half covering his face, but my finger clicked before I could stop it, freezing the frame as if he was waving a hello at me. I could see he was upset but before he could do anything he was lost as we turned the corner under the smoke screen of diesel.

Our driver told us about a place called Ronnie's which had Turkish dancing. While the Turkish music played we watched the Turkish women dressed in shiny thin dresses as they waved their arms and shook their bodies and rolled their stomachs in belly dance. It was an art as the women worked their stomachs rolling their bellies like waves flowing over each other. Much to our delight Phil and Jo gave it a go under the guidance of one of the belly dancers. The guys stood back and swigged on our beers and clapped for encouragement. It was a good evening and well worth seeing the talented belly dancers who had all eyes glued on their bodies throughout the performance.

After a quick breakfast and a thick muddy Turkish coffee which could put hairs on anyone's chest and keep one up for days we piled into the bus. Our little white bus with a yellow stripe down the side had served us well with no breakdowns or punctures thus far. It was comfortable and reminded me of an African taxi back home. At least the driver wasn't as reckless and a daredevil like our taxi drivers in South Africa who killed people daily in road accidents, one of the highest fatality rates in the world.

Ronnie the owner of the bar saw us off. Sticking our arms and heads out of the windows we waved as we sped down the main street on our way to Canakkale. Stopping briefly for a drink we carried on to Gallipoli, a place close to the hearts of all Australians and New Zealanders. I had heard about Gallipoli having seen a film starring Mel Gibson set in the World War I. I was horrified to see how many soldiers were literally cut down like a scythe through a corn field. Mike, Jeremy, Nicole and Jane wouldn't miss seeing this site for the world. This was their Mecca, no Australian or New Zealander goes to Turkey without visiting Gallipoli.

When we got out I was very surprised to see everything so picture perfect. The flower beds were free of weeds and the colours of the budding flowers were beautiful, sharp against the horizon. The grass was neatly manicured and was as green and lush as an English meadow. The sky was a deep blue as we gazed out onto the Dardanelles which washed against the cliffs on the beaches below. This was where Winston Churchill had devised a plan to land Australian, New Zealand and British forces to break a Turkish defence and put Turkey out of the war. The landings began on 25 April 1915 and lasted for nine horrific months at the cost of thousands of young lives before the Allied forces withdrew. Attaturk was the man responsible for the defence of Gallipoli. He would later become President of Turkey from 1923 to 1938. His famous face also graces the 1000 Turkish Lire bank note and to this day he is loved like a father to the nation.

The scenic peninsula is a national park with stirring memorials and names engraved on slabs that go on forever, each name a statistic that added up to on both sides to a staggering figure of between 65 000 and 70 000 dead.

The most stirring of all monuments were the words written by Attaturk himself. Under total silence while we sat on the grass staring out at the sea, our bus driver read it out to us:

Those heroes that shed their blood and lost their lives...

You are now lying in the soil of a friendly country. Therefore rest in peace.

There is no difference between the Johnnies and the Mehmets to us where they lie side by side here in this country of ours...

You, the mothers who sent their sons from far away countries wipe away your tears; your sons are now living in our bosom and are in peace.

After having lost their lives on this land they have become our sons as well.

Ataturk, 1934

I could see how this moment touched the Australians, because it touched me. He went on to tell us how the Turkish and Allied trenches faced each other and how the soldiers could hear each other singing and whistling at night. In the morning they would shoot each other. It was a war fought with respect and all Australians and New Zealanders are treated with immense respect in Turkey. Every year Anzac Day (Australian and New Zealand Army Corps) is celebrated and thousands of Aussies and Kiwis flock to Gallipoli. They remember this costly war and their country men's sacrifice who shed their blood so far from home.

It was a sober feeling as we all sat down in the bus and watched this peaceful place slip behind us as we made our way around the peninsula that linked Europe on route to Istanbul. Tom Petty broke the silence as; 'I won't back down,' sounded through the bus in an effort to lift our spirits. Lively talk soon returned with excitement at getting to Istanbul. This was our last stop and the place where our group would be scattered like seeds to destinations of our choosing. We didn't want to think of that right now, our bond as close friends had been formed three weeks ago, which now felt like months, at the coastal town called Oludeniz on the Mediterranean.

One could feel a major town was rapidly approaching. The crowds got thicker, the traffic got harder to navigate, and the volume of noise got louder with the constant hammering of the hooter for the slightest thing. *Taksi* (taxi) cars, a bright yellow like a warning symbol, bullied their way through the mess of traffic with loud impatient hooting. Bicycles, small donkey wagons brought the traffic to a crawl. The smell of a city hit our noses as thick clouds of diesel belched out of old truck exhausts along with the filth of stagnant water in street gutters.

Shutting the world out we slid the windows closed and watched as the city came into view and flashed by like a camera focusing before moving to the next shot.

People criss crossed the road at will and markets and street stalls appeared on the road sides. Suddenly we felt as though we had just crossed a border into the neighbouring country. Europe and Asia had met and one could definitely see Turkish people who looked European while others looked Middle Eastern.

This was Istanbul, the fifth largest city in the world and home to 12 million people. It is also the only city in the world to have been a capital to consecutive Christian and Islamic empires. It was named Byzantium after the Greek Colonists and then was renamed Constantinople after Constantine declared it as the new capital of the Roman Empire. In 1923 under the new Turkish Republic, Ankara became the new capital and in 1930 Constantinople became known as Istanbul.

Vehicles cut in front of us as the driver forced his way through this unending barrier of traffic nose to tail. He pointed out the Bosphorous bridge one of the longest suspension bridges in the world connecting the continents of Europe and Asia. Traffic was in gridlock on the bridge under a haze of diesel. It was cloudy and dismal and as grey as the diesel in the air. The drizzle dotted the windows as we pressed our faces against them people watching, as they passed us by in a hurry to get where they were going. The expressions worn like masks, the clothes mostly modest, head scarves wrapped around women's heads a symbol of religion, as each face became lost in the sea of bobbing bodies crowding the narrow pavements in between street vendors.

After a very long drive which was as slow and painful as watching paint dry we pulled up to a Pension offering affordable rates for rooms. The woman in charge shouted out a price which I felt was too high, and so I gave her my price. She balked at it and so I turned and told everyone to follow to the next place. To my shock these were the going prices, after all we were in a city and in all cities prices rocket. We returned to the first place and paid slightly less than what she had previously asked. I felt as though I had saved face and also saved a few Lire for my travelling companions where each dollar literally bought another days travel, especially in a poor country like Turkey.

It was an open room with a small balcony overlooking the gridlock of traffic. The Sea of Marmara was in the distant background with ferries passing under the steel suspension bridge. Washing hung from balconies like a screen curtain on limp wires flapping in the humid breeze waiting for the sun to burn it dry. Pollution hovered like a grey cloud over the drab buildings like a depressing omen. Our apartment was in old Istanbul on the same side of the river with all the ancient history of this once very wealthy city.

Walking back in the room we looked at our drab surroundings, glad to have a place and a door that locked. There were enough beds for all of us, and relieved to drop our backs where we chose we ventured out into this big city.

The first walk in a new city is always the most thrilling as adventure with each turn hit us like a wonderful drug. The sights and smells had our senses strung as we walked with urgency, our eyes hunting for an intriguing landmark like a curious cat watching and waiting, flicking its tail ready to pounce.

The backstreets teemed with vendors pulling and pushing loaded carts, while porters struggled under loads twice their size sweating as they balanced and juggled their way through the maze.

'Come look. Don't have to buy!' shouted the street vendors as they tried to lure us in as we passed each stall. There was excitement in the air as people bartered and bargained in a desperate bid to gain a sale and a meal at the end of the day.

'Where you from?' they came at us again. When I said, 'South Africa,' they looked at me in kind of disbelief. I knew what they were thinking, Africa is black continent. As others replied with their countries, they had us with the sales pitch and swarmed around us to look at their roadside stall. When they heard England they immediately rattled off English soccer players and clubs, showing off their knowledge and keen interest in the game of soccer. We didn't mind and welcomed the conversation with these friendly people who still wanted us to buy and felt quite insulted if we didn't.

Later on in the day someone offered us some hash and the movie, Midnight Express, hit me like a train. I thought of the backpacking traveller jailed for 15 years for having hash on him and the hell he endured in a Turkish jail. I took one look at the young Turk and walked away as fast as I could.

Back at the room we met up with a group of Australians who we joined up with and went for a few beers. Nick was from Victoria, a funny and smiley guy with good wit, Graeme who had the most outrageous side burns I had ever seen and he knew it, and Angelo a quiet and friendly person added themselves to our contingent.

Having heard about the Blue Mosque we set off in search of this great old monument that was always buzzing with worshippers. It was huge and quite sinister looking. Its six ruler straight minarets like pointed fingers, poked at the cloudy sky as if trying to prick the clouds. Like guard towers around the domes they could easily be mistaken for mini rockets, with scaffolding circling the minarets looking like launch pads.

The call to prayers whined through the speakers as hundreds of people converged on the site, taking off their shoes before they entered. Being inquisitive Nic, Graeme, Mike and I entered and watched as hundreds upon hundreds of men head to toe rocked back and forth. Each forehead seemed to carefully touch the floor at the same time as they got a whiff of the person's feet.

Acting as though praying with matching white hats we bowed our heads with a Turkish man with Mike making a mockery as he clasped his hands, stood straight and pushed his chest out with his face in deep sarcastic concentration. At the time it was funny but one wonders who may have been offended as we clowned around. The mosque was massive inside and I looked at the piles of sandals at the doorway and turned to Graeme and said:

'You tell me how the fuck are they going to find their sandals. They all look the same! Maybe they take the closest pair and walk off.'

After some good pictures of the mosque we made our way to the Grand Bazaar with the rest of our group. The Grand Bazaar was endless with 60 streets and 5000 shops selling carpets, silks, jewellery, leather jackets, purses, bags, wooden trinkets, shoes, Western designer knock offs, backgammon boards and literally everything one could think of. It was dark and gloomy adding to the mystique as carpets and trinkets hung from walls. Like walking through a tunnel we passed under arced ceilings decorated with inlays of hand crafted mosaics intricately designed in reds and blues. Windows built into the curved ceiling shot the light in like a spot light as it hit those particular vendors' goods, giving him an edge on his competition.

Haggling for what we wanted we moved through the stalls. Cats sat like goddesses where they chose and hardly anyone disturbed them. They were what kept the pests in control and with so many cats we never once saw a mouse or a rat. Through the market we needed to protect our group of girls from the cat calls and piercing dirty eyes that stared through them in an intimidating and lustful way. For the most part, Western women are looked at like whores while their women are treated as second class citizens. One man casually walked past Jo and grabbed her bum.

'Fuck off!' she yelled and hit him with a bag sending him running. It was certainly not what he had expected. We found a stall that was selling thick long sleeve sweaters with a hood. And in no time everyone one of us had a purple and dark blue shirt perfectly split down the middle with its two colours. With these shirts we could never get lost, whoever had one on was one of us.

Passing the leather jacket stalls filled the air with that fresh aroma of pure cured leather, soft and silky to the touch, stylish and dirt cheap. I bought a nice brown jacket and knew if I needed money desperately I could always sell it in the west for double the price.

Always ready for a beer or six we found a local bar close to us and converged on it like a whirlwind. Lined up along the bar we ordered our pints of the local beer, Tekel Birasi and knocked our glasses swilling the beer as we crowned the moment. It was always so exciting to be in a new place to see what the night would bring. In the corner behind a disused counter a man sat on a keg of beer with his head bowed and his legs crossed. He reminded me of a long lost hippy, long grey black hair with a long grey beard, meditating and totally oblivious to our stares.

At 4 am every morning like a cock crowing at first light the call of the mosque resounds. From loudspeakers this song like chant is blasted like an alarm, reaching all corners of the sleeping city. The call in Arabic is a message to all to come together in prayer and declares that God is great and that there is no God but Allah.

'Turn it down,' I shouted out knowing that this was an impossible request. Rustling in our sleeping bags we buried our heads to escape the piercing and very annoying wake up call.

Thirsty and slightly under the weather from the night of beer and socializing we surfaced and made our way to a place where we could eat. Cats seemed to be everywhere and for the most part they looked as though they were living a good life. There seemed to be one in each eating place acting as the lookout for unwanted pests. I watched the Turkish man with a weathered and wise old face, a cigarette in his mouth as he boiled the finely powdered roast coffee beans in a pot adding sugar to it. Needing a strong coffee to chase our throbbing pain in our heads we welcomed it. The bottom of the cup was always as thick as mud with the sludgy grounds at the bottom like silt in a river, but it worked its magic. I had heard of an old famous proverb referring to Turkish coffee and it went as follows:

'Coffee should be as black as hell, as strong as death, and as sweet as love.'

The proverb could not have described it any better and it served as medicine for our hangovers.

Amongst ourselves we picked a day on which we would all leave Istanbul. Our group had been together for three and a half weeks and the time of our lives had come to an end. We all wanted to leave on the same day, knowing that it wouldn't be the same if half the group had gone and half had stayed. We posed for a photo in a grassy park with our striped shirts. With smiles and emotions running high we said our goodbyes, pairing up as we wished to conquer the next country, or for some it was to return home. I think inside we all knew that these friendships had been lent to us and we knew full well that the chances of ever seeing each other again were slim to none.

Graeme and I hooked up and booked a flight to Budapest, Hungary. Excited at the thought of landing in a new city we waited at the airport watching people rushing by both excited and sad. It was dismal and dark and quite depressing. I soon got bored and walked over to a group of four floor cleaners who were pushing mops in a line across the floor and got an expressionless photo of them. Machines hadn't yet replaced the humans here.

To our shock the flight was delayed and then cancelled due to bad weather. I thought a riot was going to occur as people hit their watches and shook their fists late for business meetings and desperate to get home. The poor ladies behind the desk were verbally assaulted and there seemed no letting up. Graeme and I sat on our backpacks and smiled without a care in the world. We were in no rush to get anywhere and watched the pandemonium with keen interest.

They booked us into the Hotel Olcay, a four star hotel close to the airport and we couldn't have been happier to have a free nights stay with meals included.

'I think we just won the jackpot!' I smiled over to Graeme.

After a deep sleep on crisp clean sheets, a burning hot shower, a full stomach of Western food we boarded the small Turkish plane. *En route* to Budapest I walked down the aisle and asked the pilot if I could look into the cockpit. He invited me in, waving his hand holding a lit cigarette. His eyes were bloodshot and he looked as though he was taking us for a Sunday drive with the co-pilot looking at a map on his lap.

'We are flying over Romania!' he said in his thick Turkish accent.

I looked out of the cockpit window and saw clouds, it looked freezing cold and I was dreading winter in Eastern Europe, which would be hitting me in less than an hour.

I could still feel Turkey's warmth of friendly fun and plenty of laughter with Tom Petty ringing loudly in my ears. Now it was a memory never to be forgotten as I waited excitedly for my new adventure to begin.

Tim Ramsden

HUNGARY, CZECHOSLOVAKIA
AND POLAND (1990)

I landed in a very cold and dreary Budapest. It was another satellite state with beautiful architecture and a struggling economy. Buda was on one side of the Danube and Pest on the other with beautiful sturdy stone bridges linking the two sides. I had flown in with Graeme, who I had nicknamed sideburns for his unruly long and ugly sideburns. He was an Australian and like all Australians, a very proud one. We made our way to the Eger wine caves and tasted wine in old cellars hollowed into a mountain while gypsies played music for us with their violins.

While we sat and drank I couldn't believe my ears when I heard a couple talking Afrikaans. Here I was thousands of miles from South Africa and sitting in a cave below the ground in the middle of absolutely nowhere hearing my second language. We quickly got talking and laughed together and got chatting in English touching on hot political topics back home. The drink flowed and so did my courage as I tried to play a violin much to everyone's delight. It sounded awful but the drink covered the embarrassment.

It was quite incredible and after a day of drinking we wobbled back to the train which brought us back into Budapest.

We had heard about the Bahadla Caves, north east of Budapest on the Czechoslovakian border. We caught a train and then a bus to the Aggtelek National Park. The first record of these deep and very long caves was in 1549.

We paid a small fee and were guided in with lit torches. It felt cold and damp as water dripped off the ceilings and ran down the rocks. Stalactites and stalagmites hung and grew offering the most spectacular scene we had come across so far underground. There was a small lake with a rowing boat looking very odd in the middle. Seats in straight rows had been arranged next to the lake with massive speakers looking even odder as if a lecture was about to take place. Suddenly 'Money,' by Pink Floyd blasted through the speakers as crystal clear as one could imagine. The acoustics were unbelievable and it had us glued to the spot in total awe. Here I was in a cave over 400 years old deep under the surface of earth listening to Pink Floyd. It was as if the plug had been plugged into the rock and a miracle had transpired.

'This is blowing my mind!' I said to Graeme as we smiled not able to hear one another as it echoed through the caves. I closed my eyes and felt as though I was at a concert with the band performing right in front of me.

Walking through the caves was slippery in parts and breathtaking as shadows cast by the burning torches illuminated giant pillars of stalagmites formed over hundreds of years. The water dripped like slow rain and tasted salty. After a fair bit of walking we were told we had crossed the Hungarian border and were now in Czechoslovakia.

Hardly believing we had seen such a wonder of the world we boarded an old bus which took us to the train station. The train arrived and being in a communist state it was far behind in comfort and looks compared to its neighbor in Austria and the rest of Europe. When the borders opened most communist trains could not pass through into Western Europe as the rail gauge was a different size. Travelling through the country I saw buildings and churches that reminded me of being back in Austria. I soon discovered that Hungary and Austria were once joined, known as the Austro Hungarian Empire.

Needing more Forint's, the Hungarian local currency, I tried to change 50 Deutch Marks on the black market. I had been warned against this but decided to give it a go to gain a better exchange rate. I exchanged the money with a local on a bridge. He thrust some rolled up notes into my hand, grabbed the 50 Deutch Marks from my other hand and then shouted, 'Hurry up! Police!'

I looked around and then I saw a taxi come flying towards us. He waved it down and jumped in and was gone before I looked at what was in my hand. He had left me with about 5 Deutch Marks worth of low denomination Forint's. I had been ripped off and there was nothing I could do about it.

After nine days in Hungary Graeme wanted to head into Austria and I, needing to be back in England for Christmas, decided to head back into Czechoslovakia and head north through Poland and then cut across Germany and Holland.

It was another goodbye as we caught different trains from the Budapest station. I boarded my train for Bratislava and Graeme his for Vienna.

I as always had no idea what to expect when I landed in Bratislava. It was dark which I hated as I always tried to arrive in a new country in daylight to get my bearings. I opened up my Backpacking through Europe book and hunted for accommodation. To my surprise there were a couple of places listed but I started to wonder if they would be open. I asked a couple of young Slovaks walking their basset hound, if they knew of a place where I could stay. To my shock they spoke to me in broken English and then waved me along saying that I could stay with them. I couldn't believe my luck. They had a small apartment with hardly any furnishings. I could see they were starting out and it was no problem at all to have a complete stranger sleep in their room. Jano and Dagmar were a nice couple and I trusted them. They too must have had untold trust and intuition to allow me in to their living space.

They asked me if I was hungry and took me to a nice restaurant that would have been expensive for them, but cheap for me with Western currency. After a nice meal with good conversation in broken English they took me to a park and showed me a few statues.

It struck me as odd when I saw that they had been beheaded and spray painted with graffiti, with words that only they knew the meaning. Next to the headless statues was one knocked clean off its base and left as a worthless piece of rubble which had become a makeshift bench for people passing through the park. It struck me at how times had changed and this was the symbol, a person who instead of standing ever so importantly upright and powerful was now lying with his communist face buried in the earth.

What did this mean I wondered?

'This was our first communist President,' Dagmar said as she pointed at the torso in the middle, still standing but spray painted.

'His name was Klement Gottwald.' It was a name I had never heard of but I found out that he was a Stalinist. He nationalized the country's industry and collectivized its farms and ruled from 1948 to 1953, and died five days after Stalin's funeral.

These Slovaks must have hated the communists I thought as I looked at the giant stone torsos looking like a practical joke for everyone to sneer at. They must have turned in their graves to know their beliefs and practices were history in the total meaning of the word.

After a good sleep I was on the road again. At the Bratislava train station I met an American called Charlie. He was travelling on his own and had an address in Slovakia that had been given to him from a friend in Prague. He was heading to a little place close to the border of Poland, called Poprad.

'Come along if you want,' he asked. I had no plans and this was *en route* to get me to Poland, and so we bought tickets and waited for our train. Charlie was an odd looking young man with an afro, eyes that looked constantly glazed and a smile that was almost a sneer. He reminded me of a very young Alain Prost, a famous Formula 1 racing driver. He had a green eye and a brown eye, I had never seen anything like it before and didn't believe it was possible. Having met Charlie it definitely was.

From Poprad we took a bus and found the house of Jan where we were to stay.

Jan opened the door and Charlie presented him a letter written in Slovak. Jan looked at us, smiled and ushered us in, and then motioned to the table and we sat down. Picking up a bottle of Russian vodka he slammed it on the table, then opened a bottle of Pepsi and placed three tot glasses in the middle.

This was going to be ugly I thought. It was our welcome to Slovakia. We downed the vodka chasing it with a tot of Pepsi. There was a complete language barrier and the communication became hand and facial gestures, and amazingly enough we understood each other. Jan pulled out a calendar and flipped over the pages waving his right hand with each flip of the page. He was telling us that we could stay as long as we liked.

The house was cold and damp and very simple with the bare necessities and dated items like an old television set from somewhere in the eastern bloc.

His father returned from work and was genuinely happy to meet us and his mother got stuck into cooking a meal of meat and boiled vegetables from the market. We all sat at the table as total strangers to one another and yet we all felt at ease. These Slovaks as poor as they were took us in to their humble abode and showed us a trusting lesson in life; after all they had nothing but gave us their true family spirit.

Being poor their diet was terrible, they drank heavily, smoked without any health concerns and maybe it was because it was all they knew. They loved their lard spread thickly like peanut butter over bread and every meal was doused in salt. I looked at Jan's parents, their faces hardened and unhealthy from a life of hard spirits and high fat and I saw heart attacks coming their way.

It was evident they hated the Czechs and when I said Czechoslovakia they shook their hands as to strike it off the record immediately. It was as if I had sworn and I knew never to say that Czech word again.

'Slovakia!' Jan said. They wanted a breakaway republic with Bratislava as the capital.

Jan introduced us to some of his friends who were all hard core drinkers, and were thrilled to meet us as though we were some sort of celebrities. Vlado, Teabor, Rene and Jan took us up the Tatry Mountains which were heaped in snow. The sky was dark and there was hardly a soul around. And not being properly dressed the cold cut through our clothing with no mercy. Needing to warm up we all made our way into a bar on the mountain that was totally empty besides us and with vodka the drink of choice we warmed up and laughed the more we consumed. I could feel my liver was taking strain, I was not a spirit drinker and these doses of vodkas were lethal.

They could not believe I was South African. They kept on pointing at my skin and then at a black jacket as if to say, you are white Africa is where blacks live.

'Nelson Mandela,' I said and they knew his name with nods of confirmation.

'That's my country!' I said. They didn't seem to know about the apartheid situation and the Namibian/Angolan war, which may have been due to the difficult language barrier.

After a wonderful week we decided to move on. Charlie headed back to Prague and I made my way to the Polish border by bus. I looked out of the window and saw the depressing old polluted buildings and cars from the old communist era.

People walked to work and I could see everyone was equal, communism true to its word.

It was dark when the bus stopped a few hundred metres from the Polish border in the middle of what seemed to me, to be nowhere. I was the only passenger left on the bus and it was a very lonely feeling.

'Poland!' I said to the bus driver and he pointed down a road covered by at least three feet in snow.

I raised my hand and said thanks. Standing in the snow I fastened my backpack and began walking through the knee high snow. It was ice cold as the wind blew chilling me to the very bone. I was in jeans and a leather jacket in these well below freezing temperatures. It was pitch dark with the moon offering precious light along with the twinkling of a few stars which I drew comfort from. I trudged on shivering with my shoes filling with snow, towards a dim light which looked like a guard post. As I came closer I saw two Polish border guards with their thick great coats, visor hats and deadly AK47s hung over their fronts as they walked the fence. They stopped and looked at me as I came closer. I hoped like hell that they didn't mistake me as a threat and swing those AKs on me. As casually as I could I strutted up to the border guard inside the office passing a boom on one side to allow vehicles in and out.

I handed over my British passport; he didn't say a word and compared the photo to this foreigner standing in front of him. He swung the stamp down with his approval and gave it back to me, again without a word.

'Change money?' I asked. I knew I needed money and this was my only hope as everything would be closed. I couldn't believe it when he nodded his head. Not caring about what rate I would get I cashed a traveller's cheque and was presented with a wad of well used notes. I was now dealing with the Zloty and with a pocket full, I now had one less worry.

I tried to ask the guard where the nearest town was but he didn't understand and shrugged his soldiers. Like a lost soul I wandered into Poland along the road still in darkness with no street lamps to light my way and with no idea where I would sleep. I knew I couldn't sleep outside, I would freeze to death. I walked along the road and saw a sign that said Zakopane. I imagined there had to be a town close by and then I heard a bus coming up the road. I waved it down and bought a ticket to the train station. It was only a few kilometers away and now I had a warm place to stay. I was surprised to find the train station open and even more surprised to see a backpacker. I immediately struck up conversation and found out that he was Polish. I told him I had no where to stay and he told me that if I got to Krakow I could stay at his parents small apartment.

I booked a ticket to Krakow and waited for my train. It arrived in the early hours of the morning and once I had a seat I closed my eyes for a well needed rest.

Once in Krakow I hunted down the address which was like looking for a needle in a haystack with foreign names and little side streets, but I found it.

The parents were nice people who invited me in as though I was a long lost family member. They made up a bed for me and let me come and go as I wished.

The next day I caught a train to Oswiecim, the place with the German name that the world knows like no other, Auschwitz.

I walked through the entrance of Auschwitz I with the notorious motto welded in steel across the top, '*Arbeit macht frei,*' Work makes you free.

It was a cold grey day with snow on the ground, a fitting climate for the depressing place. I felt I shouldn't be here as if I was intruding on the Jews resting place and disturbing their souls. I walked with caution respecting the ground I was walking on.

It consisted of 16 one storey brick buildings and before the war had served as a Polish army barracks.

On 3 September 1941, 600 Russian POWs and 250 Polish inmates were crammed into the basement of the notorious Block 11 and gassed with Zyklon B, highly lethal cyanide based pesticide. This paved the way for extermination at Auschwitz, and a gas chamber and crematorium were constructed.

I walked through a passage with hundreds of photos on the wall. With each step they looked at me, their eyes seemed to pierce me. These were the innocent faces of the dead, starved and gassed and treated worse than animals. I went through another room; it was filled with suitcases, another with toothbrushes, eye glasses, little children's shoes, teeth, and hair. The Nazis had actually made carpets out of their hair and soap from their fat. It was chilling especially the little shoes, by the size alone one knows how young they were and how scared they must have been.

I felt at any moment I might hear the screams and feel the dying of the human spirit like a flame being starved of oxygen.

On the outside I took a few pictures expecting the flash to wake the dead and feeling totally uncomfortable and out of place for doing so.

From Auschwitz I, I walked to Auschwitz II-Birkenau, a German name for a village that was destroyed by the Germans to make way for this camp. This was to be the Final Solution of the Jewish Question.

I will never forget the gloom that hung over the camp. It was a freezing November day, the ground was carpeted with a fine layer of snow and it felt as the souls of the dead were alive. Almost in a reminder to never forget what had befallen them, young and old, women and little children.

The camp was totally deserted and eerily calm. I entered through an archway entrance following a railway track which entered the camp under a red brick building. There were no carriages but two straight rails of cold steel that were the lines where millions of lives ended in a lingering death sentence.

I walked into the freezing cold wooden bungalows and saw the straw used as a mattress on crude wooden bunk beds. The wind ripped through the openings like a cruel curse freezing my hands and face as I shuffled through the dead quiet bungalow. I touched the wood and knew I had touched death. The hairs on my arms were standing up with goosebumps. With every step in this camp I knew my feet were walking over the spot where a Jew was overcome with peace at last, in death. I was in the world's worst death camp.

Tim Ramsden

I could not bring myself to take a photo of the bungalows. It was just too sad to see how they would have suffered, stuffed in like animals in a cattle truck off to the slaughter house.

Barbed wire and guard towers lined the camp adding another chill to this the most horrific place I have ever walked through in my life.

While walking through the camp I met a Mexican called Raul. He too shook his head at the atrocities of man on man.

I had seen for myself where Jews in their millions were wiped away like animals with a deadly disease and cremated to smoke. To see it is to believe how barbaric the Nazis were under their lunatic leader Hitler.

I left the camps weak and only felt better when I was on the outside of those imprisoning barbed wire fences.

From Oswiecim we both made our way to Wieliczka to see an old salt mine. At 135 metres underground we walked through the cold mine shafts and saw a small museum of salt statues sculptured with great detail. It was a mine setting of the seven dwarfs all working their job assignments. Over time they had blackened and looked like stone statues. Salt was thrown over them to create the salt mine scene and it looked like a fairytale of the seven dwarfs in the snow.

Raul was also heading back to Krakow and was looking for accommodation. I told him where I was staying and we decided I would ask if he could also stay in the apartment. I thought it was a bit cheeky of me taking advantage of these strangers hospitality, but always out to help a fellow traveller I thought I would ask anyway.

After the train trip back to Krakow, Raul and I converged on the apartment and met my hosts. With their approval Raul was booked in for a small fee.

Krakow was a beautiful old city rich in history and once the capital of Poland. Somehow the war had steered clear of this wonderful city preserving the centuries old architecture. Old buildings and churches looking similar to Hungary and Czechoslovakia lined old cobbled squares and streets. Snow covered the ground as people in long coats rushed across the square braving the cold as they caught buses and trams to work.

Warsaw was the next place on my list and the following morning I was on the train and on my way to see the capital. The further north I went the colder I felt. I bought a thick jersey from an open air market below the Palac Kultury, the Joseph Stalin Palace of Culture and Science or Stalin Gothic, with its steeple lost in the mist and cold air. It was a present from the USSR to Poland, and during construction cost the lives of 16 Soviets. I met two Lithuanians and conversed with them on their lives in one of the old Soviet republics. They were glad to finally be independent of Russia. One could sense the opening of the borders judging by the items sold at the market. Cassette tapes, clothing, fur coats, food, radios, cigarettes and magazines and books from the west, spread on makeshift tables or sold from the boot of their old communist cars with each person trying to earn a living. I felt a lot warmer but was still freezing as the cold blew through me from Russia. It was Siberian cold and it reminded me as a young boy hearing about the Cold War. I thought the Cold War meant just that, countries with freezing temperatures caught in a war on the cold.

I saw the Unknown Soldier's grave with two Polish soldiers standing at attention with rifles equipped with bayonets and neatly shouldered. A bouquet of flowers rested at the head of the grave. It was like a tomb and it struck me at the importance the Polish placed on this nameless person who had lost his life in the war. The soldiers stood at attention with utmost respect as if he was an important government official who had just passed away. It was patriotic to see that this lost life had never been forgotten.

I heard Bob Geldof and the Vegetarians of Love were performing in Warsaw. Along with Dave a South African I had met at the cheap hostel I was staying at, we bought tickets three rows from the front, which were as cheap as buying breakfast. The conversation on meeting a South African always went like: 'So where are you from? How long have you been travelling? And if you were male. Where did you do your army?'

On walking into the concert hall I felt as though we were about to watch a film. Everyone was glued to their seats. Polish guards in uniforms with intimidating visor hats faced us with their backs to the stage. Their hands were held tight behind their backs with their chests pushed out in an intimidation stance.

When the concert began they looked around in disbelief, a sight their communist eyes were not used to. A group of us stood up and danced enjoying the music and then half way through, Rat Trap was played and the hall erupted in shouts and dancing. The guards were pushed back like a crowd of rebelling protesters. It allowed Dave and me to shuffle forward into the front row. I could see the sweat running off Bob Geldof's face and see every expression on the bands faces.

The very first cassette I ever bought was Bob Geldof and the Boomtown Rats, an Irish band that emerged on the New Wave scene in the late 70s. And here I was seeing him live and enjoying every second. The guards stood to the side feeling unneeded in the same way as communism had been brushed aside.

Buildings in Warsaw had been flattened by the war, but one would never have known it. They had been carefully rebuilt brick by brick to look as if nothing had ever happened. It was a test of Polish spirit. A true example of this was the Royal Castle which had been destroyed and rebuilt with the same brick.

I came across a small monument with flowers on the side of the street where Polish Resistance fighters had been caught and executed. The bullet marks were evidence where shots had been fired. It had been preserved to remember those who had their lives taken as they helped others from persecution by the German occupiers.

From Warsaw, Dave and I headed by train to a city once known by its German name Danzig but now called Gdansk.

World War II started in Danzig on 1 Sept 1939 with the bombardment of the Polish at Westerplatte by German battleships and the landing of the German infantry on the peninsula.

I saw the huge grotesque stone monument with writing chiseled into the stone that looked like a finger pointing 25 metres to the sky. It marks the site where the old town of Gdansk was leveled and where the war began. War is ugly and to me it really hit home how many millions were affected with immeasurable suffering especially in Poland by Hitler's actions on this very spot.

Dave and I met a Turk from Istanbul. His name was Sultan and the three of us walked around the wide open area that had been wiped clean of all trees by the bombardment. We came across a monument of either an old Russian or German tank placed on top of a stone base. It was freezing cold as we climbed on top of it and posed for a picture. I had my Turkish balaclava pulled over my head and ears, my only shield against the wind chill.

On 31 August 1980 the Gdansk shipyard was the birthplace of the Solidarity Trade Union movement under the leadership of activist Lech Walesa. Their opposition to communism led to the end of the Communist Party in 1989. Lech Walesa became President of Poland in 1990.

In the evening Dave and I followed a crowd that was gathering for a rally. People held candles and waved red and white flags. They were looking up at a window where a man stood and waved to the crowd. When he spoke everyone cheered. I asked a woman in the crowd who it was and she replied, 'Lech Walesa!'

I knew the name having heard it on South African television when the Berlin Wall was coming down in November 1989. I looked harder through the flickering of candles and flapping of flags and recognized his face. To see and hear the very man who gave Poland its freedom from communism was a thrill.

After a memorable night in Gdansk we made our way back to Warsaw by train. With money running low I bought a train ticket which took me through the city of Poznan to the Polish border.

In Hungary, Poland and Czechoslovakia I left people astounded that I was a white person living in South Africa. It always left me smiling and I felt privileged that I came from a country that very few knew anything about, other than the name, Nelson Mandela.

At the Polish border, snow was coming down like thick rain as I stepped onto the road and started hitch hiking. I was relieved to get a lift in a truck which took me through East Germany in the most treacherous road conditions I had experienced. I got dropped off at a truck stop and then by asking another trucker got a long lift through West Germany to the Dutch border.

It was the early hours of the morning and with no vehicles on the road and nowhere to stay I locked myself in a toilet stall on the border. Fearful of being robbed again I slept sitting up on the toilet with my backpack next to me.

In the morning I passed into Holland and caught a lift to the Hook of Holland, where I bought a ferry ticket to England.

I had been on the road for almost a year and had been through a staggering 15 countries.

The highlight of Europe, without doubt were the countries behind the Iron Curtain. With knowledge of communism knocking on our back door in South Africa along with southern Africa free from its colonial past but mixed up in communist fueled civil wars, my desire to see these countries had become overpowering.

I continued travelling in and out of Europe for the next two years, but there was a far out place in Africa calling my name, and I had to get there.

MOROCCO (1991)

To be standing on African soil again after an absence of nearly two years was an electrifying feeling, binding me to my roots some ten thousand kilometers southwards.

Parking 'The Bulldog,' (the loyal van that Wayne and I had bought back in England) below the Big Rock in Gibraltar, I pulled the key from the ignition and slid the door closed before locking it. Resigned to the fact that I would never see it again, I cast my thoughts back to some exciting travels across Europe in this reliable old vehicle. Excited and apprehensive to be setting sail for North Africa, I boarded a ferry along with a few fellow travellers, and departed from the Spanish port of Algiers crossing the Mediterranean *en route* to the famous city of Tangiers.

It was dark and chilly when the ferry docked signaling our journey's end with a new one about to begin. Unsure of what to expect we walked off the gangplank into a new world, with our eyes wide open and our senses taking in the bustling activity, under the beautiful salty smell of the Mediterranean Sea. Lucky to have a British passport my entry through customs went smoothly. It had long been a fact that no South African passport holders were allowed into Morocco with the apartheid policies of South Africa blacklisting any and all travel opportunities to this Muslim land.

A crowd of Moroccans had gathered eagerly to see what Westerns this boat would bring to their impoverished land.

'You will need a guide to show you around,' a young man with brownish teeth and piercing eyes shouted out with intimidation and authority.

'We will be alright thanks,' I politely answered, turning to Jim. He pulled out his Lonely Planet, a guide most travellers carried which was revered by many hard-core travellers as the Bible, for it listed everything that one would need to know and live by in a foreign land. Without wasting time we began to thumb through the pages under a street lamp as we scoured the fine print for a place to stay.

'You racist Jew, you have a black heart,' the rejected guide began to verbally abuse Jim. 'Put that book away or I will throw it away,' he continued with the strength of his friend's smiles egging him on.

'Get off the grass. You Westerns are all unclean. You bring the Mosquitoes to Morocco,' his friend joined in, which brought a roar of laughter from the growing circle of young Moroccans.

'You all stick together, and you will all die together,' he spat out.

Chilled by these threats Jim, Vicky, Jackie and I headed off on foot towards the lights of the city, every once in a while stealing an uneasy glance at the following throng of people. Walking down a narrow cobbled alleyway, grateful to be in a lit area, we converged on a Pension advertising a room. For a measly 50 Dirhams we booked into the Pension Place, and with four to a small room and a good hot shower to burn the sting out of our welcome to this desert land, we smiled to one another enjoying the fact that we were safely behind a locked door.

Was this really Africa, I wondered as I lay back under the confines of the mosquito netting? I could not help but feel that this was more like being in the Middle East, with the people looking and sounding more Arabic than African.

A quick two weeks overview of this land should do before I head back into Europe, I said to myself as I gladly closed my eyes.

After a deep sleep we all ventured out of our small room and through the lobby casting our eyes at the fountain and adorning green ferns, before stepping out into the real and exciting world of Tangiers. Waiting patiently at the entrance was Mohammed smiling with his hare lip and his smooth looking sunglasses, who became our guide and was branded by us as a fly for the way that he never left us alone. He led us around the old medina, down narrow alleyways upon beautifully cobbled streets with each stone fitting like a puzzle piece into the next. People and donkeys jostled by, the aroma of mint tea hung in the air as we walked along, absorbing all the sights and smells of this exciting city. Flies were in a frenzy at the meat market where camel and goat's heads sat like an offering waiting to be wrapped up in newspaper for a local dinner feast. Workers hammered on metal, while others chiseled out wood, adding to the scene. Carpets hung from shop doors and windows adding a rainbow of colour to the drab dirty walls. Pots and pans of all sizes and shapes also hung from each and every space as advertisement for what could be purchased in that shop. Fruit and vegetables were stacked in piles and in wooden boxes over a dirty table top below an overhang of woven baskets. Scales swung and wobbled as a purchase was made. People were not in a hurry, talking and smoking and sipping on glasses of freshly boiled mint tea, discussing day's events and smiling through blackened teeth. Worn Dirham notes passed between buyer and shopkeeper with a young King Hassan IIs face on each, the king that had ruled Morocco for the past 38 years. The weather was hot, under a sea blue sky with the ocean mirroring a beautiful calm as the odd wispy cloud moved with the wind in the same way as the crests of waves smoothly rolled and broke at the base of the city that towered over it.

Donkeys laboured past us sweating and weighed down with goods, a typical sight in any third world country. Flies buzzed around fitting into the scene as a welcome home to Africa where I long considered the fly to be the national bird.

Looking for some shade and a rest Mohammed led us into a carpet shop where we were welcomed in like royalty and offered a steaming glass of mint tea. While enjoying the tea it did not take long for the shopkeeper to begin showing us his carpets. Fellow travellers had warned me that once inside a carpet shop one would be forced to buy.

Remembering this I blurted out, 'We do not want to buy!' 'Oh no just look,' the shopkeeper replied. And so the carpets were rolled out before our eyes, one on top of the next, as they waited to reel us in like a fish on a hook. Time drew on and I could see the frustration building upon their olive faces with wrinkles across their brow as a mountain of perfectly crafted carpets sat before us. Like a fool I asked the price of one particular carpet and on being told it, I replied that I was just asking but did not want it.

'You have insulted me!' he screamed. 'You ask me the price and now you do not want to buy it!' Our tea was consumed, and the show was over and the two angry Moroccans pointed to the doorway for us to get out, and without another word we exited from the dark coolness into the piercing heat.

Tim Ramsden

After walking a short distance along the edge of the city a Moroccan came up to Jim, asked his name and wrote it for him in Arabic. Someone else then came up and read the paper. 'Is this your name?' he asked. 'Could be.' Jim replied. The Moroccan that had written it, shouted, 'You don't trust me!' grabbed the paper out of Jim's hand and ripped it up before throwing it to the wind.

This place was like no other I had ever experienced. These people had two faces, one to lure you in and if you did not do as they wished they would stab you with insults and brush you off like vermin. I had never felt this intimidation in any of the foreign lands that I had ventured through until now, and it certainly did not feel very comfortable.

This is not what I expected to see of Africa-the sounds were so different with the call to prayer wailing across the city through loudspeakers from tall minarets. Women covered in face shawls, with inquisitive eyes peering through the veil almost like a face hiding behind sunglasses, it reminded me of being back in Istanbul.

Sharp jabs on the hooter brought me back from my wandering thoughts as I followed a criss cross of cables reaching across the flat open roofs of houses each marked with an antenna or a satellite dish. A clothesline stretched with washing flapping like colourful flags in the afternoon breeze, adding colour to the poverty that engulfed the town. Looking back at the satellite dishes I could not help but wonder how these people could afford such luxury. They looked so out of place on these dwellings, a contrast between modern and old, a sign of the changing technological times taking them a world away into a space that for them was only recently dreamed of.

With our minds awash with enchantment we followed Mohammed over to a place called Grece, which overlooked the Mediterranean with Spain visible in the hazy distance. While eating our couscous and vegetables we saw our very first guides who openly sneered at us in sheer disgust. After the filling meal Mohammed led Jackie, Vicky and I to a wide open French style balcony where to our shock he lit up a joint filled with Moroccan hash and then proceeded to pass it quickly on to us, before suddenly leaving.

'Could this be a set up?' I blurted out to a dumbstruck Jackie and Vicky.

'Look over there, Mohammed is getting pushed around by those two guides!' Vicky nervously said.

Standing with the joint and worrying about a set up, we watched Mohammed return to us, who told us not to worry that they were just playing.

'There are two cops also smoking. Don't worry,' he said, before leaving us once again, with the words set up bouncing around our paranoid minds.

There was something we just could not trust about him, and it made us feel extremely uneasy. Mohammed would not stop trying to push Moroccan hash onto us, and even went as far as giving me a small piece of this soft brown, rubbery resin to smoke for the night.

Buzzing on the high while walking through the old medina with Vicky, I heard footsteps on the cobblestones, bearing down on us. Feeling really paranoid I think 'Police' as we continued walking without looking back. We passed outstretched begging hands, strange black faces and shopkeepers as we hurried along, navigating lefts and rights through the narrow alleys, in our quest to reach the safety of our room. It was a strange feeling to be moving so fast, while everything else seemed to stay dead still and silent except for the following footsteps.

On reaching the room we burst in and were met by three fellow travellers. Immediately the laughter began to flow, nervous at first and then with confidence all the while laughing at the tension this place had injected into us. I kept playing back in my mind at how honest and trustworthy these Moroccan people seemed to be on the one hand and yet they were all after money, with guides getting a commission for every sale from a shop whether it be a belt, clothing, a carpet or even food.

After three days in Tangiers it was time to leave or should I say 'escape' for quieter more relaxed pastures. Gladly and without a single sign of Mohammed we boarded a bus with a deep sigh of relief in the direction of a small coastal town called Asilah. On arriving Jim and I went for a stroll around the medina past colourfully painted green and blue buildings with beautifully decorated red sunbursts around the doors and window frames set in the whitewashed walls. While we were marvelling at this beauty we got the shock of our lives as we walked slap bang into Mohammed. He was really upset and quite angry that we had left Tangiers without as much as a goodbye forcing him to follow us and unsettle us at the same time. Little did he know that we were trying to rid ourselves of his clinging and very annoying presence.

'Do you want some stuff?' he began hounding us. This made Jim extremely paranoid and with an unflinching face he looked at me and said: 'I am leaving Morocco for good!' That very day we shook hands and waved a farewell to Jim as he returned to Tangiers *en route* to Gibraltar and Spain. Our group of four had become three and it was unfortunate that circumstances had forced a decision from Jim to leave, but that is backpacking, here for one day and gone the next for more wandering and wondering in this wide world.

On the beautiful open beach in Asilah I was coaxed to sit on a camel and then when I refused to pay 10 Dirhams for this luxury I was told to 'Fuck off,' which I gladly did.

Life certainly seemed more peaceful in Asilah with time to be alone to watch fishing boats laden with their day's haul, the ocean lapping at my feet and the pestering of Tangiers now a distant memory. Over lunch at a place called 'Mirimar' I met an Englishman who had been robbed of £90 in Dirhams and his expensive Ray Ban sunglasses. Funnily enough the thieves gave his Ray Bans back but took the money, leaving him to pawn his camera and glasses to keep his dream alive of a backpacking experience through Morocco. In the restaurant I got into a deep conversation about Morocco, the Muslim culture and Arabic language, and life in apartheid South Africa.

After a few relaxing days in Asilah is was again time to leave and soak up more of this land that had me hating it but also enjoying the edge that it gave one. On the train journey bound for Meknes I met a New Zealander who told me a story about an English bloke that he met who had a knife pulled on him and then robbed of £120. On arriving in Meknes I booked into Hotel Maroc with Vicky and then met another Mohammed who was getting totally drunk on Heineken. In between slurs he told me that I was the first South African that he had met.

It was a great city with high fortified walls with beautiful entrances cut so perfectly out of the wall so much so that one felt really important to pass through it below the massive overhang above. The medina was a colourful sight with many craft shops of silver and brass where designs were being hammered into the metal. Life was busy here and we could see the workmanship that was going into the metal. It was as if they were giving the cold piece of metal life with the many markings. The smell of mint was everywhere as was the succulent smell of lamb shaved onto pitas, a great filling meal known as a kebab. While strolling contently though the streets we bumped into Mohammed who told us that we would always find a bakery, a Turkish bath, a Koran school and a mosque or a doorway to a mosque on every street, and I must say he was right. During our walk he led us into his family's carpet shop and much to my surprise I bought a carpet for 250 Dirhams. Once the money was handed over and the deal was sealed we christened it with a beer and a mint tea. People in Meknes seemed more genuine and yet I am still wary of a few. I trusted Mohammed and accepted his invitation to have us around to his house. He was a real drinker and couldn't stop telling us: 'You are welcome one hundred times, one thousand times, my brother my sister.' He was thirty-four and lived with his mother, his father had died four years ago making him now the head of the house. Mohammed's family got mad at him for his drinking of alcohol, which is taboo for a Muslim and they would rather he smoked hashish. We had a few cold beers in a room just to the side of the lounge, a very well decorated room with long sofas against a freshly painted wall. He then moved us into another room that could not have been more contrasting in every possible way. The tiled floors, painted walls, wooden ceiling and immaculately laid out room were left behind as we entered through a curtain into a dingy room with dirty flaking chipped walls, burnt out matches strewn across a cluttered floor with a mattress in the corner, and clothes thrown at will around his hovel. To me it looked like a life of banishment from the main household. Again he welcomed us with more beers thrust into our open hands, and while we sipped on this despised drink he fumbled with his cassette player and played a very stretched Michael Jackson tape at ten times slower than the normal speed. Mohammed then tried to take a photo of us and in his drunken state he knocked a table that sent the teapot flying, spilling the mint tea on his dirty floor. When it was time to go he gave us a piece of hash. 'You can have it, it's nothing,' he said and then in the same breath he asked for 100 Dirhams for the beer, which we duly handed over. Mohammed then led us back through the medina in pitch darkness rounding each corner with apprehension as we passed groups of talking men and children scurrying around like rats, wide awake well past their bed time, while shop keepers noisily closed their stalls for another day. It was only when I recognized a mosque that I knew exactly where I was and began to feel a lot easier, though still not trusting this foreign culture.

On reaching Hotel Maroc Mohammed asked Vicky for some headache tablets for his mother who was suffering terribly with all the embroidery and sewing that was just a normal day's work for a woman in Morocco. With a handshake we parted company and with a sense of relief we entered the small hotel, which was more a cluster of rooms than a real hotel.

After a good sleep it was time to board the bus for a modest 12 Dirhams and head for the next adventure in Fes. The bus was packed with young and old, chickens in cages, leaving no room for our bags except on the roof, which were securely roped down, but being out of sight it was a worry, with our worldly possessions travelling above us along with at least 40 chickens with their legs tightly bound.

Our welcome to Fes was a crowd that swarmed around the bus locking eyes on our white foreign faces as if we radiated wealth from our pigmentation. They walked up to the dirty windows, tapping pointing and calling in excited chatter as if by seeing us they had miraculously won a fortune.

'Cheap hotel. Cheap hotel. Follow me!' the guide's chanted eager to lead us away from the rest of the vultures waiting to latch onto us. One of the Marocs climbed up a ladder on the side of the bus and began lowering our bags.

'Five Dirhams each,' he shouted.

'Bullshit,' I screamed back and grabbed our bags from a stunned Moroccan's hands.

As I tried to walk off, we were surrounded and brought to an abrupt halt. If looks could kill I would be dead. They stared at us as if we were the lowest of the low, forcing me to hand over the 10 Dirhams as the key to unlocking this circle that had encompassed us.

Free to leave we headed off in search of a hotel along with a hotel guide and for 50 Dirhams got a room at Hotel Jardin Public.

Dumping our bags we headed into the medina, destined never to be alone for long. First an elderly man in a white robe and then the famous 'Charlie Brown,' a youngster that could not be trusted at all, and could only be shaken off by totally ignoring him.

After getting lost we eventually found an exit out of the medina only to be rewarded with a group of five that hassled us no end. Unable to shake them off we gave in and went with one of the guides, whose name was Abdul. He led us into carpet shops, leather shops, and furniture and metal shops but was met with a continual refusal from us. The walk as always produced some extraordinary sights; goats' heads on a green bed of mint leaves, a donkey loaded and roped with seven plastic crates of full 1 litre glass bottles of Coca-Cola, a great advertisement for this world wide drink in the poverty of a third world nation.

The neatly cobbled stone and narrow alleyways led us to the leather tannery with the smell of raw hide meeting our nostrils well before our eyes locked on the round vats swirling in dirty and yet vibrant colours. The smell was vile and reminded me of the stench I had smelt of rotting corpses fermenting in the sun. Men stood in bare feet stamping the leather in the vats to get the dye to take to the leather like a man squashing grapes in a winery.

Donkeys slipped and slid weighed down with dripping leather as they were whipped forward up and down the narrow alleyways. One of the donkeys did not make it up the small incline and lay still on its side with the burden of leather still strapped to its back, its tongue hanging limply like a flag of surrender from its bone dry mouth. The eyes were wide open, not flinching at a fly, as it lay in an exhausted and abandoned heap. Its days of slave labour now finally over.

Casting an eye back at the vats of reds and muddy browns, I couldn't help but think at how behind the times this process was, and yet there was no denying at what fine leather these vats in Fes had produced.

Our guide led us away from this fascinating area and then dumped us in the middle of the medina, demanding 5 Dirhams each, which he duly got in spite of having doubled the price.

After an hour of getting lost in the maze of the medina we found ourselves at our starting point. I freaked out and had to cool down for five minutes before setting off again. Eventually we found the Principal Gate (entrance to the medina) which was like finding the key to a cell and the freedom of getting back to our room so we could lock out the outside for a while.

The alleyways were like highways with slow animal traffic; donkeys and mules labouring like slaves, draped in a wealth of dripping leather, they just kept plodding wearily on, with their heads bowed as if in shame.

Slipping, sliding and dragging their feet on the wet cobble stones, the cruelty never ending.

While in the room I got thinking about all of the millions of carpets hung wherever your eyes looked and yet all the rooms had cold floor tiles, or maybe it was just the cheap hotel I was staying in.

I thought Fes would be hassle free, how wrong I was. I bumped into a Moroccan by the name of Saiyed who I had met on the train from Asalih, two days ago who certainly struck me as one of the very few I could trust thus far.

The next day I went out to eat with a Polish Pom in a dark and very tiny room the size of a lavatory. I ordered sausages and chips expecting to have my taste buds treated to an English meal. Instead the sausages tasted like the smell of raw leather cut from a dead animal in the tannery. It was revolting and I had to hold myself back from vomiting, needless to say I never went there again.

I bumped into Saiyed again and to my disbelief even he tried to gain the upper hand on me with a bargaining deal. He wanted my sleeping bag in exchange for a robe, one chance in hell of that. This was my mattress, my warmth and my bed and I wouldn't part with it for the world.

Later on in the day I met some Kiwi girls who were starting out on a seven to eight month expedition through Africa, by thumb and backpack. Leaving them I admired their gutsiness in this continent where with each sunrise, life is a constant challenge and will bring lasting memories by the time the sun has set. Africa, a continent alive with adventure mixed with intrigue, a place that will undoubtedly leave its mark on every soul who sets foot upon it.

Went to the Merenid Tombs and got an amazing view over the medina with the snow capped Middle Atlas mountains in the background. It was nice to just catch ones breath, ponder and just chill out in the gardens, writing a few postcards without the street hassles and noises. The gardens had been neglected and left to grow wild with weeds, half empty ponds of dirty water waiting to be refilled by the next rains below tall trees offering a beautifully cool umbrella of shade.

I met a guy from England who showed us his *djellabas* (robes) that he had bought to sell in England. We all then went to to a small restaurant. It was   dark and depressing and thankfully the shadows hid the dirt very well, as we   squashed three to a miniature table. The chips were cold but filling and I was left wondering if I had been given the plate that was left on display in a small glass case as advertisement for the passers by. I dropped some of my omelette on the floor, on any other floor I would have retrieved it, but this floor was brown with filth – at an estimate I don't think it had been cleaned in the past 100 years. However, to my surprise I saw them washing dishes with Omo a washing machine detergent sold abundantly in South Africa.

After the meal I was told by a Moroccan that a bomb had exploded on a train in South Africa with 16 dead and 20 injured. Whether this was true or untrue I had no idea, but it was believable nevertheless. I also got told from another Moroccan that flights between Johannesburg and Casablanca had started up and that there was now a South African Embassy in Morocco. To me this was the signal that the walls of apartheid were crumbling, which felt good and nerve racking at the same time. With change brings uncertainty and I knew the whites in South Africa would feel it the most. Would there be reverse apartheid, I wondered?

The following day I went looking for *djellabas* with no luck, but ended up meeting two English backpackers and a Dutchman who had travelled up from the south of Morocco and said it was fantastic.

Terry, one of the Englishmen told us about his experience two years ago on his first day in Morocco. On arriving in Tetovan (considered the most dangerous place in Morocco) he was held at knife point and locked in a room for 18 hours. A few days later I heard the rest of the story. Terry and a friend were smoking opium along with a few Moroccans. When it was time to leave the Moroccans piled blocks of hashish in front of them.

'Now you must buy,' they said.

'No money!' Terry replied.

Suddenly knives were drawn and pointed at them resulting in Terry's friend's ear being cut, in order to show how serious they were.

After 18 hours they were pushed out into the medina and closely followed by the Moroccans, who chanted: 'You will never find your way out Englishmen.' Lucky for them they did and lived to tell their harrowing tale.

While walking down a main street in Fes I was dumbfounded to see people with hoses spraying down the roads and buildings while others were picking up litter. It was as if the government had said 'Enough is enough; let's do a little spring cleaning.'

But it was only this one area that was getting the attention, which made this situation even odder, until I asked a Moroccan fellow that was standing next to me.

'What is all this cleaning up?' I asked.

'Oh the President of Senegal will be here shortly,' he replied casually.

Only a few minutes later the shiniest black Mercedes that I had ever seen emerged with the Senegalese flag fluttering from the aerial. The contrast of a shiny car to a sweat soaked mule really hit me, as did black suits, starched white shirts, ties and polished shoes to a mismatch of rags and torn clothing to ripped sandals.

Here they were to see 'clean' Morocco, and saw one short street, clean for a day. A poor show for government officials where lies and untruths are hidden and covered over but somehow justified in this dysfunctional society.

The medina continued to blow my mind as I followed the narrow walkways as if I was following the yellow brick road, starved of light in some places, the stones fitting like jigsaw pieces. People and mules shared these highways like moles burrowing their way through this maze of confusion.

Another aspect of this land that amazed me was the number of blind people that I passed, which really unsettled me. Cataracts are a huge problem and with no money there is no vision.

Coming from South Africa and my privileged way of life, I found myself staring at their misfortune. Scratching my head I wondered why I hardly ever saw a person with a disability in South Africa. Maybe it was the government at work showing the white people that these sorts of obstacles did not affect the ruling minority.

Deep in thought I passed five people huddled outside a mosque under a plastic sheet pulled like a sail over their heads as the rain beat down, with unwelcome discomfort. They were homeless and desperate and I walked past them thinking, haven't they got a son or a daughter who could look after them? It was just another reminder that I was in Africa, a world away in all aspects of life.

After a meal I got talking to a Moroccan by the name of Dries, who shared a joint with me and while walking down a dark alley he passed me a piece of hash. Off guard and taken by surprise I dropped it and then panicked. My mind was racing with people pushing past me on either side.

'Police,' I mouthed to myself as I groped for it in the darkness brushing my hands over the smooth dirty cobblestones.

'Ah, here it is,' I blurted out with relief that was short lived.

'No the light is playing games.' It turned out to be a chunk of dirt.

People were pressing forward fast, like a speeding train, as Dries stood like a sentry, observing my every move.

'What if I don't find it, I have lost income for him. This could be costly.' I thought as I fumbled around desperately.

'I have got it,' I barked out with relief as the crowd of people streamed past.

After a nice latte and a regrouping of thoughts at my stupidity and the needless close call, I stepped out of the coffee house onto the road and into a steady stream of running water, which seemed odd until I saw a woman squatting two metres away from me.

Where ever I seemed to go people shouted 'Aleman.' It has taken me a couple of weeks to realize that Aleman in fact meant German. On realizing this I replied 'South African' and they would say 'Afrika du Zud' and follow it with, 'No, only blacks live there!' Some said, 'So where in the south of Africa?'

'Next to Zimbabwe,' I replied.

'Ah, Bob Marley,' one said followed by a wide grin. Absolutely no problems if you are from South Africa, you are welcome a thousand times.

Tim Ramsden

In the morning I went with a Moroccan to help him translate French into English. I have no idea why he asked me, having never spoken a word of French in my life. After 15 minutes and few caffe lattes later we packed it in. When we paid for the coffees he got really upset at the high price of the bill. It was the first time that I had witnessed a Moroccan getting ripped off by a fellow Moroccan. After the failed French translation I went looking for a *djellaba* but for 300 Dirhams I carried on walking.

After hearing that I was looking for a *djellaba* I was told by a Moroccan that a guide I had used the day before wanted to kill me for 20 Dirhams because I had not taken him with me.

What a life of threats and deceit I thought as I shook my head, wondering why I was still here and not taken the easy road like Jim, who had to be in a safer place.

On one of our walks through the medina I got lost with Terry and Martin and found an interesting sight. Before me was a display of goats' heads on mint leaves with their brains neatly displayed next to them and their glazed eyes wide open. Needless to say it did nothing for my appetite.

Once back at our rooms we shut the door with a rewarding feeling of safety. Again I couldn't help but think that in spite of how genuine the Moroccans seemed to be at first, in the end money was always the subject with everyone I have met thus far. Maybe it was all the poverty and the uncertainties that drove them that way. Seeing a white skin certainly did not help as they saw a glowing source of wealth forcing them to tap in to gain some kind of relief from their dismal poverty stricken lives.

Later in the afternoon I tried looking for the hot springs but without any luck. I ended up having four coffees watching a belly dancing show. Not only was the show painful to watch but it cost me 40 Dirhams just to see four women trying to dance.

In the evening Vicky, Terry, Martin and I went out for a few beers and stumbled on the Moroccan lottery. We ended up getting three beers for free, a very rare occurrence and something I thought we would never get away with, but we did.

I disliked the Moroccan man who ended up paying for our beers and he knew it. He constantly uttered bad comments about South

Africa, which only added to my irritation as he stabbed at my patriotic pride. After all I had been forced to risk my life in the army for my country, which after my service made me prouder to call myself a South African.

Over the beers I chatted to Terry about the Moroccan culture and how most of them have struggled. I was told that an average wage for 12 to 14 hours work was a measly 100 Dirhams, at the time equivalent to £6. On hearing this I went cold and looked around the room at the Moroccans deep in conversation and puffing with concentration on their cigarettes. In silence I admired them, because I knew they worked hard and to hear their earning capability only made me feel like a millionaire. But my life was a life of travel and I had to stretch my money as far as I could. I could not run out of money in this land, and if I did I knew I would never survive. My money had to see me through until I reached the Western world of Northern Europe and England, where I would be forced to find work.

Enmeshed in poverty I thought of what it must be like to be a child growing up with nothing and how as children they would have fought with each other both playfully and aggressively.

I thought about all the haggling and hassles that we as backpackers were dealt on a daily basis and how after having lived a life starved of luxury these Moroccan people have no choice but to view us as 'walking white money.' After all in their eyes we must have tons of money to arrive in their land from our far afield destinations.

The more experienced and persistent the haggler the more lucrative deal he would be able to extract from the average tourist. Backpackers generally ended up getting a better bargain than the normal tourist because of their tighter budgets.

It was finally time to leave Fes. I was told the bus bound for Errachidia was leaving at 1am and so I didn't book a night at the hotel. I should have known better, after all I was in Africa and when in Africa it always pays to expect the unexpected. At 1am I learned that the bus was leaving at 4am, and after kicking at the dust followed with a few swear words, I was dumbfounded to see a marriage procession snaking its way down the street.

The bride was jewelled like a beautiful princess carried carefully like royalty in a wooden box. Drums and trumpets beat out into the night along with clapping as everyone jubilantly danced around her. Blowing kisses to all in sight she disappeared with her procession into the cold night.

At 4am I boarded the bus, cold and agitated by the extended three hour wait. With my frustration rising I took it out on the baggage boy who rudely demanded 10 Dirhams for loading Vicky's and my packs. Digging into my pockets I slapped some change into his waiting hand.

Once seated, I cursed my stupidity for not bringing my sleeping bag inside the bus. Going through the Middle Atlas Mountains my legs went numb with the severe cold. Looking through the frosted windows with the Moroccans contentedly bundled up in their hooded *djellabas*. Shaking with feverish cold I saw the snow capped peaks which only sent another chill down my freezing body.

We stopped for an hour in the middle of the Atlas Mountains as if the driver was trying to further punish me, which only added further numbing cold to my discomfort.

While waiting I watched two blind men board the bus from opposite ends and begin begging with their outstretched calloused hands. To my amusement they walked slap bang into each other, then moved to the same side and walked into each other again. After a brief struggle in the middle of the aisle they passed each other and continued on.

Shortly after this comical break 'saliva king' entered the bus for his turn at earning a few Dirhams. With long dangling saliva hanging from his lips, he mumbled some words while standing directly over me and then began nudging me for money. To my horror I watched his saliva hanging by a thread ready to drip onto my face.

'Move it up!' I shouted at him harshly, but unfortunately he did not respond forcing me to be the one moving it up.

At one of the many stops to Errachidia I saw a Moroccan equal to Pop-Eye who was the baggage collector.

He would attempt to shout, 'Rushadia' (Errachidia), informing those where the bus was heading, but unfortunately he could barely shout.

I cupped my hands and bellowed, 'Rushadia, Rushadia,' which caused a ruckus of laughter from all those around me along with Pop-Eye himself.

We arrived in Errachidia late in the night, just as further proof that nothing runs on time, whether it be departure or arrival.

Eventually the connecting bus to Erfoud arrived, which transported me to this great place. A place of relaxation, friendly and in a strange way I felt as though I had left Morocco.

On the outskirts of Erfoud there was nothing but a wide main street lined with Moroccan flags adding a vibrant red to the brown mud brick houses with a beautiful backdrop of tall green palm trees.

Smiling I said to myself, what a beautiful contrast to Fes. Walking as we took in our surroundings we followed a winding road into Erfoud, which overlooked an oasis of palm trees and tall green grass with a stream running through a valley and high mountains on either side.

Vicky and I booked into Hotel Ziz and after some bargaining over no hot water for the all important shower we settled on 25 Dirhams each. It did not take long to meet another Mohammed who we named as Mohammed the third who also worked at the hotel and got us buzzing on some hash, leaving me with thoughts of, he must be after what little money we have.

Taking a mellow stroll through the town, I met Abduhl who was an African from Senegal. He wasted no time in inviting us into his house with an offer of mint tea. We met his family while quietly sipping on our steaming glass cup of tea with a beautiful fresh aroma of mint in the air. While drinking the tea Vicky passed out in the lounge chair, which created concern for the family, who honestly believed something was horribly wrong.

On leaving Abdul's house, we headed for Hotel Bar Ziz for our backpacks, and then to a pick up point for a ride into the desert. While we waited I met an Aussie and a Spaniard who were also in a quest to see the mighty Sahara desert. After a bumpy and very dusty drive in an old Land Rover a village appeared as if out of thin air and it did not take long before our Land Rover was circled with curious children. As the driver opened the door they scattered like a flock of seagulls. After another 45 minutes of driving we stopped again at a village called Hassi-L-Bid in Merzouga, and I couldn't help but think to myself, what a great place I have ventured to.

A few houses made solidly out of mud, with smoothed walls as if they had been perfectly plastered stood like lonely lighthouses along a shore of sand in the middle of nothingness. It was heaven as we entered; leaving the oven- like temperature on the outside for beautiful coolness on the inside as if someone had flicked the switch of an air conditioner.

The temperature was soaring to close to 50 degrees Celsius, cooking us literally where we stood.

Initially we planned a one night stay, but on meeting a bunch of welcoming and very friendly Moroccans, with no hassles attached we knew we would stay longer.

These people in the south of Morocco are the real Moroccan people, I said to myself. It is like a totally different country, a survival with what you have and what can be drawn from the land.

Under darkness at least 20 of us walked into the desert with our packs and sleeping bags. Just past the first dunes we stopped, dropped our packs and made a big fire. We sat in a circle round it and sang, danced, smoked hash and laughed loudly with no cares in the world. One of the Moroccans called it the 'Disco Desert,' our first taste of the Sahara Desert.

After a few hours of memorable fun, four of us hiked further into the desert towards a big dune under the light of the moon, where we laid out our sleeping bags and settled in for the night.

The experience of waking up in the morning and being engulfed in a brown sea of steeply mounded sand, was one of the most incredible scenes I had ever witnessed. I thought I had awoken on another planet. To me this was one of the natural wonders of the world and I was blessed to have witnessed it in the flesh. The higher we climbed the steeper it got and the harder it became to keep our feet firmly planted on the sliding landscape. I watched the fine orange sand flow over my feet as my footprints made a trail in a direction that looked as though no person had ever ventured before.

Stumbling forward and pulling my legs out of the heavy sand I headed along the ridge of a dune parted perfectly in the middle by the wind. With every movement as I pulled one foot out of the sand at a time I watched the fine granules flow like a cascading river down either side of the slope.

As I stood on the highest mound I drew a deep breath and sighed while gazing out into a world of nothing but sand for as far as the eye could see. A sense of pride welled up in me for not only having achieved my tiring walk, but that I was blessed to witness this peaceful splendor all around me. What a magnificent and never-to-be-forgotten sight. At this moment I felt well and truly back on the continent of Africa.

Aware of the gradual increase in temperature, I stood and gazed far below onto an oasis of palm trees offering that ever valuable shade to seeds planted in fertile soil with a slow stream of water that had been carefully directed to the small patches of earth. This life blood is what allowed this tiny settlement of mud houses to exist in an area surrounded by open arid land and a sea of fine sand, with the palm trees being the only change in colour besides the African sunset.

Naturally there was no electricity or plumbing; this was subsistence living at its simplest. There was a special hut with clay ovens for the baking of bread, two small shops with the most basic necessities and a café restaurant, which was more of a meeting place.

Donkeys were the transport and ferried water from the wells; kerosene fed the lamps and carved a path of light through the otherwise pitch blackness. This was a world where there seemed no worries, a life so far removed from the fast paced life in London, or major European cities.

Walking like movie stars amongst the small children, we passed through the small village. I remember a few of these children excitedly displaying their pets, a baby fox missing a front leg and a huge lizard both on leashes held tightly by their owners. The children appeared from everywhere with priceless smiles that children of poverty seem to display far better than those spoiled through the wealth of the Western world.

After a few days of braving the heat and cooling off in the mud bricked Caffe Loasis it was time to leave. We got up at 6am and caught a taxi to Rissani and then to Erfoud along with another 17 people, and I felt like I was back at home in SA with taxis just as crammed.

At Erfoud we booked back into Hotel Bar Ziz along with an Aussie where we slept three to a room for a very cheap 20 Dirhams.

The three of us went to visit Abduhl who invited us into his house, and immediately pushed play on his old tape recorder. Out beat the familiar sound of Juluka, a South African band of both black and white musicians, frowned on in our political world of segregation. It certainly took me back home with a wide smile during the songs duration. He also showed me a picture of a black South African man chained to a tree with Arabic writing beneath it.

Propaganda, I thought to myself without bothering to utter a word in defence. Abduhl kept on saying that I was the first South African he had ever met, and seemed amazed that I was a white born in South Africa. He stayed on the second floor of his simple dwelling and the room adjacent to his was surprisingly full of sheep.

'I have now seen it all,' I said to Vicky and our Aussie friend. To get the sheep up to the room, they would have had to be herded through the house and up the stairs.

We then took a taxi from Erfoud to Rissani, where I went on a hunt for a *djellaba*, and with all the hustlers trying to win a deal at my frustrating expense, I packed it in.

There was nothing to see in Rissani, it was just a small village which at 4pm became engulfed in dust, thanks to donkeys pulling carts, buses and cars speeding by. I did manage to fill my belly up with some very tasty clementines, famous to Morocco, or as we call them in South Africa-*naartjies*.

From Rissani I got a Land Rover taxi with Vicky to Zagora, a trip that my buttocks will never forget. Nine hours of bouncing through the desert on hardened dust roads littered with rocks.

The scenery was the odd thorn tree, a line of camels with a Moroccan man leading them to a destination only he knew, with a continual backdrop of dune after dune, along with lift-off every few seconds as my bum lifted off the seat and my head hit the roof, with a 'Fuck it, slow down!'

Half way into the journey the driver came to an abrupt stop as if he had hit something. He climbed out without saying a word, kneeled down and began praying. I had never seen anything like it, and not understanding his religion I was puzzled by the time and place he had picked to perform this ritual.

As the sun began to set it was a very soothing feeling as the coolness set in, allowing us time to rest and stretch before resuming the painful journey.

On arrival under nightfall in Zagora, I was blessed to have my first hot shower in Morocco, and I felt I had entered into heaven to have my body cushioned by a mattress instead of a thin padded seat that nailed my backside with each bump for an eternity.

'Rolex,' I said to Vicky in reference to relaxing, as I stretched out in the comfort of the bed. Venturing out into the town I found the locals very cheeky and 'out to get you' for anything they could get.

In the main town in Zagora I saw the 'Green March' parade with a lot of parliamentary figures, music and dancing and once it had passed me by I walked on to Hotel Fibule. In the afternoon I climbed a small hill and got an excellent view of the river lined with palm trees with many more clustered in a beautiful green against the mud brick of the town.

In this city everyone I passed seemed to try a bartering trick with me, wanting my watch, clothes, day bag, and my bracelets in exchange for something handmade. I ended buying some beads that originated in Mali and a Moroccan flag, a blood red cloth with the six pointed green star for 50 Dirhams.

On the third day in Zagora, Vicky and I left the Hotel des Amis for the Hotel Fibula which was a bargain for 85 Dirhams for a double room. The hotel had a bar, a luxurious swimming pool and plenty of palm trees offering a welcome canopy of shade. Suddenly we were living the good life, a life that did not come easy for a backpacker who had to stretch every Dirham to make the adventure last.

I kept on thinking to myself that if I was in England we would be paying 20 times the price, which made us enjoy it even more.

We met up with Terry and Martin who we had last seen in Fes, and went with them to a really nice coffee shop that belted out 'Sultans of swing' by Dire Straits. Tapping happily on the table, I thought what a change from all the wailing.

After a nice hot coffee we decided to go into a carpet shop for some fresh mint tea and more importantly to escape from the hot scalding sun. After being handed a joint by the shop keepers we exited laughing and were convinced we saw a moving star, which could quite easily have been a satellite.

After spending a day relaxing around the pool we climbed a mountain to crown the day with a memorable sunset. Just to sit quietly and ponder about life's ups and downs was an adventure as we took in the moment watching as the ball of fire gracefully lowered itself

Tim Ramsden

behind a mountain range radiating a spectrum of colour across the horizon. There is something about a sunset that takes a hold of me almost like waiting and then watching a show, leaving me fulfilled and never disappointed.

In the morning we left Zagora at 7am along with two Dutch, one Japanese, and an Australian bound for Ouarzazate feeling like the United Nations. In Ouarzazate we had to change buses, which ended up being an eight hour wait until we moved again in the direction of Agadir. Proof once again that nothing happens fast in Morocco. It ended up being a very hectic bus ride with a crammed bus. I sat all hunched up and didn't sleep a wink for the eight hour duration of the trip.

Eventually at 4am we arrived at Agadir, and had a quick two coffees. I could not help but notice a few locals who were well and truly out of it, pulling on wooden pipes for all to see, and barely being able to speak.

At 4:30am we left for Tafraoute on another bus, and then at 6am we passed through Tiznit. On stopping there we both got out thinking we were in Tafraoute, and I got really livid when I found out that we were still hours away.

After the driver had finished his coffee we got on the road again at 7am. With some quite scary driving around blind corners with absolutely no deceleration and a sheer drop on my side of the window the driver kept on gunning the bus full tilt up the narrow mountain pass. Hooting a few times as he cornered swinging the wheel with one hand with no barriers to prevent the bus from going over the edge, we careered forward with my arms clutching the seat in front of me and absolutely convinced that we would not make it in one piece to Tafraoute.

The driver proved me wrong and at 11am I thankfully left the bus with very weak legs and a shirt dripping with sweat. I did not know if I should thank him or tell him to fuck off. Glad to have my feet on the ground I grabbed my bag and headed towards the closest and cheapest hotel.

While walking I thought about these bus drivers who drove like madmen and yet at the same time they seemed well in control of the situation.

The next day while wandering around I met a Moroccan who I had met in Erfoud 1000 kilometres away. What a small world in this big country.

On my walk back to the hotel I saw a dead and decaying dog lying on a rubbish site with thick string tied to its paw, evidence of animal cruelty which really sent a wave of anger through me, before the awful odour drove me away.

Soon after this a few young and very cheeky youngsters with an inbred hatred for Westerners began throwing stones at us, before scattering and disappearing into a side street.

I got a really good view of the town from a mountain, and once at the top I realized what a dangerous place these people had chosen to live. Huge boulders, like I had never seen before, stood precariously above this small town of red painted dwellings, waiting like a time bomb to go off. They looked as though they could roll down the mountain onto the roadway at any moment, with just the slightest earth tremor. After the exercise we went to Hassan's shop (a local I had met) where I was overjoyed to listen to my favourite ska band, the Specials.

Relaxing in the Tangier hotel on the upper terrace I met two Germans who got us all a little wasted. They told us a story of what happened to them in Mirleft. Carelessly they were smoking some hashish in a local shop serving coffee, and were caught by the police. The cops went up to their room to do a search but one of the Germans managed to get there first and threw a huge block of hash out of the window. The police looked around the room and found a stash of grass that the German forgot to throw out.

With an *'Attensione'* (watch out), the police left them to thank their lucky stars that they were not thrown into a prison and just forgotten about in the third world system of justice.

Back on the buses Vicky and I left Tafraoute for Mirleft. These buses as always are quite an experience with three key people operating one bus. There is a driver and two people that control the opening and closing of the doors, one of whom claps twice to stop and start the bus.

On arriving at Mirleft we stayed at the only hotel called Hotel Atlas which was run by two brothers, namely Agmed and Hussien. I got to know them well and they got to know me by name and were really

Tim Ramsden

happy to hear that I too was from Africa. Jimmy Cliff, Bob Marley, you named it and they will play it.

The brothers told us stories of the hippy era when the likes of Jim Morrison visited this same area and what a wild 'flower power' time it was back then, with all the Moroccan hash, and no cares in the world, except peace and a wishful end to the Vietnam War.

In the afternoon I went for a walk along the cliffs with also no cares and no responsibilities in the world, as a beautiful sea breeze blew my favorite aroma of salt into my face which I sucked into my lungs with a smile of contentment. Smelling the sea air once again took me home to Durban to the east coast of South Africa.

I followed the high rocky cliffs as they wound along the coast towering above the Atlantic as the waves pounded the shore with a spray of white foam, which shot up against the cliffs before retreating as the next wave came bursting forward.

Further along I came to this most amazing secluded beach with not a person around to disturb the sand that had been washed clean of all footprints and human presence.

After some good navigation down a rocky pathway I found myself on the soft sandy beach as I stood with my back to the open cove and high cliffs and faced the beautiful roll of the waves as they washed up the beach, beginning with such force and ending up gently caressing my feet. I stood locked in the moment of such peace and tranquility, with a smile at what backpacking can present to an avid traveller. It was no wonder that the hippies loved this area, and chose to blow a few brain cells in the process.

Later on in the day I met a German girl who had adopted a dog in Mirleft, and who had been living here for the past two months, without a single care in the world.

I also met up with the same Aussie girl and Spaniard who I had last seen in the desert town of Merzouga, well over 1000 kilometres away. It only proved that, as big as the country was, it was small on a backpacker's trail as we criss-crossed the Moroccan map on a whim with time and adventure on our side.

After a relaxing time on the beach we headed inland and found the ruins of an old Spanish fort on the hilltop with one wall still standing and a beautiful archway looking out over the small town. A small guard lookout next to the gate was still standing as curious kids went into this tight space and stared through the slit opening. We sat on the remains of the thick walls that had long ago crumbled, looking more like a carcass as we tried to piece together what an amazing site it must have once been, many hundreds of years ago, when huge sailing ships laden with cargo dotted the horizon.

Back at Hotel Atlas the brothers prepared an excellent meal for a low price of 45 Dirhams, which consisted of an overflowing plate of chips, roast chicken, salad, bread and sauce. It was the best meal I had eaten in Morocco.

At Hotel Atlas we met four Moroccans who were heading to Sidi Ifni by Land Rover, and then were going on to their small fishing village right on the beach.

All set, Vicky and I headed off with them for a much smoother ride along the tar road.

We arrived at a row of huts below a mountain with the ocean on our doorstep and poverty with subsistence life written on each home. With a strong mint tea in our hands we sat below two big beach umbrellas with the red and white of Coca-cola adding colour to the depressing site.

It certainly was peaceful with the only sound being the odd bark of a dog over the continual sound of waves breaking. Had a relaxing day sleeping on the beach hoping before I closed my eyes, that my pack would still be where I left it in Abdul Ali's hut.

Watching a sunset over the ocean has to be one of the most memorable times in my travels. It is a time when everything comes to a halt, and the only thing that is shifting, is one's mind as a rainbow of magic appears before one's eyes. The sitting, the watching, the thoughts into the past, present and future all tie one to a place that holds one in those dying minutes before darkness wipes the sky clean.

While dinner was being prepared under the light of a diesel generator, Vicky and I were offered some tea, which we gladly accepted.

It did not take long for us to begin laughing with a warm feeling rushing through my body from head to toe. I soon learned that I was drinking opium tea and that I was completely off my rocker on a high that I had never before experienced. I was hallucinating and just could

Tim Ramsden

not stop laughing until it slowly began to wear off which felt like many hours later.

After a long night we both went to sleep on Ali's floor while he slept on a bed in his hut. Under pitch darkness I got the fright of my life as Vicky screamed out. I could not believe it but he was fondling her as she slept.

After some shouting and lots of swearing from both of us, he immediately stopped and never tried it again.

Under pitch darkness my mind ran wild as to what he could do to us, if he so chose. I thought of him holding a knife. He could get rid of us without anyone knowing. Needless to say I never slept that night.

Glad when morning dawned I rose early and sat looking at the ocean. I learned that there were 15 people living in this village, some who had been there for four to six years in this life of total relaxation. I met three other Westerners, two French and an Italian who had been there a while.

There are four cats and two dogs that also live in this village. The dogs are known as beach dogs and act as guard dogs challenging anything that seems out of place.

Ali told us how they take illegal people (mainly Africans) from countries like Senegal, Nigeria to name a couple, across the ocean to the Spanish coast for a sum of 4000 Dirhams, under the cover of darkness.

Here I was sitting in an area that was trafficking people into Europe in a highly illegal and very unsafe operation, which certainly made me feel uneasy. How many had drowned on the way, or who had died on the journey, only they knew.

After two long days of relaxation we managed to hitch a lift in a Renault station wagon, which already had four people in it and was loaded with luggage. In we crammed with our two backpacks and now the car was completely and utterly stuffed to the roof. There was a huge box of *naartjies,* (clementines) of which I ate at least 10 in the 23 kilometre stretch to Mirleft.

Agmed was really happy to see us and made a delicious meal of fried eggs and chips, which was a rewarding change from the past two nights of fish. While eating I met Paul and Paula, two really nice people from Guersney.

On the day that I should have left Mirleft I ended up relaxing for another day. It was really overcast and I decided to go for a walk through the market, and then back at the hotel we played a few rounds of cards with Paul, Paula and Vicky.

I had a good laugh with Agmed and Hussien and a few other Moroccans when I gave my camera to another Moroccan to take a photo of all of us. He had never handled a camera in his life, there was no aiming, let alone warning and with fingers all over the lens the flash went off-certainly not a camera man at all.

Bought a big block of hash from Agmed and on smoking some of it I realized I had been ripped off 100 Dirhams for the poor quality and horrible gasoline like taste that it gave off. It disappointed me that I could not even trust him and his brother. The story goes on and I look forward to finding a Moroccan that I can trust and as always people are after money. Who am I to complain maybe they were trying to curb my drug habit, or slow it down at least.

It seemed like months ago since my body had warm water washing over it, and so I boiled a bucket of water over the gas stove. Mixing it with cold water in a big plastic tub I had now prepared myself a bath, and with my body half in it I felt as though I was in heaven.

There was no electricity or plumbing in this area, a bucket of cold water, a hole in the ground and a candle, 'Naturaal,' as they say.

Sadly I left Mirleft at 8am by bus for Tifnit along with Paul, Paula and Vicky. We got dropped off on the side of the road with no idea where we were, as the bus we were on was destined for Agadir.

These buses are something else, all the seats are numbered except they are numbered completely out of order. When people are getting on the bus along a route the bus does not come to a stop, but slows down. The door opens and the doorman jumps out and herds everyone inside. Once all are aboard, he then hits the side of the bus twice as the signal to accelerate, and then he swings inside like a monkey swinging from a branch. On the journey I saw an old woman fall as she tried to get onto the moving bus. She was picked up and helped in without a single complaint, as the driver floored it before she could even sit down. After all this was Africa, where safety and road laws are not understood, and do not play a part in this backward rush where nothing runs on time.

There was a time on the journey when the bus was really flying and I was wondering where the doorman was, when he swung himself off the roof and down a ladder on the back of the bus and through the door as if it was some sort of circus act.

After waiting on the side of the road for a while we eventually got a lift in a taxi truck with open wire mesh sides, which we gripped onto for dear life for the next 10 kilometres.

It did not take long for us to meet someone, which was very convenient as we needed a place to stay. Abdulak, who soon gained the nickname, 'one and a half' in reference to his half arm with a few fingers sticking out of his elbow, gladly led us away to a hut.

Tifnit was right on the ocean, a village of only 200 inhabitants, who were unbelievably friendly and very trusting people. We slept four in the hut on a few cane mats spread over the floor, with the beautiful soothing sound of the ocean in the background.

In the morning we arose for coffee and then watched Germany playing a soccer match against Belgium, before heading back to Abdulak's for lunch. He had cooked an amazing Taginine. In the middle of the floor there was this dirty crock pot that had been heated over the fire. We broke bread and dipped and scooped the steaming food out with our hands. Seven hands were in and out of the pot as we filled our bellies and smiled at this simple life in a room that reminded me of the servants quarters back home in South Africa. This was poverty with no Western refinements, and it was a pleasure to be in touch with real life and the basic necessities for a simple existence.

After lunch I sat on a tin roof and gazed out over the sea, appreciating the beauty and the smell of salt blowing up my nostrils, and the musical sound of the waves.

After a dinner of calamari at a fellow Moroccan's house on the top of the hill, we walked back towards the sea under a full moon. What a sight it was to see the ocean under this floodlight which cast a beautiful glow on the water as the white crests rose and disappeared with that captivating sound of waves crashing all around.

In the morning we walked eight kilometres from Tifnit to Bengamoud, three kilometers from Sidi Bibi to Abdulak's house, for a meal and a night's sleep. Two donkeys carried the four backpacks, and were ridden by two Moroccans. For lunch we ate octopus, which

I had to hold while it was cut into pieces before it was thrown into a pot. Once cooked it was poured onto a big enamel plate which sat on a dirty plastic table covering with more holes than one could count. Armed with chunks of bread eight of us dug in and savoured the meal in spite of the filth all around the small room.

Anything not edible, like fish heads, bones and skin were left on the table top for the cat which enjoyed the meal as much as we did.

I started to enjoy fish, which was something strange for me; in this country I certainly trust fish over meat, fresh from the ocean as opposed to slabs of fly infested meat.

At Abdulak's mother's we ate couscous with a sauce, which I did not enjoy one bit and never even finished the meal.

The next day we met two German tourists who had been living in Tifnit for the past six months, and had not met one Westerner until they met us. They prepared some hash for us, which we gladly jumped at and it was not too long before we were flying. We thought that this would be the first day in Morocco that we would not be high, as our stash had run out the previous night. Well it was not to be.

Stoned we slept comfortably on cane mats in the hut, courtesy of Abdulak. I thought to myself, wow are we stepping up in the world of comfort, before I drifted off into a deep sleep.

It was time to hit the road again, and with our heavy backpacks we walked with Abdulak to the main road. It was like an army patrol walking through the soft sand with my backpack and the heat scorching my neck, but at least I wasn't loaded to the tits with grenades and six magazines of live ammo. We waited for a while and eventually got a taxi to Inesgane and then a bus to Agadir. I was not impressed when we arrived in Agadir. It felt as if I had returned to Europe, as we were surrounded with flash hotels, nightclubs, fancy restaurants with money literally oozing out of the walls. This was a package tourist's haven and a backpacker's nightmare with expensive prices and a distorted view of a country that was far from first world.

We got a double room at Hotel Select for a reasonable price of 52 Dirhams, which was a steal in this city. We all then went to the Eiffel restaurant and ate chicken, chips, olives, salad, bread and coffees for only 24 Dirhams, which for us was like having a meal on the house.

While walking in the city I bumped into a Moroccan that I had met 10 days ago in Tiznit, and to our surprise he gave us some hash to smoke.

In the morning and barely awake, I started to panic as I was running out of money and needed to change a travellers cheque. It was Sunday and all the banks were closed and so I went to a hotel to change the money. They tried to rip me off with a really low exchange rate.

'Agadir is backward compared to the rest of Morocco,' I pleasantly told them and took my cheque back in search of a better rate.

A backpacker is like a wandering homeless person, where both are trying to get by on what little they have. A backpacker's mission is to explore, learn and journey on to as many places as money will allow. Time for the most part is on the backpacker's side. A homeless person seldom sees the light at the end of the tunnel, whereas we backpackers welcome the struggle as an experience as we know we have created memories that will last a life time. The light we shall see, but our travels only make total sense to a fellow backpacker who has had similar experiences.

At the next hotel I got the right rate, which was worth the extra aggravation, as it put more money in my pocket.

In the afternoon we all headed to the beach which was really clean compared to the rest of the Moroccan beaches, another example of the show put on for the Westerners. While relaxing on the beach I met Hussien who was a camel rider, leading all the Westerners around on a camel, only if they were prepared to pay the price.

As soon as I told him I was from South Africa, he genuinely asked me to bring an elephant overland to Agadir so that he could lead it around with tourists on its back while I became his manager.

'What does it eat? Does it bite? Does it sit down like a camel, so you can climb on?' And so his questioning went on. Poor guy hadn't a clue.

Had a great game of volleyball along with a good laugh with some Moroccans, French and Germans, played with no worries in the world.

Back at the hotel I had a hot shower, what a luxury, my first wash since the tub in Mirleft, and with clean clothes I felt like a new man.

Managed to get a taxi bound for Taghazout, and after agreeing on a price of 17 Dirhams for the two of us, we began to load our packs in the trunk. The trunk was full and so it had to be tied closed. Sitting inside we waited for the driver to leave for the journey.

Turning to us, he said: 'Seventy Dirhams!'

'No way!' I retaliated, opened the door and pulled our backpacks out of the trunk, and then headed to the bus station.

Once in Taghazout we walked half a kilometer to a campsite and stayed in a tent for the night. I met some travellers that we had last seen in Mirleft, and we joined them around a fire where we listened to Tony, an Englishman's life story with 'Men at Work' beating loudly in the background.

He was driving a bus which was fully equipped with a toilet, cooking area and a sleeping room along with enough space for his Mini Minor that he had to leave behind at customs in Tangiers, as Morocco does not permit more than one vehicle per passport.

Tony was very funny and had done a lot of travelling which captivated our attention as we drank and laughed into the night. Our drunken walk back to the tent was another experience as we navigated our way in pitch darkness until we eventually found our home for the night.

In the morning we caught a bus to Essaouira which took four hours and felt a lot longer than that. As usual the driver was a complete madman taking the corners so tightly that I thought the bus was going to topple over. His overtaking wasn't any better as he pulled onto the dirt and then back onto the tar road with a sudden jolt as he left the overtaken vehicle in a cloud of dust. The bus was doing over 80 kilometers an hour with the money collector still on the baggage rack. A minute later he appeared and casually descended the back ladder, opened the door and swung himself in. Riding these buses is like riding the tube train through London, each and every journey you make will leave you with a good story to tell.

Once in Essaouira we hunted for Hotel Rivage where we had arranged to meet Paul and Paula, and after a few hassles and back tracking we eventually found it and met up with them.

It was strange to feel rain again, in this hot climate, something that I had not felt in many long weeks, the last being in Fes.

Under a very dismal and drizzly sky we set off in the morning for a walk around the ramparts of an old Spanish fort which overlooked the ocean with a row of cannons jutting out from the fortress wall, pointing menacingly out to sea. The threat that these cannons once imposed on the enemy were now just a forgotten relic along with the crumbling walls. Fishing boats much the worse for wear bobbed up and down like corks, adding movement to the otherwise very still and bleak surrounding.

In a spice shop I saw a few chameleons in a small cage, and felt sorry for them, with animal cruelty screaming blue murder. Wanting so badly to let them go, I couldn't interfere with their culture and walked away.

As we walked I saw this Moroccan man wearing a really thick white and grey jersey. Being damp and cold I really needed something warm, and so he led me to his shop where I purchased one of these amazing jerseys for 125 Dirhams, worth every penny. My body literally melted into it, with a warm smile as I set off to find my fellow backpacking friends.

So far I have found the people in this coastal town to be very friendly with minimal hassle.

The next day we went for a walk along the beach and at low tide we walked out to a very old Portuguese fortress, now abandoned and broken into huge chunks of rock, almost unrecognizable as a bastion of strength in its day.

Back on land I met a man by the name of Hammid, who I kept on calling the wrong name, and even as I wrote my diary his name continues to slip my mind.

We smoked kiff together and he told me about the hippy era with, in his words, freaks burning clothes and passports as a sign that they did not want to leave Morocco.

While he was telling me this story I was watching a Moroccan lady in a black shawl with piercing eyes from behind a veil, as she sneakily puffed away on a cigarette, certainly the first time I had seen a woman smoking in this country.

I met a Moroccan from Mirleft who I had bumped into a few times, another example of a small world inhabited by millions. We had a few coffees and were joined by another Moroccan who always seemed to be where we were, as if he were following us in his continual effort to do some business.

By now I had got used to the high-pitched wailing from the mosques as the call to prayer echoed across the city five times a day.

Allah was certainly the word here. '*Hum do La*,' praise Allah and '*Insh' Allah*,' if Allah wills, both very commonly used phrases in the Arabic language.

There is Arabic music playing out of every shop you pass, just another flavor from the Middle East, a sound not expected from Africa.

There are three things that one will always see in Morocco, no matter where you go except for the Sahara. Moroccan flags, King Hassan IIs photo, in shops, hung off street lamps, plastered on bill boards and the mosque.

My meals were chip rolls known in England as a 'buttie,' which were filling, tasty and really good value at 3.5 Dirhams.

Essaouira was a great town, very quiet compared with the likes of Fes and Meknes and all the hustle and bustle that go hand in hand with these two towns.

As I wrote my diary I realized that I have been here six weeks, after only planning to stay for two to three weeks, how time had flown.

The south was far more relaxing and enjoyable. It was so laid back that one tended to adopt their care-free way of life as one drifted along forgetting days and dates, and of course time is of no importance except for bus departures, but even they didn't leave on time.

This is the life of Rolex ation, without the Rolex.

I had come to realize that as far as outstanding geographical features were concerned, this country hadn't captivated my attention, but the culture did. It was amazing to see the people hard at work and the sheer brilliance of their craftsmanship. The materials and tools they used to churn out clay pots, sculptures, their metal work, woodwork, carpets and jewellery to name a few, was just amazing considering the absence of Western technology.

The country thrives on tourism for its foreign exchange, creating an income for the souks and those whose crafts are being sold by the souk. Everyone seems to support the next. The person who sells mint to the restaurant owner then makes a profit on his mint tea in his shop.

Fruit and vegetables from market and people baking bread at home, find their way on to restaurant tables as one hand helps another. It is as though everyone has a function to perform for their daily existence in this third world economy.

In my mind they are actually falling further behind the western world as their economy is not developing, but on the other hand if things did change through modern technology, thousands would lose their jobs, creating an escalation in crime, loss of self respect and dignity.

Thinking of the desert people and those in remote villages, these would be happy with their present way of life, where change would be catastrophic literally wiping out centuries of definitive culture.

But in my opinion those of my generation once given a taste of the Western world would not return to their roots, breaking a cycle of their father and father's fathers who had worked tirelessly and frugally for each and every precious Dirham.

I saw many of these young teenage children living a life of onlookers, hanging around shops waiting to make an easy Dirham by hassling and haggling with people, mainly travellers.

This country was a land of contrast, rich and poor, happy and sad, beauty and filth, picturesque and bleak, but in spite of it all it was memorable with its strong culture and a hardened smile forced from a weather beaten face, a face proud to be Moroccan.

I was still relaxing in Essaouira taking time out to wash a few clothes in between relaxing on a roof top that overlooked the ocean. It was always a sight that made me feel alive, the cresting of the waves and the crashing force as they exploded only to subside and smooth over as they receded and re-formed. Watching an ocean and staring into a fire are times that I most treasure, when I lose myself in thought and appreciation of life.

I managed to buy some hash from a Moroccan man who was selling it, and together under pitch darkness we navigated our way through these walled in tunnels with houses above them and little doorway entrances carved out of them.

After what felt like a long walk we emerged and climbed a flight of stairs with the aid of a candle in a small tin, which flickered in and out of light and shadow adding fear to the situation.

Once at the top of the stairs we entered a room and sat on the floor.

'Africa, we are brothers, cousins and neighbours,' he said after hearing of my travels thus far through Morocco.

With a small cassette player playing a distorted sound we smoked a joint and then descended the stairs, trying not to slip or trip or bang my head on the low overhead walls, in my wacked out state.

After a deep sleep we left Essaouira in the pouring rain for the famous city of Marrakech. But as always there was a problem. The baggage handler refused to load our bags unless we gave him 10 Dirhams.

'Fat chance!' we said, and threw him a 5 Dirham coin, which did the trick.

As always it was a hectic bus drive packed full, and made worse by babies crying, people shouting, and the bus stopping every five minutes. There was a leak above my head which dripped like a niggling torture, and my long legs were cramped due to my sitting over the wheel arch.

Swearing to myself as mad as nine snakes I cursed these buses and the discomfort that I would sit through for the next four and a half hours.

In Marrakech the four of us got a taxi in the rain, and after avoiding two very near accidents we arrived at hotel Kawakib and paid 30 Dirhams after the woman had asked for 60 Dirhams. It just goes to show what haggling can do even in a hotel.

We later found out that the taxi driver had told the hotel woman to double charge us, so that he could get a cut.

'Slimy git!' I said, as we wandered up the stairs and crashed at 7 pm, my earliest sleep so far in Morocco.

The toilets were an experience. A hole in the ground, with two flat areas on the thick white slab to line up your feet, before lowering yourself down into a squatting position and taking aim. Once the job was done a bucket of water was thrown down the hole as the flushing technique.

In the morning I awoke with a hive of activity happening below me. This city seemed so alive, and I really liked it.

Excited to find a better location in which to view the city square, we moved to another hotel. It felt like being in another world where we could safely watch all the activity right under our noses without the constant pestering and hassles that went hand in hand with this life and culture.

Snake charmers coaxed spitting cobras to puff out their necks into threatening hoods, while others held less poisonous snakes that could be displayed around your neck for a few Dirhams. Monkeys on leads paraded around in dirty clothes, to the accompaniment of loud drumming, trumpets and clanging of cymbals. Circles of people gathered around each act in captivated attention as flames were blown from mouths, knives juggled, all under a very gloomy sky as the drizzle put a dampener on the day but certainly not the feeling of excitement.

Walking through the activity I watched a man drink boiling water, who really impressed me as it seemed real beyond all belief. There were stalls of fruit covered by a canopy or an umbrella that were fighting the wind and rain, pulling taut on the tent pegs as it filled like a sail ready to take off with the force of nature.

I passed another stall with a table covered with false teeth and real teeth. Imagine buying another person's false teeth and wearing them as your own, I wondered, as I zigzagged through the throngs of people.

The traffic here was something else, cars, taxis and horse drawn carriages, bicycles, small motor bikes all with hooters rudely sounding their right of way. Pedestrians in this third world country did not have road rights and had to be on the alert for speeding vehicles. Miracously very few people got hit, maybe it was the good driving, but I thought it was more likely the eyes and quick reactions of those on foot.

I went into the medina with Mustafer and having learned my lesson I turned to him and said: 'I am short of cash and don't want to buy anything.'

To my surprise I spotted a nice *djellaba* and ended up bargaining with the shop keeper until I got it down to 200 Dirhams from the asking price of 350 Dirhams. I also bought a nice leather belt for 40 Dirhams, a day that turned out to be very expensive in their terms and in mine as my money was starting to run low.

It had been raining for the last two days, puddles and mud everywhere, but with signs of the sky starting to clear.

I had a good meal in the Djemaa el Fna square, totally surrounded by all the activities and acts, and the hassles and haggling that came with being a Westerner in an impoverished society. Enjoying my meal I ignored the constant comments, questions and the final insults before they left to find better entertainment.

Taking in my surroundings I went to the CTM Hotel and got an amazing view of the whole square from the hotel terrace, where I savoured a coffee as I looked onto a world that had popped into my life of travel and one that would soon be just a memory. This was travel, excitement in the moment.

Back at my Hotel Oukaimeden, I relaxed and wrote a few lines in my crumpled diary.

At dinner Vicky, Paul and Paula and I ventured out into the packed square under darkness which was well lit by gas lamps and old carriage lamps. The beat of the drums, the smell of food wafting in the air, the shrill sound of the Moroccan flute sounding like the bagpipes all made me feel alive as where ever I looked a lasting impression was stamped into my memory of Marrakech.

We had a few caffe lattes and then went for a tour with a guide around an almost deserted medina with piles of rubbish left as a reminder of the all the action that this square had generated.

While we were walking down a very narrow dimly lit street I saw a bike coming from behind me at quite a speed, so watching him I slowly moved over.

Suddenly I heard screams like I had never heard before. Whirling around I found myself staring at two sets of nostrils belonging to two horses pulling a carriage with a driver whipping the horses and screaming wildly.

In a split second I threw myself against the wall, felt the wind brush over me and heard a cynical laugh as the runaway carriage hurtled past.

With a deep sigh I walked on, very shaken at how close I had come to being trampled by two horses and then run over by a speeding carriage. It was yet another example of a vehicle's right of way.

After a good sleep and a meal of caffe lattes and toast we headed out into the square. While watching one of the acts I was immediately singled out and pulled towards the middle of the circle through a path that had opened up for me. I gripped the Moroccan's hand, shook my head and walked away.

'You are not going to take the piss out of me!' I said as I made my exit.

We had a few more minor hassles and then a comical scene erupted. Two Moroccans began fighting over us, why I have no idea. They were cursing, shouting and spitting and pushing each other, a scene I had only witnessed once before over a card game that must have had some money attached to it. They were speaking fast, pale faced, using a deep guttural *ggaa* like Afrikaans and Hebrew. Leaving them to it, we wandered on.

In the morning we left Marrakech for Casablanca aboard a luxurious bus for only 56 Dirhams, air conditioning, two television sets and the most comfortable seats I had yet experienced in Morocco. After the four and a half hour journey Vicky and I located the hotel Mirimar where we met up with Paul and Paula. After a few beers we finalized our departure from Morocco, deciding on a train bound for Tangiers at 7am.

Casablanca was unbelievably modern, just another contrast of Western world to third world, Europe to Africa, again I felt a world away from Africa and yet I was right in it.

Although I had had never seen the romantic film 'Casablanca,' with Humphrey Bogart and Ingrid Bergman, I had most definitely heard about it. I loved the name and the ring it had, saying it over and over as if I was trying to master a word in a foreign language. I am sure it brought the cities name to life around the world with its release in 1942 to coincide with the allied invasion of North Africa.

And yet in this city one thing was the same and that was the road laws. In traffic everyone edged their way forward cutting people off as they jockeyed for a place in the gridlock. Drivers barely paid attention to the colour of the traffic signal, swerving, hooting and driving as though they were the rightful owners of the road. Surprisingly I don't think I ever saw a car accident or a pedestrian get hit, a miracle on those roadways.

By now I had grown a beard, which was ginger brown and where ever I went I was called 'Ali Baba.' What that meant I had no idea but it was used on a person that had not shaved in a while. And in that case I was definitely an 'Ali Baba.'

At 7am as arranged the four of us left Casa by train and arrived in Tangiers at 1pm.

What a weird feeling it was to be back in a place that had scared the living shit out of me as a backpacker, a full 7 weeks ago. Those threats and all the hassles that had been a shock to my system after the comfort of Eastern and Western Europe, and now I was back in it.

It seemed so much easier now; I had become hardened to this way of life. With each hassle and threat I smiled back as if to say, 'Piss off, I am leaving your land!'

I got the feeling that they knew we had been in Morocco for a while, and that we knew their world of intimidation directed at the new traveller as some sort of initiation. Seeing this they left us alone.

We bought our ferry tickets for 196 Dirhams each and celebrated our return to the west with a good meal.

This left me enough money in my pocket to purchase an airline ticket back to London, only if my van the 'Bulldog' had been towed away or stolen from the parking lot below the Big Rock in Gibraltar. Being away from it for seven weeks I did not expect to see it again, and was mentally prepared to fly back.

Just before we boarded the ferry I met a Danish backpacker who in Tangiers was told to hand over 100 Dirhams, or get hurt. Standing firm he refused and his aggressors were left with no choice but to walk away with the feeling that this foreigner had been in Morocco a while.

Boarding the ferry with our backpacks was a good feeling, a feeling of accomplishment having travelled through a foreign land, with a foreign language in such a foreign life.

I must say it was such a great trip, a trip I shall never forget. The hassles, hardships, crafty Moroccan people, the buses, the Sahara desert, the fishing villages, the beaches, the medinas, and some really great Moroccans, that all made up a culture so rich in colour and intrigue.

It was a culture that was really hard to adapt to at times, one that left its mark on me. I will never forget my time in Morocco but after seven weeks it is time to get back into Western civilization and the hassle free life of the West.

I wrote in my diary that I would one day return to a very special place called Merzouga in the Sahara desert, and one day I would love to honour that.

Salaam, labass, begeer, wage, shwooia. Nana beget niet kelem la Arabia. Shoekraan and baslama Maroc. Thankyou and goodbye Morocco.

AN AFRICAN'S HEART IN LONDON
(1991-92)

London was my base and over a period of two years I came and went as I pleased. One of the main reasons I returned was to get a job and make money for the next journey. After my noteworthy trip to Morocco, I returned to Gibraltar with enough money for a flight ticket back to England. I did not expect to see my van, The Bulldog still parked in the parking lot below the Big Rock. I could not believe my eyes to see it standing out like a sore thumb exactly as I had parked it seven weeks ago. I found a note, which had been stuffed through the sliding door. It was from Jim, he had 'made it' out of Morocco, and was apologizing for his sudden departure. I was really glad to hear that he had got out of Tangiers safely.

Maybe the hairy tailless monkeys known as the Barbary apes numbering close to 200, which guarded the rock, had looked after my vehicle. I shook my head with amazement as I connected the battery.

There is a saying in Gibraltar; when the Barbary apes leave the rock that will be when Gibraltar breaks from Great Britain.

Looking up at the huge rock I fired up the Bulldog and with Paul, Paula and Vicky we drove to the border post. I was asked for my insurance papers which had expired and so after a telephone call I arranged temporary papers. After a quick check at our passports we drove out of Britain's stronghold for the last three centuries, and made our way into Spain.

The Bulldog survived the drive from Gibraltar, through Spain and Portugal and up through France to Cherbourg. I caught a ferry over the channel to Portsmouth and then made my way to a very Indian or as they would say in England, *Paki* area, called Hayes just outside of Heathrow.

Clad in a *djellaba* and looking like a long haired homeless bum, I scared the hell out of Louise, a good South African friend as I knocked on the door looking for a place to stay. Hayes became my home for a couple of very cloudy months through smoke screens of hashish and slurred speech, spent with four other very stoned South African's. Murray, Lousie, Dave, Roger and Peter had been living in the house for a few months and I took up a spot in Rogers's room on a mattress.

One evening Peter returned with a few English girls he had met in the pub. They were drunk and we were stoned. I was sitting glued to a chair watching a game of soccer when they burst through the door. We all sat dead still and stared at them in shock.

'Are you an invalid?' one of the girls shouted seeing me sunk into the chair with my legs hanging over the side and my arms rigidly holding the arm rests. Louise roared with laughter but I was still too stunned with paranoia to move at all or even crack a smile.

My van, the loyal old Bulldog stayed parked on the road until the Pakistani neighbours called the police, who told me I had to move it. With Murray's guidance I drove it between two narrow houses with Murray apprehensively pulling me forward with slow hand movements. I fought the steering wheel as I rolled the wheels scraping the drains pipes on either side of the vehicle. Murray couldn't contain his laughter as the noise got louder, while I held the wheel tight with a curled up tongue clenched between my teeth. After an agonizing ten minutes I made it through, but God only knew how I was going to get it out.

I soon got a job with the four guys at Kelly Brothers, an Irish run company running main cables under the man holes. Once these cables had been laid cable television and phones could be installed in people's houses. We worked like African labourers feeling every bit like slaves, but the money we earned made it all worth it.

When a house with a few fellow South African's came up in Streatham, south London, we gave notice and moved to the big city.

I parked the Bulldog at the very front of the house, squeezing it behind a low wall. The van had been my home and my transport. Wayne and I had lived in it for a week while we tried to get work on the beach in Zandvoort, Holland. Not being able to sleep on the side of the road we drove it into the dunes and into the middle of a race track. In the morning we were blasted awake by Porsche racing cars revving their engines. We were in the old Formula 1 race track in Zandvoort. After the race meeting and short of money we collected all the beer bottles out of the rubbish bins and had enough money to buy some food and a couple of beers each.

In France with Murray and Louise I was heading casually down a narrow road when all of a sudden a very low bridge loomed ahead. Murray scrambled to wind the sunroof down and I crept closer expecting the top of the Bulldog to be ripped off. As we drove under the bridge we all ducked and then heard this awful scraping. We all burst out laughing glad that we had kept the roof at least. After what felt like an extremely long minute of noise we emerged intact on the other side.

The Bulldog was a name known in Europe as a coffee shop in Amsterdam. On parking the van next to a beach in Marseilles, France, I was asked if I had any hash and Rizla's to roll the joint. I looked at them and laughed. I was so far from Amsterdam and yet people knew of the Bulldog coffee shop.

In London the house I stayed in had been re-possessed by the government and to our amazement we were allowed to stay there rent free. Our only expense was the electricity which worked on a metre. It did not take long before someone bypassed the coin feed giving us totally free lodging. Even the pay phone was bypassed and the calls flowed for free around the world, but mainly to South Africa.

It was an old Victorian house with at least 14 rooms with high ceilings and old floor boards with a contingent of the United Nations living in it. We were South African, Irish-Catholic and Protestant, Russian, Turkish, Spanish, a couple of black Londoners all sharing a kitchen and a house that reminded me of the way poverty-stricken blacks lived in a location, back in South Africa.

The grass was knee high, the odd window was broken, the kitchen was filthy the rubbish was normally overflowing and the toilets needed a good clean. Our money was for travel and very little went into cleanliness. Our stomachs and drug habits came first and cleaning a distant second.

Our neighbour was a prim and proper old English lady with a beautiful garden like a miniature botanic garden. Needless to say she was appalled at the way we neglected our backyard. She would read us the riot act every day which we ignored.

One day after returning from work we were utterly amazed to see the knee high grass cut with all the clippings cleared away. We knew who had done it. The poor old lady had got sick and tired of looking onto the jungle from her upstairs window. Amongst one another we laughed and were thrilled to finally have a garden.

Now we were outside all the time, sitting or playing one bounce with a soccer ball.

Jono and Sean invented a game, called 'Nut it,' whereby the soccer ball had to pass over a net without bouncing with the use of one's (nut) head.

It was great fun especially after a joint or two. The only problem was that the ball often found its way into the old lady's rose garden.

'I bet she wished she had never cut the grass,' I said pulling the ball out of some flattened flowers.

Celebrating our wide open garden we threw a party for the people we knew in the area including Buddy and Kevin who were in Balham. Peter got drunk and started a huge bonfire that was licking at the roof. He broke down fences and acquired any and all wood he could get his hands on to keep the flames rising into the starry night.

Rizza who was a Turk from Istanbul and struggled terribly with his English, walked into the kitchen and started making a sandwich. 'I like penis butter,' he blurted out. We just couldn't contain our laughter as he continued spreading peanut butter over the bread.

In February 1991, he had gone to London to work and was just outside the Victoria station when a bomb exploded. The IRA had planted it, killing one person and injuring 38. They succeeded in spreading terror through the London core. There had been bombs in South Africa and we South African's carried on with our lives as if it was normal, treating it as a slight hindrance.

And there was Pedro from Morocco who would visit us from a house up the road. He was upset at Andrew for talking to a certain lady friend. In his accented English he blurted out: 'Andrew talk to whore, look like rubbish bin. I fuck him, I fuck him now.'

Chris, an Irishman who smoked hash like cigarettes and hardly ever worked, lived in the same house along with two Australians, Gary and Craig.

One couldn't forget the lazy Russian with a thick accent. Michael was married to Catherine who worked like a slave while her husband smoked hash like a chimney, and was totally unemployable.

'Katta you fuckin' beeech. Come here,' he would say to her like a man calling a whore.

Michael set up his Russian friend to rob a pub with a toy gun, while he sat back and smoked hash hoping for a bag of money to come his way. His friend was caught running away with the money and thrown in jail. To make matters worse he was an illegal immigrant.

Peter, a South African from Pietermaritzburg, was another story. He could not handle his drink and on one crazy night shortly after having all his hair shaved off, he kicked the Boots pharmacy window in. In his drunken state he hobbled a couple of kilometers home leaving a bloody trail, with his foot so badly lacerated that he had to have at least 20 stitches.

Jim also stayed at our house. He was a tall and a very funny black guy who we branded in our South African racial way as Coloured, being of a lighter shade due to a mixed marriage. He was huge and in good shape, had an olive smiling face with perfect white teeth, long dreadlocks and a great South London accent. He reminded me of Ruud Gullit, a famous Dutch soccer player. Every now and then another South African called Brett would call him Kaffir in a joking but serious way. In our van going to work he would tell Jim, 'kaffirs in the back' much to our delight. We all knew it wasn't serious and that Jim's skin colour was of no threat to any of us. We actually enjoyed having a black friend for the very first time in our lives.

In the back we slid around as the driver drove like a bat out of hell to get us through London's slow traffic, over the Thames and down to Uxbridge just outside Windsor. We met a South African who had just started with Kelly Brothers Cable Network, who most of us in the house worked for. He went off for a diving holiday and we soon learned he had vanished. Either he drowned or was eaten by a shark, but his body was never recovered. It left us with an odd feeling especially as he was a fellow South African.

Murray and Buddy both drove the vans which were like company cars and it was a great way to get most of the house to work and back without using our own hard earned money.

On the way back we used to drive through Chelsea with pubs full of 'suits' and well to do people. Roger had an idea and wanted to shock those pressed against the window as they sipped on their ale's after a day at the office. With four of us in the back of the van, we yanked the sliding door open and then in full view of the pub, Roger dropped his pants giving them a disgusting view of his arse. People in the window looked stunned, then smiled and pointed. We rolled around in the back gasping for air as Dave tried to push Roger out of the vehicle while Murray waited for the light to turn green.

Roger, myself and a couple of others from the house went to the Castle Tavern, a South African, Australian and New Zealander hangout. Being the meeting place it was, there was always a very good chance of seeing someone that you hadn't seen for many years. This time was no different. I met Shaun a good friend from my Treverton days. Shaun was also in 1 SAI, the same unit as me and had finished his two years of National Service a year ahead of me. He went onto tell me that he had extended his service and had fought with UNITA, our old ally in Angola helping to stem the tide of communism and Marxist rule. Then to my utter shock he said that he had joined up with the MPLA, our enemy and was now fighting against UNITA. It just went to show what money can do in war with morales and justification just silent words where the greed of a dollar swung the deal. Shaun drank like no tomorrow as if trying to wipe away the past and remain firmly in the present. After a short visit in London he was returning to the Angolan bush and back to his war. I looked at him and wondered if he would die a lonely death there.

We caught up on the Castle's, served ice cold and then stumbled out catching a double Decker red London bus. We sat on the upper level and went right to the back. It didn't take long for me to pass out. When our stop came up Roger and the others got up and left me passed out in the back seat. Hours later when I awoke I found myself in pitch darkness in a bus garage with dozens of other buses. Stumbling around I found a way out and made for home which was a kilometer or so away. Roger couldn't stop laughing when he saw me, but admitted he had been worried as they had left me hours ago.

The life and times in Streatham were a good laugh, with most of the time spent as high as the hash would take us, soaring our minds and spirits far beyond the damp rainy climate that we chose to live in.

Now and then we would catch the tube into London and go to the Tattershall Castle, a huge boat docked on the Thames where many Aussies, Kiwis and South African's would go. It was always a great drunken evening meeting people that one hadn't seen in a long while.

Murray, Louise, Dave, Roger and I went to see Dire Straits in Earls Court. It was packed and was amazing hearing and seeing 'live' one of my favourite bands. 'Sultans of Swing,' bellowed through the stadium and we were standing and going crazy, an absolute thrill to see Mark Knopfler in action.

On Dave and Roger's last day before they were to leave for Thailand our Irish boss organized two strippers who met us at Jimmy's for breakfast. Jimmy ran a breakfast shop that was always filled to capacity. Jimmy was a short stocky man with a round face and a small black mustache. He was very funny, but extremely rude and always spoke his mind with women and how he wanted his way with them. It was so crude he had us rocking with laughter.

One of the strippers was a 'Ten Ton Tessie,' or a 'Roly Poly,' as they say in England and Dave was the lucky winner. Much to our delight she took his head and buried it into her rolls of fat shoving it into her crotch. Dave weaseled his way out gasping for breath. Then with her extra large breasts, she knocked Dave's head around. His hair was all disheveled and he smiled passing the show onto Roger. Roger had a great time with his stripper as he stole her feather duster and dusted her off instead.

When Roger left I took over as a driver towing huge reels of fibre optic cable and positioning it over manholes. While I rolled the reel it was pulled through the ducts and lined up on the grass before being fed through another duct.

'Watch the dog shyt!' the Irish would say. One unlucky time I was feeding the cable on the grass really fast through my hands. To my horror dog shyt flicked up into my face and into the corner of my mouth. Everyone howled as I spat it out.

Now Murray and I were racing each other in our vans from Windsor and Maidenhead, through London and over the Thames to our homes in Streatham. We had some close races but Murray seemed to lead the charge and won on most occasions.

Much to our anger a few of us were sent up to Birmingham and Coventry, home to some of my favourite Ska bands. Our job was to work with Kelly Brothers installing cable and phones in an area now live with newly laid fibre optic cables. Dave had returned from Thailand and with Karl, myself and another South African we worked in the sweltering sun installing cable. We had a place to stay paid for by Kelly Brothers, but we were all very unhappy that we had been chosen. It was this or risk losing our jobs.

In anger Karl and I devised a plan to get back at them and make them stew for sending us up there. Karl had been given a van to drive and we decided we would drive it back to Streatham and park it there, instead of handing it back. After a week they started to ask a lot of questions, but we played dumb saying that we handed it in at the yard in Birmingham. Meanwhile Steve, another South African, wanted to buy it from us and sell it on. Things became extremely heated and after two weeks we handed it in, much to everyone's relief. As though nothing had happened we continued working, making money for our travels. My eye was now set on South East Asia.

Roger returned to England from Thailand and during the customs search they found work addresses on him. Being on a South African passport he was forbidden to work. He was allowed to enter the country for a week to collect the rest of his belongings and was then deported.

Through the network of South African's in London I heard about something called Hospital courses at Guys Hospital. It was strictly by word of mouth where they needed volunteers to try out new drugs that were being tested before they hit the market. It paid £100 a day and I couldn't refuse. There was a number to call and when an appointment was made each volunteer had to go through a screening and a physical. If you came back healthy and with no traces of drugs or alcohol in your blood stream you were given a date and a time to be at the hospital. The duration of the study was also given to you.

Free meals, accommodation and a canella in your wrist with lots of reading material and television got us through the time. We were not permitted to leave the building and after 10 days it felt like jail, except with good food. I always drank lots of water to flush my system. The pill, administered orally was generally given just once on the first day of our clinic study. My longest clinic trial was 10 days and netted me £1000 towards my travels.

One poor South African cashed his cheque at the bank around the corner from the hospital. On walking out he had his complete earnings of £1000 stolen from him. I felt sick for him and instead of cashing mine deposited it into my account.

The best was when I had been accepted for a 15 day trial run by a Japanese Pharmaceutical Company. It was cancelled and I was paid out every penny. I had never won a lottery but this certainly felt like it, and I didn't have to do a damn thing.

Needing to tie up loose ends before I booked my trip to Asia, I did some work on The Bulldog, adding two mattresses, a gas stove and a few cupboards. Much to my relief I managed to sell it for £600 to some young travellers. I got £50 more than Wayne and I had paid for it.

I also signed over my taxes to a Refund agency that were meant to deposit a tax credit of £1500 into my account. One year later I would find them closed with a sign stating bankruptcy. They had taken my money and opened up another Tax refund business, and there was nothing I could do.

There were many times when we white South African's spoke amongst ourselves about our nation with that deep worry of the unknown. There was lots of TV footage emerging, some of which really rocked our world so far away in cold dismal London in an old rundown Victorian house.

South Africa had become a melting pot as the nation began to split. There was the Inkatha Freedom party, led by Chief Mangosuthu Gatsha Buthelezi who were opposed to communism and were mainly Zulu, from Kwazulu Natal.

I remember him as clear as day being asked an important and trying question to which he answered across live television: 'It is complete and utter bullshit,' with shit pronounced as sheet, which had us rolling with laughter.

There was the unbanned ANC who had a large Xhosa following from Johannesburg and the surrounding area, who hated the Zulu.

The AWB which stood for the Afrikaner Resistance Movement, under the leadership of Eugene TerreBlanche, wanted an independent Boer Republic and with their diehard beliefs we thought they would bring civil war to the country. Those belonging to the party wore an arm band very similar to the German Swastika. It was three black sevens meeting in the middle over a white circular background set in a red square, forming a triskelion. They also used the '*Vierkleur*' or the original flag of the old Transvaal Republic.

Being English we would laugh at this man as he rode his horse everywhere like a Boer from the Boer War of 1899, with a round bearded and very fierce looking face with cold unforgiving eyes. To me he was a replica of some of our permanent force leaders when I was in the army, who I loathed.

To us he was like a clumsy idiot who often fell off his horse as he rode to rallies in the uniform of the AWB with the three sevens on his arm band.

The AWB openly threatened all-out war and in August 1991 in the Battle of Ventersdorp they confronted police in front of the town hall where FW de Klerk was speaking. Three AWB supporters and a passerby were killed. Later during negotiations they stormed the Kempton Park World Trade Centre smashing an armoured car through a glass window.

It was as if our country was crumbling and the white Afrikaner was struggling to save face, while showing force with that die-hard approach never to be ruled by a black man. I believed that many Afrikaners would rather die than see the day when the black majority ruled the motherland, dictating to the white minority.

To sit by and watch helplessly as this all unfolded on a TV screen so far away in London, was like watching a volcano erupt in slow motion as it began to spray heat and flame like a war scene, wiping away any barriers in its path with the fuel of hatred adding to the fire.

South Africa was on alert, and while many held their breath, others prayed and people prepared by loading up with guns and ammo for a civil war that seemed inevitable.

On 10 April 1993, Chris Hani leader of the South African Communist Party and chief of staff of Umkhonto we Sizwe, was assassinated by Janusz Walus, a Polish far-right immigrant.

The tension that followed the assassination led many to believe that the country would erupt into a bloodbath.

Nelson Mandela, not yet President, stepped in and appealed to the country for calm:

'Tonight I am reaching out to every single South African, black and white, from the very depths of my being. A white man, full of prejudice and hate, came to our country and committed a deed so foul that our whole nation teeters on the brink of disaster. A white woman, of Afrikaner origin, risked her life so that we may know, and bring to justice this assassin. The cold blooded murder of Chris Hani has sent shock waves throughout the country and the world....Now is the time for all South African's to stand together against those who, from any quarter, wish to destroy what Chris Hani gave his life for – the freedom of all of us.'

Whatever was to be with my country and my people was in God's hands, and I just knew that things would work themselves out.

No matter what happened I would always be a South African, a birthright that was my privilege to carry.

With political unrest on my mind it was time to hit the road again with a full wallet and sharp curiosity.

THAILAND (1992)

Many years ago, when I was a teenager in the 80s I heard a song about an oriental city with bars and temples, a muddy old river and reclining Buddha's in a country once called Siam. It was a catchy song titled, 'One Night in Bangkok,' and became an instant hit in the clubs and bars across South Africa. Little did I know that I would one day venture out to this faraway land on another continent?

Totally ignorant as to what lay ahead I boarded my Air Bangladesh flight that was to land in a place called Dhaka, which at first I thought was the capital of Senegal, in West Africa. I soon realised it was Bangladesh as we landed in the simplest airport I had ever seen. Thousands of Bangladeshi onlookers with nothing else to do pushed against the fence and stood on low buildings to get a glimpse of what had flown in. I felt like someone very important as their eyes locked on us like lasers. There was a single building at the end of the bumpy runway and we were ordered off the plane and had to cross the landing stretch to get to it. While the plane was being refuelled I had a cup of tea and took in my surroundings.

These Indians look like ours back home, I thought. They were dark as the Ace of Spades like the Tamils in Durban. If the airport was run down I could only imagine what the actual capital looked like. Shit, I hope Thailand is a little more advanced than this. It didn't take long before we were back on the plane and in the air with Bangkok a short flight away. I had no idea what to expect and I didn't want to know until I landed. Ever since Greece I had made a point of never building up an expectation of a country in my mind. Through my conjured up thoughts Greece had been a letdown.

The landing was smooth and as everyone started to vacate the plane I felt totally alone. I had a year ahead of me. What would it bring? It reminded me of a Circus cartoon book that was read to me when I was small.

'If you want to find out what it will be, just open the flap and then you will see.' Now I had to open the flap to see where my life would journey to, through Thailand and onwards for the next long year. It was scary, but I had to do it. I had committed myself and there was no turning back.

With my thick 'Bible,' South East Asia, Lonely Planet on a shoestring, and Murray Head's song, 'One Night in Bangkok,' swirling through my mind, I waved a taxi down. 'Khao San Road,' I said. This is where I had been told to go as this was a Westerns hangout where connections and friendships could be made. He dropped me at the top of the road and I started looking for a place to stay. I quickly found a single room with a shower and a window, and most importantly a door that locked.

Khao San Road was a hive of activity as I walked down the street with nightfall having already covered the area, and like Christmas lights on a dark tree the little restaurants and fluorescent lights shone like flickering ornaments. People were talking over tables filled with Singha beer bottles and laughter flowed onto the street making me feel that much more alone. I felt like an outsider looking in through a window at a scene of backpacker comraderie, and I knew I had to meet people to be a part of it. I had learned a long time ago that in travel one is seldom alone and I drew comfort from this.

Bangkok was alive with Sex clubs and seedy sex shows. Young innocent girls as young as ten had been plucked away from their parents in the rural north and sold into the sex trade. Parents had actually sold their daughters for a pay cheque. I shook my head and couldn't fathom the guilt of this life sentence. I saw it only to believe it as young girls stripped and performed indecent acts, with ping pong balls, poles, bottles and men and women for the entertainment of the bar crowd. The price was in the beer which covered the sordid show. The girl's innocence had been taken and a glazed over mask replaced her sweet face. Her eyes were ringed with sleep deprivation and drugs were written in etched lines over her aged face. The beauty had been replaced with the work of the devil. I felt sick to see it but it was part of the experience and I had to sit through it. After a couple of expensive beers we returned to Khao San Road, courtesy of the three wheeler taxi called the Tuc Tuc.

The 'Lady Men' was another story. These were Thai men who dressed up as women to lure the Westerners. They had caught many unsuspecting travellers in very embarrassing situations.

'It is a man,' one traveller had exclaimed in utter shock at the realization of what stood naked before him.

I had to laugh as I watched one Westerner after the next move in on these 'Lady Men,' with no clue. I kept well away and watched people get lured in like unsuspecting fish.

'Look at the adam's apple and the wrists!' someone had told me. The wrists were bigger than a woman's and the Adam's apple was very noticeable. From then on I could pick them out like flies on a wall and smile to myself when I spotted a fellow traveller flirting with a young Thai man.

Prostitution was as rife as poverty in a third world country and the AIDS statistics vouched for it. Many travellers, old, young, ugly or average picked up Thai girls and travelled with them. The Germans seemed to lead the way with many pot bellied men beyond their prime here to lead another life with a young Thai girl in tow, less than half their age. It looked like a sin as men old enough to be their fathers used them for their selfish needs. In Thailand it seemed as though it was anything for money with morals on the back burner.

There were many second-hand book shops along Khao San Road. While I looked through the book shelves scanning along the spines of well read books one title caught my eye. It was titled Selous Scouts-Top Secret War written by Lt. Col Ron Reid Daly as told to Peter Stiff. I had always had a keen fascination for the Rhodesian War, but other than that I thought nothing of it as I thumbed through the dog eared pages totally engrossed in the story. Little did I know that 15 years later I would have my very own book published by Peter Stiff.

I soon met Pernilla, a Swede from Malmo and we hit it off immediately sharing stories from our past travels. She had come from Japan where she had worked as a hostess and was heading to Australia. I on the other hand was following the wind and I would go where it took me. I knew I needed to get out of the sauna temperatures of the city for the cooler and more exotic island setting. Pernilla decided to stay a few extra days so I set my sights on Ko Samui. Pulling out our Lonely Planet's we picked a place to meet and ringed it in blue pen. We would meet again at the Sun Rise beach resort.

The day was sweltering and the sweat ran like a river off my brow. My backpack was stored underneath in the baggage hold and I boarded the bus with my day bag with all my valuables. The engine revved to life and a freezing chill blasted out of the air conditioner. We were on our way to Surat Thani. I was suddenly freezing my nuts off after being boiling hot only a few seconds earlier. I tossed and turned cursing myself for not packing a jersey in my day bag. The cold air was blowing through my vest like an arctic chill. A couple of hours into the journey I began to feel sick as though I had heat stroke in reverse, like a feverish chill.

I had been warned to be careful on the buses. I had heard about Thai children who had been trained to climb under the seats and look for money belts and wallets belonging to unsuspecting Westerners. I had also heard that a drug is often blown through the air conditioner to put the passengers to sleep, which becomes the ideal time to rob.

My bones ached and I allowed my firm grasp on my day bag to slacken. After hours of driving through the night we eventually pulled into Surat Thani as the sun was coming up.

I felt drunk as I got out of the bus, glad to have my day bag and with a quick check my money belt too. I thought to myself I should have had this around my waist, as I waited in line to order a coffee. When it was time to pay I noticed my wallet was thinner, with my last exchange in Baht now only a few notes left. Then in panic mode I tore open my day bag and grabbed my money belt. I unzipped it with shaking hands and to my utter disbelief I looked at my travellers cheques. A fat wad of £4000 was now paper thin. I had 11 cheques left at £10 each. My face was white, my legs were jelly and my breathing was rushed. I was sick to my stomach and totally lost. I looked again to make sure that my eyes weren't playing a cruel trick. My passport was in the money belt, which I found strange.

'I have just been robbed,' I told those around me with an expression and voice that almost sounded as a joke. A young Thai woman called the police. I remembered the Germans behind me and my gut told me it was them. One had long leather boots which looked so out of place

Tim Ramsden

in Thailand. The more I stared at his boots the more I believed that my £3890 was wedged in there. But I had no proof and all I could do was stand there in a lonely space and wait for the police. In the end I was taken to the police station while the rest of the travellers on the bus made their way to the ferry. I hadn't even been in Thailand a week and my year long trip was looking like an impossible dream. After an hour of translation and a statement to say I was robbed, I was told to call Thomas Cook and notify them of the missing traveller's cheques.

'Have you got a credit card?' a voice in England bluntly asked, to which I replied: 'Yes.'

'Well you better use it until we recover all the stolen cheques and only then will you be paid out!'

I couldn't believe what I was hearing. And so with no choice I had money put on my Standard Bank Master Card, thanks to my Dad after a frantic phone call. Feeling better with some money to my name I caught the ferry to Ko Samui. I had to put it behind me and move on, with the experience chalked up to a hard lesson learned. From this day on my money belt remained around my waist. I knew it could have been worse. Had I lost my passport I would have had to fly back to London and that would have been a bitter pill to swallow.

Years later after talking with many people, I realized without a shadow of doubt that I was drugged to sleep and robbed by the Thai driver and his group of pilfering scum.

I found the Sun Rise resort, a simple area with little huts dotted under palm trees with the beach a stone's throw away. There were huge rocks in the front of my hut where I sat and gazed out into the ocean in total peace and tranquility. The water was calm and as blue as the sky. It was like being inside a photograph with paradise all around. I felt as though I had been crash landed in this remote place with a jungle of palm trees behind me, a beautiful beach in front of me and a mesmerizing ocean ebbing and flowing with soothing calm. I had found paradise and I basked in the glory of finding this spot.

After a few days I was really surprised to see Pernilla standing in the restaurant with a Canadian traveller. She had struggled to find the place and we were thrilled to see each other. The Canadian man on the other hand wasn't happy at all and wandered away leaving us to catch up.

Hiring a motorbike we toured the island two up on a little 125 CC which had a lot of zip. It was not compulsory to wear crash helmets and this always resulted in many head injuries mainly from out of control travellers. It was heaven as the wind blew through my hair and the sun beat on our backs under the ocean blue sky which cocooned us into our little world of paradise and seclusion. The palm trees waved their arms like scarecrows in a field, and fishermen pulled their nets from little fishing boats adding colour to the deep aqua blue ocean. I smiled a smile of pure satisfaction to actually be in the most exotic place I had ever seen in my life. Everything was so make- shift and used from the land. Thatched roofs on the little grass huts on wooden stilts, all facing out onto the ocean. We spotted some monkeys, as big and scary as baboons on chains. They had been trained to climb palm trees and pick coconuts and it was quite comical to watch. It was also just as funny to see a Thai man scale the tree just like a monkey as he too picked them.

The bars were pounding out reggae music with Bob Marley's voice a cry to all pot smokers to light up and be mellow. It was everywhere, the sweet smell drifted like a breeze where ever one went. It went with the culture of the island with the travellers bringing all the tourist dollars to an economy in dire need.

After a few days we decided to catch a ferry to Ko Pha-Ngan to a place called Bottle Beach that could only be reached by boat. Feeling on top of the world we were chauffeured from the ferry dock and out to sea and around a rocky outcrop to a place even more picturesque than Ko Samui. There was nothing but huts, palm trees and wild bush backing onto a mountain. The beach was unspoiled, white and cool to the touch of our bare feet. To me this was a five star hotel and for the equivalent of 50 Canadian cents we had a hut facing the ocean that was a coconut throw from the waters edge. Each hut had a hammock to sway the stresses and strains from our bodies as we lapped up the beauty with smiles that spoke a million words.

While I lay in the hammock I wrote a short note on relaxation:

Watching the crystal clear waters ripple their way onto the white sandy beach, I sway peacefully from side to side in the wooden hut, shielded by two huge palm trees offering precious shade. I gaze at the splendour before my eyes. Coconuts lie scattered beneath the towering palms, imprinting themselves into the soft surface. Boats, the only access to this remote part of the island of Ko Pha-Ngan on this Bottle Beach, bob merrily like corks in the peaceful waters as they await their passengers, before being propelled away from this paradise. For those that remain so the tranquil beauty of this natural island lingers on.

There were a few other backpackers on the island, from Canada, Norway, Germany, France, Australia and England. There were about 20 of us. People played volleyball, swam, lounged in the eating area to escape the heat, swayed in the hammocks and just milled around in total freedom. I took a long walk through the thick bush and got an amazing view of the island with the palm trees and ocean in the background. It was postcard material and I felt like we had this paradise to ourselves.

All food, cool drinks, and beers were entered in a book under ones name and when it was time to leave the island the Thai owners tallied the bill with what we had written down. The business was run purely on a trust system, one like I had never seen before.

At night we all congregated in the restaurant and drank Singha beers and played cards under some hanging lights powered by the generator that kept the night awake. It was fun with lots of laughter in true backpacker spirit. So many nationalities made the world so much smaller and us all the wiser with worldly knowledge.

After five days it was time for Pernilla to leave and make her way back to Bangkok for her flight to Australia. It was a sad goodbye but as all backpackers realize friendships are lent for a period of time through the journey of travel. Travellers are like seeds blown in the wind moving in the direction where circumstance is leading them. One can never hold someone back, but rather wish them well with a safe journey and an unforgettable experience.

I stayed a couple more days and then took the ferry back to the main dock at Thong Sala with an Aussie called Nick. Nick was funny and very cheerful with that 'all to live for' Australian mentality. As soon as I got off the ferry I saw Karl and Desiree, a couple which had stayed in our rent free repossessed house at 61 Mitcham Lane in Streatham. They had left for Thailand a couple of months ago and I never believed I would actually see them here in this country where they could be anywhere on any given day. It was a great reunion and the four of us decided to go to Hat Rin Beach and revile in a Full Moon party, where drugs were consumed as normal daily life for all Westerners. It was so laid back with the smell of marijuana blowing in the breeze as people rolled up their joints where they chose. Restaurant owners sold it like food and it was known that the cops had been paid off to keep away. It was a wild island and we heard that a Westerner was shot and killed just before we arrived. One could only assume drugs had been the cause. It shocked me and I instantly thought of his parents. They most probably didn't even have a clue where he was. I knew mine didn't and if I died somewhere in the world I don't know how they would ever have a body to bury.

We got a hut adjacent to each other and lazed in the hammocks as the humidity sweated us dry. When the sun started going down we all wandered onto the beach and sat in the sand feeling as calm as the evening. The four of us decided to have magic mushrooms, something we had never tried. It was served in a cup with hot water and we sipped it like tea with chunks of mushrooms floating like thick tea leaves. When I had thrown back the hot water I chewed on the vile brown bits of mushroom. It didn't take long for it to kick in as we broke into fits of laughter like deranged lunatics in a Loonie bin. My body started tingling from head to toe and I became warm all over as if I was bundled in a tight blanket. I looked into the trees that seemed to stretch into the dark sky almost reaching the murky moon that shone like a torch on a thick misty night. A bright rainbow of colours erupted from the tree as faces and shapes appeared and disappeared like shadows. I was hallucinating like no tomorrow with the LSD kicking in and the song Lucy in the sky with diamonds playing in my mind, a song written about LSD. Bob Marley songs added a mellow background beat as the high soured us to a level I had never been. This certainly was a Full Moon Party.

The lady who had served the magic mushrooms became very worried as she felt she had given us too much. We looked at her and smiled a goofy smile before bursting into laughter. I didn't want it to end; it was the greatest feeling with a rush that would have made a drug addict jealous. When it started to wear off I started becoming sad, cold and disappointed. I began rubbing my arms and legs to keep warm hoping the rush was on its way back. When we all resurfaced from the ride our stomachs became really sore as though needles were trying to push their way out. It was excruciatingly painful and I held my belly as though I had been kicked in the gut.

I didn't sleep well that night with a cloudy hangover feeling in my head and a stomach that had been poisoned.

We laughed about it the next day and vowed never to try it again. I heard a story about a few travellers who had also indulged and hallucinated on swimming to Ko Samui. They attempted it and drowned in the process. I considered myself lucky with only a sore stomach and couldn't have imagined a long swim.

The marijuana smoking continued with us but the mushrooms were something of the past like a bad experiment gone wrong. There was nothing to do at night besides smoking weed and watching videos in different bars. The Doors and Jim Morrison played by Val Kilmer was very popular and another great music video was 'The Commitments' which I thoroughly enjoyed.

Yearning to see another island we caught a boat to Ko Tao, known as 'Turtle Island.' We took a boat 44 kilometres north of Ko Pha-Ngan seeing nothing but ocean and all of a sudden a mountain loomed out at us. On getting closer we saw huge rocks and huts on stilts built into the mountain side amongst an overgrown sea of green. It looked wild and untouched and was by far less inhabited than any of the other islands. The boat slowed to a crawl and the Thai boatman cut the engine and tilted it saving the propeller from being smashed to shreds by the rocks below. We had arrived on the west side of the island at a place called Ban Mae Hat. Paradise just got better as we surveyed the scene. It felt as though we had the island to ourselves. There was hardly a soul around. We met the Thai owner and wrote our names and passport numbers in a book and then she booked us in, pointing up the mountain at a hut high up on stilts. We followed a path and climbed our way up until we got to our wooden hut. It overlooked the island and across the ocean for as far as the naked eye could see. There are three small islands that in low tide are joined by a narrow stretch of beach, and we were told it is the only one in the world. It was stunning with the crystal clear water a turquoise blue with pure white sand enhancing the sharp colour.

We just looked at each other and smiled huge radiant smiles as if we had all secretly won the lottery and didn't want to let the world know. Being a backpacker this was a five star hotel with a view to die for. There was a veranda and a hammock with small benches to sit and feel the ocean breeze caressing our skin as the heat beat down without forgiveness.

There was a really small beach that had big boulders encroaching on the small patch of sand. We had heard this area was great for snorkelling so we dived in with our masks and air pieces. I had suffered from claustrophobia my whole life but I was determined to shake these demons to see what lay hidden below. At first I struggled as my mask filled with water and I coughed for breath and then calmness settled over me as I absorbed the beauty in a kaleidoscope of colour. It was out of this world as fish darted playfully from the coral and shoals split with me feeling like Moses parting the Red Sea. Past me they reformed back into a dark shoal. An eel swam by and I could see its eyes and teeth, and for a moment I thought it might attack me. I snorkelled for a couple of hours, totally entranced in this underworld adventure. Eventually I walked back onto land and with my thoughts fresh I jotted down exactly what I felt.

I called it the 'Unseen beauty,' and this is what I wrote.

The huge blue mass laps lightly against the giant boulders. Rooted to the seabed they lie concreted in a horseshoe at the base of the cove, standing tall as if guarding the unseen beauty beyond.

Floating peacefully, head buried below the crystal clear waters, eyes transfixed on the splendour as a whole new exciting world opens before me. Red, yellow, green, purple, black, white and blue, the colours are endless as they snake their way through the coral in an exploration of their world. Barracuda's cutting through the surface in search of easy prey, parrot fish at play on the seabed, interwoven with hundreds of shapes, sizes and colours all moving in harmony to their surroundings. Below me, feeding frantically off the mushroom like coral, the yellow and black angel fish hover above their feed undisturbed by my monotonous breathing and invasion of their privacy. Further on a swarm of fish split as I try and pass through them. Reaching out to touch as they dart past my outstretched fingers, they reform perfectly past me, all this in the silent picturesque paradise.

Lifting my head from the cool waters, I part from the paradise below and return to my world, sad but grateful to have witnessed 'the unseen beauty.'

After the snorkelling the four of us got into a rowing boat and headed for the three islands. We were determined to explore at least one of the three land masses, quite sure that not many people had ever ventured onto them. The winds became strong and the waves slapped at the boat sides and the harder we rowed the more we stayed still. After a futile hour of struggle we abandoned the idea, but did manage to get some nice photographs.

After a good shrimp curry and rice in the restaurant we wandered back to the hut and dropped onto the benches with one lucky person in the hammock. The bong came out which was a crude piece of thick hollow bamboo with a pipe in it. Karl went to work crushing the marijuana and packed it into the pipe. While one sucked another held the match to get it going and then with a thick plume of smoke it was passed onto the next person until we were as high as kites. Time sped by and before we knew it a black curtain had been pulled over the blue sky. We became restless with hunger as the munchies gnawed like worms in our growling bellies. Making our way tediously down the rocky path with a torch to direct the way we stumbled, laughing like mischievous children into the makeshift restaurant. The owner was quick to enter his restaurant like a guard alerted on watch duty. And when we asked him to make us some food, he sneered at us and waved us away. With little choice we turned and made our way up the path.

'I saw some bottles of Fanta!' I told the other three, planting the seed of a nice bottle of fizz to wet our dry throats. In a split second we did an about turn and headed right back into the restaurant. And with a bottle each we marched like victorious soldiers up the hill with our trophies, fighting hard to keep our laughter at bay.

'Fuck him! He didn't want to serve us now he is short a few bottles,' I laughed as we collapsed in our hut in fits of laughter.

I had a small cassette player that I had brought over with me from London and on hitting 'play' Jim Morrison's voice echoed into the night as another bong was passed around.

A storm was brewing and the rain hit the thatched roof with deadly force. Thunder rolled as if the gods were at war and at this precise moment 'Riders on the Storm' began playing. Like a blacksmith striking an anvil with vengeance, sharp cracking bolts of lightning shot like sparks across the ocean. We sat stoned, eyes glued to the storm afraid to turn our heads in case we missed the next bolt. It was as though we were watching a show with the music perfectly choreographed with each drum roll of thunder and shuddering crack as the lightning lit up the sky in the most spectacular way we had ever seen.

After a surprisingly dry sleep we packed up and boarded the boat for Ko Pha-Ngan for the quieter side of the island. Nick and I shared a hut and in the middle of the night we got the fright of our lives as an animal rustled in the thatch roof and I felt at any moment it was going to land on my bed. We never found out what it was but it succeeded in scaring the crap out of us.

The following day Nick felt really ill and left the island for Ko Samui for the Sun Rise resort. The three of us stayed an extra day and then I became ill. Instantly I felt like there was something wrong with the island and so with this in mind we all decided to leave.

Back on Ko Samui, Karl and Desiree left for the north, and I made my way to the Sun Rise resort where I found Nick in a terrible state. I was no better and I could feel my body slipping away as I struggled to put one foot in front of the next. Once in my hut I collapsed on the bed and broke into a high fever. I sweated worse than any army patrol in the midday heat as water droplets ran off my body soaking the mattress and my sleeping bag. I tossed and turned in delirium and couldn't even move to leave the hut. For days I stayed in the hut like a lonely hermit with not the slightest ounce of energy to lever myself up. I didn't need to urinate; my bladder had been sweated dry. My joints ached, my bones felt like brittle twigs ready to snap and I had the most excruciating muscle pains. I was as stiff as cardboard all over. After four days I forced myself up, literally rising from the dead. I opened the hut door and rays of light speared into my already sore eyes throwing me off balance. I shut them tight and held onto the door for support. Like an old blind man I felt my way down the stairs and onto the flat ground. I stood like a pale outcast feeling very cold on a sweltering day. I needed water and managed to buy a bottle along with a bowl of soup. I slurped it down and it was like filling a container with a hole in it, it instantly shot right out the other end. I could barely squat on the toilet

let alone get up. My body ached and my eyes were killing me. I couldn't move them and look out of the corners. It felt as though something large was pushing behind my eyes hurting them and forcing them out of their sockets. I managed with all my energy to flip the soaking wet mattress over and then flopped like a dead weight back onto it. I stayed in the hut a further three days and on the seventh day I started to feel better.

On speaking to Nick who had suffered in the same way, he told me he had seen a doctor and was given pills to treat Dengue Fever, also known as break bone fever. I can understand why as my bones felt as though they were breaking and it was a fever like one only sees in the movies in the tropical jungles of Asia or Africa. This is an infection transmitted by mosquitoes and I soon learned that it can be fatal. I thought I was dying and I couldn't help myself. I had ridden it out totally alone, a very scary experience in the middle of nowhere.

Rejuvenated and ready for the next adventure we decided on Malaysia. Catching a night ferry we left the island for Surat Thani and caught a train which took us to the border.

MALAYSIA (1992)

A s soon as we crossed the border at Rantau Panjang we were met with huge billboards with writing painted in big letters on the walls that read: '*Awas*!,' Death! And then in English, 'That's the mandatory sentence for any (*Dadah*) drug trafficker in Malaysia.'

This was our welcome and it scared the crap out of us. We met a traveller who told us two Australians had just been hanged and two Dutch nationals were on death row awaiting their fate for trafficking.

'We are not touching weed here,' I told Nick with a face as serious as if I was staring death in the face myself.

We had decided we were going to hitch hike through Malaysia and so with our thumbs out our journey began. Our first place of call was the Perhentian Islands. It was an easy journey in a truck which dropped us at the pier where we would catch the ferry to the island. Thrilled to be in another country it was a beautiful feeling to be on our way to see an island that rivalled its neighbour's beauty.

On the island we got a tent at the Coco Hut, threw our bags down and walked along the untouched and unspoiled beaches with sand as white as a sheet and an ocean as clear as bath water. Palm trees dipped into the water at peculiar angles and the island had a remote feel to it as though hardly anyone ever came here. Once again I felt like a survivor from a plane crash marooned in paradise.

For dinner we went to the only eating place on the island, a tent run by a few Malaysians. We met a few travellers who were also in heaven with nothing around but peace and beauty. Music played and the beers flowed. In Malaysia we were drinking Tuborg, imported from Denmark and it went down very nicely.

'What's this crap playing?' Nick shouted across the tent in reference to the local Malaysian music. The mood changed instantly and with the Malaysians feeling totally insulted chased Nick out of the tent area and into the darkness. Too much drink had definitely been the cause, and to make matters worse they came looking for him in the tent we were sharing. They were shouting and I knew they wanted to beat the crap out of him, and being in the same tent I imagined myself getting a beating too.

When morning dawned the new day brought peace which was refreshing to both of us. I think Nick learned his lesson as no music from then on was deemed as crap.

I had to call London to see if my traveller's cheques had been cashed, and so I had to catch a ferry back to the mainland. I made a call from a windup phone and couldn't believe my ears when I found myself talking to a Thomas Cook agent. My cheques had still not been recovered which meant I had to continue racking up credit in worthless South African Rands.

Having had enough of the beach we set out for the Cameron Highlands. We caught a jungle train that took us through some wild terrain as we snaked our way through each turn stopping at small stations hardly worth mentioning on a map. Piet and Willeke a Dutch couple were also on the train and we all instantly hit it off.

'*Kom nou julle klootsakke!*' 'Come on you ballbags!' Willeke shouted to get us back on the train as it blew its whistle and pulled out from the station. We got off at Kuala Lipis and then headed for a small place called Raub where we persuaded a disgruntled Chinaman to open his bar and serve us. Yoke was his name and he wasn't happy as he served us one Anchor beer after the next until we had him smiling and drinking with us.

From there we hitched a lift in a truck which took us all the way into the highlands, winding up the hills in low gear, allowing us to take in our surroundings from the elevated position. The Cameron Highlands were a green oasis as green as Ireland with damp and chilly temperatures ideal to grow tea. The British always with a cuppa in mind had found the perfect site to grow their tea.

I was astounded at how many Hindus were in Malaysia and we joined a large group of Sri Lankans round a fire with beers in hand. It also happened to be Eid, a three day Muslim holiday marking the end of Ramadan, the Islamic holy month of fasting. With Hindu and Muslim alike we joined in their celebrations and wished everyone a happy Eid. There was a little boy called Christmas who was no more than seven and he was sipping on a can of beer and became the centre of the celebration.

From the highlands we hitched to Kuala Lumpur. We got a lift with two business men in suits in a BMW that struck us as suspicious. They dropped us just outside Kuala Lumpur and told us they needed to take care of some business and would be back in half an hour. Before we knew what we had done they drove away with our packs still in the boot. I started to panic. What if they planted drugs in our packs and used us as mules to ferry it safely through Malaysia. We would be hanged, not them. I was shitting myself. In an hour they returned. I looked in the boot to see if our packs were there and cast a quick look to see if they had been tampered with. I couldn't see anything and so we went with our guts. Once in Kuala Lumpur we grabbed our packs and disappeared into the nearest accommodation. In the room I stripped my pack down to nothing, searching each zip up pocket and crevice until I was certain that nothing had been planted. I was sweating when I finished, and relieved I dropped onto the bed.

At the very place we were staying we funnily enough met Piet and Willeke again which was reason for a round of beers. Des from England and another Dutch girl joined us and we had a great time swopping stories which all ended in laughter.

From Kula Lumpur we made our way to Melaka an old Portuguese, Dutch and English seaport with old junks still sailing the rivers. There are still many reminders of the old colonial days, as well as intriguing Chinese streets and old antique shops. The buildings are old and dirty adding further nostalgia to a once thriving little trading port. Again, for the third time we bumped into Piet and Willeke and along with Des we all went to an Old Portuguese restaurant. We met the owner Michael, who was a pleasant old man with large rimmed glasses and a smile that one could instantly trust. He served us the most delicious shrimp in typical Portuguese fashion with heart and passion and a sense of pride. We sat at a table under the stars with the night noises as backdrop music. He waited on us treating us like kings, smiling as we devoured his cooking. Michael went on to tell us that he was a prisoner of war under the Japanese and had built the bridge over the River Kwai. I could see his face wince as he relived the barbaric torture that the

Tim Ramsden

Japanese meted out to their prisoners of war. With a great evening had by all we shook Michael's hand and thanked his wife Nancy for such a wonderful meal and the memorable time in his restaurant.

The following day we crossed into expensive and ultra clean Singapore. We had been told it was illegal to chew gum and I could believe it, as the city was spotless. The subway train glided silently over the rails as smooth as silk as we navigated our way through the city in our hunt for cheap camera shops. I found a Pentax 105mm zoom that I wanted and bargained it down and Nick got a small Cannon also for a good deal. Accommodation and food were expensive so we decided to eat cheap and only stay two days. We walked over into little India and suddenly we felt as though we had crossed the border into a very filthy and poverty stricken country. While we ate in a small little dirty restaurant I saw a greyish white rat the size of my hand with a long pencil thick tail scurrying through the fridge between the bottles of coke and sprite.

'Look there's a rat!' I exclaimed to the owner. He looked at me and smiled.

'Eskimo rat!' he said and turned without a care, let alone a worry in the world.

'This is more like India than Singapore,' I said to Nick as we ate our cheap curries, keeping one eye on the rat.

Thrilled to have our cameras we crossed back into Malaysia and headed up the west coast with our eyes set on getting back to Thailand. Back in Kuala Lumpur I finally managed to get my cheques paid out at the Bank of Hong Kong. All the stolen traveller cheques had been cashed with a forged signature and this was proof enough that I had had nothing to do with it. It was common practise in Thailand to sell your travellers cheques and then report them stolen. I was ecstatic and felt rich with £1900 to my name, and the means to see my year out in Asia.

We followed the west coast stopping in Telok Intan and then to Lumur and Pankor before arriving in Penang. It is the oldest British settlement in Malaysia and with all its Chinese writing could be mistaken for a town in China. With our Lonely Planet at hand we made our way to Lebuh Chulia for affordable accommodation. It was like the Kao San Road of Thailand.

It was Nick's birthday and we converged on a small bar with a few other travellers sitting at a table. We soon joined a party of English, and Scandinavians knocking back Tuborg beers like no tomorrow. A long haired Indonesian man with a bushy moustache and olive black skin sat to the side of the table with his guitar on his lap. He was very mellow and smiled at us with slit eyes giving away the fact that he was high on something. While we chatted and laughed over stories from home and travel he began playing.

'Have you ever seen the rain?' came flowing from the corner as he sounded every bit like the famous Creedence Clearwater Revival band of the 60s and 70s, with the emotion of the song etched in frowns on his forehead. He strummed the guitar and tapped his foot as his body moved with the rhythm he had created. We joined in feeling the connection of the song and united as one, we sang it with the same deep-down emotion. Our group couldn't get enough and we asked him to play it again, which after a few more beers he did. It was just amazing to be connected like this in a faraway land in a place most of the world had never even heard of.

With a hangover and a smile we passed through Georgetown and headed for the border crossing at Hat Yai. After a hammer-strike stamp in our passports we were waved out of Malaysia and back in Thailand.

THAILAND

A quick month had passed by as we travelled from north to south in Malaysia. I was now in my third month in Asia and the days were flying by like lightning flashes.

Krabi was our next port of call where we would have to get a ferry over to Ko Phi Phi, an island we had heard wonderful things about. The island was another breath taking scene of tranquility with a pure blue ocean lapping up on the white sand with huge cliffs covered in greenery filling the background. Long boats broke the peace as propellers cut through the water ferrying in supplies and taking travellers out fishing. On our way to get accommodation we met Loica, a Frenchman who we instantly became friends with. With three in a hut the price became that much cheaper which helped Loica who was short of money. He chose the floor which made the arrangement that much sweater. Loica also smoked a lot and it didn't take long for Nick and him to make a bong and within a few minutes we were wandering around the island like three zombies, laughing at the most stupid little things that crossed our path.

Nick wanted to go fishing and so we encouraged him to catch dinner for us. After a few hours he returned in one of the long boats with a broad smile and a massive fish at least three feet long. He filleted it with his pen knife and a restaurant cooked it up for us. I had no idea what it was, but it tasted delicious and we ate until our bellies were bursting at the seams.

The following day we took a walk around the island and met Linda, a nice English girl who joined us as we demolished a few more precious brain cells.

Feeling as though we had seen enough of this island we caught a ferry back to Krabi with the bong concealed in Nick's backpack. This was a risk and could get us in jail if we were searched. But with our thoughts clouded, and before we knew it we were on another ferry to Ko Lanta.

Ko Lanta was by far the most untouched island we had seen. It was off the tourist trail and this is what drew us to it. We got a hut right on the beach at the Lanta Miami Bungalow. The restaurant was quite modern by Thai standards and had been built with cinder blocks. It was really mellow as we sat and watched life pass ever so slowly by. Water buffalo were common and walked in small herds through the sea. Little fishing boats bobbed on the ocean under the backdrop of the most beautiful sunsets I had yet seen. Our cameras were put to work as we clicked off pictures capturing the sinking fireball with a fishing boat passing through the orange glow. There was an abandoned bar called the Easy Bar. It had a beautiful rustic look to it, made completely from wood. An old buffalo skull hung from the entrance and an ox wagon wheel hung below it as decoration. I sat on the floor with my feet in the sand and watched the day slip into night. It took me back to South Africa with the beauty of the ocean, the magical calmness of a sunset and the gratitude and warmth that it brought me. I had now seen a lot of the world, but my heart always told me South Africa is your home. It was a time like this that my African heart swelled with pride, and I knew there was nowhere else in the world where I would rather settle. With a wry smile on my face I knew when my journey was over, I would be returning to the land of my birth.

Nick and I found a school on the island and walked in as though we were late for class. The little Thai children took to us as we clowned around and made them laugh. Even the teachers stopped and smiled shyly as we stole the moment. After half an hour we left with a good feeling at having touched some lives that had in all probability never ever seen a white person before.

Heading back along the water we stopped at a little fishing village and mingled with the locals. There was an old man who caught our eye as he mended holes in his fishing net. Feeling like journalists for National Geographic we snapped off pictures as he posed with a toothless grin.

The First Bar, run by a small Thai man who we called Thai, became our Pina Colada hangout for our sundownwers. To sit in a simple chair hacked from the forest and look over the ocean with the sun setting on the horizon was like watching a movie at a drive in. We sipped our drinks and smoked away with no cares in the world. There was no boss to answer to, no business deadlines, and no bills to pay. We were in heaven for as long as our money lasted, and in Thailand we were stretching it well.

Nick woke up one day and told me that he was heading to Bangkok where he was going to book a flight to the Philippines. Something told me that I needed to stay on and so I did.

I moved to a cheaper hut and got talking with Zabong, the owner. He had a monkey which was tied by a chain to a tree. The poor little creature ran along a circular path as far as the chain would allow. It saddened me and I approached Zabong asking if I could take him for a walk along the beach. I was shocked when he said yes without any hesitation.

Like a Dad bonding with his newborn I led the monkey on the chain. He darted for the ocean and skipped over the waves with glee and it was a pleasure to see him having such fun. I had a banana and passed it to him, which he snatched and peeled it like a human. He climbed onto my shoulder and ate it like a little curious child. He squawked and made laughing sounds baring his teeth as if he was smiling with joy. After a good few hours I returned him to the tree, and feeling very uncomfortable chained him to his post.

I met a German while walking down the beach and we exchanged stories. He had been travelling with a Canadian girl. She had been followed and cornered and then beaten up and was lucky not to have been raped. I then went on to tell him how I had been robbed on the bus, losing almost £2000.

Later on that day I bumped into the Canadian girl, Karin. She had already heard what had happened to me. Having been told her story I made it clear how lucky she was with her awful experience.

It didn't take us long to hook up and hang out together. Karin was a nice girl, very smart and very beautiful with a healthy brown tan and a smile that lit her youthful face that had a cheeky look about it. She had been working in Japan as a sales rep for a Japanese hospital and to my surprise could speak the language fluently. I couldn't believe the money she had made over the last year, with her job and teaching English on the side.

We hired a motor bike and toured the island two up. We passed an old disused bar area on the beach with the international Hard Rock sign in faded paint, and strolled through the crumbling hangout. The island was very untouched the further inland we went. There were vast open stretches of lush green with mountains and palm trees as far as one could see. A dirt road hugged the ocean offering a spectacular view over the beach and ocean with not a soul around. We sat and watched as the calmness and peace fell over us like a hypnotist putting us in a trance. Feeling hot we decided on a swim and found a shallow lagoon where we cooled off under the midday heat.

I moved into Karin's room, which worked well and saved us both money. I had stepped up in the world from a wooden thatched hut that creaked and groaned in the wind, and was now in a solid little brick room with a window and a bathroom.

The First Bar also became our hangout. I introduced Karin to the bong which Nick had left behind in Thai's room and I showed her how to self destruct and lose a few brain cells. Laughing like crazy we ate crab legs and followed it down with Pina Coladas as the sun began to set. It was a magic time and became our place to see out the end of the day, every day for a week.

'Where is the bong?' I asked Karin, as we finished eating.

'There he is over there,' she pointed at Zabong. I looked around trying to see where she was pointing and then I realized where she was looking.

'No not Zabong! The bong!' I cried with laughter and so did she.

We had a great time on the island but as a traveller it was time to be on the move again. Packing up we caught a ferry to Krabi. The ferry was packed and we all sat still and watched the water hitting the side of the boat as the spray lifted off the ocean and settled on us like a mist shower. All of a sudden there was an almighty explosion of splintering glass. I thought a bomb had just gone off. People sat motionless as if in a trance. The woman in front of me was bleeding and she didn't even know it. Then the adrenalin kicked in and everyone started to move and see what had happened. A huge fish had been lifted out of the water and had crashed through the front glass window leaving shards and a massive hole. The fish, a couple of feet long flapped on the floor in the alleyway next to my feet. I was bleeding slightly but nothing like the lady in front of me. We were lucky and I wanted to tell the man at the helm to stick to fishing with a rod.

From Krabi we made our way to Bangkok. I had now been away nearly four months and the travel bug was still biting loud and strong. Karin and I were talking about Sri Lanka and India, two places that I had not thought much about, but as a traveller I was open to the next challenge.

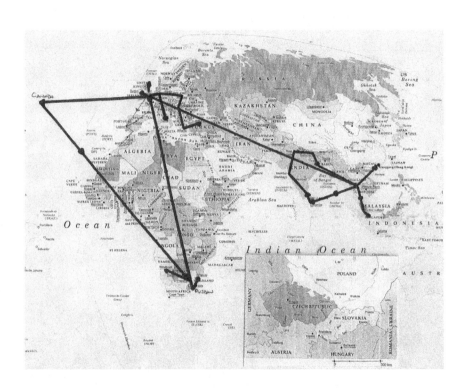

Map showing the countries I travelled.

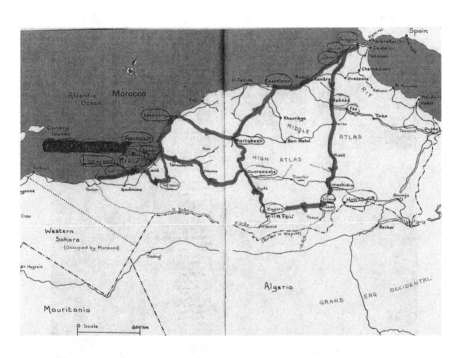

Map of Morocco-1991.
The route I took which I plotted in my guide book.

Ireland-Galway-1990. The author, Ian from Australia, Tony and Bruce from South Africa with our backpacks in search of accommodation.

East Germany-East Berlin-1990. Standing in No Man's Land.

Turkey-Ephesus-1990.
The group I travelled with.

Turkey-Selcuk-1990. In a Turkish bath. Lt.-Rt. Chuck (USA),
Jeremy (Aus), Pat (USA), Mike (Aus), Darryl (Can), the author,
Phil and Joe (Eng), Jane and Nicole (Aus) and a stranger.

Morocco-Sahara Desert-1991.

Morocco-Merzouga-1991.
Talking with the children of the desert.

Holland-Zandvoort-1991. Wayne (my good army friend)
and the author with our loyal van, 'The Bulldog.'

Germany-Munich-1991. Murray and Louise, friends from
my hometown Hillcrest in South Africa and the
author at the October Beer Fest.

Thailand-Ko Samui-1992. Travelling the island on a 125
without wearing a crash helmet; there are so many
head injuries and yet it isn't the law.

Malaysia-Melaka-1992. Lt.-Rt. Piet and Willeke (Holland),
Nick (Aus), Des (Eng), Michael the restaurant owner and the author.
Michael was a Japanese prisoner of war and helped
build the bridge over the River Kwai.

Thailand-Ko Lanta-1992. Taking Mr Wong, a Lopburi monkey for a
walk along the beach and stopping for a rest break and a banana.

Sri Lanka-Tangalla-1992. Dumega and myself drinking Arrack at the Seth Siri Guesthouse with Simon behind us on New Years Eve. Getting fuelled for the celebration.

India-Agra-1993.
The Taj Mahal in all its magical glory with a
rough looking South African in front of it.

Portugal-Evora-1993. Statue of Vasco Da Gama, a Portuguese
explorer, which was given to Portugal from the Province of
Natal in South Africa. In 1497 he sailed up the coast of South
Africa on Christmas day and on seeing it he gave it the name
Natal, the Portuguese word for Christmas. I am kneeling
next to the side inscribed in Afrikaans, my second language.
A proud moment being so far away from my country.

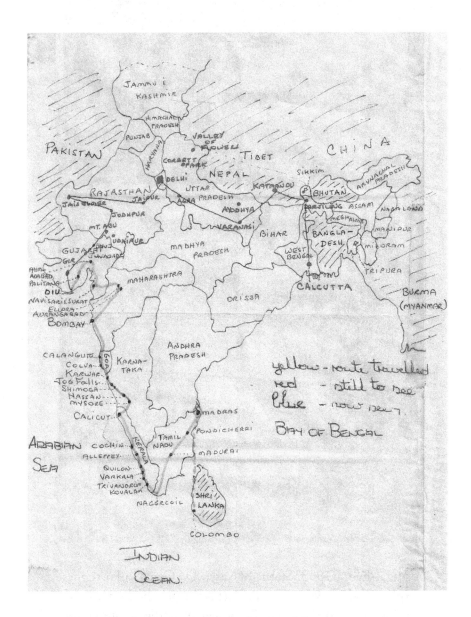

Map of India-1993. A rough sketch of the journey taken.

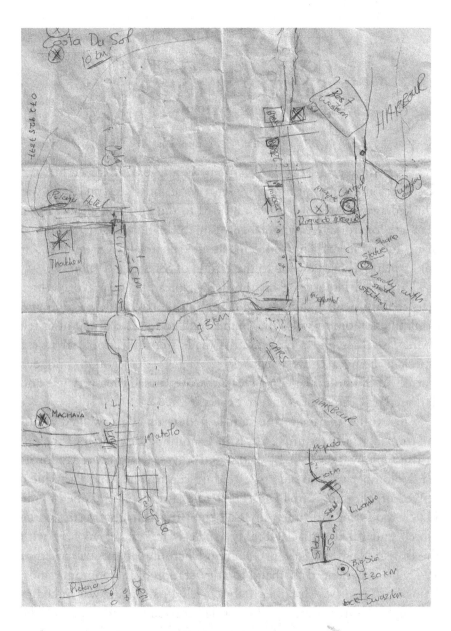

Rough map of Maputo in Mozambique to
get us to the Machava Prison.

SRI LANKA 1992/93

It was sad to say goodbye to Karin as we hugged and kissed before I stepped into my waiting taxi. With a wave and a 'see you later' I was whisked away by the driver who headed to the Bangkok airport like a man late for work. Weaving dangerously through the traffic he arrived in no time and with no problems at all I boarded a very empty Air Lanka plane which flew me to the capital of Sri Lanka, Colombo.

I travelled like a king on the flight, spreading myself over three seats. I think I made up for the empty airline as I ordered food and drink like no tomorrow. Wine, brandy and coffees, luxuries not tasted in the last three and a half months made me smile from ear to ear especially being a cheap backpacker as I felt I had got my money's worth. At 8pm on the 14th of December we landed on a very wet and dark night, with no idea what to expect.

On exiting the plane the rain lashed at us as we walked across the runway to the terminal. I was in Colombo, the capital of the old British Colony once called Ceylon, and still very famous today for its tea. Colombo was the old spice trading centre when the Portuguese arrived on the shores in 1505. Their rule lasted 150 years before the Dutch took over. And then in 1802 the British finally overthrew the Dutch and ruled until 1948. My Uncle Mac had served here with the British Navy and was in Colombo when the Japanese attacked in 1942. He experienced firsthand the devastation of the bombing raids. Being born to a British father, I always felt a part of me was linked to the mighty British Empire which ruled for crown and country. The thrill of being here in old Ceylon was mind blowing. Those postage stamps that I collected as a young boy with the name Ceylon always had me wondering about this land. Now I was here in the country now renamed Sri Lanka.

Walking through the airport I felt as though I was back in Durban with all the Indian faces and customs so unique to this culture of people who had been shipped to Natal to work in the sugarcane fields during the British Imperial Days. After changing money at the airport I hooked up with an Australian and an Englishman and we all boarded a taxi to Negombo. After forking out 400 Sri Lankan Rupees along with a 10% service charge between the three of us, we had a very basic room. Looking out of the dirty front window we had an amazing view of the ocean lapping on to the beach without a soul around. It was dead quiet and felt quite eerie. At 70 Rs to £1, I felt we had a good deal and a safe enough place to put my head down for the night.

After a relatively good sleep we caught a bus back to Colombo. The driver was in a hurry and drove like a madman. Little did I know this was the norm in Sri Lanka. He nearly hit a cow in the middle of the road and also missed hitting a few vehicles as he bore down the tarmac as if he owned it. He pushed on his hooter like a musical instrument as a warning to clear a path. There was no doubt he seemed in charge of the roadway.

Glad to have made it unscathed we found a room at the YMCA for a night which cost us 85 Rs each. With a place to stay now taken care of we were free to explore. We took a walk through a market which caused a ruckus of bargaining as we were pestered to buy belts and watches and you name it. The aroma of incense drifted from the market stalls. I hated the smell as it needled my nostrils as the aromatic plant materials and essential oils burned away the foul odours. Needing to eat we stopped for a curry and I had the hottest of my life. My mouth burned like a furnace while sweat ran off my forehead like water. I thought I was going to lose control of myself as I fought the heat of my meal.

I saw lots disabled, many with one leg or missing an arm and many more blinded by cataracts left to feel their way around in a world of blackness. They waved their stumps like a begging salute hoping to gain a valuable Rupee. It was sad but it was reality. This was my welcome to an impoverished third world country with no health system. I kept on thinking our Indians in South Africa are so well off compared to these people. At the Change Bureau I met five Muslim South African's who were attending a festival. It was strange to speak to a non white like a friend, but they were South African and I could feel my apartheid shackles being loosened. There were still many Sri Lankans that just couldn't believe I was a white South African. I smiled and walked tall feeling even more proud to be born on African soil.

Old faded red London double decker buses traversed the streets spewing out clouds of diesel and cast iron pillar boxes, now dirty and used as advertising posts with paper stuck haphazardly over them, were two of the many prominent British reminders. The old Clock Tower which was also referred to as the lighthouse stood in good condition on the main street next to the Central Bank of Sri Lanka.

In the morning I rushed to catch my train to the south which hadn't arrived and yet was meant to have left. It was another reminder that I was in a world where time was just a word and nothing ever kept to it. Finally when the train came it was as though we were drawn to it like a magnet even before it came to a halt. People pulled and pushed fighting for a seat and I couldn't believe my luck when I got one right by the window. Sitting with my pack at my feet I looked out of the dirty window and admired the scenery as the train snaked its way through towering palm trees with the ocean on one side and a forest of green on the other. Local people hung from the train carriages by one arm, some to get a better view, others only too glad to be on the train where there was no limit as to how many could be crammed in. We followed the coastline and the beauty shone through like a diamond in the rough. We passed huts and makeshift dwellings where people stood on torn up and disused railway lines and watched the train chug by while the ocean offered a beautiful backdrop. Old fishing boats with dulled and flaking paint had been pulled up on the beach after their day's work on the sea. I sat back enjoying the glimpse I had into their lives as people went about their chores. My eyes were digging for information and adventure as this new culture was opened like a page being turned in a book.

Everyone was trying to sell something on the train from peanuts to pineapples. One man had a pineapple in a bowl on his head and when he stopped to speak with someone the pineapple spun around in the bowl and yet the bowl remained glued to his head. He ducked through the doorway and entered into the next carriage without even putting a hand to it. He could get a job in a circus I thought.

After three hours and only 45 Rs I reached Hikkaduwa a place 'claimed' by Australians from the surfing world. It was a quaint and very quiet town and in no time I had a place at the Curry Bowl which was an old building with lots of character and palm trees all around it. It overlooked the beach and the sound of waves was definitely music to my ears.

I saw the Englishman from the first night in Negombo at the Pink Palace while I was scouting for cheaper accommodation. Needing money I went to the exchange office in Hikkaduwa. The paperwork baffled my mind as I watched one man fill out a form; it was then taken downstairs where it was stamped and brought back upstairs. I was then presented the form and had to take it back downstairs to get my money. I felt exhausted and very rich with a wad of dirty, crumpled and useless Rupees in my money belt.

On the way back to the room I got caught in the rain. It literally poured down washing everything clean and filling my nostrils with that beautiful scent of wet dust that had me sniffing for more. Ravenous I could not stop eating avocado spread over toast. In the end I consumed eight pieces in almost as many minutes.

From the highly glossed red polished veranda of the Curry Bowl I could see the fishermen bobbing merrily in their boats. It was so peaceful to just sit and take in my surroundings with no time limits or distractions. Walking through the courtyard I passed the big fish pond and briefly watched the fish darting under lilies as I got too close.

Strolling down the golden beach I enjoyed the soft hot sand between my toes as the water rushed to my feet and then as quickly retreated. I went to the Blue Bar disco and met some travellers sitting at tables on the beach under the stars as the music beat from large speakers. With a cold beer in my hand the evening was perfect as I tapped my foot enjoying the moment. I felt totally at ease trapped in an atom of peace and solitude.

I had heard snorkelling was amazing and so I headed to a small run down building with a rusted tin roof and hired a pair of flippers and goggles. I swam out to the coral 250 metres from the shore. The fish were teeming as they moved through the beautiful coral reef darting in and out of holes as if playing hide and seek. To my amazement I saw a huge old turtle which swam in front of me with such grace and agility like a fat person floating in space. I could not take my eyes off it until it left me behind as it headed further out into the ocean. With my concentration on the turtle I was pushed by the current into the coral and a barnacle sliced my finger like a razor blade. Blood poured from it and I began thinking of sharks and wondered what the Sri Lankan waters held. After a couple of hours engrossed in my underwater adventure I headed back for the shore.

On the way back to my room I stopped at a batik shop and looked at their wonderful works of art. With my eye set on a beautiful sunset I purchased it, wanting a special reminder of this beautiful place. Needing a better place to stay I moved to the Sea Lion Guesthouse along with Aussie Bryan who I had met in Hikkaduwa. I continued satisfying my appetite with the avocado sandwiches, a good change from the roti's and curries, even though I loved the roti's. They were made from wheat flour and scrapings of coconut with chopped green chillies and onion. They filled them with potato and peas and I couldn't get enough of this filling meal ordering two and three at a time.

Being so close to the main road I watched the buses scream through the town blasting the horn at cows and people and hardly slowing down. Apart from the sudden whirlwind of noise it was paradise as I enjoyed watching the sea and sitting on the beach with the palm trees acting like tall umbrellas to shield the fiery sun as it beat down with venom. I watched a snake lying peacefully in the warmth of the sun on a thatched roof and it left me wondering if it was poisonous. It looked as though it was and being a safe distance away I wasn't perturbed in the least.

On the beach I met the crowd from the Blue Bar at the Royal Beach Resort and we all had a mellow evening around a fire with the sound of waves crashing and the crackling and popping of logs. It was so therapeutic and enjoyable until a wave came too close and put it out, and by doing so killed the moment. I felt angry that such a peaceful moment was destroyed so suddenly like a fire sweeping across an open field.

In the morning I got a flip flop and a pair of shorts repaired for 50 Rs which was nothing in the Western world. As a traveller I had to keep my wardrobe going and when it was cost effective I did. Back on the beach I met a crowd from England on their way back to India, but they were encountering problems with their Air India flight as the pilots were on strike. Apparently there where no flights until mid January and that is when I had to be out or extend my visa for £25. I decided to wait and see and hopefully save the 25 quid.

I went to another bar on the beach and on arriving I could see the people were well and truly wrecked. Fire crackers were flying in all directions like tracers in a military manoeuvre. I watched as an Englishman let off a fire cracker inside the bar that whooshed over the heads of those in front of him and then shot towards the beach missing a person by inches. He recoiled as if he had been shot and his eardrums must have suffered for the blast.

The bar had a monkey and I uttered some monkey sounds to it. It looked at me and slapped me across the face as if to say: 'Who do you think the monkey is?' I had to laugh along with those that had seen it.

Needing to explore I set off for Galle and looked at an old fort which had been built by the Portuguese and then modified by the Dutch a century later. It is the largest remaining fortress in Asia built by European occupiers. It is so well preserved and stands steadfast on the peninsula with a lighthouse close by. As I exited the fort a young boy asked if I wanted to buy some coins. I looked at the old coins flipping them over in the palm of my hand. One was a big five cent coin with Sinhalese and English dated 1890 with a young Queen Victoria and the country as Ceylon. The other two were VOC coins with a coat of arms and a date, 1742. I gladly purchased them as souvenirs of a bygone era where the British had ruled with such power close to half a century ago.

On the main street I couldn't take my eyes off an old Coca-Cola truck from the 1950s properly painted in red and white with one litre bottles of Coke and Fanta in wooden crates. It was a trademark still alive in the most poorest of countries. Walking along the streets I watched naked men to the waist lugging bags of rice as they layered them like bricks in a truck until the suspension sagged and the truck tipped to one side. The streets were dirty and while some sat, others moved with the urgency of slaves driven on by their invisible masters. Galle I was told exported rubber, rope, tea, coconut oil and coconut fibre and judging by the workers in the street I knew this little city was thriving by Sri Lankan standards. Old wooden two wheeler carts pulled by lean shirtless men with sarongs tightly wrapped around their waists and feet clad in sandals and flip flops ferried supplies from store to truck. It was a bustling area with everyone besides the beggars working bloody hard for their next meal.

I was glad to find the bus station and then without any hassles we caught a local bus to Unawatuna. Bryan and I met two Austrian girls and we stayed there until 8:30pm and after a great day we were very lucky to get a bus back. The bus ride was an experience with a very drunken Sri Lankan trying to talk to me, nothing of which I understood. He stood up and gave me his seat, which at first I refused. He then forced me to take it with some loud and annoying slurring. To shut him up I did and enjoyed the ride back to Hikkaduwa in the crammed bus with not a westerner aboard.

Looking for more adventure and a change of scenery I took a bus to Galle. I then had to change buses and got the run around as I was told to go there only for another person to point me in the opposite direction. After some loud cursing I eventually got a bus which took me another four kilometres to Unawatuna where I spent the day lazing on the beach. Back in Ambalangoda I got a room with a family for 75 Rs and stayed in their house. The father of the house was called Uncle and he was in his late 70s. He was well educated and spoke good English and he didn't have a bad word to say about the Colonists. He went on to tell me that the country was a better place when it was called Ceylon and belonged to the mighty British Empire. Uncle also told me that Aravinda Da Silva, a famous and very well respected cricketer from the Sri Lankan national side was in town. Everyone was crazy and so uncontrollably excited to meet their local hero.

I met an Israeli at one of the wooden bars with thatched roofs circling the water's edge. On talking with each other we quickly realized how similar our two countries were, one with the Palestinians and the other with blacks. Both parties looking for equal rights and fair treatment from their ruling governments.

On my way back to the room I desperately needed to urinate and so I shot into the bushes along the road. Suddenly I heard a rustling sound and to my shock I whirled around only to see a cow urinating right next to me. With a nervous smile I was on my way. I had difficulty opening the old rickety gate to the property, but after a great deal of groping and pulling I eventually found the lever and walked through the garden to the back door.

Tim Ramsden

I had a great sleep in the simple room on an old wooden bed with a mattress filled with straw. It was very dark and there wasn't an ounce of decoration besides a faded brownish yellow wall.

Walking along the beach I was pestered into buying a wooden carving of an elephant which I had to bargain hard for, saving 120 Rs from the original asking price of 200 Rs. Every step I took I was asked to buy things ranging from a cactus to a pineapple. In spite of it all I found the Sinhalese to be extremely friendly people.

Feeling better about my claustrophobia I went for another snorkel and saw a turtle which I followed for about 10 minutes. It was as graceful as a bird and just a little smaller than the one I had seen in Hikkaduwa.

In the afternoon I went to Galle with two Austrian girls and an Aussie, four up in a small three wheeler Tuc Tuc. It was a great ride with the little two stroke engine over revving as he gunned it down the narrow single lane 'highway,' like a slow prehistoric wagon minus the oxen.

In Galle I was asked if South Africa was in Europe and after answering them they told me how much better life was under British rule in the old Ceylon. Galle was a nice old town with a mix of Portuguese and Dutch influence. The old Portuguese and then newly acclaimed Dutch fort was still intact and so was the old Dutch Groote Kerk (Great Church) built in 1752. I always loved the feel of a town that had an influence of Europe to it. The mark these two rivals had left as they conquered this little island was a testament to their workmanship that had stood for hundreds of years.

Back in Unawatuna we all had a very drunken Christmas along with three Austrians and an Australian. Sitting at a table on the beach Eva, Bryan, Peter and I threw back our chilled Lion beers, brewed by the Ceylon Brewery. We all followed this with shots of London Dry Gin which cost us 220 Rs for the bottle. It soon got the better of me as I staggered around and then vomited in the sand after which I felt as right as rain and continued on with the beers, the lesser of the two evils. The more we drank the more fireworks we shot off into the starry night exploding in a shower of cascading and spiralling twists and turns as they cracked the night awake. There were some near misses and we were lucky to have the armour plating of the alcohol which chased any fear away.

As the night wore on we joined a group of Sinhalese who were beating on drums around a fire. The fire crackled and embers shot up into the night with stars hanging so magically in the sky. The drums added to the feeling of peace and hope as we celebrated Christmas all so far from home. Before long the gin and beers got the better of me and I passed out next to the fire for an hour. When I awoke I was glad to have my money belt on and then zig-zagged back to the house, but before I reached it I walked straight into a tree banging my head. I cursed like a trooper as I held my head, which hurt like hell as I tried to steady my balance.

With a hangover and a bruised head I walked along the beach needing a tea or a coffee to clear the throbbing pain and on the way met up with the Austrians. We went to Menza's restaurant and ate a potato curry which was excellent and drank tea, unfortunately coffee wasn't on the menu. Had another great evening with the same Christmas crowd, but this time it was with a little less drinking. At 12:45am I tried to get into the house. I knocked madly for 10 minutes causing every dog in the area to bark their heads off and then finally a German girl came to my rescue and let me in. Surprisingly enough she wasn't upset at all and only then did silence once again reclaim this very quiet part of the island.

In the morning I saw the two Austrians girls off who were heading back to Colombo for their flight back to winter in Austria. I lazed around for the rest of the day feeling a cold coming on. It was a sign to slow down and detoxify my body and I listened to the message as a warning.

I wrote a poem in my diary while I relaxed on the beach, calling it, 'The Power of Beauty,' referring to the beauty of picturesque Unawatuna.

Palms standing tall
And towering over all.
Below the sea a gentle blue,
Cascades and foams about you,
And then rushes up the golden beach.
With this paradise there is nothing out of your reach.
Smiling you absorb the beauty,

This is the life completely.
Relaxed and with a peaceful mind,
You forget what you left behind.

This area was beautiful and I was quite content to watch the ocean in the circular bay for hours. Palm trees lined the curved beach and road way as fisherman weighing down their flimsy wooden catamaran boats fished the waters. There was hardly a sound besides the waves breaking ever so slowly and peacefully.

I bumped into a traveller from the Netherlands and so I practised my Afrikaans on him. He thought it was really good, *goed* in his words and followed it with a *dank u vel*, thank you. I was bumping into people throughout Western Europe, making the world that much smaller by the day.

Needing to see something new I went with Bryan by bus to Weligama 30 kilometres from Galle followed with a walk along a fine sandy sweep of beach to Metigama. I met some very friendly stilt fishermen and a few fishermen who had caught a small shark and a stingray. They stood stiff and very proudly almost scared to smile as if to conceal their joy as they displayed their catch with the father holding the metre long shark by the tail.

The sun beat down in its normal way as we waited for a bus. Each one sped by not even slowing down, some were crammed with people and others were an express service. Finally we stuck out our thumbs and got a lift for nine kilometres and then we managed to catch a local bus with my seat being the floor. I watched as a Buddhist got on and he was immediately given a seat, suddenly I was wishing to be a Buddhist too. Standing up I stretched my legs and looked out of the front window and watched a long snake slither in side winding movements across the road. The bus didn't even slow down and the snake made it by a few inches.

The buses and the beds are two conversation stories here on the island. The buses are dented and worse for wear with hardly any padding on the seats. The drivers are maniacs and drive the roads as if they were on a Grand Prix circuit. There seems no fear and it is pedal to the metal all the way with the breaks hardly being used. The beds are more like sleeping on a flat rock with a sheet spread over it. Sacks are sewn together and filled with coconut fibre but for 75 Rs what can one expect. The buses and beds tortured my back as if to knock the Western crap right out of me as if to humble me into being a third world citizen.

I spent a whole day in Galle, walking through a part of the town that was a slum. Beggars lay sprawled in gutters along the road side like trash swept from a side walk. They hardly moved as the flies buzzed around them, their eyes staring into nothingness, their souls having long abandoned their bodies. I watched a one legged beggar using his hands to push his body forward and his leg to balance himself as he stood and swayed like a pendulum on the side of a busy road. Still fascinated by the beggar I managed to dodge a mouthful of snuff as a Sri Lankan spat it out, just missing my face.

Back in Unawatuna while walking down the overgrown road to the house I was staying in, I heard a rustle in the palm trees. I cupped my head with my hands expecting a coconut to drop right onto me and split my skull in two. To my relief I saw a monkey swinging and jumping through the palm trees, but nevertheless it still scared the crap out of me.

In the morning I hitched a lift in the pouring rain with two Hong Kongites to the bus station and then caught a bus to Matara. While sitting on the connecting bus to Tangalla I watched the people streaming on either to beg or sell anything they had. Some had sweets while others had mandarins. There was a beggar with one arm and a huge lump growing grotesquely over his eye. His face was hideous and looked like a mask to be worn on Halloween. Again I stared like a kid in a candy shop with disability shielded from my privileged South African upbringing.

I came up with a name for these buses which ran the roads in the most unsafe fashion; I called them the shake, rattle and rollers, hoping never to see or worse be on one that rolled. On the way we passed some construction, the scaffolding was bamboo and was tied together with rope while workers balanced 40 metres up. I shook my head, thinking that health and safety were not part of the Sri Lankan vocabulary.

The cars in this part of the world are a collector's paradise; Austin's, Peugeot 204s, old Mercedes', Morris', and Austin Cambridge not to mention a couple of vintage cars. How they kept some of these antiques running I have no idea, with money and parts in short supply and the country in total ruin where ever one looked.

Walking along the coast I got caught in the rain and then spotted a huge iguana on the roadside. It was at least a metre and a half long and as thick as both my legs and looked more like a crocodile to me. I stayed a safe distance fearing that I might lose part of my body to it. I made my way past it as it waddled on its short stubby legs and hissed before thrashing its way through the bush and disappearing in the long grass. Relieved to be back in the safety of the Seth Siri Guesthouse I told my story to those I saw who smiled as I excitedly rattled it off.

Hungry as usual I placed my dinner order of hot curry at 4pm after paying 53 Rs. We had been told to get our orders in early so the kitchen staff could buy what they needed from the market and get it prepared. At 8pm it was served and it was enough to feed two people. Twelve of us, 10 of whom where German travellers from various German towns sat down at a table covered in a white cloth under the stars, and we feasted like kings with cold Lion beer close at hand. Backpack travel brings a new experience every day, one does not know what it will be, but one thing is for sure it will be an experience. We laughed and joked with our fellow travellers as our Sri Lankan hosts waited on us like peasant servants to royalty, serving and earning income with each order. It was their guesthouse and their business and for us it was cheap and the food was amazing.

Someone at the table spoke about the average wage for a labourer in Sri Lanka which ranged from 50 Rs to 150 Rs which was about £2. Everything keeps on going up especially their diets of rice, vegetables and meat. This was their land and their hardship as my mind drifted back to South Africa and our blacks in the same situation with the poor getting poorer, hungrier and more destitute.

Strolling through the markets was an adventure with all the sounds and smells connecting with my senses, intrigue and disgust coming to the fore. Flies buzzed around the fish and the bloody chunks of meat as if they were playing a game. Looking at the crude cuts of meat I said, 'Todays special. Five free flies for every slice.' Rusted and dirty scales hung and wobbled with fish, balanced with weights to denote a price.

The fish was no better and stank to high heaven. I thought back to Unawatuna when Eva and Bryan had eaten tuna and had got fish poisoning. Bananas and pineapples and beautiful red apples hanging in large upside down pyramids added colour to the market. Worn dirty notes changed hands as heads nodded with an odd smile sealing the deal.

'Where you go? What's your name? Are you married? Where you from?' They asked as I weaved my way through the multitude of people.

'Give me one cigarette!' they finally demanded as I turned my back unable to answer each and every question. They are very friendly and mean well and I have been told that this place is a pleasure compared to India. I knew it was matter of time before I would be the judge of that.

Back at the Seth Siri Guesthouse a huge fight erupted between two family members with alcohol the cause. The drunken man who caused the fight was given some hefty slaps which resulted in cries and shrieks for half an hour with lots of slurred apologizing. Dumega, a funny Sri Lankan who loved alcohol himself, came to the rescue and as much as he had drunk he seemed to restore peace and instil calm.

I took a walk along the beach which stretched for miles and miles with not a soul about. Fishing boats lay like markers on the beach waiting for the next sea voyage to ferry fish to the market all for that vital income where subsistence living ruled this impoverished island. The golden sand massaged my bare feet as the heat beat on my back and the water caressed my legs like a soothing spa. The palm trees lined the shore like a wall with the branches blowing together in one synchronized movement. The silence was so peaceful and I became lost in thought as my mind revelled in this beauty and solitude.

New Year's Eve was spent with 18 of us around a table in the garden of the Guesthouse under a star-studded sky as they shone so brightly. I stared upward like a love struck teenager captivated by the pull they had over me. There were no city lights to dim the sheer beauty of the evening and no noise to dispel the calm that cloaked the night. There was peace and hope in spite of us being on an island that was still in civil war and had been for many decades.

Food was served and we devoured barbequed tuna, noodles and vegetables in a curry sauce followed with a few Arrack's. Arrack is an alcoholic drink made from fermented fruit, grain, sugarcane or the sap of coconut palms. It has a golden amber colour and knocked the shit out of us. The food was brilliant and the company was great as we bounced stories around the table from our travelling experiences. As the countdown began we walked to the beach and let off my sky rockets that shattered the calm and decorated the night sky in an array of colour. I had a very close call with one just missing my ear. I felt a whoosh as it flew by but the alcohol made it feel as if it was a million miles away.

With a throbbing head I went to the Mulkirigala Rock Temple which was carved into the side of the rock face, with Beniva from Switzerland, Nic from England and a German. After climbing an endless number of steps we arrived weary and exhausted at the top and had a great view over the surrounding countryside.

In the bus while we waited to be taken back I saw a six fingered, one handed, stump footed man with his toes pointing up at 45 degrees with a really sad face as he begged for a rupee. I had to stare to actually believe what I saw. I turned away feeling really guilty for not throwing a few coins his way, but inside I went cold with shock at his misfortune.

I stood for 20 minutes in the jam packed bus holding my head down as each bump drove me up towards the roof. My head hit the roof many times until I forced myself down, wedging my body into a sitting position anticipating each bump. There are no doors on the buses allowing more and more people to fill the crowded space like a flood covering land. People hung out of the openings with each body equating to another Rupee. It was hell and my head hurt from the early pounding into the roof.

Catching another bus Nic, Benwa and I left Tangalla for Mirissa and on arriving there we were stunned to find that there were only two options of accommodation. One was too expensive and the other had only one room available for the night. After bargaining we chose the one room at the Beach Inn and paid 175 Rs, needless to say I slept on the floor.

I had a really good vegetable curry served for breakfast which cost 60 Rs along with an avocado shake with ice cream which for 12 Rs was a steal; it filled me up and was like no other.

Standing on the side of the road with our three packs the buses sped past totally ignoring the fact that we wanted a lift. When I finally had enough of being ignored I walked into the road forcing the next bus to slow down and come to a halt in front of me. It stopped inches from me and I felt like the Chinese man in Tiananmen Square holding his shopping bags as a tank rolled up to him. With my adrenalin racing and sense of victory raging in me, we made our way to the bus door. I got another fright as a bicycle came out of nowhere and nearly hit me forcing me to jump out of his way.

Once in Polhena we found accommodation with a family, very friendly and poor. While walking along the coast and getting lost in the beautiful and tranquil scenery we came across a few locals playing cricket. We joined in and played amongst the palm trees with the pitch a worn path and three sticks used as the stumps. The cricket ball was a tennis ball and the bat, a carved out piece of timber with a handle. They loved the sport and had gone to great lengths to keep enjoying the gentleman's game no matter how poor they were.

The Tamils are really funny when they shake their heads from side to side. Their heads roll on their necks like a bobble head as if they are saying 'no,' but in fact they are saying 'yes.' Highly confusing but it looks funny as they have a big smile flashing those pure white teeth. They also chew on Areca nut a seed from the Areca palm which is commonly referred to as betel nut. It is often chewed wrapped in betel leaves and when broken down is red in colour. Needless to say their teeth are a filthy red and one has to be on the lookout for people spitting, as they will spit anywhere. Every second person seemed to be puffing away furiously on their beedi's, a thin poor man's cigarette with tobacco flake wrapped in a tendu leaf. It looked as though they were just smoking tightly wrapped leaves and being so poor I wondered if they were.

Thirsty I went for a tea at a locals shop and saw a Sinhalese with a 5 Rs coin in his ear. Two minutes later I saw him with two 1 Rs coins in his ear and laughing to myself I realized this was his wallet to store his loose change.

Nick, Benwa and I went into Matara to change money and then caught a bus to Mirissa for the day. We all played a game of cricket on the beach under the blazing sun. Needing to cool off we dived in to the warm ocean which was so unbelievably refreshing.

Tim Ramsden

Our meals were eaten at our normal cheap place and after a fruit salad and an avocado shake with ice cream for the equivalent of 30 pence I was full and felt as though I had robbed the owner for paying so little.

We stayed three to a room and rotated one night on the floor and the next on a bed. Benwa had an infected sore on his leg and I watched him as he operated on it with a needle with lots of deep sighing, some blood and pain etched into his face. For the first time in months I watched the world news in the family's small living room area which instantly connected me back to the outside world. I also saw highlights of South Africa playing India at cricket with every Sri Lankan glued to the screen, clapping and commentating as each ball was bowled and driven by the batsman.

I left for Tangalla needing to get to the Post Office where I was expecting a call from Karin who was still in Bangkok, Thailand. The journey took one and a half hours with one hour spent sitting on my pack with 40 people crammed into a 20 seater bus. Finally I got a seat right in the front and knowing their driving skills I felt I was better off on the floor if we were to have an accident. I felt as though I was in an African taxi back home.

I made it to the post office on time and it was magic to hear Karin's voice. We chatted for about 10 minutes and I was heartbroken when she told me she was thinking of going back to Canada. I so wanted her to come to Sri Lanka and then we could head off to India together.

'Whatever will be, will be,' I said to myself.

Feeling down I went to a local restaurant and had a few teas and some cake to digest the news. The plate of cakes and buns were left on the table in front of me and when it was time to pay they just charged me for what was missing. It was a really filthy place which is why it was dirt cheap. The plate of cakes and buns is passed around from one dirty hand to the next from table to table. The bill arrived in a plastic ashtray on a small scrap of paper.

Tangalla was a very sleepy town with some beautiful untouched beaches and old fishing boats that made for some picturesque photo opportunities. I wandered around deep in thought and feeling quite lost wondering about my future travel plans. I thought about India and I really didn't want to go alone. But if it was meant to be I would.

In Thailand Karin and I had become very close and I had to accept the fact that it looked highly unlikely that she would fly down to Sri Lanka. I thought about her as I wandered around aimlessly and watched cows wander with total freedom down roads, through gardens, into bus stations and where ever they chose. They had total freedom of the town.

I saw a family of five come towards me on a black bicycle with long mudguards that was the standard across the island. It reminded me of the BSA bicycles in South Africa, which at school we had named, the Biggest Shit Available. Not believing what I saw I asked them to stop so I could take a photo. The father rode the bike while his wife sat side saddle across the frame cradling a little boy who dangled his feet over the handle bars while a young boy and girl sat on the carrier at the back.

The Sri Lankans made transport look easy as they used what they had to get where they needed to go without having to pay for a bus fare or taxi. Water buffalo pulled old ox wagons laden with coconut husks to market while others earned income selling water from a red tank on a wagon as an old ox pulled it down the busy road. Life was certainly backward and lived at a very slow pace, but it was so interesting to watch it in motion. There were many times that it felt as though I was watching life pass me by in slow motion, where their seemed just no urgency at all.

I left Tangalla for Matara still thinking of Karin and the phone call. There were four Westerners on the bus all heading for Colombo. We paid for our tickets and then the ticket collector pulled out a coin and started banging it on the railing in the bus.

'What the fucks going on?' I said to a Westerner next to me.

Suddenly everyone was passing him coins. Then the bus stopped and out he jumped and put them in the coffer at the Buddha Temple. This procedure happened twice on the way and it was like passing the hat around at church.

Once back in the capital we all got a room at the YMCA along with a hardened traveller from Germany. He had come overland through Turkey, Iran, Pakistan, India and then a flight to Sri Lanka. I looked at him with utmost respect; this was backpack travel on a shoe string.

Walking around the city at night we hunted for a place to eat that served us what we wanted but we had no luck and settled on a vegetarian restaurant. I had a potato curry kind of roti and a tea for a good price of 20 Rs. We found it impossible to get a simple curry and rice at night; this seemed to be only a meal served at lunch for some unknown reason. At 8pm we noticed the city was in curfew with hardly a soul in sight and yet I heard a man bellowing over a microphone. He was trying to sell something and I can assure you he couldn't have sold a thing as there was no one to sell to.

At 5am and dead to the world I was awoken by what sounded like a herd of elephants walking down the passage. But in fact it was a group of Sri Lankans that didn't know how to step lightly, who were on their way to work.

In the morning I caught a train from Colombo to Kandy. We were now on our way into the Hill Country.

'*Whattee, whattee, whattee, whattee,*' which was a small curry biscuit with a shrimp, echoed through the train as a man tried to make a living.

'*Skileyar, skileyar,*' which is a pineapple was shouted along with, '*Juicy lucy, lucy,lucy, lucy, juicy,*' as the chorus of sellers echoed through the carriages as the train wound its way through spectacular scenery. Looking out of the window I stared down onto beautifully terraced rice fields as green as the Irish countryside. The locomotive worked hard as it pulled the carriages up the winding railway as it chugged up the mountainous route with open land far below on one side and a rock face on the other. I felt pushed into my seat leaning back as the train wound its way like a snake through the mountains. When we stopped at one of the hilltop stations a one legged man boarded the train and dragged himself through the aisle on his bum, wiggling his stump and holding out a worn and very calloused hand. Very few paid any attention and only a few coins were dropped into his open palm.

The platform had thousands of peppercorn seeds spread out to dry. I watched as an old woman walked over them accidentally and then like standing on marbles her legs shot out in front of her and she fell back slamming into the platform. It looked as though she had waited for just the right moment to perform this act for us.

'She didn't even do a somersault!' I complained to Karin in my sarcastic humour.

Finally we pulled into Kandy with crowds of people waiting on the platform. I made my way out of the station to the Pink House which was a family Guesthouse. I was shocked to bump into Bryan and another American who I had last seen a couple of weeks ago. We all went out to eat and caught up on our travels.

I called Karin and was over the moon on hearing that she was flying into Sri Lanka after all. I couldn't wait and didn't even bother asking what had made her change her mind.

I went for a walk into the Botanical Gardens with Bryan and Geoff. This was nature and preservation at its best; it was truly beautiful, colours so vibrant and exotic. Feeling energetic we walked up to the big Buddha and got a spectacular view over Kandy. An elephant with a chef riding high on top decked with his chef's hat and a white uniform with advertising draped over the elephant on the side and with a red headdress was led down the road. This was advertising at its best and had every person staring his way.

Beggars lay sprawled on the sidewalks either missing a limb or two. Some even looked as though they were sun tanning. No one gave a second look except for me. I saw a sight that made me feel cold and ill. A man with drooping sad eyes cradled his young son, a victim of polio, stiffly in his arms. His son's legs were like two very straight thin rods and I knew this poor boy had been dealt a life of suffering with no help for his disability. He would never walk and it was written all over his loving father's face.

I saw at least 20 monkeys swinging in trees and eating out of a rubbish dump. The locals threw stuff at them and I knew they hated them like vermin for their cunning ways, stealing their crops and depriving them of a living after they had slaved over their fields for a harvest.

Needing to get back to Colombo to meet Karin, I took an express train which was at least 20 minutes faster. I was very excited at the thought of being with her again after a month apart.

I killed time in a restaurant having attracted an audience as I tried to speak some words in Sinhalese. The laughter that arose from the room was quite amazing, especially as it was all at my expense. Writing my

Tim Ramsden

address for them created more of a crowd. What they saw on the piece of paper was wealth and riches in a land far from their hopelessness and poverty. One person left and returned with a camera. He must have taken 10 shots with me and one Sri Lankan at a time in the frame. I left feeling that they had taken me for some sort of down to earth celebrity that chose to eat in their humble restaurant and mix with them instead of a five star hotel. But, little did they know how poor I was. I had made their day and they had made mine.

Now I needed to get to the airport and waved an airport taxi down, which was a small bus. For a taxi it was slow, overcrowded and stopped every 100 metres to pick people up. It then came to an abrupt stop as the radiator overheated with steam gushing out of the engine like smoke. Half of the bus had to climb out so they could refill it. As much water as they put in at the top flowed out the bottom forming a muddy pool below the engine. If I wasn't in a rush I would have thought it very comical as the driver look dumbfounded and lost for words. Eventually after two hours we pulled into the airport. I still made it on time and then found out that Karin's flight had been delayed by 1 hour and 20 minutes. Things are going wrong today I said to myself as I wandered around the small airport looking for something to pass the time.

I was really excited when I saw Karin and it was just so amazing to reconnect. She had met another Canadian on the plane and the three of us caught a taxi for 310 Rs to Negombo at the ungodly hour of 2:30am.

To my horror we arrived to find everything shut up for the night. I have no idea what possessed me to think that we would find a room at this time of the morning. I knew Karin was upset, tired and frustrated. We went for a swim to wash ourselves and then slept on the beach until the sun came up.

We were awoken by a few locals who were ready to launch their old wooden fishing boats into the sea. Karin started putting in her contacts and all of a sudden she had an auidience. Three Sinhalese were absolutely dumbfounded as they watched her put her 'eyes' into her face. The smiles of amazement were priceless.

After a quick breakfast in Negombo we caught a bus for Colombo and then took a three hour train ride to Ambalangoda where we stayed with a great family at the Sea View Guesthouse, the same place I had stayed at a month ago. They were thrilled to see me again and meet Karin.

This small town is known for its mask carvers. They reminded me of our Africans back home as they chiselled out beautiful works of art from useless stumps of wood. So impressed with what we saw we both left with a mask. Mine was an evil looking red face with a flat nose and piercing black eyes that looked like bullet heads sticking out an inch from their white sockets with a headdress of cobras ready to strike. There were also cobras slithering out of each nostril and through a mouth full of teeth. It was certainly a work of art and a scary piece at that.

We had a day of relaxation as we explored the little town together. Karin learned her first sentence in Sinhalese, '*Air bohoma pieceominya*' which meant, I am crazy and then she pointed to me much to the delight of the Sri Lankan crowd.

Back in our Guesthouse I spoke to Raj who we called Uncle. He loved his politics and told me about the good old Ceylon days and what respect he had for the British and their style of running the country, from education to politics. He was very unhappy with the present government allowing its people to live below the bread line. He told me that 70% of the Sri Lankan population was Sinhalese and only 20% Tamil. And then he went on to talk about the Tamils in Northern Sri Lanka who had been shipped in by the British to work in the tea estates as the Sinhalese were not prepared to do the work. Today there is the problem of the Tamils wanting an independent north and the Sinhalese refusing to allow this to happen. This has resulted in civil war with the north cut off from the south with tourists forbidden to enter the north. The war began in 1976 and was still waging with the Liberation Tigers of Tamil Eelam (LTTE) wanting a separate Tamil State in the north and east of Sri Lanka. The Tamil Tigers or LTTE have been labelled as a terrorist organization with bombs and assassination attempts, killing and maiming in an effort to achieve an independent country.

This is when I first heard of suicide bombers, and couldn't believe their disregard for their own lives and those of innocent people. I was told the Tigers pioneered the use of suicide belts. When I was in England I heard the former Indian Prime Minister Rajiv Gandhi had been killed by a Tamil Tiger. This terrible incident put Sri Lanka on the map for me.

Karin and I felt really relaxed with the family as they began to bond with us. Meals were eaten in the small dining room on an old colonial solid oak table. The chairs were plaited with cane and needed repair. Pictures of Jesus and a cross hung on the wall along with a sign that said Happy New Year 1993 with some coloured tinsel adorning the drab pink walls. I thought they must be catholic with all these symbols denoting their Christianity. Their parrot named Patta watched us eat while they waited on us like servants, which brought back memories of life in old apartheid driven South Africa. They kept on telling us how good we looked together and we enjoyed their conversation as we ate our meals with no cares in the world. We watched Patta who was fed red chillies at breakfast and then broke into banter of Sinhalese.

'A parrot talking Sinhalese. What next!' I smiled looking at Karin as we laughed not believing our eyes or ears.

'*Hari honday!*' 'Okay,' I replied back in Sinhalese to the parrot.

In the afternoon we went for a swim in currents that were the strongest I had ever felt along with huge dumping waves that really knocked us around. Poor Karin was completely knocked off her feet and slammed into the sand and her bathing suit was filled with sand. Forcing herself up she stumbled around as though she had lead weights strapped to her feet.

Before the sun was about to set we sat on a roof top and drank tea and waited for the sun to drop and radiate its glow through the palm trees and across the ocean. It was spectacular and we sat without moving until the burning ball was gone and black sky had covered over the beautiful surroundings once again.

At 8:30am we left for Colombo by train to get a visa extension for Karin. This involved going to eight different counters which really pissed me off. Finally she had an extension and then we went to book our flights to India. The excitement we felt as we booked them was indescribable; our dream of seeing India together was coming true. This was a travellers dream and we were in it and living it.

I watched a beggar with a stump for a leg lying in a pathetic heap on the road side holding out a hand for a pittance. An hour later I saw the same beggar in a totally different place and quite some distance from when I had last seen him. Then funnily enough at lunch time I saw him in another place with his back to the passing crowd as he shovelled down a curry with his right hand.

'He's on lunch break,' I said to Karin with a grin.

At 5pm we caught a bus back to Ambalangoda and arrived at 9pm totally exhausted. We had fought through all the traffic jams in Colombo, and all the unnecessary stops on the way. It should have been a two hour journey, but four hours on a packed bus was normal for this island and absolute hell for us.

We arrived at the house to a very worried and welcoming family. They were so relieved to see us and their smiles said it all. Dead to the world we collapsed into our bed which shockingly broke in the middle of the night much to the fright of the family and us. The floor became our bed and we still slept like logs.

In the morning Uncle showed me a magazine in Sinhalese about South Africa and the old apartheid regime. Any link to South Africa always awakened my dormant pride no matter how positive or negative it turned out to be.

In the evening Karin and I bought some Arrak and took it back to the family. We all drank like no tomorrow and got quite drunk with the men of the family. It was gone in no time with us staggering around and slurring as we looked for more.

With cloudy heads Karin and I headed for the post office and shipped off parcels to Canada and South Africa, a procedure which took a very long and drawn out two hours. It was here to there, back to there, confusion, wait, nothing happening, back to where we were, blank looks with no urgency in the world. My parcel cost 569 Rs plus 10 Rs for a cup of tea for surface mail which worked out to be a very reasonable £8. Unfortunately prices had also just gone up by 25 percent on the day we chose to send our packages.

We caught a bus from Ambalangoda to Hikkaduwa and got a place at the Sea Flower where we booked in for two nights stay. The beds were rock hard, the fan was broken and the mosquito net was filled with holes. For 150 Rs it seemed a rip off. At 1:30pm we were told to clear out as the boss of the guesthouse had a group of German friends who were arriving. I had a big argument with the Sri Lankan who broke the news to us.

'Fuck this. I will show them!' I said to Karin as I hastily packed my backpack and summoned her to do the same.

And then we walked right past the owner in disgust without even paying for the night's stay or the two cuppas' (tea) we had recently had. He was mad and shouted abuse at us and together we walked without a care in the world.

'That's what happens when someone bullshits me!' I said to Karin still shaking with a rush of adrenalin, expecting to be rushed at from behind by an upset Sri Lankan.

We walked half a kilometre down the road and got a bed at the Restaurant and Rooms. What an excellent room with a soft mattress, a proper bathroom and a good view of the ocean from the balcony. For 150 Rs it was a steal compared to the shit hole we had just walked out of.

While sitting on the roof pouring tea from a tea pot we watched the sun set through the palm trees. It was so tranquil and beautiful as we angled our cameras for that perfect shot lining up the orange ball between a cross of palm tree trunks with the branches adding a spectacular silhouette finish. Not even the pestering mosquitoes could distract our vision as we stared at the sunset until it was sadly gone for another night.

From Hikkaduwa we set off for Unawatuna in the afternoon. We hitched a lift into Galle in an old Renault with the air conditioner pumping arctic temperatures onto us. It felt good to escape the heat but mighty cold at the same time.

'Una-wa-tuna. Uuna-wa-tuna!' I couldn't stop saying this word to Karin as I rolled the Uuna off my tongue followed with wa-tuna. I was speaking another language and I felt fluent with it.

For 125 Rs we got a place at the Tourist Rest, a nice foam mattress which was like gold compared with the coconut husk mattresses we had slept on.

Our first meal in Unawatuna pissed me off as there was a problem with the bill.

'I am really getting tired of being ripped off,' frustrated I said to Karin. Finally we sorted out the bill after being overcharged around 200 Rs. I thought of the Sinhalese as sharks when it comes to money, they never lose out and never fail to politely rip you off.

Another shop keeper also tried to rip me off over some cool drinks. I wasn't having any of it and paid him the normal price, much to his disgust.

'Don't ever come back!' he barked at me, to which I smiled and nodded my head.

While walking around Unawatuna I bumped into Bryan for the third time. It was good to catch up and hear where he had been and what he had seen.

We decided to have a curry at Menza's Restaurant which served the most delicious meals on the island as far as I was concerned. While we were relaxing after having puffed casually on a joint we were shocked back to our senses as a few police came running in. They started to search the place with flashlights and intimidating faces. I felt myself getting nervous as I had a little bit of grass in my pocket. Karin and I sat stock still and waited. There was nothing I could do without drawing attention to myself. One cop stood guard by the entrance while the others conversed and searched.

Finally much to our relief the police left and then the restaurant owner rushed in and told us to leave. In a hurry we did and went to Amas Guesthouse to see Bryan off.

I spoke with Ama who knew me from the time I had been through the area before Karin arrived. She reminded me how very impressed she was that I came from South Africa. She took myself and Karin inside and showed us photos of her son. She then brought out a glass bottle filled with ashes and a few teeth, some hair and nails from a coffin. It felt quite spooky and uncomfortable as she spoke of her 26 year old son who had been killed two years ago. With tears running down her face she told us that he was killed by the Tamil Tigers. I felt helpless as I watched her openly grieve for a young man who looked so alive in his Singhalese camouflaged uniform cradling his rifle.

In that instant I thought about myself as a young conscripted soldier and how close I had come to being killed at least three times. The friendly fire incident on the SWA/Angolan border rushed back at me as I recounted bullets cracking over my head and getting lower with each spray of automatic fire. That pitch dark night engraved in my memory.

Tim Ramsden

Deciding to tour the island on a motorbike we hired a Honda XL125R from Amas Guesthouse for 300 Rs. With a mighty kick I revved the bike and with Karin on the back and no crash helmets protecting our heads we headed down the beautiful coast. What a pleasure it was to watch the Indian Ocean breaking through the palm trees as fisherman rode the waves on flimsy wooden boats. The sun shone with vengeance as we covered our faces in sun block which only collected dust and dirt like a magnet to iron filings.

At Tangalla we stopped and rested our bruised arses in a little restaurant. Thirsty we gulped down some sodas and then met a few Singhalese from the Seth Siri Guesthouse. Ordering a tea we spotted an interesting man sitting alone. We moved over to where he sat and drank tea with him. He was a nice old man with glossy and glinting eyes and more hair on his ears than his head. He could literally comb his ears and having never seen such a sight we posed for a photo with the man. Naturally he had no idea what we were saying to each other and why we wanted a photo of him.

Back on the bike we headed off further down the coast with the wind parting our hair as Karin held tightly onto my waist. At Hambantota I saw a huge iguana which was easily two metres long and wider than both my legs. I kicked out the stand and parked the bike and started following it. I ran into someone's garden and got really close with my camera drawn to my eye like a soldier with a rifle ready to shoot. I clicked the shot and as I did so the flash went off. Suddenly it hissed at me and bared its teeth and flicked its thick trunk-like tail in my direction. I understood this warning and backed away, thinking it was about to attack me.

We continued riding all the way to the Yala Park which was a 140 kilometre journey from our starting point. We set up our camera and took a picture of us in the Yala Park with water buffalo drinking out of a water hole in the background. Scared that we were now so far from our starting point we decided to turn around and head back for Unawatuna.

At 330pm we set off, our arses numb from all the bumps and uncomfortably thin seat. I cranked the XL 125R with our destination solely being Unawatuna, there were to be no stops or photo shots, we had to make it back before nightfall.

We rode through the rain and the darkness missing cows, dogs and bicycles as we tore through the night with the small headlight opening a small passage like a miner in a dark tunnel.

Totally fucked we arrived back at 7pm after riding pretty much nonstop for seven and a half hours and 240 kilometres. We were filthy, tired and so sore. My bum was numb and I could barely walk. I hobbled into our room feeling as though I had just run a marathon. After a quick wash we collapsed into bed and slept a deep sleep with a scenic trip to be remembered.

Still tired and stiff we got up at 5:30 am and rode on our motor bike to Medigama where we watched the sunrise with at least 25 fisherman perched stiffly on stilts in the water. They are known as the stilt fisherman and it looked like torture as they held onto the stilt while balancing on a piece of wood nailed into the pole and yet they still managed to fish and leave with some catches.

On the way back, still riding with no crash helmets we were pulled over by a policeman who wanted to give us a spot fine. I stood my ground and told him it is not the law in this country and I wouldn't back down as he tried every possible trick to get a bribe. He took Karin's licence and the insurance book for the bike. I wouldn't allow him to intimidate us with his authority and continued to stare at him as though he was absolutely stupid. Finally after about 20 minutes I realized I needed to apologize and with a sly smile he nodded his head and handed back our documents and then he waved us on.

Once back in Unawatuna we were quick to hand back the bike glad to have incurred no fines or damages. While walking along the bay area in Unawatuna I met a South African girl who was totally amazed at my travels, the places I had seen and some of my experiences. She filled me in on South African news and I was shocked to hear that National Service was only one year, citizen force soldiers were refusing to do camps and South Africa was changing dangerously by the day. The harsh and unkind laws of apartheid were very much history now. She had been in India for a few months travelling on a South African passport in spite of there being no South African embassy. One could now see and feel the embargo against South Africa having been lifted. The whites were out of the wilderness and free to travel where they had not been welcome before. She went on to tell me how a fellow South

African lost his passport and the hassles and frustration it took to get a new one.

In the afternoon I went snorkelling over the coral in a half metre of water. The sight of the colourful fish and the beautiful untouched coral was amazing until I found myself above the sea world with no water to float in. The waves brushed me over the coral and in the process I nearly lost a flipper and with no alternative I stood up and faced the waves. By standing on the coral I could feel I was damaging their world as pieces broke away as I struggled to stay standing.

Needing to eat I went to Menza's Restaurant and ate a very filling curry and found out that they had been fined 6000 Rs for the sale of alcohol with no licence. They had eight beers on their premises of which the policemen took four. This is what the search the other night was all about.

At 8am we got on a bus and travelled along the coast and then wound inland passing some exotic scenery as we climbed into the mountains. We passed the Ella falls which was so spectacular seen from our dirty bus windows. Finally at 10pm we arrived in Nuwara Eliya, a very English hill station used by the British as an escape from the heat and a place to relax in the home of the famous brand of Ceylon tea. It was the longest and cheapest bus journey I had ever been on. Four buses from Unawatuna to Matara, and Wellawaya to Banderawela, a total of 14 hours travel for 54 Rs which was the equivalent of a whooping 75 pence, a journey that would have cost me a fortune in England.

We booked into the Mount View Tour Inn which to our absolute surprise had hot water and absolutely exhausted we dropped onto the bed freezing in the damp room. Water droplets trickled off the wall and mould grew in the corners as we shivered under blankets with our sleeping bags layered over us.

In the morning we walked past an old horse-racing track that looked worse for wear and surprisingly was still in use. I imagined well-dressed English businessmen placing their bets and escorting ladies in big hats hanging off their arms. We then made our way to the tea plantations of Nuwara Eliya. We watched Tamil women hard at work as they plucked leaves from the tea bushes and dropped them into a basket cradled on their backs. I learned they earned around 59 Rs a day, close to a figure we had just paid for our trip to get here. It was scenic and beautiful and very quiet as we walked through the tea plantation feeling like very privileged whites in this poor country. Wanting to see the tea factory we went to Labookellie and watched the process as the tea leaves were sorted along an old conveyer belt which looked as though it had been kept running since the British departed in 1948 when the island gained independence. But it wasn't until 1972 that the name Ceylon was changed to Sri Lanka when it became a republic. We enjoyed a cup of Ceylon tea, on the house after seeing the whole process which made our tea taste that much sweeter. The name of the famous tea had lived on through all the political changes.

After a freezing and very damp sleep in the misty highlands we wanted to leave Nuwara Eliya and find a bus that was heading to Adam's Peak. Finally we boarded a bus that was heading to Talawakelle and after changing at Hatton we caught another bus to Maskeliya and then at 8:30pm arrived at Pelhouse at the base of Adam's Peak.

A Sinhalese woman met the bus and asked us if we wanted to stay with her family for a cheap price. We knew we just needed a place to drop our bags and get a few hours sleep as we would be climbing the peak in the early hours of the morning. At 2am we started the gruelling walk which was an ascent of 2224 metres, walking up an endless conveyor belt of steps cut into the mountain with wood and rocks set in place to keep them from washing away. We wound our way up stopping for the odd tea and rest at tea shops. It was freezing cold and we shivered the higher we climbed needing tea to keep us warm. Tamil men passed us carrying 30 cool drink bottles in wooden crates balancing precariously on their heads to refill the tea shops. We were told they took about two hours to get to the top and were paid 200 Rs for this heavy workout.

At 5am we arrived at the summit and with another piping hot tea we waited for the sun to rise. Luckily I had brought my sleeping bag and together we stayed warm as we sat and waited for a new day to dawn. As the light began to creep in, I felt as though I was in an aeroplane looking out of a window. We were above the clouds with mountains silhouetted against the fresh morning glow of orange that burst its way in, slowly expelling the darkness. It was the most amazing sight I had seen unfolding before my eyes, where our little world was christened with the most memorable start to a new day.

Once the sun was up it felt like a heater had been turned on and soon we were sweating as we made the descent. We stopped to eat, and drank a few teas while we enjoyed a well-deserved rest. We met a few locals who we spoke with as we caught our breath and marvelled with them at the beautiful sight we had just seen.

Once back on level ground we swore never to do this again with my army language of '*opfok*,' (punishment) coming to the fore. We grabbed our bags from the family's house and caught a bus back to Hatton and then bussed it through the day until we pulled into Kandy at 6pm, totally exhausted and beyond tired.

In the last three days we had been on 12 buses, experiences and nightmares with short distances covered in such a long time. Packed to capacity and thrown around with reckless driving along the mountain roads, our arses had paid the price.

After a good sleep we just relaxed not wanting to do a thing other than stroll through the main town marvelling at all the prominent British buildings still standing proudly as though the British were still ruling this small island. We were in the Hill country and it was beautiful, very calm and pleasant.

We went to an old small theatre and watched Kandyan dancing with loud drumming and dancers dressed in reds, yellows and whites. With the drumming coming to a crescendo a man in yellow banging two sticks ran bare foot across a bed of fiery hot coals. The dancers, sweating and shaking their bodies gave the audience their money's worth. For 150 Rs it was a treat to see live entertainment after being in Asia five long months.

In the morning we set off for Pinnewala to the elephant orphanage. It was sad to see what man had done to some of these poor Indian elephants, having worked them like slaves in the forests some still with chain marks on their thick tree trunk legs. We watched a baby being fed milk from a bottle as the young calf gulped it down with its small trunk curled around the bottle like a baby to a mother's breast. Further down at the river we watched as the elephants were led into the water and then on command they lay down on their sides in domino effect. A Sinhalese man stood on them and proceeded to scrub them with a hard broom, jumping from one to the next as though he was practising for long jump. This was their bath time and it was amazing to watch.

Opting for a quicker mode of transport we decided to hitch a lift and got back to Kandy in half the time that the bus would take. Looking for something to do we went to the Archaeological Museum and somehow managed to get in free which always felt good for a poor traveller. For lunch we went to the Botanical Gardens and relaxed under a tree overlooking a huge pond and made cheese and tomato sandwiches with absolutely no one bugging us. It felt like heaven to sit undisturbed and be allowed to enjoy our meal, the peace and the beauty without it being shattered by a pestering salesman.

In the late afternoon we went to the Temple of the Tooth which houses the relic of the tooth of Buddha. The relic, since ancient times has played an important role in local politics. It is believed that whoever holds the sacred relic holds the governing body of the country and with this in mind Kandy was the last capital of the Sinhalese kings.

It was a very calm setting with the Bogambara Lake sprawling in front of the temple. The golden canopy over the main shrine offers a spectacular glint in the sunlight, drawing one's attention to the temple, now a world heritage site. Part of the temple was destroyed by a bomb blast planted by LTTE terrorists.

Walking back up the main road we passed an old elephant chained to a stump. It was throwing logs into the road and pulling on its chains with such force that I thought it was going to break free. It rose up on its hind legs and trumpeted as we passed, its tusks long and thin and ready and willing to spear anything in its path. We were told that it had gone mad. It was a sad sight to see.

I met a white South African from Durban who had been deported from India on his South African passport. I questioned the policies of the two countries and if the governments were talking, after all apartheid was over and South African whites were now permitted into India.

I was thrilled to eventually sell my old camera to a British traveller for 1600 Rs which worked out to £22 and was a stack of worthless notes that would go far only in this country. I felt I had got my money's worth as I had had it for three years. It had done me proud freezing that special moment in time in many out-of-the-way places I had ventured through.

Tim Ramsden

On the trail again we caught a bus to Dambulla and went to the rock temple, but unfortunately because the entrance fee was in US dollars and was a steep rip off, we chose not to go inside. But instead we saw the huge rock of Sigriya in the distance looking every bit like Ayers Rock. Starving we went to a shop for a chunk of bread and a dhal, and then we were pleasantly surprised as they invited us back to their house. The whole family watched us eat our meal as if they had never ever seen Europeans in their lives. They mentioned a place to stay and we booked in at the Celonica for 125 Rs for the two of us.

We paid $10 US which was 440 Rs to get in to see Sigriya, equal to six nights of accommodation which was our bread and butter over the luxury of seeing a huge rock up close. In an hour we climbed the massive rock and saw some amazing fresco's of the 'Sigiriya damsels,' many hundreds of years old and the remnants of a fort on the top of the rock which was built 1500 years ago.

It was an insult to have had to pay in US dollars in a country so poor and dirt cheap for Westerners. The price for the locals was way above their means and therefore was only set as a money grab from the tourists.

'I am not paying this sort of money again!' I said to Karin as we made our way to the bus still feeling ripped off.

We headed to Polonnaruwa still with our day bags, our packs having been left at Kandy in the family guesthouse where we had stayed. It was much easier and lighter to travel without it and in no time we got a double for 100 Rs at the Samudra Hotel. After checking out of our room we went to the find the Statue of Parakramabahu I, close to the Potgul Vehera Monastery. A huge boulder had been chiselled away with a 3.4 metre stone sculpture depicting a majestic figure deep in thought or prayer with his eyes half closed and holding a yoke or book in his hands. It was a work of art with mind-blowing detail, especially as it had stood undamaged since the 12th century.

From there we went to some of the ruins climbing through fences to avoid the steep US charge. At Quadrangle we saw more fascinating ruins with guard stones and moonstones, and while taking a few photos we were caught. With a quick dumbfounded look that I feigned so well we apologized and left. We made our way on foot to the Northern ruins and again walked in for free. There in front of us was the Kiri Vihara dagoba. There were also three images of Buddah cut and chiselled so perfectly into rock called the Gal Vihara. There was also a 17 metre high cathederal known as the Lankatilaka which was 800 years old.

In the late afternoon we left by bus to Anuradhapura and got a cheap place for 150 Rs at the Paramount Hotel. There we met a student called Lashman who promised to guide us around the back areas of the ruins to avoid the charges.

True to his word he met us on his bicycle and brought another two bicycles along. All with our new mode of transport we cycled off to the ruins cutting through thick bush following narrow paths. We saw the Abhayagiri dagoba, which was the biggest and oldest in Sri Lanka and had recently been restored. It was over 2000 years old and with its white paint it stood out of the green bush prominently with its golden spire pointing to the heavens. Anuradhapura is the most important and extensive ancient city of Sri Lanka. It became a capital in 380 BC and was lost to the jungle and only rediscovered in 1845. It was an amazing feel to be lost in the ruins and see huge pillars, massive dagoba's and moon steps with animals so intricately chiselled into them as though it was done yesterday. Today it is a city now deemed a UNESCO world heritage site.

After a great day which saved us a fortune, Lashman invited us to his house and prepared lunch for us for absolutely no charge. There was not even a hint of a business motive from him. He was a genuine person who had taken a liking to us and from his heart he had been proud to show off his country.

At 330pm we left for Mihintale which was off the Trincomalee road to see more ruins which was no comparison to Anuradhapura and Polonnaruwa. As we wandered around I couldn't help but notice how badly neglected the dogs were up here compared to the rest of the island. We passed a dead one with hardly any fur. It was covered in scabs which looked disgusting with yellow pus oozing from its sores. Flies buzzed around with the heat intensifying the smell, forcing us to gasp for breath as we rushed past.

Needing to get back to Anuradhapura, which was 11 kilometres away we hitched a lift in an old truck from the 1970s, testament to a third world economy where everything that can be kept going is. We were continually stopped at road blocks manned by the Sri Lankan army as soldiers clad in camouflage uniforms came wandering over to us with their rifles at the ready and intimidating faces prying holes into us. We expected this; after all we were in the North and very close to the area of Sri Lanka that was a haven for the LTTE wanting their independence for a breakaway Tamil country. Karin and I had both spoken of going to Trincomalee but due to us running short on time as we were flying out to Madras in India on 7 February we decided against it. In the newspaper the following day we read of a bomb planted in a pumpkin that had killed and maimed in Trincomalee. I often wondered what would have happened had we gone or was I still invincible like I had been as a young National Serviceman soldier.

Our lift dropped us at a bus station and then we caught a bus for 26 Rs to Kandy. I am positive these buses can only become road worthy based on the noise of their hooters. The buses are falling apart and yet the hooters work like clockwork. The bus swayed and shook, and then we had a blow-out on the back tyre. Two hundred metres up the road a car had collided with a mini bus which was blocking the road. People had to have been injured I was sure of that but sadly we were tired and wanted our tyre changed so that we could get back to Kandy. I wasn't a doctor and people were helping out so we remained in the bus and waited.

At 1030pm we arrived back in the Hill country and to our shock we found that our family house was full with other travellers. Our packs were still in the house and with no option we went to the Pink House to sleep the night.

Long journeys always put us into a comatose sleep and then in the morning we collected our packs and headed for the train station. We were excited to board the train for Colombo, a distance of 115 kilometres which held the key to our next travel adventure.

It was just so amazing to stretch out in the seat and put my feet on my backpack that lay on the dirty floor. It felt as though I was relaxing in a Lazi-Boy enjoying a cool breeze through the open window. I pulled my walkman from my day bag and with my head phones in my ear I was literally in another world. The Specials and their emotionally charged political song, 'Nelson Mandela,' reverberated through my ear drums as they sung 'Free Nelson Mandela.' I knew it would not have been received very well by the Apartheid government when it came out in the early 80s, and I am sure it had been banned. It reminded me of Peter Gabriel's song, 'Biko,' which was definitely banned along with a film titled 'Cry Freedom.' It was about a black political activist called Steve Biko who met a brutal death while in Police custody. It was filmed in Zimbabwe because our government refused to have any dealings with it in South Africa.

And then there was the number one hit around the world, 'Another Brick in the wall,' by Pink Floyd who sang, 'We don't need no education.' This too was banned, which just went to show how we had lived without free speech and freedom of the press with the government totally in control of our lives both black and white.

On arriving in Colombo we picked up our flight tickets from Let's Go Again To George Travel on Bristol Street. For 3300 Rs which was £45 we had our tickets to Madras on Indian Airlines. We couldn't contain our excitement, our dreams now almost reality.

With no worries in the world we boarded a bus to Ambalangoda a distance of two and a half hours away. On arriving we made our way to Uncle's place, the family we had stayed with three weeks ago.

They were thrilled to see us and all came out to greet us with genuine happiness. Uncle's face lit up and he had a huge banana smile minus about 50 teeth, hugging us he then led us into his house.

In the morning we relaxed on the beach not wanting to do a thing. It was Poya or Poya Day which is the name given to a Buddhist public holiday on every full moon, at which time they visit their temples for rituals of worship.

The family was so hospitable bringing us tea and cooking us a delicious curry lunch. We spoke about the Buddha temples and they told us that there were five offerings at the temple, incense for the smell, flowers as an offering, drums for sound, food for the mouth and light for sight. There was also an oil lamp burning next to Buddha which we had seen. I was so surprised to see so many monks in orange in a country that I thought had only Indians in it.

I was now getting so excited about India. Just the word India made it sound so remarkable to be only one step away from seeing this great land. While I wrote my diary I remembered I had been away exactly three years to the day. It was the 6 Feb 1993, how much had changed in three years, my attitude, my country and my worldly outlook. How could I have known that I would be in Sri Lanka or even Asia after flying out of Johannesburg and have been through an unbelievable 30 countries and cultures?

I wrote in my diary: 'It has been wonderful and at times extremely difficult but at the end of the day it is an experience whether it be good or bad, it is all part of travelling. A time I shall treasure and never forget.'

In the morning we said our farewells to the family who had become our adopted family in this beautiful and foreign land. With handshakes and hugs and sad smiles we waved goodbye and left for the train station. Uncle and Nimal came with us and waved us away as the train pulled out of the station towards Colombo and the next adventure.

On the train we met a German who we had bumped into three times as we travelled the island. The ride was smooth as we sat like excited school children staring out of the window with India consumed in our thoughts.

We arrived in Colombo and headed to a small cheap restaurant for a meal and then caught a taxi to the airport preferring getting there hours too early rather than late. We waited four hours for our flight and then we were cleared to board. We carried our backpacks onto the runway and then we were told to get it security checked. One person told me to carry it onto the plane and another told me to take it off.

I felt the disorganization had begun and the fun was about to begin.

'India here we come,' I said to Karin with a wide smile.

As we flew out I looked down on this beautiful paradise and said: 'Thank you and goodbye beautiful Sri Lanka. See you later!'

Sri Lanka was now in the past, a cherished memory and India was going to hit us in less than an hour. India was going to make us and break us and there was no turning back now.

INDIA (1993)

BUSSING, BOATING AND CHILLING; TAMIL NADU, KERELA & GOA

When I first heard of the country called India I envisioned adventure and intrigue with colonial masterpieces left behind by the mighty British Empire. It seemed too far away, almost like an impossible mission, that my worldly wanderings would actually lead me to this vast land of teas and spices, magic and intrigue blended in a culture far removed from any Western democratic society.

'You haven't travelled until you have been to India,' came ringing back to me. These wise travel words had been spoken to me in Turkey, by a well travelled backpacker from England.

'Everyone gets sick,' he added along with, 'You will love it and hate it at the same time.'

India sounded romantic and filled me with that yearning to see and experience for myself the harsh reality of poverty mixed with beauty. There was also a voice inside of me that wanted to be able to say that as a backpacker I had in fact travelled through one of the most difficult countries in the world.

While in Thailand a 16th century mosque in Ayodhya, an ancient city sacred to the Hindus in India was demolished on 6 Dec 1992. A mob of Hindu fanatics who alleged the mosque stood on the site of Rama's birthplace had gone on a rampage. The riot quickly swelled to 150 000 people resulting in more than 1000 deaths as the turmoil swept across the country, plunging it into a depth of uncertainty especially amongst foreign visitors.

Backpackers and tourists alike began to change their plans, cancelling airline tickets fearing a trip to India to be too unsafe. Traveller talk on

Khao San Road in Bangkok was spreading like wild fire with rookie backpackers and hard core travellers opting for alternative countries like Vietnam, Nepal, Cambodia and the Philippines.

Karin and I had spoken in depth about India and wanted to experience this vast country in spite of what had happened at Ayodhya.

Excited and nervous we flew out of Colombo on Air Lanka destined for a city I had never heard of, a place called Madras. Madras to me sounded as though we were flying to another planet that was a utopia of hot curry and sticky rice. It was a good flight which took just over an hour and culminated in a scary bumpy landing on a very dark night.

Walking out of the airport I realized I had set foot in one of the poorest and dysfunctional economies in the world.

It was the 7th of February 1993, two months and a day after the Ayodhya bloody rioting, and there was still a lot of uncertainty in the country. I knew seeing India would change me in some way, I just didn't know how and what it would change in me. I still believed I was invincible, those memories of army life still shrouding me, along with a few racist seeds still sprouting. After all I was from South Africa having lived a privileged white upbringing, and with it racist thoughts and actions that for the most part I was not aware of, thanks to life under the South African apartheid government.

Trying to find a taxi we met Mark a Dutchman and Nick an Englishman and together we boarded a yellow and black Ambassador. Like a snake slithering around obstacles, the Indian driver recklessly tore down the roads honking and weaving around slower cars and bicycles as he tore a hole into the night.

'Yes this is India, chaotic,' I thought to myself as we all sat in silence staring out of the windows as our just impressions of India began to sink into our consciousness.

We found a place at Sam Mansion for 70 Rupees for a double. It was 1 am and we were wired wide awake. Glad to rid ourselves of our cumbersome backpacks we went for a walk in search of a drink to whet our appetite with this experience of a lifetime.

Right outside our mansion I saw a sight that I had never seen in my life. People lay like litter on the dirty street, totally homeless and deprived of a simple shelter. Babies cried the night awake, raspy coughs echoed the hardship and bodies turned to find a better sleeping position. Cows roamed the streets near the sleeping forms, grazing on litter with the smell of a sewer pervading everything. Dogs wandered unwanted and unloved, scrummaging for scraps, adding another sad note to the plight of India. In spite of the darkness and depression, stars tried to pierce holes in the night as if trying to encourage hope to these lost and worthless souls.

I had never seen anything like it, and here I was seeing poverty close to its worst in the very first hour.

Karin and I looked at each other in shock. 'This is fucked up,' I commented pointing at the homeless life on the streets. It felt odd, but I thrived on it in a perverse way absorbing it like a drug induced addict.

I immediately thought of the blacks in South Africa, and quickly realized that as tough as their lives were in the locations, these conditions were a hundred times worse.

It was the Muslims New Year and there were still thousands of people milling about at 2:30am.

Feeling safe to be back in the room we lay down under the overhead fan that spun like the rotor of a helicopter as it propelled coolness onto our sweaty bodies. I decided to leave the windows open onto the corridor.

It proved to be a bad mistake as I watched a hand snake its way through the curtains flapping like a fish out of water as it sought anything to grasp hold of and steal.

'Fuck off,' I shouted and like a tortoise's head darting back into its shell so the man's arm retreated.

After slamming the windows shut and moving our backpacks closer to the bed we closed our eyes with uneasy excitement at what tomorrow would bring.

In the morning the four of us strolled around town with the sun heating up a stench as vile as fermenting crap.

In spite of the smell we were hungry and curry and rice filled the gap, but I was wary of the water served in a dented jug with a few years of filth dulling the metal. I had often been told not to trust the water, and instead decided to pay a premium and have bottled water.

I must be on my toes in this place, I told myself, with that ever present fear of sickness lurking like a serpent ready to strike at any time.

I saw a woman begging with her child, a child so small that it should have been in an incubator. It was squawking its head off in an unpleasant and distressing way. Its cries certainly made me feel uneasy and helpless, not that I wanted to help. In all probability it was near death, and the mother was using its life as leverage for a valuable rupee or two.

Madras was a haven of disability with each step revealing another hardship. Dirty kids latched onto me screaming, 'Give me one rupee!'

I carried on walking shaking them off like clinging *haak en steek* bushes as I pulled free with an air of, leave me alone you are suffocating me.

Being white, Karin and I soon realized we were viewed as being ultra rich and living a life of luxury in the West, after all we had enough money to get to India in the first place.

I have never seen people so poor in my life, it made our South African blacks look like royalty for the most part, with clean clothes, food to eat, and a dwelling even if it was a tin shack.

In the afternoon we went around town on a bicycle rickshaw pulled by a thin Indian. I felt really bad with that air of a king as I looked over a sea of humanity living out their hopeless lives in this slum of filth.

We visited the Kapaleeshwara Temple, which took hours of walking in the midday heat, which punished our sandalled feet like red hot pokers drawn from a furnace.

It didn't take long before we abandoned the idea of the walk and we hailed a tri-shaw which scooted us to the temple in no time.

The temple was grand and decrepit and had been left to slip into ruin, making the scene even more interesting with age and time mixed with the predicament of the country.

We visited the Madras beach which was like walking through a squatter camp with makeshift tents dotted over the sand amongst litter, while plastic and paper blew with the wind.

Others enjoyed the water as the waves crashed past them and cleaned the beach by pushing the line of litter further back.

Back at the hotel we had a problem with the hotel manager over our room. On paper we had been checked out, but physically we were here. There was confusion and arrogance with me leading the way with arrogance. The Hindu manager broke out into his language leaving me further frustrated.

'Fucking foreign bastard,' I mumbled.

'Typical fuckin India, no easy way out of a minor problem.'

Eventually two room numbers were swopped on paper and we had our same room back.

We decided to hire some bicycles and Mark, Karin and I rode around for five hours dodging speeding cars, taxis and trucks that honked as they flew by scaring the crap out of us. The roads were chaotic with no rules, one had to just go and hope like hell that the motorists had bloody good vision.

It was bedlam with horns blaring, bicycle bells ringing and tyres screeching while a wall of people walked were they chose. Cows grazed and stood where they pleased, as if they were watching the chaos themselves, before shaking their heads and then lowering them to eat more litter.

They were the rubbish trucks and they did quite a good job.

'This place is fucked,' I mumbled as I dodged an Indian who walked into my path.

'Fuckin watch out!' I screamed. This place was working on my patience with the heat, the flies and chaotic life spinning me back to my army days.

In the evening a group of us; a couple of Israelis, Dutch and Karin and myself went to watch an Indian dance which put me to sleep only waking up when it was all over.

In the morning we headed with our packs to the bus station and waited for a bus to Pondicherry. Even though we were told a time of departure it really didn't mean a thing as nothing in India runs on time. It was like watching a clock that never kept time, and this was normal in the everyday running of things in this backward land.

When it did finally arrive people swarmed like flies to the bus doorway shoving their way in as if they feared an end to the world and this was the last bus leaving for safer pastures.

Being a gentleman I waited and watched as people pushed us aside, until I realized if we didn't move we would not get a seat.

'Fuck this,' and I levered my way on, motioning Karin forward and pushing old and young away with my pack which acted as another clearing device.

Out of breath we sat down, the only white faces in a sea of black with brown prying eyes staring at us as if to say you are rich, why the hell are you riding in this dirty over crowded bus.

Four hours later we arrived in Pondicherry, a smaller town than Madras and with a strong French influence.

We got a room at Fenns Lodge for a really cheap price, after all we only needed a place to safeguard our packs and rest our eyes for a few hours.

Again we hired a couple of bicycles and Karin and myself set out to Auroville, which was a city in the making, some kind of Utopia where there is no religion. It is a collective community modelled on the lines of a Kibbutz where all must work a minimum of five hours a day.

It gave me a weird feeling looking at all these backpackers dressed in Indian clothes with long unkempt hair, as they wandered like lost souls having escaped from their Western worlds.

There is a huge dome called the Matrimandir which is used as a meditation centre with cool marble floors and huge marble pillars, creating an atmosphere of peace and tranquility.

The building of this Utopia began in 1970, and even though the grounds had not been finished one could sense that it would be a Garden of Eden with a botanical garden walling it in.

Back at the lodge I had a cutthroat shave on the main street with the hustle and bustle passing before me. I felt nervous as I watched the skilled Indian barber draw the well-used blade, as sharp as a carving knife, down my lathered cheek giving me the smoothest shave in my life.

It was blazing hot and I felt lousy, nauseous and weak, I think I was suffering from heat stroke.

After the shave with a face as smooth as silk, I felt like a new man relieved that my face hadn't been butchered to shreds, my fate totally in his hands.

We sat down for a meal and a coffee. The coffee was brilliant and for a moment I thought I was back in France as I savoured the latte with a broad smile. I ordered a masala dosi which took care of my hunger pangs.

Immediately I had to go the toilet with the milk or the heat stroke driving me on at speed as I tore through the kitchen and up the stairs to reach the toilet which were both equally as filthy.

Walking back through the kitchen I realized why the food went straight through me, caked-on dirt and filth was part of the makeup of this place which was the same right across India.

'Everyone gets sick in India!' reverberated through me again. One had to get accustomed to the food and the life until your stomach became like iron and only then could you survive India.

The next day I was confined to my bed, sweating, weak and nauseous and suffering heat stroke.

As sick as I was I couldn't just lie there, so I staggered out slowly through the throngs of people trying to find shade as the heat engulfed me.

My body ached and my head seemed detached from my neck. Suddenly I felt this slap on my day bag that I had slung over my shoulder and as I turned I saw a cyclist speeding away becoming lost in the sea of humanity.

I soon realized that he had tried to snatch it as he rode past using his bicycle as the getaway.

I had my brandnew Pentax camera in it, recently bought in Singapore, and this would have been a great loss, for I never travelled anywhere without it.

I managed to hold down a meal of curry and rice with yoghurt while watching Pakistan play South Africa at cricket.

Since apartheid had been abolished, South African sporting teams were once again welcomed into the international arena.

It was a good feeling to see our cricket team doing so well after decades in the wilderness.

I remembered a rebel team from the West Indies headed by Viv Richards who visited South Africa in the early 1980s and played a few Test matches against the Springboks, to the absolute outrage of the world.

Money had defied the ban and what they were paid was enough to compensate for being blacklisted for life from the gentleman's game.

Karin and I left Pondicherry for Madurai, a journey that was eight hours of bumpy hell, that we needed kidney belts for.

Tim Ramsden

While sitting on the bus I stared out of the dusty window and watched a man on his bicycle which had a mountain of straw tied over it. It was huge and I could not imagine adding another single piece of straw to it.

He waited patiently to cross the road and I watched with interest as a few water buffalo strolled ever so casually up to him. One of them began to nibble on the straw, and to the man's horror his whole load slid to the ground.

Cows are the sacred animal in the Hindu religion and have total right of way and freedom to the town 24 hours of every day.

To see traffic brought to a halt by a cow crossing a main road is comical to watch and even better to see a cow standing still in the middle of the road as a queue of cars wait patiently for it to move puts the cherry on the cake.

We went to the Gandhi museum which was definitely worth a visit. To view old photos and learn about this wonderful man who had visited South Africa at the turn of the century. It was the discrimination that he suffered in racist South Africa that became a turning point in his life. Thrown off a train for refusing to move from the first class to the third class coach, beaten for not riding on the foot board of a stage coach to make room for a European, barred from hotels and jailed for a non-violent protest, influenced his social activism. Mahatma Gandhi helped found the Natal Indian Congress in 1894, binding the Indian community into a strong political force. The person who stood for peaceful change no matter what the cost might be, had been born. He was in South Africa from 1893 until 1914, serving in the Ambulance Corps in the Boer War and the Zulu War of 1906, where Indians were used as stretcher bearers to treat wounded British soldiers. In 1914 Gandhi attempted to recruit combatants for war but in a letter to the Viceroy's private secretary he wrote that he 'personally will not kill or injure anybody, friend or foe.'

In 1915 he returned to India with social injustice in South Africa having set the tone for the martyr he was to become. Mahatma Gandhi lived to see India gain its independence from British rule before being assassinated in January 1948.

We bumped into a girl also from Durban who had been away for three years and who also had used England as her base from which to springboard her travels.

You are never alone in this country; with a billion people what can one expect.

'Hello, what is your name? Give me one rupee.'

After a while I wanted to say, my name is Fuckoff and leave me alone.

With loud hailers blaring Hindu music, the never ending toots of horns, the constant stream of humanity, the smell, the heat and the flies became for me the ultimate test on my patience.

I was cracking and I knew it, but this was real travel with an experience to be remembered and we had to move forward. This was no package tour to an all inclusive beach resort, this was living the hardship through the eyes of the local people and suffering while doing it.

There is no comfort in poverty and we saw it with outstretched hand after dirty hand, expressions pained and eyes pleading with mercy. In a distant trance I looked down on them knowing that hope had long deserted them, they were destined for a very lonely death.

I watched an elephant being ridden down a road and had to smile as its trunk swayed around as it sought out food. Market stall keepers were on guard as they protected their fruit with alert eyes and on one occasion its trunk had to be shoo'd out of a shop with shouts and waves.

We sampled a few local Kingfisher beers at a really small and dirty Indian bar. The label read, 'Most thrilling, chilled,' and thankfully it was. Satisfied with the taste and the amount we had drunk we then headed off to our jail cell room that was a hive of noise.

After one night's lack of sleep we realized what 40 Rs got us. No sleep, and we were both itching like crazy from bed bugs and our bodies were dotted with red bites like chicken pox.

For double the price we moved across the road to the Ramkrishna and were rewarded with a deep sleep and no bites.

In the morning we went to a sound and light show where we met the girl from Durban and her Danish friend. After the show we all went to dinner at the Mahal restaurant where we caught up on some

Tim Ramsden

South African news. It was always good to meet up with Westerns and catch up on news from the outside world, especially involving our own countries.

We watched a wedding procession that came marching down the road with trumpets and drums beating into the night, amplifying the joyful union of marriage.

In the morning it was back on the bus again as it shook, rattled and steam rolled forward towards Nagercoil, which took five hours of hell. After that it was a smooth Rolls Royce ride to Trivandrum, a two hour journey. We had entered the green paradise in the state of Kerala.

We ate our first 'hand curry' off a banana leaf with our cutlery being our right hand. The left hand was reserved for wiping your arse and one could never be seen eating with your left as that would be vile. On seeing a person with only his left hand, his right having been amputated, I was left to wonder how he would eat.

I noticed there are plenty of toilets in India, choose your wall and piss. I have also been blessed many times by accidentally walking through buffalo and cow shit which is everywhere. They are like land mines except the only explosion is some heavy swearing when your foot sinks into it.

We learned never to travel without a few rolls of toilet paper and when on the road the open bush became the toilet.

In Madurai the river runs through the town and people are washing their cows, washing themselves and using the river as a toilet. One hundred metres downstream people are bathing, washing clothes and drinking the water totally oblivious to the smell that stinks to high heaven and blind to the defecation happening upstream.

We waited half an hour by a sewer for a bus to Kovalam, and killing time our eyes focused on an Indian dwarf who was totally deformed. He had a crooked body and sat on a four wheeled trolley on which he pulled and pushed himself with his hands bandaged in grubby rags. His hands were worn and calloused as he begged for his survival. It was a case of only the tough survive, and in India I believed he would surely die.

This was one of the worst cases I had seen and in India one just has to look away, as one is seeing it all the time.

We arrived at Kovalam beach, which after being in Thailand was nothing to write home about. The beaches were dirty but it was a holiday from the constant sea of city humanity and constant begging that went with it.

But people still try to sell you anything from bananas and pineapples, to *lungi's* which is a bed sheet cum sarong. After a while this too became so annoying that we meted out the silent treatment to each and every salesman.

There are plenty of restaurants in Kovalam with Western food and videos that took us back to our home lives a million miles away.

At one of the restaurants I met a Swiss guy who I had last seen two months ago in Tangalle, Sri Lanka, which only went to show how small the backpacking world was.

Topping this story of a backpacker on a trail, was an Englishman who I had met in Athens, Greece, and then two years later I bumped into him again on Ko Pha-Ngan in Thailand. The majority of Westerns on this island are stoned out of their heads on weed and magic mushrooms, and we were no different. He like me had been on the road nonstop soaking up adventure in country after country with time the least of his and my worries.

Karin and I went to a few beach parties with crowds of drunken and stoned people crowding a huge fire that ballooned into the dark like an erupting volcano. Music blared as people stumbled and danced in the sand.

There was a Westerner who was shooting flames as he gulped kerosene into his mouth and sprayed an arrow of fire that pierced the night. Kerosene was dripping like water from his mouth and I honestly believed I would see his face catch fire. He held a burning stick inches from his face as the kerosene ran like sweat dripping onto his shirt. He was totally drunk as he continued to blow the flames and to my amazement he kept his face and was applauded for his drunken and heroic antics.

At 5:30am we left Kovalam by bus, our preferred transport, and two hours later arrived at Valkala still under the umbrella of darkness.

We got a room for 50 Rs paid to the local doctor cum manager and yoga instructor.

It was a very beautiful area and totally peaceful until the ungodly hour of 4:30 am when the temple wailed an annoying noise for the eternity of an hour.

We walked along the cliff which had a sheer drop far down to the ocean below. Palm trees covered the area and we were in a sea of green as they waved with the force of the wind. It was a beautiful scene and we both marvelled at the sheer beauty that we had literally stumbled across.

We met a bunch of Brits and had a really mellow evening talking and drinking around a fire on the beach. Life was just too easy, not a single problem in the world as we watched the fire flickering through the logs under a star studded sky.

In the morning while wandering along the beach I saw a dead dog lying by the water's edge getting pecked over by a swarm of crows. It was a dog eat dog world but this time it was the dogs turn to be eaten.

While sitting at the clifftop restaurant I saw a crow on the verge of dying and a local told me that it had eaten poison. I thought back to the dog and maybe it too ate poison and then in turn the crow that pecked at it also became poisoned.

Karin and I walked into Valkala and explored the town. We stumbled across a very seedy bar and decided to have a beer. It was served in record time, a nice chilled Kingfisher but before our first sip a vile stench of stagnant urine wafted over to us. We sat and sipped and battled to hold back our nausea with each sip reducing the smell thanks also to a breeze that blew some fresher air over to us.

We met a few locals who were knocking back rum and whisky and after spending three beers worth of time with them we stumbled back to our home. This temporary home actually felt like home as there was no one around to bug you with that, 'Give me one rupee,' bullshit.

We had a tea from Sri Lanka, a beautiful country that we had both fallen in love with, which we enjoyed with two Brits also staying in the lodge. We sat around an old table in cane chairs, the only furniture in the house, as we enjoyed each other's company through the evening.

Karin, and the two Brits, Matt and John and I went for a four kilometre walk in search of a festival we had heard about. Soon we had a marker as the noise directed us to it. There were 21 Indian elephants all with a head dress of studded gold and red trim with a rider sitting on top and another person of importance holding a red umbrella. It was out of this world as the elephants trooped past like a convoy of vehicles perfectly positioned from one to the next. Leading them were drummers as they pounded out noise with sweaty faces. Along with them were the flute players who added their shrill piping to the music, while others danced with an air of absolute joy and contentment. People were dressed in bright colours with multi coloured ribbons tied to their wrists. As they waved their arms and moved with the beat, the ribbons ebbed and flowed like waves in an ocean. Their faces were smeared white and enhanced with red lipstick. We four and another family were the only white people that had stumbled across such a magic moment. It just seemed odd to have witnessed something so exciting off the tourist trail. This is what backpacking was about, totally unplanned and unexpected adventure, and most importantly another memory of this country.

When the procession had passed and the noise was in the distance we made our way back, but managed to get lost. We ran into a three wheeler taxi that saved the day and steered us home in time for a late curry over excited conversation.

We went to the beach and a thick oil spill lined the sand which, after seeing the filth of India, only fitted into the surroundings. In spite of the smell we still managed a swim. We spotted two dolphins that at first I mistook for sharks and was out of the water in a flash.

Back on the cliff I had a plate of chips cooked in coconut oil, savouring the welcome taste of anything but curry and rice.

While eating I met another Brit who had travelled Africa and had also been to South Africa. He did not find it beautiful, the fruit according to him was low quality, the roads were bad, it was hard to get around and overall he didn't think much of the country. As far as beauty goes, I felt the same for his grey land, but it was the first and only person that had ever given South Africa such a bad rap to my face. I knew it was beautiful with some of the best roads in the world and lots of tasty fruit. Yes it can be hard to get around but that should never dull one's experience of a lifetime.

The next morning we had our very first train experience as we departed from Valkala to Quilon which was a 45 minute journey. It was overcrowded and I ended up sitting two to a seat with an old Indian man.

We then got a Tuc Tuc with an English guy to the boat which we would use to get to Alleppey. It was a huge old wooden boat with a motor that chugged along and looked as though it was in desperate need of repair judging by the splattered oil. It was run on diesel which spewed out behind us as the Indian steered out down the canals and waterways with palm trees tilting towards each other from either side. It was sheer paradise as we glided undisturbed through it, with not a soul to pester us. Fishing boats with makeshift sails worked hard with their nets as they struggled at their day's work. There was a bloated dog that we passed rotting and stinking, just another testament to the untold numbers of stray unloved dogs that lived and died totally uncared for.

We spent the night in Alleppey at the Sree Krishna Lodge for a measly 42 Rs and then christened the night at a bar in town with a few memorable Kingfishers.

We arose tired, hot and sweaty at midday, had a curry breakfast and then we left on a pleasant two hour bus ride to Ernakulam. We had a good feel about this town that seemed very Westernized with everything from ice cream shops to modern jewellery shops. It was always our priority to find a room, and it was no problem getting a double at the Basoto Lodge, and then free of our packs we were set to explore the town.

Money change was always interesting, a simple process that took hours with untold manual writing, stamping, triple counting, passport checks, and a million and one questions. And then finally a wad of crumpled and worn notes, with many torn due to the way they were stapled together would be shoved at me. The rate was anywhere from 30-45Rs for £1 which was a lot of worthless money that went far in such a poor economy.

We got a ferry over to Fort Cochin, which was granted to the Portuguese in 1503 where it remained under their control for 160 years. But in 1683 the Dutch captured the territory destroying many Portuguese institutions, and they held onto their possession for 112 years. Then in 1795 the British took control by defeating the Dutch. What a historical feel this place had as though we were wandering through a very dirty and dilapidated Europe. Taking in the history we walked to the Jewish Synagogue which was built in 1568, my first experience inside one. The floors were tiled with hand painted designs from China along with lots of hanging lamps, a gift from Belgium. I just couldn't imagine too many Jews in India, and I must say it was an unusual sight in this part of the world.

We also went to a Dutch palace which housed a fantastic museum in excellent condition with some fine oil paintings.

Old Cochin has plenty of character with a mix of old houses built by the Portuguese, Dutch and British in these colonial periods along with churches and buildings, all suffering years of decay.

In the evening we set off for Bolgatty by ferry to see the Kathakali dancers. We watched them being painted with olive green faces, black lines around the eyes and red around the lips. The men wore a circular headdress with a red cloak and lots of bangles. Kathakali means a story play which was acted out with no words but music in the background. It was entertaining and well worth the ferry trip.

In Fort Cochin we saw some old Portuguese and Dutch churches dating back hundreds of years when these colonies ruled India. I found it amazing that their mark on this land had survived all this time.

The name Cochin implies 'co-chin,' meaning 'like China.' Cochin had looked like China when the Chinese came to the region in the 14th century and built their huge fishing nets.

We watched the sunset through an old Chinese contraption of poles and a massive mushroom like net that was lowered into the water like an umbrella. It was a beautiful sunset with these old fishing nets in the background, setting up a picture perfect photo shoot. It was amazing to think that after 500 years the Chinese influence had remained and was still used for fishing the waters to feed hungry mouths.

After the beauty had faded away we caught the ferry back to Ernakulam and went to watch a movie at the cinema. The screen was half the normal size and the seats were rock hard.

Back at the room, I was squatting over the hole doing my business when a rat darted out right underneath my buttocks. It gave me the fright of my life as it disappeared into our room. Karin was on top of the bed giving direction as I hunted for it with my phobia of rats making me sweat. To make matters worse it stayed hidden for the rest of the night.

Tim Ramsden

Then it was the cockroaches' turn. While I was sipping on my coffee I felt something crawling over my foot, it was a humongous cockroach. And then to my horror I saw another peering out of a hole in the wall. There are plenty of them in India as it is certainly dirty enough for them.

We saw where Vasco da Gama was originally buried in St Francis Church in 1524, which immediately took me thousands of kilometres southward to my country. He was the Portuguese explorer who landed on the east coast of southern Africa on Christmas day in 1497 and named it Port Natal.

It was back on the road again and we caught a train to Calicut, a five hour journey for 42 Rs. Passing through the state of Kerela was far more beautiful and green in comparison to Tamil Nadu. The rice paddies, endless lines of palm trees and long stretches of coastline made it so much more colourful than what we had seen so far. Even the people seemed friendlier with more opportunities to earn a living.

It still amazes me at how many different answers one can get for the same question.

'What time is the train leaving?' a question I asked eight to ten people and got a different answer each time. It just goes to show that because nothing runs on time, how can there ever be a right answer and a right time, unless it is by pure fluke.

It is a game of patience as you try to curb frustration as you wait and wait lugging your pack and then sitting on it, but never allowing it out of your sight. The persistent beggars are everywhere. Every two minutes a new face appears riddled with pain and suffering. Many are blind their eyes either sunken in or removed totally while others are simply glazed over with cataracts. Some have really bad facial burns, their faces in all probability scalded by hot oil or water over primitive cooking fires and others have stumps for fingers due to leprosy. We would be broke if we gave money to every outstretched hand, it is just too sad to see the condition of some of these people. As always we looked beyond it and took the scene in like a Halloween movie as it played out before us without us getting involved in it.

The heat as always was unbearable along with the filth as crowds of people weaved past trying to sell anything and everything, all looking for a business opportunity with a couple of dirty white skinned backpackers. There was a chatter of noise as passengers passed the time in a normal way for them, never seeming to complain about the wait.

I thought about my time in India, I had already been here a month and it felt like two years as I struggled through each day. Travel should be enjoyable but this was more of an experience involving double doses of hardship.

I was lost in my worldly travels, on the road in Asia backpacking for the past 6 months since landing in Bangkok, Thailand, on 26 August 1992. I had arrived with £4000 in travellers cheques, my Lonely Planet bible, 'South-East Asia and West Asia on a shoestring' on an adventure filled with scares and not a single fact known about Asia, let alone the language and India of all places.

I had last contacted home at Christmas after lining up for a phone at an exchange in Bangkok. Many postcards had been written on my journey but by the time they reached their destination, which could take as long as six weeks, I had long since moved on, and in some cases I was in a new country. As if I was lost to the mission of travel, no one could get hold of me and no one knew where I was. An adventure that had started off with a six month ticket that I thought I would extend to a year had now become three years and I was still going strong, in spite of the daily challenges.

Alone I learned quickly how to move through this vast continent.

The train was packed inside with people spilling out of the corridors and hanging off the sides, while others sat on the roof looking as comfortable as if they were in a seat. Karin and I hugged our packs watching for any straying arms that came too close. It was a known fact that most travellers were robbed on trains.

Once in Calicut we got a place at the NCK Tourist Home for 80Rs for a double. The town gave us an odd feel with stare after stare directed at us in a very uncomfortable way, almost as if they had never seen a Western traveller or a white face before. After a couple of beers at a local bar and a few more inquisitive stares we ambled off to our room.

The next morning we had an easy time booking a bus to Mysore which turned out to be a five and a half hour journey sitting on the edge of our seats. The bus driver to put it mildly was a fuckin lunatic and drove like a bat out of hell. We had entered the state of Karnataka and the bus driver was on a mission to beat the clock, which defied

India's transport system as nothing ever ran on time. He just missed hitting a cow, a goat and a dog as he gunned it through a town. He also narrowly missed a truck transporting eggs.

I had had a similar experience in Sri Lanka when an over taking manoeuvre nearly ended in our deaths as the oncoming truck and the bus I was on careered towards each other with neither letting up. Seeing my life pass in front of me, the truck slowed allowing us passage.

Well, I went fucking crazy at the bus driver for putting our lives at risk.

'Look where you are driving,' I shouted, but this was a mistake as he turned around and started shouting at me with his hands waving as the bus was doing 120 km per hour on track for another head on collision. All I could do was point to him and make him look back at the road at another bus charging down on us. He looked forward again and I shut up as he swung the wheel avoiding disaster while the oncoming bus flew by, as if this was the normal road procedure.

We were in God's hands and I dared not divert his attention from the road. I became shit scared as we drove along the side of a mountain with a sheer drop. There were no barriers and therefore no survival, if we went over.

We were going up a very narrow mountain pass and another bus was coming down. To make matters worse Karin and I were on the cliff side and looking out of the window it was a drop straight down to death as far as we were concerned. The back of the buses wheels were right on the edge and if there was a time in my life that I thought the end was here, this was it. No one else on the bus seemed to worry and our fear of riding on the edge was evident on our nervous faces. The oncoming bus shot by and then our driver steered us back into the middle of the road, and with the turn we breathed a deep sigh of relief to have survived what we thought was disaster. We often read in the newspapers of bus crashes in India, and this one had looked so much like another story of numerous deaths and injuries.

Once in Mysore we saw the Maharaja's Palace, a sprawling castle like Buckingham Palace with open grounds of fine green grass. The halls were wide with high ceilings and bright hanging lights. Sculptures added to the absolute beauty of this palace while a stone's throw away people were surviving in a slum. We walked through it and marvelled at this museum of wealth and then we sat on the grass and watched the sun set over it. We snapped away recording the moment with our cameras as the light diminished while the sun sank behind one of the gigantic domes. At 7:30 every Sunday the lights are switched on, and this is what we were waiting for. From total darkness the palace became ablaze with little lights. It was breathtaking and unbelievable that something so beautiful could emerge from the poverty and squalor on its doorstep.

In my diary I had written: India, one massive over-populated, poverty stricken, religious feuding, and wonderful cesspit of a nation. I think this summed up the country.

After the amazing light-show we got a place to stay near to the palace called Hotel Parimala.

After a deep sleep and a curry breakfast Karin and I walked to the train museum where we lazed around amongst some really old steam trains that had run the rails at the turn of the century. But most all we were really grateful to be away from the starving millions that, like flies, never left us alone for one precious minute.

When we emerged onto the street we saw Indians covered in pink, blue and purple powder. As we positioned our cameras for a shot we were blasted with handfuls of the same coloured powder from passersby. Our faces were covered and we took it with a smile and deep wonder as to what had brought it on.

As we walked each step brought another dumbfounded stare. The Indians just couldn't get enough of Karin and I covered in this fine powder that was as bright and colourful as a rainbow. We soon learned it was all to do with the celebration of harvest, known as Holi, the Festival of Colour and we had been included where food was riches.

On the way back to our room we came across a few Indians who were dressed up and dancing to music with huge *papier mache* heads with over exaggerated expressions. Those without their faces hidden glowed in happiness as they enjoyed the moment in their celebration.

Karin and I had had a small fight, my patience and frustration over hard travel coming to the surface, and I ventured off on my own. On the terrace of the Dunbar Hotel I met a Korean girl, who was talking with a few blacks from Kenya. They looked as out of place as a few Englishmen lost in a jungle in Africa.

It was brilliant looking down and watching people scurring like rats as they weaved their way through converging throngs of humanity.

The Kenyans I soon learned were studying in Mysore to become lawyers. They knew about South Africa and the life that was dictated to blacks, and yet they were very friendly towards me. It was as if they realized one cannot judge a person for his countrys policies, whether they are just or unjust.

We decided to go to the zoo and got a horse drawn pony. It proved to be a terrible mistake as we witnessed animal cruelty at its worst. The animals were living like prisoners deprived of all human kindness. The cages were small and dirty with the animals living in their own filth. I watched a lioness walk in a figure of eight for hours as she continued to wear a path into the concrete in a trance-like state, her eyes staring blindly ahead with her life extinguished years ago. Having seen lions in the wild in the Kruger Park in South Africa, it was just too sad to see an animal jailed like this.

The monkeys were the most unhealthy as they scratched at scabs on their skin, their fur falling off in chunks.

At the monkey cage there was a sign that read:

Appeal:

1) Visitors are requested not to feed the animals and to refrain from offering cigarettes etc
2) Please do not stand on the parapet, see the animals standing near the parapet.
3) If you throw stones at the animals they return the stones to you with a stronger force. You will be injured. So keep off this practice.

The zoo was so dry and arid in places, with any grass long gone. There was no water in the enclosures and the heat was boiling our brains and as a nature lover it sickened me to sip water while they thirsted under vicious animal cruelty.

Wealthier Indian families came to view the animals with their children. One could see how much they enjoyed getting this close to wild animals only dreamed of. A vicious lioness, a 70 year old Indian elephant chained up for three months which had lost its marbles, some African rhinos black and white, some African elephants as well as Asian rhinos. There was also a small gorilla that sat alone like a lost child in a patch of green grass. An old black bear, with sad eyes drooping and a furless face half stood in a cage as big as the animal itself. It was as though the bear had been placed in solitary confinement like a prisoner awaiting punishment.

It made my stomach turn that they did not see the condition of these animals and the prison they had been confined to. Shipped from the wide open savannas of Africa, they would die like innocent slaves on foreign soil in a jail simply for the sake of show. To me it was like a freak circus from the Victorian times.

I said to Karin: 'I would love to take those in charge and put them behind the stinking bars and teach them about animal care.'

Space, water and clean cages, but I forgot this was India, there was no space, water was costly and clean was a word for the elite.

Glad to leave we went to Chamundi Hill and saw Shiva's bull Nandi, a huge black stone sculpture that towered over us decorated with flowers and paint.

We sat in an Ashram and spoke with a local for a while, enjoying the shade and the peace and quiet before we headed back to Mysore.

From Mysore we had a hell of a bus ride to Hassan. At one point the bus came to a sudden stop. The driver got out, borrowed a hammer from an Indian and started hitting the engine. The bus miraclously roared to life and all of a sudden it was going three times faster than it had before. We were at the back of the bus and with every bump we were catapulted up like a jack in a box. When we came down we hit the unpadded seat with the force of a hammer, and did it hurt!

'Drive like a white man,' I mumbled to Karin, my racist South African upbringing coming to the fore.

Thankfully we arrived with our arses intact, and for 63Rs we got a place at the Hotel Sanman with a balcony overlooking the town. We went out and bought four beers, some bread, tomatoes and cheese and sat on the balcony. What a pleasure it was to sit like two flies on a wall and not be bothered by a single Indian, it was as though we were in a trance looking over the town. To have a meal other than curry and rice was heaven. To sit quietly eating and drinking while we watched the crowd dwindle as darkness enveloped the town, was a great ending to another hectic travel day.

I woke up with a slight touch of flu, feeling very weak and drowsy. We still caught a bus to Belur and Halebid to see the Hoysala Temples dating back to 1117. Built along the Yagachi River we entered one of the temples with impressive sculptures chiselled out in such detail, along with ornate pillars which had also been hand chiselled while others were turned on a lathe. There were sculptures of 650 elephants charging, symbolizing stability and strength. Above them were lions which symbolize courage and further up horses symbolizing speed. Above the horses were floral designs signifying beauty. One could see the thought and the precision that had gone into this old temple. Again it seemed strange that such history and beauty could exist in this poverty-filled country.

While we were walking I saw a cow push open a gate and sneak through into an Indian's yard. The cow ducked its head into a sack and emerged with a big onion hanging out of its mouth. It was incredibly comical to see the cow leave through the gate with its windfall as the Indian politely scolded it. Cows get away with murder as if they know that they can never be harmed due to their sacred nature.

The bus got us back just before the heavens opened and a deluge came down, washing away the filth temporarily or at least moving it to a lower lying area. When it cleared up we ventured out and I saw the worst disabled person in my life. I had to stare at her in order to comprehend what I was in fact seeing. She was old and frail and managed to break a smile through a few rotten teeth that hung in her mouth like bark ready to drop off a tree trunk. Her arms had grown in hideous right angles like zig zags as if they had been broken purposely and then left to grow. It is a well known fact that many babies are deformed by their parents in order to create an income through begging, and so playing on the emotions of others for survival. Her legs were so thin and weak they trailed behind her like two tails as she hopped along on her bum. A pathetic sight to see.

'Money,' she blurted, looking up at me and smiling painfully. She held out her weathered hands as her stick thin arms struggled to hold them up. Needing to get away I dropped a Clementine into her waiting hand.

On the 12 March 1993 I got hold of a newspaper and the front page showed ugly carnage. Even though I could not read what it said, the picture said a million words. Destruction, blood, death and people maimed. It was a bomb blast in Bombay and I soon learned by asking an Indian that 200 had died and there were 1100 injured. We were on our way to Bombay, and there was no stopping us.

I awoke feeling very sick and drowsy, a dose of the flu, but we still left as planned for Shimoga a four hour journey, that would be a nightmare especially due to my condition. The conductor tried to short change Karin by 10 Rs. It was the action that angered me as I watched this con artist handing her six 5 Rs notes to cover his trail. I forced it out of him and eventually he handed over the remaining 10 Rs. What a sly bastard I thought, but again this was India and people did what they had to do to survive.

The driver was a kamikaze. It was the normal bus story of nearly hitting a truck, almost going over a small bridge to avoid a cow and missing a few civilians as the bus tore through towns. The buses have only one door and bars along the window like a jail cell. Don't ask me what would happen if there was an accident or a fire. To board the bus people fight and push like no tomorrow with the women being far worse than the men, all to gain that valuable sitting space. Some casually hand a cloth or a bag through the bars to book their seat. At the beginning I had tried to be polite allowing women to go in front of me, but after hours of standing and getting thrown around I said fuck that and fought to get a seat for Karin and myself. It is first come first served, as simple as that. To survive our overland travels through India, a seat is a sought after luxury, there to renew our strength and resolve as India threatened to break us mentally and physically. Relieved to get to Shimoga, and still feeling deathly weak we quickly booked in at the Shimoga Tower Lodge.

At 9am we got a bus and surprisingly a seat that we didn't have to fight for. We took a pleasant three hour scenic bus ride that took us to the Jog Falls. There wasn't much water flowing over the rock face but enough to see what it would look like during the monsoons. The flowing of the water gave off the splashing sound that captivated our attention. We decided to take a walk to the bottom, a descent of 1001 steps and the reward of a cool swim with the misty spray blowing over us massaging the aches and pains, and washing the dirt from our pores like a powerful showerhead. It was so silent and peaceful away from the crowds, and we enjoyed watching the antics of a couple of apes in the overhanging trees.

Back at the top and feeling like new people we met Mohammed, a 60 year old red headed Indian, with round rimmed glasses, drooping blood-shot eyes and hairy ears. I don't know if he realised how bizarre he looked with his dyed red hair, a safe bet that he was the only redhead in India. He was a Muslim and a hardened drinker, a retired soldier, a chef and a doctor, or should I say a bone clicker. He held a glass of neat spirits in one hand and came up to me swaying and slurring. He grabbed my hand and then took hold of my thumb and before I knew what he was doing he pulled it and then pushed it back towards my wrist. I heard a loud click, but felt no pain leaving me with shock as to what had just happened. He then proceeded onto my neck for more clicking and in a polite way I refused. This left him no choice but to practise on a local who had his neck, ear, scalp, and arms all clicking like a springloaded toy. It was weird to watch as the local smiled and the red haired Mohammed glowed with pride at his workmanship.

He pulled out a small bottle of Arrack more like jet fuel and passed it to me. I took a quick sip and thrust it back as I choked on its potency. Mohammed took the bottle back like a grateful alcoholic and downed it like water without a single wince or frown at the sheer strength of the spirit.

Mohammed had taken a liking to us and he invited us around to his house, which was a simple dwelling in the middle of nowhere. He clicked the TV on and for five minutes we watched cricket, India's national game as they hosted Zimbabwe. As we sat with me trying to explain to Karin what this game called cricket was all about, Mohammed nipped out to the shop to buy us food. He so badly wanted us to take a photo of him and I think this is what drove him out to get food for us.

He didn't return so we went looking for him and it didn't take long before we found him swaying like a drunken bum clutching a loaf of bread and two eggs. He so wanted to cook us a meal, but we had already eaten a tasty Thali and the last thing we wanted was his eggs and bread as he swayed like a sail boat in a hurricane.

We left Mohammed and took in the tone of the town, so quiet, peaceful and friendly that we had to pinch ourselves to realize that we were in fact still in India.

What a reward it was to find a room without any fuss or pestering. For a steal of 50 Rs we booked in at the Tunga Tourist Home, and got a beautiful clean room with two very comfortable lounge chairs and an even more comfortable bed. Paradise we thought as we dropped our heavy packs to the clean wooden floor.

In town we bumped into an East German girl from the old communist DDR. Having lived her life in East Berlin, she was now free to travel the world with the Iron Curtain and Berlin Wall now just historical facts. It still felt odd to meet someone so far from home who had been impoverished in monetary terms by the harsh communist system that, just over two years ago had the *Stazi*, the East German Secret Police watching peoples every moves.

With India's unpunctuality we waited from 11:30 until 1 pm for the dreaded bus that should have arrived at 11:30am. I asked the locals what time the bus should arrive and they shook their heads, not knowing. I kicked at the dust in frustration as the heat prodded my sanity like a blow torch.

'If they don't know their system how the hell can we rely on their times,' I shouted to Karin.

My feet in my leather sandals were filled with dust, I was sweating like a pig and my patience had long run out.

I thought about the word 'patience.' In India you either have it in you or you acquire it very quickly, or plain and simply you catch the next flight out. I realized I had to become patient very quickly or this world would drive me round the bend.

I stood for two hours on the bus journey along winding roads as I swung like an ape from one side to the other. Thanks to someone getting off I sat for the last two and a half hours which was a real treat, allowing me to nurse my arms that had stretched with each sudden turn.

We arrived in Karmar, a small town on the coast with a large fishing community. Back on firm ground we booked in for a night at the Udipi Anand Lodge. The room was really small with a low roof and a fan that spun like a rotor inches from my head. With my back to Karin

I heard an almighty smack and then heard a scream from Karin. She had been chopped by the fan. I was looking for blood on her head but found none. She was holding her hand and wincing in pain and then I feared she had lost a finger. As luck would have it the fan hit her flat on the hand, and she was lucky not to have lost a finger or two. In no rush for a haircut or a flatter head I walked around like a hunchback for the rest of the night.

Refreshed, we packed and headed for Colva beach at a place called Margao. In the normal way it was a bumpy and unpleasant journey that lasted three hours, leaving us two hours away from the downtown core. We had arrived in the State of Goa, an old Portuguese enclave famous in the 1960s in the hippy era, when groups like the Beatles performed and relaxed there. Being stubborn I refused to pay for an auto rickshaw as he was set on ripping us off. We decided on another bus and after a lot of asking and finger pointing that had us on and off buses, we finally found the right one.

Once in town we darted off to the bank to change money, but by then it was 2 pm and they were closed.

'This is bullshit,' I cursed with another obstacle planted in my way. I thought it was only in Africa that you expect the unexpected but fuck no, this was the way in India too.

With no option we angrily waited for a bus to Colva, but half an hour later with our tempers rising we opted for a rickshaw and 30Rs later we arrived in Colva. Our luck seemed to turn as we found the most amazing place to stay, and for the measly price of 40 Rs we booked in at the Roiz Cottages. Needing a beer or two we shot off to the restaurant that was facing the beach and with one Kingfisher after another we drowned out the difficulties of the past and thoroughly enjoyed the present.

While sitting on the beach a qualified ear cleaner who presented his very worn but stamped certificate to me, proceeded with his sales pitch.

I played along as he carefully looked in my ears like a doctor would a patient.

'Very dirty Sir,' he remarked and he pulled out a long dirty ear bud that was the longest I had ever seen. Before he tried to poke it into my ear, I jerked away and told him to, 'Piss off.'

Tired of the beach we went into Margao for the money change never wanting our cash to dwindle into the red and run on reserve. I had a shave on the street and felt as smooth as silk once again, the bristles and filth cleaned off my face.

We experienced a sad day for the locals as one of their own was swept out to sea as they were playing in the water. It is a terrible fact but many millions of Indians cannot swim and when the sea gets angry the tide will pull you in and never give you back. His body was never found and the locals were left at the water's edge staring with heavy hearts, their eyes fixed on the horizon as the sea teased their feet.

We had some brilliant cocktails in a restaurant overlooking the beach and for a drunken moment I thought I was in a Western country. We were drinking Fenny's, orange and pineapple juice known as a Fenny's Cooler, which was potent and got rid of all the frustrations after a few heavy sips. A vegetarian sizzler made up of carrots, potatoes, chips, onions, and cabbage fried in butter helped coat my stomach lining. And after the meal I met a Swiss national who I had met back in Sri Lanka and again in Kovalam Beach, just another example of how small this backpacking world really is.

On the bus again we reached Margao. To my astonishment I saw a travellers truck called the Celtic Tattoo with paintings on it. I had seen and photographed this very truck on the ferry crossing from Spain to Morocco an incredible one and a half years ago. It was moments like this that made me realize that there were many backpackers like myself and Karin, travelling by various means of transport and wandering the world for years at a time. Spain was a long way from India and one and a half years was a long adventure. I thought about my wanderings; three years, where had the time gone?

From Margao we got a bus to Panaji and then a short half hour trip to Calangute, a town filled with bars, restaurants, shops and intriguing little markets. On wandering the streets we met a hippy, a white Westerner, his long straggly hair unkempt and his beard left to grow as it pleased. He was dressed in the local dress, a thin white shirt and matching pants, now no longer crisp and white. To our horror he was actually begging, a white man begging amongst the poorest of the poor. It seemed like a story that someone had got wrong. I had to look twice to believe it when he poked his white hand at me and asked for money.

'Sorry,' I calmly replied, knowing full well his money had gone on drugs and now he was lost in this society with no way back. I had heard stories of travellers burning or selling their passports so that they could remain in this rural culture free of Western life pressures.

'If I am ever in this situation, I leave. I will not be a beggar, especially not in India,' I commented to Karin as we shook our heads at this pathetic sight.

We stopped at a very mellow bar with a terrace and good Western music filling the air. With a Fenny's mixed with Limca in our hands we slowly got wasted, sitting and watching life pass us slowly by.

Wanting to relax we wandered through a few markets and then decided to laze on the beach, which was far from relaxing as people selling pineapples and clothes bugged the living hell out of us. It was like an alarm clock on sleep mode, every five minutes we were pestered to look and buy until we just got up and left.

We got a very clean room in an old brick house that was starting to crumble with neglect, missing the odd brick and roof tile that only added character and blended into the surroundings. A cluster of palm trees added some nice shade. There was also a cool pillared veranda from where we could see the beach. It was an old Portuguese house built many years ago when the Portuguese still exercised power in this part of the world. What a pleasure it was to have a proper toilet and a clean one at that, and a luxury shower that worked. I felt like a king as I stood under hot water that pounded my body compared with the filth of a dirty bucket and a small jug to scoop cold water that I had been used to. India had been a survival course and now we were enjoying a milestone of luxury.

Outside the room a farmyard of animals scrounged around for scraps from snorting pigs and annoying roosters to stray scavenging dogs and wild looking cats. Flies and mosquitoes bugged the crap out of us but were just commonplace and went with the territory.

Karin and I along with two local Indians went for a walk along the beach. As much as everyone raved about the sheer beauty, Karin and I looked at each other and without saying a word we knew nothing could compare with the exotic islands of Thailand. Thailand was paradise, palm trees and beautiful beaches that stretched untouched for miles. We came across a kitten not even a week old, abandoned by its mother, lying helpless in the sand. Crows circled like vultures waiting to strike. Like a Good Samaritan I picked it up and placed it in a thicket of bush. But lo and behold as we walked away it followed us for at least three hundred metres. Again I picked the poor kitten up and handed it over to an Indian household, and when we left a child of four years old was clutching it lovingly. I had saved a stray that was doomed for death with only the strong surviving in India, and this applied to both animal and human. The strays on the beach or as we called them the beach dogs, scabbed and scarred and in many cases stripped of fur, roamed in packs. It was scary to see them looking like hunting dogs living off the land with no love in the world. They were like the beggars, except the beggars were less scary as the thought of rabies came flashing like a lightning bolt at me. We decided that we would not wander in unlit areas at night.

In daylight we went for a pleasant stroll along the beach and rocky mountain to the weekly market at Anjuna. It was full of way out hippies wandering like lost souls amongst the many stalls that were selling hand crafted bags with round chips of mirrors sewn into them and racks of tie-died clothes, sari's, you name it. I met the same East German girl who I had last seen at Jog Falls, another example of the backpacker trail. After a relaxing day feeling too lazy to walk for 40 minutes back to our room, we caught a boat that for a measly 20 Rs saved our legs and our bodies some intense heat.

Back in Calangute we headed out to Tito's Bar cum Indian disco in the open air with tables and chairs arranged below tall palm trees and music pumping hard into the night. We met an English couple and shared a few travel stories over some cold and welcoming Kingfishers. On the walk back we met Mahendra, a young Indian who was studying in Bombay and had come down to Goa for a break. He was staying in the room next to us and invited himself over. After a couple of beers and a few photos taken of us he started to get out of hand. He leaned over to Karin and whispered into her ear what he wanted to do with her. He also told her to open the door that linked the two rooms and when I was asleep he would sneak in and have sex with her.

Karin told me and I flipped. 'Get the fuck out of our room right now,' and he looked at me as if to say, what did I do that was so wrong.

'Fuckin perverted curry muncher,' I said to Karin as I slammed the door after him.

On our walk over to a restaurant for breakfast we saw a thin furless dog covered in pus-filled scabs and scars. It was a walking statement of animal cruelty as it was shoo'd away like contagious vermin. And then when we thought we had seen it all with the beggars another scene emerged. A man with no use of his legs pulled himself along the beach with his hands like a beached whale stranded and struggling. Then there was another with no legs to the hip and missing an arm.

'How did he get here,' I asked Karin dumbfounded that he could be here in the first place.

Needing money we went to Panaji for a money change with £1 getting me 46 Rs, and I also managed to find some comfortable leather sandals that were less than £1 and yet in the Western world they would be 10 times the price.

So far this was the longest we had stayed in one place. We were now on our fifth day after only planning one day in Calangute. We had already put 100 Rs down on a coach trip but decided to stay an extra day so it was either we lose the money or we try and wangle our way out of it. Needless to say I wangled our way out of it.

At the Sunset restaurant we met the owner and had a really decent conversation with him on what we had seen, where we had been and what we should see. Unfortunately when it was time to pay he tried to overcharge us and I wouldn't have any of it. He backed down and charged us the correct amount. Again it was a story of being sneaky with what seemed everyone's intention, to gain that extra buck out of each unsuspecting traveller. Little did he know that we were poor? What little money I had in my pocket was all I had in the world and I had to stretch it for a year.

We saw the same lost German soul begging for money with a cigarette and a beer. He had been roughing it for a month. His white robes were still dirty and his hair was a matted mess. Through an Indian we heard he was trying to sell his passport so that he could buy hash and deal it to earn an income. He wasn't leaving India in a hurry.

TRAINS, MORE BUSES, CAMELS AND ROWING BOATS; MAHARASHTRA, GUJARAT, DIU, RAJASTHAN & UTTER PRADESH

At 3pm we left for a 16 and a half hour bus ride that covered 586 kilometres. At the ungodly time of 7:30am we entered the famous city of Bombay in the state of Maharashtra.

Men at Work's famous song, Down Under hit me with a line denoting Bombay. 'Lying in a den in Bombay, With a slack jaw and not much to say.'

Tired we stared out of the dirty windows, also with not much to say as we wondered what den we would be staying in.

I had always been fascinated by the name Bombay; it gave off a flavour of intrigue and mystique along with a very important place on the world map. Bombay along with Delhi in the days of the British Empire were the jewels in Queen Victoria's crown as she ruled with such power over this huge land. Bombay is the most populated city in India with approximately 14 million people, and the second most populated city in the world.

We had a rude awakening as we hunted for a cheap place to stay. The going rate was 200 Rs and we got a room at the India Guesthouse with no bathroom which was at least three times the price we had paid so far.

It seemed as though we were in London as red double decker buses travelled the busy roads except these buses were badly in need of a repair job along with some panel beating and a coat of fire engine red to bring them back to their former glory. Cast iron post boxes, now a faded and very weathered red with the inscription of kings and queens stood dirty and covered with pasted on advertising. The British influence was still prominent after all these years. In 1947 India gained its independence and broke free from British control with the mighty Union Jack lowered forever. The old historic Victoria Terminus which serves as the headquarters of the Central Railways buzzes continually with a human tide that ebbs and flows like an ocean. This famous landmark in Gothic style was built as the headquarters of the Great Indian Peninsular Railway. It was designed by Fredrick William Stevens and took ten years to build. It was named Victoria Terminus in honour of the Queen and Empress Victoria, and opened on the date of her Golden Jubilee in 1887.

The traffic is a nightmare with the continual hooting and diesel that is ready to suffocate you as the stream of traffic stops and starts and rolls forward. Cars, trucks, taxis, buses and human rickshaws converge on each other as people and bicycles weave like a thread through the jam. Cows wander along undisturbed, looking up and staring at the traffic. As they shake their heads to shoo away a fly it looks as though they are actually shaking their heads at the stupidity of the traffic congestion while they stroll away unhindered.

We walked past the Stock Exchange on Dalal Street that had been destroyed by the bomb blast. Glass had been blown out and one could only imagine the sharp shards flying like knives embedding into people. The metal frames were still a twisted mess with makeshift scaffolding surrounding the devastation. We could still see the scars in the walls and could only imagine the mutilation on the bodies. Nineteen people from the building were killed and close to 200 were killed in total. The bomb had been placed in a car that was parked in the basement and it was quite obvious that this had been a very powerful blast that had inflicted such carnage and soaked the streets with innocent blood.

It was a time to take in the surroundings as we walked and looked and photographed. We bumped into two Egyptians who had worked on cargo ships, one of whom had been to Durban, 10 years ago.

Thirsty, we stopped at a pub and ordered a couple of ales. They stared at Karin and me as though we were some sort of alien creatures.

'What's your problem?' I said sharply as I stared them down. Suddenly they looked away sheepishly and fell back into their conversation leaving us to sip quietly on our cold beers. With Dutch courage I ventured out into the street and had a street shave with a blade that must have shaved every second Indian in Bombay. Most importantly it didn't draw any blood but it cleaned my face making me look years younger and took my tan with it.

I went to a travel agent and bought a ticket with Birman Air for £400, which was meant to be an open one year ticket. To my shock it was only valid for three months. I had been scammed and now I was screwed, down £400 on my shoestring budget was an enormous sum of money. There was nothing I could do except to see how my travel days would turn out. Only time would tell, and I still had a lot of time.

We walked and bussed our way through Bombay and found a place called the Dhobi Ghat, which we had been hunting for. It was the biggest open air laundry in the world with filth and squalor and makeshift dwellings under plastic and metal sheeting. It was a sinkhole of poverty with a smell that reiterated the condition. People washed their clothes in the small square concrete-walled blocks and watching them at work I could not believe the clothes would come out any cleaner than when they were thrown in.

Wandering away we saw some dogs that looked much bigger than we had seen up until now. Maybe it was the city life with more scraps to scavenge off. The city with its bustling population brought with it an abundance of homelessness and beggars along with a hefty portion of disabled.

In the morning Karin woke very sick with a fever, stomach pains and diarrhoea which made us think back to what we had eaten. We put it down to the milk we had had in a coffee which had tasted slightly off. We still ventured out, and at breakfast met two Kenyans who had been studying sociology for three years in Bombay. I ordered a dahl fry, a vegetarian meal which came swimming in fat and tasted very meaty. On arriving in Sri Lanka and India I had become a vegetarian. One could not take a chance with meat stewing in the sun with flies laying eggs in it as it hung dripping blood or lay on a dirty chopping block waiting to get hacked by a filthy bacteria-ridden blade. I loved the vegie meals, my favourite being Aloo Ghobi which consists of chunks of potato and cauliflower in a spicy thick sauce which makes me hungry just thinking of it.

With full bellies we walked past the Air India offices which had also been the target of bomb blasts recently. The walls were scarred etched like lines in a tombstone, marking the place where innocent people had been torn to shreds by this violent and cowardly act. There was plenty of security with swarms of police looking busy with sticks and old Lee-Enfield rifles as if they were trying hard to prevent another blast.

It reminded me of what Karin had said as we drove into Bombay.

'It looks as though the whole of Bombay was bombed,' pointing out the dilapidated buildings with peeling faded paint and creepers twisting through cracks in old colonial buildings. Piles of rubbish and rubble waited for collection with a job half done, and the road had pot holes like craters while discarded papers blew about everywhere.

Parts of the city looked as though another bomb had gone off years ago. But it was the gradual descent from being a rich Empire to an independent country where the shift in rule allowed many key functions to slide and crumble.

Some of the buildings are really splendid, showing off the majestic British grandeur, looking even more spectacular at night as the darkness like a black paint brush blotted out the ugly background. One building that stood out was the Prince of Wales Museum. There was another beautiful building that was a photographer's dream, and ironically there was a makeshift sign that read, Kalimpong Art House. It was a balconied two-storey building with ornately decorated pillars supporting graceful arches. The stone, once a shining marble white, was now a dirty unwashed brown. A tree had grown on the top of the building like a flag and staff blowing with the breeze and cracking the stone as the roots took hold, growing like thick ropes as they snaked and twisted their way through holes as if to reclaim this spot by throttling the building.

We took a stroll to Chowpatty beach and amazingly enough did not spot one cow but instead saw a herd of horses, chickens and a multitude of homeless people living in makeshift tents made from anything and everything. It was a collage of bits and pieces of all shapes and sizes matted together to make a home, with some degree of privacy and shelter against the elements.

As we surveyed the pathetic scene an Indian came towards me with his horse at full gallop. Shitting myself I stood my ground and then when I was thinking it was too late, he veered past me with a callous smile.

'Fuck off!' I cursed as I pulled a zap sign at him to further amplify my anger, and only then breathed a deep sigh of relief.

From the filthy beach we walked to the Hanging Gardens, which were dry and quite boring besides a few animals carved into hedges that were works of art. It was peaceful but nothing to compare with the beautiful Botanical Gardens of Sri Lanka.

As if we hadn't had enough of Chowpatty we returned for more people watching. Again an Indian on a horse came towards us, except this time he was cantering but blow me down if he didn't lean over and pull my cheek. I lost my temper and smacked him across the shoulder and then told him to, 'Fuck right off!'

'No one touches me like that,' I said to Karin as we hurriedly began to walk away from the beach. I had thoughts that he was going to round up a few people on horses and then who knows what could happen. We did not feel welcome and were relieved to vanish into the streaming crowd.

We caught a double Decker bus to Falkland Road and went into the red light area. It was fascinating as we watched people lining the road ready to ply their trade in small dirty rooms. The women were mainly Nepalese and Darjeeling and as we walked by they begged us to pick someone. I looked at their faces so much older than their years. Their eyes were like lifeless torches, once so bright with wonder and excitement and now all they could see was an existence of chosen slavery without dignity. Make-up plastered over blank faces to entice that customer that had hundreds to choose from, each woman hoping to earn an income to feed a hungry mouth.

'Come I find you a nice woman,' an older woman remarked. 'No thanks,' I replied as I saw AIDS and disease written on each face, not to mention it would be the last place on earth I would think of sleeping with a woman.

Turning to Karin she said:

'I will get you a nice woman,' and smiling we walked on as dirty men scurried out of rooms like rats to the gutter, now even poorer than they were half an hour ago. It was eerie, with the roadway barely lit as the women danced, dressed in the most expensive and brightest eye-catching clothes for this poor part of town. The women seemed genuinely happy as if they were getting the most out of their jobs.

Karin and I caught a horse and carriage with wooden wheels and metal rims and Victorian carriage lamps to light the way. For 50 Rs it felt as though we had stepped back into the 19th century as we surveyed the poverty and prostitution like a king and queen. I sat there feeling above the filth and degradation of their world. When the carriage stopped, so the beggars crept forward like crawling insects ready to scavenge a rupee or two from our tight pockets. In the darkness a man hopped up to us with a leg and arm and three fingers missing. He was cleaning windscreens at the traffic lights to earn a living.

Back at the room I made a huge mistake. While chatting to the owner I left our room key at reception. After eating out we realized the blunder and to our amazement we lost nothing. We had been warned many times that in India your stuff gets stolen, and when you think of the poverty one has to believe it is just a matter of time.

'Never let your guard down,' I said to Karin as I apologized for what could have been a very stupid and costly mistake.

In the overcrowded Bombay train station we organized our tickets which took an hour to obtain. Bumping, sweaty faces, foul odour and crying babies were all part of the experience to ride a jam-packed Indian train. It seemed exciting and a change from the sauna-like buses.

We couldn't leave Bombay without seeing the Gateway of India, a huge basalt arch 26 metres high made from yellow basalt and reinforced concrete. It is a combination of Hindu and Muslim architecture, the arch in Muslim style and the decorations in Hindu style. The Gateway of India was built to commemorate the visit of King George V and Queen Mary to Bombay in December 1911. In the earlier days the Gateway was the first thing visitors would have seen on approaching by boat. After a ceremony on 28 February1948 the First Battalion of the Somerset Light Infantry passed through the Gateway, being the last troops to leave India after independence in 1947.

For some crazy reason I couldn't stop eating, and instead of the usual two meals a day I was eating five meals, which led me to believe I had Indian worms crawling through my gut.

With time to kill and no room to stay we wandered around part of the city and then after dinner we sat with our packs in a corridor lined with solid pillars built by British workmanship and Indian labour. Right next to us an Indian woman began stringing up white sheets, from the wall to a pillar, and then from the pillar to the next pillar and then back to the wall.

'What's she doing?' I asked Karin as we watched with intrigue and satisfaction that now our waiting time was serving a purpose. It didn't take long for us to realize what was going on as we watched men walk in and out totally undeterred by us being there. She was plying her trade and therefore earning a living on a filthy street, with equally filthy men drooling over her.

'Not even the prostitutes have a room' I remarked as the moaning drove us away.

The train left Bombay at 10:30 pm and for 75 Rs each we rode second class with sleeping berths. I didn't sleep much, keeping one eye open for the long- fingered Indian thief that had no scruples about lifting a money belt or anything of value from a 'rich' backpacker. The trip took 10 and a half hours which was an orchestra of snores, coughs, and throats sucking back phlegm, sneezing and farting. It was played out in stereo as the snore and cough worked in sequence with the odd sneeze and the drum roll of farting. Hardly sleeping a wink on the train for fear of having our money belts stolen, we constantly guarded each other like sentries on duty. We had heard of many travellers having their money belts cut off them as they slept and we were determined that we wouldn't be another case.

As the train passed through stations we looked out onto the platform, which was covered in sprawling bodies who had no homes to go to. It was just another reminder of the millions of worthless lives that this country had, clinging for survival like stray dogs curling up anywhere and looking for scraps of food, that driving force to stay alive ever present.

We arrived at Aurangabad and glad to be off the foul smelling train we got a small, dark and dingy room for 60 Rs at Anand Lodge, and crashed dog tired onto the bed with the overhead fan beating down a breeze on to our sweaty bodies.

Rejuvenated we ventured out for a meal and tried a beer called Khajuraaho, which was absolutely disgusting and tasted solely of liquid yeast.

In the morning we went to the Elora Caves which were built between 600-800AD with massive sculptures cut from rock. There were Buddhas, Hindu gods, elephants all so precisely chiselled from the rock face. We found the Kailasa Temple which covers twice the area of the Parthenon in Greece and is one and a half times as high. All the caves had been cut from the rock starting from the top and working down to the bottom, it was unbelievable. To sculpt the temple 200 000 tons of rock had to be removed, a remarkable wonder of the world.

We decided to find another room and found a cleaner and bigger room at the Hotel Dwarka that was even cheaper than our previous lodging.

Lunch was the most spicy curry we had ever had, spurred on by the fact that we kept on telling the kitchen staff that we wanted it as hot as possible. With a Ghobi masala in front of me I sweated like a pig, with my mouth burning like a furnace. An audience of Indians watched us with interest, enjoying watching us squirm. Digging into the Rita we soothed our taste buds before assaulting them with another mouthful.

After being congratulated for eating one of the hottest curries they had ever made we were glad to be in the open. We passed an old hotel which was totally abandoned and overgrown, and there in front of the entrance was a cow about to enter, after all it was called the Welcome Hotel. We laughed at the sight and snapped a couple of pictures with the cow a welcome symbol anywhere.

Karin and I were talking and starting to get really annoyed at all the stares that were literally boring holes through Karin's clothes. Only when we glared back at them with a 'fuck off look' did they break the stare and look away as if they had been caught. We felt we couldn't trust anyone and needed ten sets of eyes to keep some of these slimy people at bay. It wears one down being continually alert like a soldier in an ambush position. Expecting that something terrible could happen to one of us, whether it be sickness or an accident, an attack to steal our money and our few possessions, all played on our tired minds. We fought off the people like a tidal wave that kept on coming at us, wearing us down with each new wave. I could not imagine being out of money, lost in a remote area that could not even be found on a map, it would be pure hell. I looked over at Karin as the thoughts swirled through my mind like that wave that kept crashing down on us. I was so glad to have her company, her love and companionship and her watchfullness over the bags as I shot off to buy the tickets, respond to nature's calls, or getting us something to eat. We both appreciated each other for this and we knew we could not have attempted to travel overland alone. It would have been a long and lonely, tiresome and aggravating journey especially, as nothing ever goes according to plan.

There were many times that we were the only Western faces in some of the remote areas that we ventured, far off the tourist trail. The longing to see a white face became quite overpowering.

People, people wherever you look, wherever you stand, they swarm to you like flies to a rotting corpse. There is no escape. I stood with Karin for five minutes in a secluded Muslim area filled with makeshift shacks. All of a sudden 30-40 people emerged from nowhere and gathered around us. They were mainly children, dirty and snotty nosed and dressed in clothes that were bullet ridden with holes. They were undernourished and forgotten in this slum, walled behind sheets of corrugated iron that made a shelter. Dogs scavenged and the area reeked of a sewer and yet the kids smiled at us with their ivory white teeth and inquisitive button brown eyes. I believe this was the first time that they had ever seen white people. Unfortunately for us it became time to escape, to be alone and like Morocco there was only one place to escape to, that being our room. India reminded me of Morocco where the persistence of the people was much worse, but the intensity and the sheer volume of humanity crowding every square inch of space and the harmless yet extremely frustrating bugging and begging was like slow Chinese torture. To be polite all the time is impossible and to be patient is a pre requisite for India, but it was impossible to remain patient indefinately. The constant travelling told on Karin and me, and there were many times when it came out in our relationship as the frustration erupted like a pot of boiling water spewing over.

We left Arangabad by deluxe coach for a 10 hour journey to Surat, but unfortunately got a raw deal on the seats. We were at the back of the bus with no reclining seat. We were mad and ignored our seat numbers and found two others. On being checked by the ticket collector, we did a great job at acting dumb and gave them a sorry story about Karin having a sore neck. After giving the same story twice we secured our comfortable seats. In spite of this being one of the most comfortable journeys we had had thus far, we were still bounced to oblivion and were forced to listen to shrieking Indian music which pierced the old eardrums until 2am. Wide awake we watched a Hindi film until 3:30am, without being able to understand it.

On arriving at Surat, we had entered into the state of Gujarat, a Muslim enclave from where many Indians had been shipped off to

Africa, namely, Kenya, Uganda and Tanganyika, (now Tanzania) and South Africa. Many were slaves either working under their colonial masters building railroads or working in the fields.

We sat on the concrete station floor waiting for dawn to break, with the early morning chill adding further discomfort to our wait. Our packs became our cushions as we watched the city awaken from slumber. I had two coffees to stay awake but it was overloaded with milk which must have been off. To make matters worse it made my bowels run like a runaway train.

We tried to find out about a ferry crossing over the Bay of Cambay. Some didn't know, some would pretend to know, some wished they knew, some would say yes, others no, then no and then yes we could make the crossing. Not knowing what to do we decided to try, and therefore defy the language barrier and our bible, The India Travel Guide, which had no information about a ferry crossing.

Tired, not having slept the previous night, we set out to Dandi with our fingers crossed. We clambered aboard a crowded bus with an idiot of a driver who got us stuck in a narrow roadway with traffic blocking us in. After a nightmarish one and a half hours he eventually manoeuvred the bus out of the jam and got us to the bus station. Then we all had to get off for half an hour while I presume the driver and conductor had tea. Then we got back on the same bus which was even more packed as we readied ourselves for another 45 minute bumpy ride. Thank God the Imodium worked as I could quite easily have emptied the bus.

'I hope we can cross,' I said to Karin dreading the fact that we could be wrong which would mean retracing our journey back to Surat, and then a further two days travel to Palitana.

Finally we met two really nice Indians, a husband and wife who had spent their lives in Zambia, involved in the copper mines, before immigrating to Leicester in England. They had left in the mid 1970s when Zambia gained its independence from British rule and Kenneth Kaunda was sworn in as the first black president.

'You cannot cross the Bay of Cambay,' he told us with all the confidence in the world that we so needed to hear. Now we could make a sound decision. We left for Navsari, no longer tired but ravenously hungry. Eating became the priority and then we found lodging for 60

Rs for a small room at the Hotel Sarvoday, an old colonial building, from the British past.

I saw a doctor about the ringworm on my leg that was getting progressively bigger by the day. It had started in Sri Lanka three months ago and was now the size of a tennis ball. I was given cream for it which I gratefully rubbed onto the red rough patch. I had tried many creams before and I hoped this one had some magic powers as the itching was beginning to drive me crazy.

We booked a train for Ahmedabad, the place we could have reached by the deluxe bus which would have saved us a lot of hassle and two days of travel.

'We are going to stick to the travel guide. They knew what they were doing when they wrote it,' I said to Karin as we laughed loudly at our mistake that cost us time but gained us a story and an experience. After all, this is what real travel is about, getting off the beaten track and seeing where it leads you.

We boarded the train for Ahmedabad, this was our third time on a train and it was as crowded as an Indian market. There were no spare seats so I stood amongst the sweaty stench of humanity, swaying like a pendulum as the train followed the curve in the old railway line that had been planned by the British and laid by the Indian. I got a seat towards the end of the five hour journey as we arrived in the most berserk city we had yet seen. We were in one of India's biggest textile centres and also the place that was used as one of Mahatma Gandhi's bases during his campaign for independence. It was the first time I had seen donkeys and camels in India, pulling carts laden with sacks of supplies and textiles along busy roads packed with trucks, cars, buses, tuc tuc's, Ambassador taxis, bicycles, motorbikes, pedestrians and cows as another moving obstacle. It was just so weird and comical to see a truck and then a car followed by a long necked camel with big teeth and huge pursed lips smiling stupidly with wide eyes frowning over the traffic ahead, as it stood patiently like a fish out of water. A massive bus sat behind its cart in the row of traffic ready to force it forward. The noise was mind blowing with all the hooting amid the pollution as diesel spewed like clouds from exhausts while dust blew like a storm churned up from the roadsides. It was chaos as the traffic literally had

Tim Ramsden

every vehicle in a jam and everyone in a frustrated panic, except for the nonchalant camel.

While walking I had my back grazed by a bus as it rolled past making sure that no one else was going to get in front of it. It was a driving skill of, 'I am first and no one is going to get in front of me.'

'I want to get out of here, this place is just too chaotic,' I said to Karin during a lull of noise as I sucked down another lungful of dust.

We got a room at Apna Ghar Guesthouse for a reasonable 50 Rs and then we went to the Shaking Minarets. It is a mosque and we were told off for exposing our skin by wearing shorts and vests and for trying to take a photo. It just went to show how little we knew about the Muslim religion and how unprepared we were for a visit to their holy place. Nevertheless it was a good learning experience.

After a brief look we went to the Dada Harini Vav, which is an intricately carved octagonal well built in 1499, with steps that led us down into the coolness of the underground. It has been cut from the rock with support pillars and a ledge preventing one from falling over. There were three to four levels with sunlight pouring in like a giant flashlight from the overhead opening.

Needing a drink we searched for a bar and after asking a few questions we were directed to an area with benches and tables in a cubicle. It faced the busy street and as soon as we placed our order two curtains were drawn walling us into the cubicle space. We sat facing each other with not a soul visible, feeling as though we were in a secret establishment about to watch a highly illegal sex show. It seemed odd, but we quickly realized we were in the 'dry state of Gujarat,' where alcohol was taboo for Muslims. Sipping on our Kingfishers we tapped our bottles together in cheers and smiled at what lengths we had gone to, just to have a cold beer in our sweaty hands to wash away the stresses of the day.

At 1pm we were on the bus for Palitana which was a five hour trip through stifling dry heat. On the way the bus driver decided to stop on a main road and have conversation with a passing bus, so he waved it down. Blocking the traffic in either direction the bus drivers had a great conversation as cars and trucks backed up behind them. No one seemed to be bothered in the slightest, apart from myself.

'Fuck India continues to amaze me. Do as you please, block the road and stew the passengers in the dry heat!' I complained as time ticked by and we sat like confined inmates tortured with wait and heat.

Dave, an Englishman we had met in Ahmedabad was travelling with us. He was a lively Londoner with brown eyes, a dark olive tan, wispy brown hair, good looks with not an ounce of fat on his body, and he had the inbred British gift of witty humour. It was great to have another person travelling with us, not only for friendship but another set of eyes to drive off any potential thieves.

Sapped of energy we arrived and got a double at the Hotel Shravak. For 100 Rs we felt like king and queen with a beautiful clean room decked with a table and chairs, a comfortable bed and a spotless bathroom, a commodity hard to find in India, especially on our travel budget. For some reason we could not find a restaurant and so we bought some tomatoes, bread and cheese along with some spicy snacks from the market and ate dinner in our room. We sat on the balcony and relaxed, so glad to be out of the crowds and filth for a few welcome hours.

In the morning we got into a horse cart, at least 100 years old with old wooden wheels with spokes and a covering for shelter from the penetrating heat. The old beast which looked more like a mule than a horse came to a stop at the base of hill. Looking up we saw all the Jain temples perched at the summit. This is what we had come to see but it would be a test to get to the top. There were 3500 stairs for a distance of two kilometres to reach the top. We watched as wealthier Indians paid the price and were carried up as they sat in a hammock-like seat while one Indian took the pole at the back and the other at the front. It was like watching slave labour at work as they sweated while the rich man lazed like a king puffing on a cigarette. It took us a gruelling one hour and fifteen minutes to complete the monotony of step after step.

The temples were again brilliant pieces of work, built with such skill from rock that had been carried up piece by piece from the bottom, 1000 years ago. It was an amazing view standing in such splendour as we went from one temple to the next enjoying the coolness from within.

On the walk down we saw a sickening sight. A stray dog lay with its paw hacked by a machete. It hung limp and broken as blood pooled where it lay. On lifting its head we noticed more blood. Someone who had just walked these stairs had hacked this dog and left it to suffer until death would end its misery.

'What fuckin thing would do this?' I blurted out.

Turning we left the dog to die and I am sure before we reached the base it was dead. Again the example of only the fittest survive came shining through, which applied to man and beast, with no mercy for the weak.

Back in town I couldn't help noticing all the pigs running around, which I suppose was due to the fact that we were in a Muslim state and naturally pigs were not on the menu.

At 5:30am we got a bus to Una which took four and a half hours. We had a very nice *thali* there and then caught the connecting bus to Diu, which was only a half hour away. Shortly before the end of the journey, water started spurting from the radiator and landed on Karin. It was boiling hot and began to burn her.

'Look,' I shouted at the driver, wagging my finger at the eruption in front of him. He looked at me and laughed, and carried on as though it was all part of the normal routine with bus transport.

'Bloody idiot,' I mumbled really glad to know that Diu was in sight and after that I couldn't give two shits if the bus blew up and took the driver with it.

Diu is a city in Diu District in the Union Territory of Daman and was an old Portuguese enclave. It is famous for the battle of Diu in 1509 when the Portuguese defended the territory from a combined attacking force from Turkey, Egypt, Venice, the Republic of Ragusa (now called Dubrovnik) and the Sultan of Gujarat.

We soon learned that there was really cheap alcohol to be had, at only 16 Rs a bottle. Gujarat was a 'dry state' due to the fact that it is Muslim. Taking advantage we all threw back a few and laughed, so enjoying this old Portuguese paradise with hardly an Indian around to bug the shit out of us.

Hiring bicycles we rode eight kilometres to the beach at Nagoa, which turned out to be a letdown but the exercise did us some good as we sweated the cheap alcohol from our pores. Diu is known for its fishing, and the fishermen were hard at work casting and reeling in the catch that would bring food and money at the same time.

On reaching the old Portuguese Fort we rested amongst the ruins. The fortress was completed by Dom Joao de Castro after the siege of 1545. It had already withstood the siege of Diu in 1538 by the Ottoman Empire and the Sultans in 1537 and 1546. It gave me an odd feeling to be sitting in a prominent vantage point where the seas were guarded from intruders from this very place, knowing that battles had been fought, ships had been wrecked and sunk, and people had died. I thought about southern Africa and how the Portuguese had landed by ship and colonized Mozambique and Angola and how they had buried their dead in these faraway lands, just like Diu. The walls had crumbled but the boundaries were still clearly marked by piles of rock and stretches of wall that had been built like a castle. We watched the sunset over the ocean, a very calm feeling settling over the three of us.

Diu is a Catholic territory due to the Portuguese founders, and St. Paul's church with its pearl white walls stands prominently and well maintained as a Portuguese reminder from its colonial days. Easter is still celebrated, where as just over the river it is a strict Muslim culture almost like another country. It felt as though we were in Portugal, with the quaint architecture, the Portuguese language and the laid back approach that is so evident in Portugal.

Almost down to my last Rupee, I went to exchange money and as luck would have it the English Pound had got stronger which gave me the best rate I had got so far at 46.85 Rs for £1, a sweet deal. As normal the paper work, counting and stamping took an hour to seal the deal. I walked away with a stack of bills tucked away into my money belt that made me feel profoundly rich in such a poor country. Walking down the street I had to remind myself that we were in India and not strolling down a back street in Portugal. It felt like a holiday, free from the pestering and constant hassle, not to mention being bombarded by people on every bus journey and around every turn. Savouring the moment we had a few beers as we reflected on our Indian travels thus far.

Relaxing on the beach which was a little rocky in places we tapped into the sound of waves crashing and then stillness as the water receded. The cycle of crashing and quiet was heaven as we read and wrote in our journals while the sun beat down on us. Bored, the three of us took a walk along the old wall around the city ascending and descending over parts of the wall that had collapsed through age, erosion and battle. The wall was narrow in parts and overgrown in others, but amazing nevertheless that it had withstood the ravages of time, a good 447 years later. On our walk we met an Indian man who to my amazement came from Mozambique, another former Portuguese colony. He was a pleasant man with a trusting smile, grey hair and a matching handle-bar moustache. His house was in the dry moat around the big wall and he seemed very happy to be out of Mozambique that was still trying to rebuild after decades of civil war.

Back at the room we listened to Western music, a nice change from the Indian shrillness, and played cards as we swigged back the beers with much laughter and teasing during each round.

After a clouded sleep we left Diu by motorbike rickshaw for Sasan-Gir. There were five of us and five backpacks in the rickshaw as we headed at top speed to Una, lambasted with every bump. After a long wait in a crowded station we finally boarded a bus and three and a half hours later we got an excellent room at the Lion Safari Lodge with Dave, Karin and I in a room.

At 6:30am we were up and in a jeep that took us into the Gir forest. There were five of us, a guide and a driver and after numerous charges, for entry fee, a camera charge and a kilometre charge we entered the park. In a matter of minutes we saw spotted deer, a few antelope, monkeys swinging from trees, peacock that strolled like royalty through the forest screeching as if they were in pain, and one big turtle that crossed the road with all the time in the world. Unfortunately there was no sign of Asian Lion in this really dry reserve. At 4pm we went out again for a three hour game viewing stint but only saw some spotted deer. This time the guide explained things about the park and nature so much better than the first. We were eight in the jeep with the driver navigating over the bumpy and very dry terrain that had us chocking on dust. There were few waterholes and a forest of dead teak trees, a carpenter's dream, lying like firewood ready for burning. On the drive we saw a jackal and a one and a half metre snake that disappeared as quickly as we saw it.

At 6:30am we again woke from a deep sleep and were bundled into the jeep. After a bumpy and chilly drive we returned to camp having had no luck. I looked at the game wardens and could almost understand why the animals were eluding us. They had no weapons, no radios for contact, no emergency first aid kit, and the jeeps themselves were dilapidated. One of the wheels nearly fell off and the other jeep's transmission packed up. The jeeps were like the park, little to no maintenance had been administered to either.

After a rest we went out again in the afternoon and this time we saw a crocodile and a few more deer. The closest we came to the Asian lions was a fresh kill that had happened only two hours ago. The paw prints were fresh and so was the blood and the bare carcass of a cow. It was boiling hot and Dave and I swam in a fast flowing river that flowed through some concrete drainage. We then tried to act like Tarzan as we swung from long creepers that hung like thick plaited ropes over a dry rocky river bed. While we made idiots of ourselves a monkey sat and watched us with keen interest, looking as though it was seeing if it could learn something from us. While we played a couple of Indians tinkered on the jeep hitting this and that in their efforts to get it working again. As mechanics they looked as out of place as a couple of bushmen in suits. But miraculously they got it started. It was strange to find out that there were many local people; mainly Muslim, who lived in the park with their cattle in small rural dwellings and cultivated land to grow their crops for survival. The cows are easy prey and along with the buffalo become the most hunted by the Asian lion. The locals are not immune from attack and many become statistics as they roam the park.

At 9pm we caught the last bus to Junagadh, one and a half hours of the usual bumpy ride. At the train station we went to the restrooms and funnily enough met the same two young English girls from Gir. They had four beds in their room, and Karin, Dave and I were thinking this would be easy and cost effective to just stay here. The landlady like a prim and proper English woman totally disallowed it.

'No unmarried girls to sleep in same room as unmarried man,' she said allowing the fact that Karin and I were together even though she did not know we were unmarried. So Dave was the one in question. After an hour of bargaining along with an interpreter we decided it was best to move on and find another place.

The three of us caught an auto rickshaw to another hotel which turned out to be too expensive. With our packs we walked in the pitch darkness down lonely desolate streets. Rats scurried across the road in front and behind us. Dogs barked furiously and under the dim light of a street lamp we saw two packs of street dogs squaring up for a fight. They snarled and growled with their teeth exposed ready to rip each other apart. They were completely wild and it scared the shit out of me. We were right next to them and all I could think was, if they attack us we will die of rabies.

'Let's get out of here and find another place. They could attack us at any moment!' I quietly spoke with panic evident in my voice. Karin and Dave both agreed and we walked fast to distance ourselves from this dog fight.

Walking at a brisk pace we bumped into a drunken bum who told us to fuck off. We asked three more people about accommodation, but every place was full. Now we were getting nervous, we had to find a place, any place as now the price did not matter. There was no way we were going to sleep on the street and get chewed on by the dogs. After walking for an hour we finally found accommodation, booking two rooms at the Capital Guesthouse that met our budget, even though that was the least of our worries. It was midnight and we were incredibly relieved to be inside a room with a locked door. Dropping our packs to the floor we laughed and flopped onto the beds totally exhausted.

In the morning we met up with Dave and the English girls at the old fort and then went on to the zoo, where we saw Asian lion and tigers in far better spirits than we had seen in god awful Mysore. Shade was still lacking but more importantly the animals were cared for. Putting our stomachs to the test we all indulged in brilliant chocolate milkshakes. I sipped it savouring the taste with one hand ready on the table to lever me up for a run to the closest bush.

At 5am we surfaced, packed and washed our faces and at 6am we were on the bus set for a nine hour sauna bus ride to Bhuj. We passed an overturned truck with its contents of metal pots and canvas sacks spilled around it along with a couple of squashed dogs to add some horror to the scene. People milled about almost glad to be doing something with their unemployed lives.

The long drives were becoming torturous, what with overcrowded buses, the heat, being rocked around on a thinly padded seat as the driver rode like an out of control lunatic. I felt as though I was back in the army sitting in a Samil 50 troop carrier on a *roofie* (new recruit initiation) ride getting bashed against the metal, holding on for dear life.

I sat in a trance and watched an Indian a few rows ahead of me clear his throat and spit out of the window. The wind took the phlegm and blew it onto my face. I was pissed and I made him know it. The sounds were disgusting as people coughed, spluttered and sneezed all around us.

'These are the kind of sounds that would frighten an animal in the wild,' I commented to Karin and Dave, who nodded sleepily.

Glad to be off the bus our next mission began as we hunted for accommodation, settling on the City Lodge for 70 Rs.

Free to explore, the three of us hit the town and went to a few palaces. One of them had at least 100 stuffed animal heads all from Africa, ranging from impala to a huge African lion. They were the hunting trophies shot by one of the maharajas at the turn of the century when the world's elite would converge on wild Africa and hunt at will. The old black and white photos now discoloured and yellowed of dead animals and serious-faced Indians holding guns had been frozen in time by the click of a camera set on a tripod, capturing the moment for eternity.

The three of us took an auto rickshaw to a village on the outskirts of Bhuj called Bhujodi. It was very rural and I am sure they had never seen foreigners before. They were very friendly and we had a *chai* with them, before hitting the road again. We decided to hitch a lift and in no time we had flagged a truck down. Sitting in the back we headed for Padhar. On arriving we felt as if they were expecting us. They welcomed us like we had never been welcomed before. This was by far the friendliest place we had found on our journey through India thus far. No one could talk any English but that didn't matter as we all communicated through hand signs and expressions with smiles and shaking of the head. It was an unbelievable experience as we shared another *chai* with the man of the house, some women and children. The women and children were dressed in red dresses adding beautiful colour to a backdrop of white painted mud walls of thatched huts.

'This is just like Africa,' I said to Dave as we sat in the coolness of the hut on the ground that had been covered with cow dung now long dried and hardened like wax to keep the dust away.

We couldn't stop laughing as a tame pigeon kept on hovering around the headman landing on his head as if it was a tree. He looked at us without a smile, almost not understanding what could be so funny about this.

Karin sat with the women as they showed her how to roll and bake chapattis along with the clothes that they made by hand as they wove threads through a wooden contraption with pedals that divided threads through a set of wires.

Glad to have had a glimpse of their way of life we waved farewell. While we waited for a lift we heard this awful squealing of distress. Looking around we saw four wild looking dogs, one of which had a piglet hanging from its mouth. Right behind it came a furious sow with another piglet from its litter following close behind. The dog made his getaway and must have feasted on its steal.

'I guess the dog isn't Muslim or Jew,' I mumbled as we were reminded it is a survival of the toughest.

Back in Bhuj we had a mellow day as we strolled through the town and then went for a visit to one of the best museums that I had seen in India. All the exhibits were displayed in an old palace and we found it very interesting.

In the evening we were invited by an Aussie to a local Indian's place for dinner. The four of us converged on his dwelling, a simple concrete house with flaking paint and cracked walls. We entered a small dimly lit room with candles flickering, illuminating pictures of gods that hung like clutter on a wall. Ushered in we were directed to sit on the floor around a feast of food laid out on a white sheet. Like starving beggars we eyed the food waiting for the green light to pig out. While we ate we talked, with conversation touching the sporting world of cricket with respect being heaped on Hanse Cronje's captaincy of the Proteas, to citizenship in Australia, England or Canada. Each one of us was from a foreign country, Dave, Karin and the Aussie's countries had been picked as suitable immigration routes, but South Africa was not on the list. The man asking the questions was married and yet he still asked if there was a woman in one of the three countries who could marry him and give him citizenship. He was the oldest of six brothers and one couldn't help but assume he had a plan in mind with each leading question, whetting his appetite for a world away from his. But inspite of this it was an enjoyable evening with decent people and tasty food. It was as though he had laid out the food as an investment, and he was hoping for a return on it.

At 2pm we left Bhuj for the dreaded 17 hour trip to Jaisalmer, nicknamed 'the golden city,' a town in the state of Rajasthan. The government bus was half empty so we could stretch out with a seat to ourselves. After a good rest we arrived at 6:30am with only five people on the bus. It made me wonder where all the crowds were, and I had to ask myself why no one had wanted to come to Jaisalmer. Was it the Thar Desert and the burning heat that had kept them away? We would soon find out.

For me this was the most exotic city of India, it was like a medieval stage set in the middle of the desert. It was once a very important staging post along a traditional trade route traversed by the camel caravans of Indian and Asian merchants. The strategic route linked India to Central Asia, Egypt, Arabia, Persia, Africa and the West.

The old walled city is dominated by the ancient fort with all its Jain temples. It is like a huge sand castle with a structure of rock-hard sandstone walls built like a fortress with an open view all around. In the sunlight it had a beautiful golden glow about it as the sand reflected a rich colour onto the openness of desert like a lantern in a sea of black. The 800 year old sand castle with its narrow alleyways and curved arches was like a maze as we wound our way through the fort ascending steps and inclines until we reached the top. We booked in to the Paradise Hotel and rejuvenated ourselves with a short nap thanks to the heat that sucked at our energy with no let up.

Excited to see our surroundings again we sat on the terrace and admired the view, staring into a dry heat haze that shimmered and blurred over mud walled houses and burning hot corrugated tin roofs. It cast a reflection into the barren distance like a mirror making me thirsty at the thought of being lost in this sea of nothingness except for this castle that was the lighthouse in the desert.

After a good breakfast of tea, eggs and toast we sat in an embroidery shop as Dave and Karin bargained for three hours for a deal on bed covers and cushion slips in colourful designs with little round mirrors sewn into them. Glad to be moving on after the deal was sealed we booked our camel trip. We each paid our portion, so excited at the thought of being in the wide open desert with a camel as transport, sand as a bed and the stars and moon for light. My eyes soon began to hurt as the dry heat and sand blasted them like a blow torch at temperatures over 40 degrees Celsius and climbing.

Looking for shade we went into a building full of windows covered from all angles, it was called a Havali and meant winds passing through. It felt cool with a nice breeze passing over our bodies. It was such a unique town within this fort, a paradise within a paradise and the people seemed friendly and not out to beg and bug us like we expected. Walking through the narrow cobbled streets we met a Frenchman who we thought was mad. A cow was blocking the alleyway and so he calmly walked up to it and hit it. Well, to his shock it charged him and he had to jump out of the way as we roared with laughter.

The sunset was glorious as we sipped tea watching the sandstone change colour in the dying light as a cloak of coolness settled over us.

Ready for our camel trip we were joined by the mad Frenchman, Bertron, along with Peter from the United States with Dave, Karin and myself making up our group of five, a colourful United Nations. Crammed into an old jeep we drove south west of Jaisalmer, stopping at a few villages before arriving at base camp three dusty and very bumpy hours later. We were now in the middle of the desert, heaped dunes clearly visible in the near distance. The heat rose from the dunes in a haze, like a death threat to anyone who ventured further. Not to be totally prepared both mentally and physically along with water and navigation would have been a suicide mission.

We met a few locals at the camp and took some photos. Bertron suddenly noticed that his hat and a used roll of film were missing. I chased after a group of small boys and shouted: 'Give it back!' They were startled and so was I, as I did not know if they had in fact stolen it at all. Sheepishly one boy with wide sad eyes handed it over much to Bertron's joy. The Indian in charge of our camel trip took him aside and we could see the verbal abuse he got as his finger wagged and his voice rose.

The camp consisted of three mud huts, one of which was used for cooking with solid rounded mud walls with a dome thatched roof and the other two were derelict with hard mud bricks scattered like rubble. I felt as though I was back in rural Africa, expecting to see a few Africans herding goats and living off the land. The huts were surrounded by a mud wall with a small courtyard in the centre where we slept. Gazing into the heavens took me back to my hated army days as I lay in the bush in South West Africa, and also back to Morocco and beautiful memories in the Sahara desert.

My mind raced back to 1988 when I was a Citizen Force soldier in the bush positioned close to Ruacana in South West Africa awaiting an order from Pretoria to attack a Cuban Motorized Brigade that was bearing down on the South West African border. I had laid there in my sleeping bag on the ground absolutely petrified like a stiff corpse in a body bag. My eyes remained locked on the stars in the very silent cold night as if I was staring death in the face. They were my angels radiating hope while the night was the devil with its cloak of death ready to smother us and take some away when and if the ugliness and horrors of war began. The stars are what got me through instilling hope as I prayed for my young life to be spared, like a man on death row.

But in the Thar Desert there was silence and peace as the stars glowed like shiny diamonds twinkling in the blackness. The moon, a shiny silvery ball shone light like a bedside lamp onto the desert. Like a child that needs the light on to scare away the bad people it was encouraging to have light. The stars and the moon mesmerized us into a deep sleep with the ground feeling softer as our eyes became heavy and closed on the most peaceful scene so far.

At 6am we were awake in the morning chill. After a wash at the well which again had my army days rushing back at me as the cold water hit my face with a slap, we were ready to get our camels. Karin's was called Buri and mine was Bagna who was a Great Dane of the camel world. It was weird watching them stand up as they push themselves up arse first which almost throws you over their head. When they raise their front legs you feel as though you have risen above the clouds and just keep rising. Feeling really comfortable we all sat on our camels like statesmen representing their countries, after all we were the United Nations.

Tim Ramsden

It didn't take long before we encountered our first problem. The camel drivers did not have camels and they asked if they could climb on ours. Blatantly we replied no ways, as they had been paid by us, which covered camels for them. So while we rode they walked with long faces, muttering to each other as the sand burned their feet.

After a short journey we stopped at a village of only a few huts like a dot on a map. We met a few locals and had a hot *chai* from a blackened kettle pulled from a fire. Some of the women smiled, covering their faces in embarrassment as Karin clicked off a few shots that caught them off guard making the pictures more natural. These people had never seen cameras or TVs and had no idea that we had flown into India from a world away from theirs.

After a welcome rest we were back on the camels that rose like Citroens except this wasn't romantic Paris, but rather the furnace of the Thar Desert. As a group we got the camels into a gallop leaving our Indian chaperons in the dusty distance. Again we complained about them not wanting to get a camel for themselves so that we could all ride at the same pace, without us waiting for them to catch up. After three hours of riding we came upon a little thatched mud hut in the middle of absolutely fuckall to put it mildly. Glad to be in the coolness with the outside temperature a blistering 45 degrees Celsius, we sat on the sandy earth and waited for lunch to be served. I soon noticed ticks crawling in the earth and then they were crawling over us, which had us constantly brushing them off.

Lunch was great, a chapatti, rice, dahl and a vegetable curry cooked over a small fire. With a full stomach we rested in the hut allowing the midday heat to pass us by without sapping every morsel of strength from us. At 5pm our camels were saddled up and we were off again in far more comfortable and cooler temperatures. To our amazement a sixth camel had arrived on the scene as if it had been dropped like a gift from the heavens. The Indians were riding it two up and smiling like two Cheshire cats.

What a delight it was as we headed into the dunes which became a perfect backdrop for a photo session with our United Nations group sitting proudly on our uncomfortable camels. Our guides became agitated with us as we snapped off pictures, feeling that we were wasting time. We became furious and reminded them that we had paid 700 Rs for the trip and therefore could do as we wished with our time.

At the base of some biggish dunes we stopped and settled in for our second night. A fire sprang to life and we crowded around it for warmth and entertainment like a family around a television set. Sipping on tea and spooning down our curry dinner we were all totally at peace with our lives. Our five Indian guides sang into the night as the fire flickered and the stars twinkled. It was like being at a theatre as the soulful voices moved us and kept us sitting dead still while we revelled in this unique experience of being in the Thar Desert, a place most would never find on a map. Dave pulled out his walkman and recorded the performance, and when they finished we clapped showing our heartfelt appreciation.

When the singing stopped and the fire burned out we got into our sleeping bags and slept on the dunes. The stars were there in their plentiful clusters so close and yet so far away. It didn't take long for sleep to take us away into dreamland. Like being woken from a nightmare we sat bolt upright as a sand storm swept across the desert like a fire over dry grass. The dust particles hit our faces with a force to be reckoned with, and like a soldier ducking for cover we immediately lay down. I felt as though I had swallowed a fair portion of the dune as I ground my teeth through the grit. When it passed we again lay back staring up at the sky and marvelled at the stars. Deeply content at being in the wide open spaces at the mercy of the elements, I felt a sense of joy and accomplishment of making it to the Thar Desert. I had never heard of this place before, and now here I was not far from the Pakistan border with all its radical beliefs. With a smile that only a backpacker knows at seeing a new place for all its worth, a place way off the rich tourist maps, sleep once again enveloped me.

At 6:30 am we rose looking like stiff cardboard cut outs as we stretched our aches and chills away. At the camp fire breakfast was being made. A warm bowl of porridge was thrust into my hands along with a partially burned piece of toast, now dried and covered with a generous helping of jam. Sipping on my tea for warmth we sat in the sand in a line and filled our stomachs, needing all the energy against the heat that was waiting to attack us. I watched one of the camel drivers approach Bagna with a stick that had been sharpened like a spear.

Bagna had a growth the size of a tennis ball on his neck, and to my horror I saw the stick pierce the ball and from it spurted a milky fluid. Surprisingly Bagna didn't even wince or utter a cry as this technique seemed to relieve him.

At 7:30 am we mounted our camels and began a slow but very pleasant ride that continued until 10:00 am when an early lunch was called. We felt it was too early so we left them to prepare the food while we continued to ride. Bertron's camel started uttering some obscene sounds which caused Bagna to bump into Dave's camel and then lunge at Bertron's. Bertron saw what was happening and as my camel was about to topple onto his, he jumped clear. It was quite scary to be so high up and nearly fall onto another camel. Bertron decided to change his camel and then off we went. Our group came across another village where it was obvious that the people had never seen a white face or a camera in their lives. Glad to be on the ground we entered through a gate made of sticks with a wall of dead bush surrounding a cluster of mud huts with neatly thatched roofs. Laying claim to this village we walked in with all the authority in the world, poking our heads into the huts while the locals watched us as if we were aliens from outer space.

With hunger dictating we arrived back for lunch. Sitting under a lonely tree we ate sticky rice in a soup of curry vegetables which was filling and tasty. The heat gnawed at us like a burning rash as we scratched and shoo'ed away flies that buzzed around us annoyingly. Dave couldn't take it any more and seeing a hut close by we ambled over to it. The door was locked which seemed ironical, a hut in the middle of fuckall. There seemed no reason for it to be locked. Dave without hesitation used a little force and the door and the frame broke free from the doorway. It was like an oven inside and yet cooler than the furnace outside. All of a sudden we heard a scary scratching sound and saw a wild cat with pointed ears which I thought to be a Serval. It dropped from the rafters which held the thatch roof up, hit the ground once and sprang up the wall then bolted like lightning through a small hole and back out into the desert. Stunned we all sat down enjoying the cool earth. Then to our amazement another cat with the same pointed ears scared the shit out of us as it also dropped from the rafters onto the ground, and in its panic ran right over Peter and made a bee-line for the door. Peter was in shock and so were we. These were wild hunting cats, twice the size of domestic cats and could quite easily have bitten one of us and left us with not only a nasty bite, but disease in the middle of the Thar desert. After all we were miles and miles away from any medical help.

While I sat I pulled off a few ticks that had crawled over my skin from the camel or the sand we were sitting on. Karin being the only woman was getting hassled by our guides who at times became complete idiots as they stared at her with those kinds of undressing fixated eyes.

At 5:30pm it was time to mount our camels for the last leg back to base camp under a cooler afternoon as the golden ball began to drop down on the horizon. It was like watching a painter brush the last strokes onto his canvas as the sun splashed its splendid colours across the darkening desert, completing a magnificent picture perfect sunset.

The nine one litre water bottles that we had started the trip with were now empty and all that was left was water that had to be boiled over a fire. It tasted smoky with embers of ash and so we all decided that a cup of tea in our metal mugs was the way to go. While I rested my cup of tea in the sand a small dog from the base camp came over to us wagging its tail in a playful mood. The bloody thing knocked over my tea and I nearly lost it as I watched the liquid sink into the sand. All I could do was launch my cup at the dog which resulted in a quick squawk. My thirst gnawed at me as I waited for more water to boil.

There was a small stagnant watering hole that the camels milled around and I thought about my thirst. I asked Karin if I should drink out of it.

'No, it's filthy, you wouldn't do that!' and that was the dare that I needed. In a push-up position I lowered my mouth into the stagnant pool of filth and drank away. While I drank I noticed a couple of dead scorpions floating upside down in the ugly brown water. The dead scorpions and the smell didn't deter me, nor did the camels droppings not to mention what else had gone into this hole. With a full belly I raised myself up and smiled at beating the dare.

I had my tea and then all hell exploded in my stomach. It felt as though it was being cut open from one side to the other with a sharp carving knife. I was wincing in pain and then had to take flight into the dunes as I began losing control. Immediately I felt a fever rack my body as my gut continually felt as though it was about to spill open on the dunes. I popped a couple of Imodium's and hoped like hell that it would sort out one end as I held my stomach as if I had just suffered a barrage of punches to it. And then I began thinking about the scorpions and what had killed them. The parasites were no doubt in my stomach. The pain was absolutely intense and I imagined it was similar but not exactly on a par with a woman giving birth. But with invincibility riding with me I knew I would just have to bite the bullet and shake it off.

It was a long night but with my stomach made of cast iron I arose as if last night was just a nightmarish dream. I was fine and smiled, so glad to be out of that intense pain. After breakfast, and staying well away from the camels' drinking hole we clambered onto the rickety old camel cart that had accompanied us on our trip with all the food supplies. We waved farewell to the harsh desert as the five of us and our packs bounced around until we got to the bus stop.

I didn't believe a bus would ever come. After all we were again in the middle of nothing besides a narrow old cracked tar road and a faded sign with black lettering in an Indian language. To my relief we saw a bus come hurtling towards us with a trail of dust billowing behind it.

Thankfully it stopped but it was full. With no choice we were ushered onto the roof. Like blind people feeling our way through we found a place to sit along with another 30 odd desert people. Hanging onto the luggage rails for dear life we watched the dunes whip by as the driver floored the old bus in total disregard to our safety. We were on our way to Pokaran, which we gathered was two hours away. Anything could happen in two hours on an Indian bus, judging by their driving skills and the accidents we had seen on our travels. With a nervous smile I held thumbs as the lunatic tore down the potholed tarmac. Just when I thought I had seen it all, the ticket collector emerged on the roof and as cool as a cucumber he began writing out tickets and collecting money. He balanced his bum on the side of the baggage carrier and with both hands free pulled out a pen and wrote out a ticket in one hand and collected the money in the other. It was one of the oddest sights I had seen, like a trained seal doing tricks out of water. I could see he had done this many times, the speed and danger meant nothing to him because this was his job and he was bloody good at it.

Relieved to be in Pokaran we had to wait for an hour to catch the next bus for Jodhpur which was another four and half hours of misery. We said our farewells to Bertron and Peter who went their different ways, their travel plans dictating the route they had to take for that next adventure. When the bus arrived the people went crazy, pushing, pulling, elbowing and swearing as Dave, Karin and myself fought against the tide to get a seat. I lost my patience and cracked.

'Fuck them,' I swore. 'We must have a seat. I can't stand for four and a half hours.'

'Survival of the fittest!' I blurted to Karin as I forced my way through the throng of people like a steam roller, my pack a clearing device as I knocked people aside creating the open path I so needed. I got a seat for Karin and seeing how riled up I was she handed it back and chose to stand for an hour, before a seat became available.

At 3:30 we arrived in Jodhpur and checked in at the Ghoomar Tourist Bungalow and for 150Rs for a double we slept three in a room. Dead tired we did absolutely nothing but relax and drink bottles of lemon sodas, the heat and the long journeys having taking their toll. Jodhpur was located on a strategic road linking Delhi to Gujarat where there was a flourishing trade in opium, copper, silk, sandals, date palms and coffee.

There was no rush to get up and so we rose really late and then took a walk to the Mehrangarh Fort located on a sheer rocky hill, with the unkind heat itching at our necks. Seeing how steep the ascent was to the fort we quickly decided an auto rickshaw was the answer. With three of us crammed into the little three wheeler, which looked like an overweight black and yellow bug, the Indian driver grabbed on to the handle bars and steered us away as if it were a motorbike. The two stroke engine over-revved and struggled as he worked the motor with total abuse. As soon as we hit the hill leading up to the fort, which was 125 metres up from ground level, the speed began to slow, and half way up we were at a mere crawl. Without hesitation we all jumped out, much to the pleasure of the driver, and after paying we began a leisurely walk.

There was a water station on the roadside which was run by an old man who looked like a cross between an Indian Father Christmas and Charles Manson. His beard and hair were as white as snow but his eyes were as piercing and devilish as Manson's. His job was to give out fresh cold water ladled from big old clay pots that chilled the water as a fridge would. The fort towered over us with its beautiful design and open arches acting as windows without glass. Unfortunately after seeing the fort in Jaisalmer this was no match, even though it was still amazing with a breathtaking view over the city of Jodhpur. We were now in the old city of Jodhpur in the largest fort in India, with construction beginning in 1459. The walls around the old city stretched for 10 kilometres and encompassed a fascinating maze of cobbled streets that suggested a long history of treasures, adventure and intrigue. The walls are 36 metres high and 21 metres wide with well preserved cannons protruding menacingly from designed openings. It is also known as the 'Majestic Fort' as it stands so proudly above the city, a landmark that can be seen from miles away.

Back at the base of the fort we saw four vultures drinking from a puddle of water. I crept up to them and got within five metres, my camera clicking off a couple of shots. These ugly but useful birds played an important role in India as they cleaned the streets from dead rotting animals, which were in abundance in India.

At 8:30am we got a direct bus to Pushkar. Feeling like royalty the three of us walked onto the packed bus with tickets in hand. I had bought tickets at the office instead of the counter which had saved an agonising wait with at least 50 people ahead of me. The bus was full and so was the roof carrier with people and bicycles packed as tightly as sardines in a can. With a deep sigh we sank into the seats in the best possible position for the five hour journey ahead of us. Pulling my walkman out of my day bag I pushed the head phones into my ears and hit play. The cassette which I had taped back in London held my favourite songs, it was all 2-Tone, with the likes of The Specials, The English Beat, Bad Manners, The Selecter and Madness. Instantly my feet began tapping the floor and my hands began drumming on my legs as the catchy and very fast tune of 'Hands off, she's mine,' reverberated through my eardrums. Nothing could touch me now as I drifted off into the Western world.

Further on into the journey more passengers were herded onto our bus, picked up from their stranded and broken down vehicle in the middle of nowhere. The aisles were now jam packed, but we had seats and comfort, which was a very good and soothing feeling.

Once in Pushkar we walked from the bus stop with the aid of a local who guided us to the Pushkar Hotel. Dead tired we all slept a few hours and then headed out to the Peacock Hotel which we had heard was excellent value and had a swimming pool. Unfortunately it was full so we stayed where we were. There were many tourists in Pushkar and it had this ultra relaxed feel to it as though once again we were free from the clutches of poverty and desperation. We ate a great buffet at the Sarovar Restaurant which included chips, tomatoes, tomato soup, egg plant, curry and dessert. We topped it off with a Bang Lassi which banged me around for hours thanks to the high content of alcohol.

Karin was complaining of a very sore bladder, and so we decided to go to the hospital to have it checked out. The hospital was in a bungalow style and in a state of disrepair. After quite a long wait we saw a doctor who looked at Karin and felt her stomach and then prescribed some tablets for her. Ever since Jodhpur my stomach had also been racked with pain and I put it down to the water. Two weeks ago we had started drinking tap and well water in Bhuj and should have known that parasites lurk in the water. There was no doubt that they were swimming in our guts and inflicting such pain.

From the hospital we walked across a wide open area of rubble and litter, which to me looked like a rubbish dump. Not too far from us I spotted a stray dog that was hunting for scraps and immediately I was on alert with a one litre water bottle clenched in my hand.

To my absolute shock, Karin enticed the dog towards us as she imitated a dog barking with a 'Bow wow wow,' at the top of her lungs. Suddenly the dog came towards us with its eyes fixed like lasers and baring its vicious teeth as it snarled. It was scarred and had lost most of its fur and looked as though it was a walking disease on four legs. Karin shot behind me and I was left to fend off this beast. I was shit scared as it came at me and all I could think of was rabies and a slow death. With quick thinking I yanked my day bag from my shoulder and I hung it in front of the dog like bait and then I lifted my arm with the water bottle and waited for the attack. It grabbed my bag and then I swung. To my great relief it let go and ran before I could connect it.

Tim Ramsden

'Don't ever do that again,' I said to Karin as I reprimanded her like a father would a daughter. 'We could have got rabies!' I carried on. She had got the message the instant she jumped behind me. Walking across the open area it did feel good to have shown Karin that no matter what, I would protect her from any situation.

The more distance we put between ourselves and the rubbish dump the better we felt. Close to the town centre we saw a dead piglet lying on its side with all four legs sticking straight out, looking like a wooden carving that had been knocked over. It lay on the roadside opposite a busy market as people walked by not casting a second glance.

Needing better accommodation we moved to the Bhagwati Guesthouse where Dave got a dorm bed and Karin and I got a room. Hungry we went to Shiva's Restaurant for a dinner buffet. While we stuffed our guts with anything but curry we watched a wedding ceremony coming towards us in full procession. India was full of surprises both good and bad and this was a wonderful surprise as we sat glued to the event as if we were watching a play. To top it we had the best seats in the house as we stared down onto the street from the roof top. Trumpets, drums, clanging cymbals, clapping, singing and dancing marked the joyous occasion. A man walked behind the procession carrying neon lights that were wired to a generator that was being pushed along adding a disco kind of feel. To me it was like seeing the Indian version of a strobe light. The groom was smartly dressed in a suit sitting atop his horse and looking as petrified as if he had just seen a ghost. Either it was his first time on a horse or it was his bride. Being an arranged marriage this would have been the first time he had clapped eyes on her, which explained his pale face and nervous chewing.

At Sarovar Rest we ate lunch in the garden and played with the tortoises that roamed the property at will. Picking them up we placed them on our table and fed them tomatoes and bananas and played with them like real toys. Like a windup car I picked one up and watched its legs clawing and moving forward as fast as it could and expecting it to take off as it hit the surface. But instead it idled forward towards the chopped up food, which it guzzled down.

On May 2 the headlines of the Hindu Times read: 'Premadasa (Prime Minister of Sri Lanka) Assassinated on May Day.' He was killed by a LTTE (Liberation Tigers of Tamil Eelam or also known as the Tamil Tigers) terrorist with a bomb strapped to his body, in Colombo.

'We left at the right time,' I said to Karin as we thought back to our wonderful time on this small island over shadowed by such division and violence, especially in the north. Hindu and Tamil had been at war since 23 July 1983. The Tamil Tigers were a separatist militant organization set on creating an independent Tamil state named Tamil Eelam in the north and east of the island.

Always welcoming the coolness of night we decided to sit on the roof top with Dave's radio complementing the beautiful stillness with a light tune. Below us we stared down on at least 40 homeless Indians as they slept next to a bus. Huddled under shawls they coughed and squirmed in discomfort. The scene couldn't have been more polar opposite, solitude and comfort on the roof top and absolute destitution on ground level.

There was an abundance of pigs and wild boars trotting around and lying in puddles on the roadside. We watched a small piglet trying to mount an adult pig and as the adult tried to break free it held on behind it running on its two raised up legs still firmly latched on. The adult shot under a parked bus and then we heard a smack as the piglet hit its head on the undercarriage finally freeing the adult from some bad omens of incest parenting. We all bent over laughing at the comedy that had just played out before us.

Groggy and tired we rose at 5:30am and clambered into a waiting jeep to Ajmier, a three and a half hour journey away where we would catch another bus to Jaipur. On arriving we waited an hour and then boarded the bus that was filled to capacity. We were told there were no seats and we had to put our bags underneath in the baggage hold.

'No way!' I said. Our rule was never to allow our bags out of our sight, and so we kept them on the bus sitting on them as seats in the aisle. People stared at us as the bus pulled away with a jerk swaying all of us backwards. Soon we became frustrated as the bus drove for 20 minutes and then stopped for 20 minutes, then drove another 20 minutes only to stop again and wait for more passengers. People got on, but hardly anyone got off. Above my left ear I spotted a speaker and out of it screamed a shrill of Hindu music which drilled deep into my bruised eardrum. Now I could understand why most of the older generation were stone deaf. I remained patient until I finally succumbed to the torture.

'Please turn it down,' I asked politely holding back my anger and frustration, and it paid off as they kindly followed through on my request. I was soon rewarded with a deep sleep which got me through the journey.

Once in Jaipur we booked into the Evergreen Guesthouse, dropped our packs and hit the town. We had three things we had to do. Post Karin's package to Canada, which took half the normal time. Then it was the bank for more rupees which I used my Master Card to purchase, saving my traveller cheques for another time. Now we had to see the Palace of the Winds. In an auto taxi we set off to see this pink facade which was nothing too exciting but nevertheless worth seeing.

My stomach has started to feel a little better since leaving Pushkar, with the Western style foods upsetting my hardened gut. We have become very observant on sealed bottles of water and soda drinks. Many of the seals had been broken and refilled with tap water while the merchants charge 10 Rs a bottle making 100% profit. It was easy to spot when one knew it was happening. Many soda bottles had a different cap that didn't correspond to the label on the bottle. I would point it out to a few merchants who acted as though it was normal practice, but it wasn't them. There was also Tiger Balm with turpentine oil, and different items in non corresponding packaging.

I have never seen such cunning moves to sell merchandise as some of these money-grubbing, long fingered businessmen, that given half a chance would steal the shirt off your back and sell it in half a second.

Three up on a scooter we hunted for another bank needing another money change which proved fruitless as the system was down.

Having been in India for three months we were now on our way to Delhi. The bus left at 9am and five and a half hours later we were in the famous city called New Delhi.

We got a room at Indian Deluxe for 100 Rs, very dirty and over-priced but this was an expensive city. 'One night here and then we move,' we said to each other. Walking around the city we bumped into an English couple that we had last seen in Sri Lanka, now many months ago. They helped us out with better accommodation directing us to Navrang Guesthouse which was cheaper and cleaner so we won on both sides of the coin. We began meeting many travellers all with interesting stories. It was so good to see and speak to white faces for a change, without having to explain yourself all the time. Walking along the Main Bazaar Street we noticed many down and out Westerners, either down on their luck, hooked on drugs or simply out of money. One down and out Westerner ambled over to our table. He was slurring and mumbling and had lost his marbles through some good drugs that had rotted his brain. It just seemed so ironic that he was in worse shape than the average local.

Back at the guesthouse I had a terrible sleep with the sticky heat an unbearable itchy discomfort, with the whirl of the fan trying to drown out the clanging of pots as a kitchen cleaned up and closed on another day of business.

I got a surprise from the Post Restante as we collected mail. We had told people to mail letters here many months ago, with our intention of making our way through Delhi at some point. It was great to get some South African news touching on family, politics and sport. We also got our visas for Nepal after handing over 620 Rs for the stamp in our passports.

Along with Martina, a French girl, the three of us got an auto rickshaw to the Lotus Temple which acknowledged the Baha'i Faith. The architecture was amazing all in the shape of flower petals. The inside was furnished with wooden benches on cool spotless marble floors, and the silence was deathly. From the outside it has a strikingly similar look to the Sydney Opera House minus the water and the backdrop of the Sydney Harbour Bridge. After we had enough of the silence we all headed over to the Red Fort with its rich red brick work. Construction of this massive fort began in 1638 and took 10 years to complete within the walled city of Old Delhi. The fort had also been used by the British as a military camp. Significantly the Prime Minister of India raises the flag of India on the ramparts of the Lahori Gate of the fort every year to commemorate Independence Day.

After we had seen enough of the fort we went over to the Jami Masjid mosque, also known as the 'World Reflecting mosque.' It was completed in 1656 and is the largest and best known mosque in India. The courtyard can hold up to 25 000 worshippers. Feeling energetic we climbed 130 steps striped with white marble and red sandstone, not that we paid too much attention as we scaled one of the minarets. Eventually 41 metres up we were presented with a magnificent view over the fort and Old Delhi under heat that could cook an egg. I was drinking water like there was no tomorrow and sweating target rings of salt onto my vest. Delhi for an Indian city was clean in comparison to what we had seen, but the lungfuls of exhaust fumes did little to help the environment as the diesel fumes spewed into the air like dust in a dust storm.

The road on which we were staying was a people watchers' paradise as crowds of both Westerners and Indians ambled by. Many were walking barefoot, dreadlocked, skimpily dressed in Indian outfits and all tanned a healthy brown. No one seemed to care how they looked or how they smelt as many tried to find themselves in this land that couldn't, in my opinion find itself.

While sitting with five other Westerners casually minding our own business and sipping on a delicious *chai*, I watched an old woman beggar who seemed slightly deranged. She walked right up to us and to our shock grabbed the nearest *chai* and proceeded to drink it.

'A little forward,' I said to the group as we watched her enjoy the tea.

I was quite surprised to meet a lot Russians who were here on business rather than travel. They were buying cheap clothing to resell back in their homeland.

Power failures in New Delhi were common and so far the record was three in two hours. The intense heat without a fan wasn't very pleasant and it started to stew our minds with frustration. Generators broke into action and I couldn't decide which was worse, the noise or the heat. Luckily we found a restaurant which to our amazement had air conditioning, and so we sat there and ordered some food. The spelling on the menu had us in hysterics. *Smashed Potatoes, Paincakes, Porched Eggs, Mushed Potato, Enscrambled Eggs, Colldings, Skumbale Eggs, Beard, Sugger, Custarred, Sandwitch, Soap, and Suop.*

We hoped like hell that the food was better tasting than soap and the rest of the outrageous spelling but nevertheless it was painfully funny. More importantly it was a welcome shelter from the niggling heat.

After an early night we rose early and boarded the train for Agra at 7:45. Unbeknown to us we were sitting on the wrong train but thanks to the usual delays we had enough time to get out and board the right one. This was the line where most Westerners were robbed; losing their money belts to long fingered Indians with sharp blades. After all, no traveller can go to India and not see the Taj Mahal. The train was packed and Karin and I sat on the top bunk with one sleeping as the other kept watch.

We were now in the state of Uttar Pradesh, and arriving in Agra was pure *Agra vation,* as touts and throngs of people began circling us like vultures shouting and pestering us for accommodation, and begging for a rupee donation.

'Cheap accommodation,' they shouted holding up a worn and very creased photo of a place to stay. We needed a room so we picked a place and followed the obliging Indian who took us to a basic guesthouse, which was what we needed. We booked in at the Sikander Guesthouse for a measly 50 Rs a night. The room was huge and clean and the bed was comfortable. Bags dropped like dead weights to the floor and with our day bags we locked the door with a heavy key and ventured out in search of the Taj.

With our Lonely Planet in hand we navigated our way to the Taj Mahal, one of the wonders of the world and also one of the most photographed. We walked like two excited school children on an outing, with the excitement mounting with each hurried step. Finally we were at the gate and for a ridiculous 2 Rs each we had our tickets to see the most breathtaking and inspiring sight that India has to offer.

Before us was the most magnificent structure that one could imagine. It felt as though we had stepped out of the Indian filth and into the most pure and beautiful place on earth. It was like a fairy tale palace, beautiful white marble looking as clean as a hospital and built to perfect precision. This stunning piece of architecture was built by the Shah Jahan as a monument in memory of his deceased wife as a gift of his love. It took 20 000 people 22 years to build, starting in 1631 until its completion in 1653. It had us mesmerized like two lovers gazing into each other's eyes. We could not stop staring as it pulled us closer along the path beside a long rectangular pond of water perfectly positioned to offer a spectacular reflection of the Taj. We came to the bench were Princess Diana was photographed. This was the famous photograph that sold millions of copies as her beauty and charming smile graced the covers of magazines and newspaper tabloids all over the world.

It was like a gift from heaven. It had us lost in amazement that something so beautiful could be built without modern machinery, literally cut from heavy slabs of marble to produce a wonder of the world. And we were staring at it, so gob smacked at the overwhelming size and beauty.

We were trapped in the moment and nothing else in life mattered. It was like a powerful omen had fell on us absorbing our being like a magician would an audience. We spent hours taking picture after picture as if this magical sight was about to disappear and we wanted memories to live on forever.

Walking around Agra we came across a man who was selling meat in the filthiest conditions I had yet seen. The chopping block was as dirty as the ground with old caked on blood. His knife was equally dirty and rusted and so was the scale that hung from a makeshift arm that propped it up. The old man sat like a guard over his fly infested meat that had literally been chopped to shreds. Glad to be 'born again' vegetarians we walked on, sickened by the sight, wondering if he would sell any of it and make a living.

The following day we were up early wanting to see the Taj as the sun came up. It was spectacular as we watched the marble change colour as the morning light brought it to life like a candle casting a glow and breaking through the shadows. It was so tranquil to be trapped in the moment with this wonder before our eyes.

On our way to breakfast we met two English girls and a guy from Canada. We were all starving so we headed on to a roof top for some eggs and bacon. It was fantastic to give our stomachs a break from all the rice. Conversation quickly got going as we chatted about India, where we had been and what we still wanted to see. People and food entered the conversation and so did the shits, as no one comes to India without getting chronic dysentery. The experiences were all similar and it felt good to be understood in a land where one struggled daily to keep one's sanity and a clear patient head.

Needing to see the Taj one last time we headed up to the gates. I stopped when I saw a beggar. He was no more than 10 years old and was suffering from enlarged feet that looked as though they were rubber. His feet were so huge and bloated that his toes were sticking out at all angles looking more like stubby disfigured fingers. I thought it had to be some sort of elephantitis and guiltily I walked up to him and gave him a few rupees. It was one of the only times that a human face touched me in a way that I felt I needed to give. After all he was only a poor kid.

The Taj again absorbed us in its tranquil beauty and it was hard to pull ourselves away, back into the real Indian world. As we were walking out Karin saw an amazing photo opportunity. She wanted to take a picture of the Taj through the entrance archway. The only problem was that a million and one Indians were passing through blocking our photographic path. Realizing I had to help Karin I shouted, 'Please get back. Photo!' Karin readied herself for the shot as everyone stepped back. But as always someone had to stick a head into the frame.

'Get back!' I screamed, and as he ducked his head Karin clicked. She captured a photo of the Taj that I have never seen elsewhere, one worthy of the National Geographic. It was like looking through an open window with the Taj Mahal perfectly positioned in the background. This was our farewell salute and from palace to poverty we stepped back into reality as the stench and filth hit us like a welcoming hello.

Torn notes were an ongoing problem in India with many locals and shop keepers refusing to accept them. The bank starts this problem as they allow the notes to be stapled together like pages of a thick book. On being pulled apart a hole is made which gets progressively bigger leading to a tear and then it becomes difficult to get rid of it. Again I shook my head at the logic that starts with clever business men at the top and filters down to uneducated peasants at the bottom. Rich and poor, educated and uneducated, logical and illogical the class steps in Indian society.

After a memorable stay in Agra it was time to get back on the travellers trail. We encountered untold hassles as we tried to book a train ticket to Varanasi. After two trips to the train station which was five kilometres away from the guesthouse, we stood in a queue that curved like an endless snake. Apparently the computers were down and there was no manual backup. We stood there for an hour only to find out that the trains to Varanasi were booked up until the 14th of May which was four days away.

Tim Ramsden

I was as mad as a hatter. An Indian bothered me and I told him to leave me alone. He continued so I had no choice but to tell him what I thought of India in a very rude manner. I felt bad but the chaos was starting to work me over like torture and I was cracking.

'Fuck this; we are going to bus it!' I said to Karin with my face pulled as tight as the gut of a tennis racket.

On a mission we marched to the bus station, totally focused on the journey ahead. First of all we went to the wrong bus station that had me screaming blue murder and four letter words into the air. I didn't give a continental fuck as we had to get going.

Finally we arrived at the right station and got two tickets on the devil with four wheels. How we cursed this method of transport and yet we depended on it and so far it had delivered us to our destination.

Relieved we went back to our room and then went on a long walk behind the Taj, and met a very thin and small middle-aged Indian. He was as bald as a coot and had a long beard which covered his mouth like a creeper growing over a doorway. He was hard at work adding logs to burning fires.

Unbeknown to us we walked into this open courtyard with pillars holding up a roof. There were two fires burning and one smouldering. Then it struck me.

'This is a fuckin burning ghat!' I shouted to Karin who looked as though I had lost my mind. I pointed at the fire and the bones and then we smelt that awful smell of burned flesh. And then on the outside of the building we saw a funeral pyre that had just been lit. This is the crematorium I thought as we surveyed the scene like a detective looking for clues.

Suddenly the same small Indian emerged waving a stick. 'No photos, no photos!' he screamed trying to protect the souls he had incinerated.

When he turned his back I took a photo as if to say fuck you, I can do as I wish. I still shook his hand and posed for a photo with him and a body burning in a shallow hollow. On leaving, the charred smell hung in the air and remained in our nostrils until the diesel pollution cleared it away.

At 9pm we boarded the bus and took our seats right at the back. At 10pm we left. The aisle was packed with boxes, suitcases and people. It was like a market on wheels, packed to the brim with humanity. If they could have squeezed another person on they would have.

Half an hour into the trip there was a huge commotion on the bus. A thief had been spotted hanging on the back of the bus trying to steal a few bags from the roof carrier. This time for some strange reason our bags were on the roof which sent a wave of panic through us. To lose our bags would be one step towards homelessness. This was our walk-in cupboard, our survival pack and our worldly possesions. The thief had untied the ropes and was so close to off-loading a few bags. The woman next to me had spotted the thief and had alerted the driver who brought the bus to a sudden halt. When the vehicle stopped the thief had disappeared with the speed of a lightning bolt.

Our bus made it to Rakpur at 5:30am and after changing buses we set off at 6am for Varanasi. Our packs stayed close like newborn babies to parents. They were not going to be out of our sight. With nowhere to put my pack I had it on the seat next to me.

'You English fool!' a voice shouted out from behind me, with a finger pointing at my pack for occupying a seat. Finally I found a place for my pack and placed it under the conductor's seat.

'Now come and sit on my lap!' I told the fat Hindi lady that had called me a fool. She became as mad as a snake and felt as insulted as if I had spat at her. The man next to her gave up his seat and then turned to me.

'Now I am going to sit on your lap!' he said, to which I burst out laughing and told him where to go. Finally one of the complainers took the open seat next to me. It was a tense bus ride and to make matters worse I noticed that someone had vomited on my backpack, either on purpose or accidentally. Either way it didn't matter but it stunk to high heaven.

At 2:30pm we arrived. It had taken us 16 hours from Agra to Benares now called Varanasi. The first bus was seven and a half hours of pain and suffering and the last was eight and a half. To put it mildly we were fucked mentally and physically. Stumbling out of the bus like two drugged animals we orientated ourselves with our feet firmly on stationary ground. We hailed the first auto rickshaw and got a room at the Sandhya Guesthouse. To shower was like standing under a waterfall as it cascaded over me taking with it all the stress of the last day, which had felt like a week.

In the afternoon we met a Dutch couple. Unfortunately the girl was so sick and weak suffering from the normal vomiting and diarrhoea that India deals to every new traveller wishing to venture through this massive country.

There was adrenalin and excitement pumping through us with the thought of being in this the holy of holiest places for the Hindu religion. Without a second thought we rose early in time to see the sunrise streak across the greenish waters of the Ganges River. It was like watching a tree blossom as the sun rose and brought life to another day with colours as bright and beautiful as a magic carpet. People in boats rowed down the river while others were hard at work thrashing laundry onto rocks. Others washed and played at their different Ghats.

Karin and I got a row boat and we passed masses of people all so absorbed in this holy place as funeral pyres burned thick clouds of black smoke. It was this rite that was the ultimate wish for any Hindu to be burned and have their ashes thrown into the Ganges River. It gave us an eerie feeling as bodies were laid in white cloth on a bed of logs with more logs covering them. There was calm and yet for us it was unsettling as the flame was lit and the cremation began in open daylight.

It was forbidden to take photos here with the dead totally respected almost as if the flash would somehow destroy their soul and give them an unpleasant after life.

We soon learned that some people are not burned. Babies and poor children below 10 years of age are thrown into the Ghats. Also anyone bitten by a snake, small pox victims or a holy person escape the fire and are thrown in. Men are wrapped in a white cloth and women in any colour cloth as they are laid on a pile of logs and then covered with more wood before the burning begins. While it is burning, water from the Ganges is sprinkled over the funeral pyre along with some sand. We managed to sneak a few prohibited photos as the smoke and flames set an eerie tone to an outside crematorium. Walking to the water's edge we saw charred remains being thrown into the water and piles of ash. Right next to it people swam, drank and bathed in this holy water. The ashes could not halt the throngs of people that flocked to this holy site in this the most spiritual city in India.

Taking another rowing boat out on the Ganges we manoeuvred the old small wooden boat to the far side. To our shock we saw a corpse floating face down, an awful sheet white colour and decomposing. A vulture sat on the corpse's back and feasted on the flesh while a wild dog, which had swum five metres from the shore, ripped off chunks eating as it doggy paddled. It was a scene out of a movie, hard to comprehend as nature did its work. As we moved closer, the carrion eaters dispersed leaving us to look at this dead person alone, its flesh falling off like boiled chicken from a bone. On the shore we spotted a skull smiling at us with long teeth and deep hollow eye sockets. It was another sinister moment as we realised the tide was pulling those unburned victims onto this side of the river.

The Ganges was filthy and to our amazement we spotted a dolphin. I had been told there were dolphins here but couldn't believe it. I had never heard of a dolphin living in fresh water. The Ganges River dolphins are on the endangered list, dying off through hunting and toxins dumped into the river. Those that remain are going blind due to the murky and very polluted water.

Back at the room we rested and then ate. In the afternoon we met two English girls and a Canadian and went back to the Ganges for another rowing experience with the sun setting over this magnificent and death-filled site. It was beautifully calm as the sun drew a line down the still water, as it   hung in the darkening sky like a fire-ball losing its heat.

After enjoying the sunset and the rowing we all went out to eat. While we consumed a few beers we played cards and kept talking about India and the experiences we had lived first hand. It always struck me how similar they were even though we had travelled through different parts. It again reminded me of being a conscripted soldier back in my latter teenage years in South Africa. Years after my National Service, I would meet others who had served in different units across the country. The places and the bases were different but the core experience was the same.

One of the English girls was really sick. It was that old Indian sickness of stomach cramps and chronic diarrhoea with vomiting, something we had all been through on many occasions.

I was amazed at how many albinos I had seen in India, somewhere between 100 or more. It seemed odd and out of place like an albino in dark Africa, and I knew there were many there too. They seemed accepted and like Africa their skin fried and reddened into a scabby freckled burn that seemed to make them uglier than they were before the harsh climate burned them and made them look like outcasts.

Turning away from an albino I watched a cow as it casually strolled from an alley and into a house. In the next second it came bolting out, chased by the screams of the house owner, as he protected his food supply.

Further up the road I watched Karin as she snapped off pictures of a buffalo. In the very next instant another buffalo, which was at least 20 metres away charged up to Karin and stopped exactly where the other photographed buffalo was standing. The buffalo twitched its tail and snorted as it stood posing for a picture. It looked like a prime example of jealousy and waited perfectly still for the photo shoot to begin. It was extremely comical, where the animals had become like the people looking for opportunities.

People continued to bug us. 'Buy this or buy that, change money or do you want a ride in a rickshaw?' The torment continued as each person fought for a rupee for that ever important next meal.

I had an argument with a boatman while we were on the Ghats. It was about the amount of time we had paid to rent the boat. Under his breath he muttered something in Hindi with a vile face, which I took as an insult.

'*Marra chute*!' I shouted back to which he retaliated, '*Chello, chello.*' 'Go, go.' He waved his arms as he dismissed me from his sight. Thanks to this our ride along with two Dutch travellers was cut short. Back on land I could only think what a money-grubbing swine he was.

We met Ilya from Canada and Liz from England for breakfast. It was always good to swop stories and gain valuable information to make further travels that much smoother, cheaper, and easier without missing out on an important point of interest.

In the afternoon we went on our fourth boat ride which was just as exciting as the first. The funeral pyres never stopped as body after body burned. I watched those who walked up to the water's edge with a small urn and poured their loved one's ashes into the Ganges. This was the next best thing to being burned on the banks of the Ganges. And then there are those that have come from afar to cleanse their bodies and souls in the muddy and dirty water of the Ganges.

'Very nicey!' I said to Karin as I made reference to Varanasi. I just couldn't get enough of this magical place, famous for its silk, sitars and the afterlife for Hindus. Crazy as it was with bicycle traffic, cows and water buffalos in their hundreds, the burning Ghats, the crowds, the colours, the smells, the noise, the filth, the side stepping of cow shit and yet it was a place that one had to sit back and soak up to fully appreciate. It was like watching a knotted ball of string slowly being unwound as chaos began to harmonize into a setting live with activity.

I have never seen a place like it, nor do I think I ever will. For me it was as if we had made the pilgrimage that so many millions have made to get to this very spot. As a backpacker I felt blessed to have been guided to this city by word of mouth and our Lonely Planet, West Asia on a shoestring.

After three long and hard months in India it was now time to cross the border into Nepal for a change of scenery and some cooler temperatures.

Tim Ramsden

NEPAL (1993)

With thoughts of the snow capped Himalayas in our minds we boarded what we called a 'deluxe' bus direct to Kathmandu, a place I would visit for the catchy name alone. Broken windows, seats hardly fastened down, suspension that was nonexistent, a groaning diesel spluttering engine and to top it off we had to stop for a two hour wheel change. This bus was far worse than the average government bus, but without complaining too much we were on our way to see another country. Two hundred Rupees poorer and an 11 hour numbing journey behind us, we arrived at 8pm at the Nepalese border post.

The journey had come to a temporary end and we were all ordered off and slept for free at the border on the Nepalese side without having our passports stamped. I could feel the colder temperatures and that was a sign in itself that we were out of India.

After a deep sleep in a dormitory style bungalow, we crossed back into India on foot and got our passports stamped. Now we were legitimately leaving India. And then at another desk a Nepalese man swung the stamp down on our passports with authority, allowing us entry into Nepal.

At 8:30am we were on a bus for Kathmandu. Immediately we felt the difference of being over the border. This was like a holiday, there were less people, hardly any noise, it seemed less intense, and the landscape was a lush green with beautiful mountains with a calming cooler temperature. It felt as though this was heaven.

'This is a holiday away from a holiday,' I said to Karin as we soaked up the new surroundings like young children on a school outing. The exchange rate also gave us something to smile about as £1, which seemed to be gaining strength got me 76 Nepalese Rupees.

At 9pm we arrived very weary in Kathmandu. Thirteen hours on the road which was smoother than India but it was still a long day.

We went straight to Freak Street and got a place at the Monumental Guesthouse for 110 Rs. The room had no carpet and later we found out that it had no hot water. I complained twice and was as mad as an antagonised snake ready to strike at anything, but to no avail. In the morning we left and feeling ripped off we paid them 60 Rs instead of the 110 Rs, as a fuck you for no hot water.

Feeling strong for standing up for ourselves we booked in at the Sugat Hotel for 132 Rs. Our room overlooked the market square with a great backdrop of huge mountains that seemed to poke at the clouds and surround us like a fortress wall. It was so peaceful and picturesque, two words that could not be used to describe India.

Excited to be in a new place we took a stroll around the town, darting in and out of stalls, and restaurants for a tea and a snack. Suddenly I had the runs and like a 100 metre sprinter in the Olympic Games I broke all records as I headed to the nearest toilet four times in as many hours. I am sure I broke another record for toilet sitting. I blamed the milky tea and the suspect meal that I had just ingested.

Feeling stronger I decided to sell a bottle of whisky I had bought in India. I managed to get 160 Rs which was much the same price as I had paid, and with the money I bought two knitted Nepalese bags.

It was great to be in Nepal and we met umpteen people we had last seen in India, all so relieved to be enjoying a holiday from the hardest place on earth to backpack through. Or that is what I had been told. Having done it I could now believe it.

Kathmandu held a fascination for us with each turn presenting another noteworthy scene of interest. I thought of it as medieval and rich in history and religion. It was so exciting and we were thrilled to be here.

We went out to Swayambhunath known as the 'Monkey Temple', which is the oldest religious site in Nepal. It is perched on top of the hill and is visible almost anywhere in the valley. The white circular mound forms the base and a golden spire adorned with colourful flags stands above all, as the painted blue eyes watch over the city and every soul in it. The temple is said to be over 2000 years old. We walked amongst ducks and dogs and a few of the holy monkeys that looked at us as if to say, 'you are in the wrong place, this is our temple.' We called it the 'Eye Temple' as the eyes of Buddha looked in all four directions with the word 'unity' in the main Nepali dialect between them. Now we understood why every second Westerner had a T-shirt with Kathmandu and the eyes embroidered in vibrant colours on them. The view of Kathmandu Valley was out of this world, so unspoiled and picturesque with miles and miles of open land untouched by man's greedy hand.

At the temple we met Andy and Kate, an English couple we had first met in Sri Lanka and now here they were again. Catching up on traveller stories, we had a pizza at a small restaurant. It was expensive but more importantly delicious as the Western flavour came flooding back, striking my taste buds like a needle scratching skin.

With full stomachs the four of us got a taxi ride in a car to Freak Street. It was given its name during the 'flower power' hippie years in the late 1960s and 70s. Droves of Westerns lost themselves as they mellowed with drugs and an attitude of peace not war, at a time when the Vietnam War was raging. I sat in the front seat and like a young kid on an outing I took in my surroundings with a broad smile on my face. The last time Karin and myself had been in a car was five months ago in Sri Lanka when we had hitched a lift from Hikkaduwa to Galle.

After an early night we got up early and headed out for breakfast where we bumped into the two English girls we had been on safari with at Sasan-Gir, in our quest to see the elusive Asian lions.

Pissed off we had to move out of our cosy room as it had been booked. Like nomads we wandered over to the C.G. Lodge and for 70 Rs settled for rather a dirty room with no hot water. Power cuts added to the frustrations that were as regular as the chiming of a cuckoo clock, always at the worst possible moment.

Needing to renew our visas for Thailand we went to the Thai Embassy and after waiting all day and spending 600 Rs we were legal to enter back into Thailand on our way out of India. From the embassy we walked to Patan and into Durbar Square which was really quaint with all the market stalls and levelled pagodas. I couldn't believe my eyes as a dead dog lay stinking in the middle of the square with a swarm of flies buzzing around it. As though it was the norm people walked on by, waiting for the next person to move it.

'What a great place,' I said to Karin as I made reference to the Nepalese who we both loved for their friendliness and easy going manner. They are full of smiles, have a wonderful sense of humour and are easy to bargain with, which every backpacker loves. This fact alone allows every traveller a chance to stretch a Rupee to buy another travel day in this paradise, with each day a memorable experience. Most definitely a world away from the day to day routine of sleep, work, eat, television, think more about work and sleep.

For a capital city it was strikingly quiet, easy going and so clean. It was like being back in the West with treats like chocolate cake, pizza, rump steak and potatoes. It was like looking at a mirage. For the last five months every meal that I had eaten was something curried and it involved rice. Holy shit was I sick of this and now I could choose what delicacy I wanted that would rocket my taste buds back to my homeland a million miles away.

Ten of us, all from England except for Karin and me, went to the Cosmopolitan Restaurant. It was brilliant as we sat out in the open on cane chairs with the stars above our heads as we drank beer with no worries in the world. Not even a half hour power cut could dull the great time we were having. I had a delicious pizza with all the toppings and tons of cheese. I looked at it and thought diarrhoea, with the power cut worked into the equation.

'Fuck that, it looks too good,' I said to Karin. My saliva was running like a hound dog and if I was to have the runs in the morning so be it, was my thinking. There was no way I was going to pass up this magnificent Western delicacy. It was a great evening where the talk flowed as fast as the beers with conversation ranging from politics to travel and from laughter to complete awe as the stories rolled off our tongues.

After a short but deep sleep we were up at 6am and on a bus for Nagarkot, with a change at Backtapur. While we were changing buses I was hit with a stomach pain that felt like a knife had been thrust into my gut and turned. Suddenly I could no longer stand upright but had to walk hunched over like a man three times my age. It was excruciatingly painful and yet I walked up a hill, with the gradient helping my bent-over back while we hunted on for some kind of chemist. I couldn't believe my eyes when we actually walked past a shop that was selling pills and Pepto Bismal. I had two hours to get myself back to normal before our bus left from this very rural place.

I threw back the pills I was given and downed half the bottle of Pepto Bismal and then my stomach erupted like Mount Souevious. Thank God for a hut close by. I hurried like a crippled man holding my gut and squatted behind it. I emerged as if a miracle had been performed standing as straight as a ruler. The pills and Pepto had definitely cleared the pain and rid me of the bug. We were back on the bus for a few kilometres and then we stopped for a *chai* and a snack. We started hitch hiking and caught two trucks that took us to the top of the mountain. Suddenly we had the most spectacular view in the world of the snow capped Himalayas that stretched before our eyes as if a magician had waved his magic wand opening an invisible curtain. We sat and gazed totally absorbed in the moment like two drugged- out teens staring into oblivion with Cheshire cat smiles.

'Isn't that Mount Everest over there?' I said to Karin with my finger pointing to the most famous peak in the world. This was where many men and women had conquered the summit and also where many more had died in vain as the wind, altitude and fatigue had swept them away forever. Edmund Hillary, a 33 year old climber from New Zealand and his Sherpa mountaineer Tenzing Norgay from Nepal scaled the summit and on 29 May 1953 they became the first known people to stand on top of Mount Everest. Sir Edmund Hillary like Neil Armstrong was the very first person to ever set his foot where no man had been. It was Queen Elizabeth's II coronation and word through telegraph quickly reached Buckingham Palace adding further glory to a proud day in the British Empire. A young man from the British Empire was an overnight hero having conquered the unconquerable.

Suddenly I was as right as rain sitting dead quiet enjoying one of the most peaceful and tranquil moments in my life as I thought about Hillary standing on top of the world.

While we were on the bus back to our room the heavens opened and a deluge hit the roof like a rolling drum beat. Thunder and bolts of lightning shattered the calm as flashes lit up the purple black sky. It was like sitting in a movie as we watched the zigzags of lightning splinter the skyline and then in a flash disappear. After all it was the rainy season and we had somehow picked the worst season to visit Nepal.

Safely back in our room and a little wet, we reminisced over the day. We could actually boast that we had in fact seen the Himalayas and Mount Everest.

While I jotted the day's events into my diary and Karin was writing in hers, within a five minute time frame Karin had said something at the exact time that I had been writing it. It was weird and uncanny as I thought about how many other times we had thought and spoken aloud at exactly the same moment. Having been together for so long we were now thinking the same.

At 7am we got a bus for Pokhara and just to remind us that we were still in Asia, the driver drove like a bat out of hell. To make matters worse he navigated winding roads that with one mistake would give us a one way free flight into the Bagmati River for a cold swim. Over bumps and dips my bruised arse must have left the seat at least 15 times with my head barely missing the roof each time. He covered the distance in six hours, which in my book was close to a record. Thankfully we climbed out of the bus with our legs feeling like jelly, and my mind a mental mess. I thought the Indian drivers were reckless but this Nepalese man certainly took the cake. I wanted to give him a piece of my mind, but what good would that do, I said to myself. Hitting the ground in an awkward way I steadied myself against the bus and walked through a crowd all thrusting lodging cards into our hands. An orchestra of shouting erupted as each sign holder fought for our business all to gain our precious Rupees. Eventually four of us got a taxi to the lake. For 100Rs we got a room at the Butterfly Lodge, with a nice garden to relax in, and more importantly a hot shower. There were many makeshift stalls that sold clothes and handmade items, wallets, belts and bags just to name a few of the commodities. Food stalls were in abundance all filled with friendly chatter and the luring smell of tasty food. The locals seemed friendly and it was as though we had finally set foot in paradise. A huge muddy lake with the greenest of grass surrounding it was positioned in front of the snow capped Himalayas in the distance, as bait to any avid photographer. The air was fresh and the temperature cool, and there was no pollution. Sucking in lungfuls of clean air was therapeutic and it felt as though we were on a natural spa treatment program to clear the toxins from our bodies. It was heaven and I couldn't cut the magnetic pull that the Himalayas had on me.

Karin and I had decided to do a trail and so we caught a bus at an early hour with morning waking the sleeping town. We rubbed our hands to keep warm as we sat on the bus that would drop us at the start of the trail. The drive was scenic as we passed rice fields terraced into the slopes with trees and grass as green as an Irish shamrock. Water flowed through the valley chilled like wine as the fresh morning cold hung in the air like a misty blanket with a powder blue sky above. It was a picture postcard and we so wanted to stop the driver and aim our cameras to capture the moment.

After an early breakfast we set out on our short trek with our decision made due to time and weather conditions. After all, we had timed our travel through Nepal at the worst possible time, it was the rainy season. A trekking permit was also 1000Rs which was quite steep for us. We began walking around the lake with our day bags slung over our shoulders like two teenagers walking to school. Nepalese women dressed in red walked past, forcing a smile as they followed a meandering stone path. They were bent over and had a mound of dried grass balancing on their heads while others lugged bundles of dry wood fastened to their backs, that one could see were extremely heavy.

With map in hand we looked for the Sarankot turn off but thanks to some poor navigation on my behalf we hit a jungle. Trekking through some thick bush we followed an old overgrown path that lifted our spirits somewhat. The two of us were suffering severe bouts of diarrhoea which certainly didn't help with the climb. After an hour's walk with constant side swipes of branches we amazingly enough stumbled over some steps that were the correct path that we needed to be on. Taking a well needed rest we absorbed the magnificent view literally soaking it in like a sponge. It was breathtaking looking over the valley with the lake sprawled below the green carpeted mountains, with rice paddies terraced into the slopes like pieces of a jigsaw puzzle. Thatched houses far below marked their plots of fertile land with a few trees, standing like markers offering shade with a meandering sea of green as far as the eye could see.

Rejuvenated we climbed another hour and then to our relief we found ourselves at Sarankot, 1600 metres above Pokhara. After catching our breath we celebrated with a chilled bottle of soda in our hands. The heat was now sweltering and we looked forward to the evening chill that would soon caress our skin. Needing a *chai* to perk up our spirits we sat with our eyes glued on the Himalayas like two children gawking at their toys. The snow- capped peaks looked so close and yet they were many days walk away. How many people had climbed these mountains and how many had died as they tried in vain to conquer the almost impossible. I looked on with awe at the courage people must have to even contemplate challenging nature on these terms at an altitude where man seems an outsider with odds that are heavily stacked against him.

Back on our feet we set off on a flat walk to Naudanda, with the ascent well behind us. It was a pleasant walk along a path on the edge of the mountains with the scenery jumping out at us like frames from a 3D movie. We were immersed in it almost floating in awe as the scenery washed over us like a soothing massage. Locals were hard at work in their corn fields and rice paddies as they waded through mud. Porters rushed past us as if they were rushing to beat a timed cut off, carrying huge loads of camping gear having returned from the mountains.

'*Namaste!*' we greeted them with a hello and goodbye as they shot by. Needing a rest we stopped at one of the many *chai* stops and ordered two teas to wet our dry throats and cool our bodies from the fierce afternoon heat.

'Where do you come from?' a Nepalese man asked me as he stooped over the well used tea cups and proceeded to pour boiling water from a blackened and dented metal tea pot through a sieve. He frowned as he looked up at me.

'South Africa is where I come from,' I replied knowing quite well that he did not know where in the world South Africa was other than a far off place somewhere in Africa.

'Where in Africa?' he replied, just as I had suspected. No one seems to know that South Africa is a country and not just a place South of Africa. Someone in the stall amazed me when he blurted out, 'Nelson Mandela.' To me it felt as though there were a few people in the world that were actually following world politics, especially politics close to my heart. And here was a man in one of the poorest countries in the world who in my mind had put many educated people to shame, for example

Tim Ramsden

I had met many Americans that knew little to nothing about South Africa. They did not even know that their government had pumped in millions of dollars to help South Africa eradicate communism on the South West African/Angolan border to fight the communist threat of Cuban, East German and Soviet involvement inside Angola.

Forcing ourselves to march onwards we finally reached Naudanda, which was three and a half hours from our starting point in Sarankot. Having been in the army I was used to the many *opfoks* that came our way. This time I had volunteered myself for a three and a half hour *opfok* which was weird and yet so rewarding. We got an excellent room at Chandra Lodge for a price of 20 Rs which became the cheapest place I had ever stayed in my three years of backpacking travel, which in British currency worked out to be 13 pence. For once in my life I honestly felt I was ripping off the man running the lodge. The view alone was worth $200 by North American standards and here I was forking out a big 13 pence. As a backpacker one takes it with a smile knowing full well that each cent counts for another day on the road and this alone had bought me a week at the very least.

The room had a magnificent window that offered a view to die for, a comfortable bed and to top it off it was surprisingly clean.

Really tired we had an early dinner of mashed potato and deep fried samosa's, and then hit the soft mattress for a deep sleep.

Like old timers going to sleep early we were early risers wanting to see the Himalayas as the sun rose. It was a little hazy but the mountain range was clearly visible as it broke through the haze like an open mouth of white smiling teeth. They protruded through the clouds and dwarfed everything else.

'Look at the colour contrast,' I said to Karin as we compared the green mountainside to the powder white of the Himalayas and the sky, an ocean blue which appeared through the white fluffy clouds like a window being opened. It was as if a flag with green, white and blue was waving all around us with each colour at its very sharpest.

Eventually we tired from the splendour and we started feeling hungry. With a hot mug of coffee to die for and a plate of food we concentrated on our meal with that thrill of where it was taking place. It was like climbing inside a photo page in the National Geographic.

At 2pm we left Naudanda and followed the road to Suliket, and then like a bad dream the rain came down and lashed at us as if to drive us off the mountain. Thankfully we had hired a couple of ponchos and hurriedly we covered ourselves as they flapped like torn sails.

We found a short cut used by the locals and followed it cautiously over a rocky, muddy and very slippery path. Naturally I had to be different and was walking in flip flops which made it harder, but I enjoyed the challenge. After all I had hiked up the mountain like this.

We passed a makeshift station which looked as though it had been thrown together with pieces of tin, wood, thatch and canvas. Rocks acted like weights to hold the tin roof down. It was used as a supply centre to ferry goods up the mountain. Mules loaded with supplies stood in a daze as Sherpa's added weight to their already buckling backs. Had we chosen a longer trail this is the service we would have needed.

With only a few minutes to spare we arrived with the bus idling and ready to take off. Glad to be out of the rain we whipped off our ponchos and dropped into a double seat, ready for the half hour drive to Pokhara. The bus dropped us outside the town, and along with two New Zealand girls we caught a taxi to the lake. As we arrived the skies opened like a sluice gate and a humungous storm erupted. Thunder and lightning hit out as if the forces of nature were at war, set on turning everything upside down. The rain lashed at us like an angry slave master as we ran for shelter to the closest little stall. Diving through a crack in the canvas we looked like two drowned rats. Glad to be under cover we stared at the Nepalese woman shop keeper, and she smiled back motioning a hand towards the coffee. Cold and shaking we nodded our heads and accepted two mugs of steaming coffee. As she passed them over to us another contagious smile was directed our way. The rain beat at the canvas for an hour as if it was determined to drive us out and drench us. Once it let up we went to the Butterfly Lodge and picked up our backpacks that had been locked in a storage area. We paid 200Rs and got an excellent room with a hot shower and a Western toilet, no hole in the ground this time. We were doing it in style and were also rewarded with a spectacular view of the mountains.

Hungry, we went to the Bamboo restaurant and ordered a large cheese and tomato pizza which Karin couldn't finish, nearly vomiting in the process.

An early sleep and an early rise we went down to the lake and watched the mist rise off the lake like smoke. With cameras in hand we took photographs of the mountain and the scenery that were postcard material.

Seeing a rowing boat we hurriedly tried to agree on a price with haste as we were after that elusive photograph, like a journalist after a good story. When the boatman told us that he had to fetch his oars we discarded the idea as we knew the clouds would have enveloped the mountain and the haze would have destroyed the shot while we waited. A great pity as this is why we had got up early. He arrived five minutes later and the price had doubled.

'You stupid idiot,' I shouted angry that he had lied and wasted our time.

Off we went to the next boat looking for the first price that was quoted. Exactly the same thing happened, the price had doubled.

I lost my cool and kicked water at the boatman and then threw a carton of water at him. Wet and angry he came at me like an antagonised bull. Thankfully he backed down as I was getting ready to run.

'You are bullshitting us!' I cursed, feeling I could now go on the attack.

'This wouldn't happen in India. Once a price is agreed upon things go ahead!' I added, disgusted at their greed.

Finally we ended up taking a five minute boat ride for 20 Rs to a small island in the middle of the lake but by now it was too late to get that picture.

Needing some more Rupees I changed £20 on the black market and got 77 Rs to £1, a slightly better rate than a bank would give along with service charges.

With a need for fresh air and scenery we took a stroll to the lake and got an excellent view of the mountains. It was like the crest of a wave glistening white in the sunlight with the lake in the foreground.

We had to hand in our ponchos which we had hired for two days, but when it was time to pay suddenly we were ordered to pay for three days.

'No ways!' I told him with my face contorted with rage at reneging on a deal.

I handed over 28 Rs, the agreed amount for the two days. He picked it up and threw it back at me, at which I turned and left it to blow away.

To my shock I saw the man at our lodge complaining to the landlord at what had happened. The landlord was a great person and took no sides. I explained the meaning of principle, but he didn't want to understand. Karin went berserk and said her part and then stormed away. It was the first time I had seen her so angry with someone other than me, and it felt good to watch.

I explained the principle of the story once again, and then added, 'Sorry. A deal is a deal,' and turned away leaving the poncho man to stand there with a sign of defeat on his face.

'They have to learn. They just can't rip us off because we are Westerns! A deal is a deal. Once agreed upon it cannot be altered unless agreed on by both parties.' I said to Karin on meeting up with her back at the room. It was our worst day in Nepal and we were glad to be leaving Pokhara for Kathmandu the next day.

After paying 130 Rs we were on yet another 'deluxe' bus which turned out to be less bumpy and a smoother ride. On the way we met a traveller from Zimbabwe who had also been away travelling for the past 3 years, but on a Zimbabwean passport. In China he was nearly arrested as the officials at the border post did not believe such a country existed in the world.

Glad to be back in Kathmandu we got a room at the Anapurna Lodge for 150 Rs, which was really comfortable and with a hot shower it was worth every penny.

The food in Nepal had been a culture shock to my stomach and I had paid the price having had stomach pains for the last two weeks. It didn't help that I was eating cheese rolls, apple crumble and thick gooey cheese pizzas. I felt like a drug addict, hooked on Western food and I did not care what the repercussions would be. I needed a change from curry and rice every day, breakfast, lunch and dinner.

Wandering around the town we bumped into Martina, the French girl we had last seen in Delhi and Agra over three weeks ago. The backpacking world was certainly small as travellers seemed to follow a path that led to a central point where fellow backpackers had been or were about to converge. We spoke about India and had a good laugh about past experiences in this mind altering land.

After dinner we went to the Snowman which was the best cake and pastry shop in town. Our mouths were watering as we looked at the apple crumble, pies, chocolate brownies, and other delicacies from the Western world. My fix was an apple crumble and it tasted brilliant.

To kill time we looked for an embroiderer and found a tailoring shop where we placed an order for a few shirts with the name Kathmandu and the eyes embroidered into the T-shirts. We left him 85 Rs as a deposit.

Karin and I passed by the shop the next day and to our disbelief we realized he had made a total mess of the shirts.

'Karin he has just cocked up the shirts!' I complained as I looked at the poor job that this man had done.

There was argument and real annoyance on our part for his wasting our time as we needed the shirts because we were leaving the following day. Standing my ground he handed us our 85 Rs deposit back. And then we went to Thamel and hung around waiting for our bus that would go via Karakavita before it made its way to Darjeeling back in India. With some time on our hands we found an embroidery shop that completed three shirts in as many hours. We just couldn't believe our luck and the most amazing job they did.

Feeling like lottery winners we rushed back to our lodge, grabbed a bag of cheese rolls for the journey and then went to the agency to wait for our bus.

Our bags weighed a ton and it wasn't the cheese rolls. The odd souvenir, extra clothes, at least a dozen rolls of film and some warm clothes made my bag feel as though I was carrying a house on my back.

The Nepalese man at the agency told us that we had to walk three kilometres to get on the bus.

I went mad and wanted to strangle the man as no mention was made when we paid 475 Rs for our tickets.

'Fuckin typical!' I voiced my anger to Karin.

'You lied to us!' I turned on the man in my anger. To my shock he paid for a taxi and we arrived at the bus ready to face the next problem.

Then to my disbelief we were told we did not have the seats we had booked with the agency. Our seat allocations had been changed by the bus company.

Lengthly arguments ensued while we sat firm like stubborn protesters standing up for principle.

'Once again we have been bullshited!' I said to Karin fuming at being fucked around as if we were just two pieces of extra baggage.

It felt good when the bus started and began to roll forward to begin our 16 hour journey to Karakavita, on the border with Nepal.

The roads were dreadful and I heard heads hitting the roof as the bumps catapulted people from their seats. I smiled to myself and looked over to Karin, the reason why we wanted the front seats now very obvious.

At 830am we arrived at the border crossing, ate a free breakfast and then got our departure stamp from Nepal, confirmation that we had checked another country off the travel list.

Nepal had been a great trip but it was time to get through India *en route* to Thailand.

BACK INTO INDIA

TAXIS, TRAMS, HUMAN RICKSHAWS AND THE DREADED BUS THROUGH WEST BENGAL

We crossed over the border on foot. It felt like ages since we had last been in India. Along with two Australians, two Scots and the two of us we hailed an Ambassador taxi and headed to Siliguri, which amazingly enough was included in our bus ticket.

The drive was spectacular as we wound our way up mountain roads through curtains of mist and wet roads until we finally stopped at Darjeeling. We were now in the heart of the tea plantations at an altitude of 2134 metres and it felt as damp and dreary as London.

It was late afternoon when we booked a room at the Samrat Lodge for 100 Rs along with a 10 percent government charge which we thought was another scam to get more money. The room was dark and dripping in dampness and was as cold and depressing as climbing into a fridge to sleep. The shower consisted of two buckets of hot water which we had to tip over ourselves. The uplifting factor was the tea, the famous Darjeeling tea which warmed us up and brought a smile to our faces with this new experience unfolding around us.

Needing to see our surroundings we took a short walk around the cool and very damp town. It reminded me of being back in my home town of Hillcrest with the cool nights and thick blankets of mist, a blessing from the sweltering days. In India again it was back to spicy food and we filled ourselves up before entering our damp room for an early night's sleep after a long day on the road. It was always the most amazing feeling to have been in two so vastly different places, and countries for that matter, in the course of one day. This was travel on the backpacker's clock.

'A person could be blindfolded and led over the border from Nepal into India and they would know which country they were in purely by smell!' I said to Karin.

'And I don't mean the food!' I added.

The putrid Indian smells of filth had come back with a vengeance. The holiday break in Nepal was over. We smiled, welcoming the adventure to come.

After a deep and chilly sleep with water running off the walls and mould growing in the corners we were up and ready to walk the town in the glorious morning light. Our eyes took in the scene with mountains all around us and mist that hung like a cloud in the valley obscuring all visibility. We overlooked the corrugated iron rooftops with peeling paint and through the tall trees into the wall of white. After staring for a while we wandered over to the market where we bought a small wooden chess set, and over a cup of tea Karin taught me chess and thrashed me in the process. The second game I managed to win, I think more through fluke than anything else.

With hunger dictating we stumbled across an old British restaurant. Well worn wooden floors welcomed us into the dark room. Wooden chairs where many a colonist had sat lined the walls, brass tea pots and jugs stood on a silver tray on a colonial table, and faded black and white photographs hung on the walls as they had over half a century ago, depicting a bygone era. It was strange but so rewarding to be in an old part of the mighty British Empire, and I felt proud that my Dad had been born British.

Walking around we were shocked at all the graffiti we saw. We always came across the words Gorkha-Land and soon realised that these people wanted to break away from India and become an independent state.

Darjeeling back in the 1800s had belonged to Nepal and used to be known as Dorge Ling, known as the 'Place of the Thunderbolts.'

It all made sense to me now as the people certainly looked more Nepalese than Indian, but the pollution and stink was Indian and the beautiful tranquil setting was every bit Nepal.

Tim Ramsden

Wanting to see a tea estate we went down to the Happy Valley estate and walked into the tea plantations. Women were hard at work picking the tea leaves and then throwing them over their shoulders into a woven basket which was held firmly against their backs by a padded strap across their foreheads. They performed their monotonous jobs as if they were working a line on a conveyor belt. As they filled and refilled we laughed and joked with them which brought a shy smile to their weathered faces. Somewhere on the journey I had bought a box of cigarettes, waiting for the right time to hand them out. I knew the opportunity had presented itself and Karin and I began handing out the cigarettes which were accepted gratefully in exchange for warm and very shy smiles, and like photographers on a National Geographic exercise we snapped off frames that spoke volumes.

The woman looked exactly like the Nepalese. There was no doubt their roots were from Nepal and yet they were Indian from the standpoint of the boundaries.

We were then taken for a 10 minute tour of the tea factory. It was over 100 years old and looked every bit its age with old machinery held together with anything they could find to keep it going. The manual practice of sorting the leaves which the British had introduced all those years ago was still in force. We had been into a tea factory in Nuwara Eliya in Sri Lanka, but in spite of it being old it was well kept and extremely well run. One couldn't say the same for Darjeeling, but it was worth the visit and the tea tasted great.

Having heard about a small train with a steam engine and carriages in tow called the 'toy train,' we sought it out hoping for some good views. It rode along the road side puffing clouds of smoke as someone furiously fed coal into the furnace to produce the steam needed to drive it up the steep winding tracks. On the ascent the little engine pushed the carriages up like a work horse. The beautiful journey took us along at a snail's pace and presented us with the most spectacular views. Forty five minutes later we arrived at Ghoom, walked around a bit and had a *chai*. Painted in thick green paint on many walls I noticed the words: 'We want Gorkha Land,' wanting so badly to break away from India and rule as a country called Gorkha Land.

We decided to walk back and covered the eight kilometres with plenty of sweating and cursing for not taking the train back. Arriving back in Darjeeling we had a quick curry and then a nap from the tiresome walk.

'Isn't travelling a difficult job?' I said to Karin as I closed my eyes.

It was 2 June and it was my birthday, so we headed off to the Flamingo Restaurant and Bar. Unbeknown to me Karin had arranged to have a cake made for the occasion which was short lived as Nema, the barman blurted it out as I returned to the table from the toilet. It was an enjoyable evening as we had a few wines to toast my 28 years on the planet. We had a craving for French fries and were presented with a mountain of fries overflowing the plate. Along with a bottle of tomato sauce we got stuck in immediately. With our craving satisfied we followed it with chocolate cake and rich coffee in proper European style. Karin gave me a nice address book and an embroidered T-shirt with 'Canada' and a Maple leaf worked into it which she had had done back in Nepal. It was a very special time together feeling like we were living normal lives again, well away from the struggles and hardships of backpack travel. I had been on the road for over 10 months staying no longer than a week at the most in one place, and the strains of travel had begun to show in frustration and short tempers. This birthday was like a ray of sunshine after weeks of gloomy skies. As wonderful as travel is with adventure beckoning every day, one just needs to stop and literally smell the roses and be in the moment.

Wanting to get to Siliguri, we tried to organize a bus which turned into a nightmare of frustration. Stand here, no stand there, in typical army fashon. Taxi drivers beckoned as they pointed to their taxis which looked so inviting but expensive. Eventually Karin decided to get an express bus ticket. She ran off leaving me to stand guard over the overweight packs with the zippers ready to explode. For 40 Rs we had two tickets and now it became an Easter egg hunt for the correct bus. Relieved we found the bus after some time with our packs weighing us down and pissing us off as people bumped into us, throwing us off balance.

There was a cane basket on the bus' roof filled with about 30 live chickens. I watched with interest as it was lowered off the side with a lot of loud squawking, and then two metres from the ground it was dropped. It hit the ground with a thud and then dead silence.

'Look at that for animal cruelty!' I said to Karin knowing in the Western world what an outcry this would raise among animal rights activists.

Three more baskets hit the ground and I was sure some must have broken their necks. It was off to market for them and into the curry pot. I knew people didn't understand animal cruelty, after all how could they, in a society where humans are also treated without dignity especially those trying to live below the poverty line.

I kept on thinking of Calcutta and the end of our overland journey through India.

'I can't wait. These buses have sucked the life out of me!' I said to Karin needing the end to come quickly.

The journey was hair raising with the driver gunning down the narrow winding mountain roads. The speed, the rain, the thick mist and the fact that it was our last trip on an Indian bus made it even more nerve racking. One mistake and it was a sheer drop into the valley. My hands dug into the worn leather as my foot tried to brake. I was sweating as I thought how many people had died so close to home near the end of an excursion just as they thought they had arrived safely.

Suddenly we passed a sign that read: 'Keep your nerves round the curve.' Show that to the fucken driver I thought, but I was hoping for a sign that read, 'slow to a crawl.'

I was shitting myself and closed my eyes, bracing for what lay ahead.

'Look over there!' Karin exclaimed. I half expected to see something terrible like a sheer drop or an impossible turn. Instead we saw the snow capped Himalayas.

Before leaving Darjeeling I had commented to Karin that in five days we had not seen the Himalayas once. The mist had parted like a window being opened and we saw the snow capped peak for a brief few seconds. As quickly as the window opened it was shut again as a thick wall of mist hid it like a treasured secret. It was as if the Himalayas were saying *sayonara* to us.

At 4pm we arrived at Siliguri and got a room at the Patna Guesthouse for 70 Rs. Our destination was Calcutta and after paying 150 Rs we had a ticket for our very last bus trip in India.

On arriving in Siliguri the traffic, noise and pollution hit us like punishment, but I think it was to get us ready for Calcutta. We relaxed and wasted the day waiting for our bus that was scheduled to leave at 8pm. I read JFK for most of the day, a President I have been fascinated with my whole life. His assassination a mystery, leaving the assumption that there was a plot to prevent him from leading the American superpower. He had come close to starting World War III with Nikita Khrushchev due to his unrelenting determination to stand firm against the Soviets. In my opinion this is why he was assassinated.

On the bus we had excellent seats with more leg room than we could have hoped for. The trip started off well with a smooth road, not too many stops and a thunderstorm in the distance. Suddenly rain began pelting down like no tomorrow.

The bus came to a stop at a railway crossing and I half expected the bus to be across the tracks. For half an hour we waited as the rain poured down the windows and then we heard and saw the train hurtle by. It was a delayed reaction compared to the Western world. Suddenly the traffic started moving as if everyone had woken from a trance causing a minor traffic jam that we had to laugh at. One could not experience traffic anywhere that was more disorganized than the system and driving ability in India. The oncoming lane of traffic had a two kilometre line of trucks and buses still waiting for the barrier to be lifted. I suppose when in India it is better to be half an hour late and safe rather than sorry and dead.

The trip went well until 5am when the driver went crazy on the hooter boring a hole into my brain with each sharp hoot. The bus was crawling forward through some traffic and he was using it unnecessarily, like a blind man feeling his way forward with a cane. It was bringing my anger and frustration to dangerous levels.

Back on the open road he floored it, and now wide awake I was watching this idiot. He started overtaking another bus at 100 km/hour and then we were neck and neck and the bus being overtaken was not going to let us in. Both buses began hooting madly and to my horror I saw a truck rapidly approaching us.

'What's this fuckin arsehole doing now?' I shouted to Karin.

'This shit for brains is going to kill us!'

My hands were sweating as I thought back to all the accidents we had just passed. There had been five, burning trucks, head on collisions, a bus in a ditch and some mangled wrecks.

Could that be us I wondered as we braked and skidded and got thrown around in our seats. The driver ducked in behind the unrelenting bus again as the truck slowed slightly and then sped by.

Without thinking I jumped up and ran up to the driver swearing my head off at him. I thought I would have the support of the bus but everyone looked at me as though I had overreacted and that he had had our lives in control all the time. I turned back to the driver and carried on.

It wasn't clever because he turned around, and with no eyes on the road rattled off in Hindi which sounded like machine gun fire.

With my face as vile as I could make it I pointed to the road and shouted for him to turn around. Eventually he did and I walked back to my seat with my hands even more sweaty and clammy.

'Come on Calcutta,' I mumbled as I sat down. I felt I was losing it.

Finally at 10am we rolled into Calcutta, a miserable 14 hours later. For five hours the hooting had gone on and I was slightly deaf and beyond mad. I felt like a tortured soul, numb from the noise and aching from hours of sitting and jarring. I felt like a drunkard as I lurched out of the bus and stood on land once again. We were now in the place where Mother Teresa had cared for so many, a place I knew to be one of the poorest in the world. I had heard a lot about Mother Teresa, an Albanian Catholic nun who had devoted her life to helping the poorest of the poor. She had founded the Missionaries of Charity in Calcutta in 1950 and had lived out her life helping those from the slums. I am sure the Nobel Peace Prize she won in 1979 meant little to her compared with her tireless dedication to helping the sick and dying.

This was the old British capital before it was moved to Delhi and it felt exciting to be here, our very last stop in India.

Wanting to get to our accommodation quickly we jumped into a waiting Ambassador taxi and for 20Rs we arrived at the Modern Lodge and got a nice room for 100Rs. Unfortunately we had to wait until four other travellers returned to get their packs.

I needed to change more money and so we went to the bank where I withdrew 4000Rs on my MasterCard. It all worked out so well having made it into the bank half an hour before closing on the Saturday afternoon. Banks were closed on Sundays and there was to be a strike on Monday, so for once luck was on my side. I had to have cash to buy a flight ticket as I had three days in India before my visa expired. I booked a flight with Bhutan Airways costing me 2800Rs, which worked out to £60, a very cheap flight.

To celebrate our finalised plan of departure we went to eat at the Blue Sky. They served the most amazing *Lassi's* and egg, cheese and tomato sandwiches.

Back at the lodge I crashed on a sofa at the reception for four hours while we waited for our room to become vacant. Finally the travellers returned for their bags and left and we moved in with speed. A cold shower and clean clothes after nearly two days in the same sweaty filth made us feel on top of the world again.

We walked around parts of the city and then caught taxis and beaten up trams to witness the depressing scene. We came across the Victoria Memorial, a marble palace completed in 1921 with a very solemn and not at all amused statue of Queen Victoria. The palace was beautifully preserved with carefully manicured gardens and a small lake in front of it. We had seen the good and now we wanted to see the bad. From a palace of pure white marble reflecting money and opportunity we crossed the Howrah Bridge over the Hooghly River. People and traffic streamed like a fast flowing river. Buses, trucks, trams, taxis, human rickshaws, bicycles, motorbikes raced by adding chaos to the scene we were about to walk into. Over the bridge we encountered the Howrah slums a disgusting area of dirt and squalor with people looking like scavengers having being cast out of society through poverty. In less than an hour we had seen the polar opposite in this monstrous slum. People slept where they could in makeshift housing on the roadside with a bridge as a roof and an old disused tram as a wind breaker and a home for others. It was a sewer of filth with standing water and a toilet where one wished. Fires burnt on pavements and it reminded me of the film, 'Escape from New York,' where the city had totally collapsed and everyone did what they could to survive. It was a mess as people milled around like zombies with no place in Indian society. I had often thought that blacks in South Africa had it bad, but having seen these slums I felt our blacks had a better life and more of a chance to find work to dig themselves out and live a happier life.

'These people are fucked!' I said to Karin believing that they were doomed to die as beggars and worthless human trash.

Further on we saw people eating mud to stay alive as they hoped the iron would give them some strength.

Passing through throngs of people we saw a man sprawled as naked as the day he was born on the road. He was as dead as dead can be. He was thin and frail and his eyes stared ahead as if he was looking for his God. A few coins lay around him like small bits of litter as a donation towards some wood for his funeral pyre. His clothes and shoes had been pilfered giving the next man a free roll of the dice with a bonus second set of clothes. I looked at his face hoping to gain an answer to his hard life but all I saw were weathered lines covered by a beard and a face that welcomed the end.

People raced by offering a casual glance with no time to stop. It was everyone for themselves with that motto of, only the strongest survive.

We walked away leaving him to stew in the sun like road kill.

'This is their problem not ours,' I said as we made our way to the ferry. For 1 measly rupee we got a ticket down the Hooghly River and watched the poverty from the comfort of the ferry.

And when we had enough we got a taxi to Sudder Street and then home to our lodge. Hungry, we had a good Chinese meal and when we left the restaurant we were rushed at by a beggar who had leprosy. Karin and I jumped a step back as he thrust his arms at us. It was as if he was waving a flag of surrender as he displayed both fingerless hands.

'Quite a lot to swallow after eating that excellent meal,' I sarcastically commented.

Feeling really bad we gave him some biscuits and a cigarette which he was really happy with. He smiled a wicked smile of brown teeth as he puffed on the cigarette using both his palms to take it out of his mouth.

I enjoyed Calcutta with the remnants of the British past still present in many buildings and palaces. As time marched on the buildings had started to look worse for wear. There was the odd pillar post box now a dull dirty red with advertising stuck over it, a reminder to the colonial past.

I looked at my watch after hearing a clock strike and noticed that it was 15 minutes fast. For some unknown reason there was a 15 minute time change between India and Nepal and I hadn't acted on it. My watch had been fast for the last eight days. I looked back at some of my cursing for buses not running on time and smiled.

It was 7 June and we had left Sri Lanka four months ago. I thought about time and how incredibly fast it had flown by.

Calcutta was on strike and the streets were deserted of vehicles. Instead a team of people had created a makeshift cricket match as the bowler bowled at the batsman with a box as the wickets. The British had also left the game of cricket deep in the hearts of all Indians.

We wandered over to the Blue Sky restaurant and had breakfast before it closed for the strike.

There was no noise and no traffic. It was unusual and we felt out of place. The air was cleaner and everyone seemed more at ease away from the hectic and chaotic speed with which Calcutta functioned.

Walking down a street with homeless sleeping in gutters I saw a woman with a bloodied face. Blood was dripping like rain as it ran off her face. Her eyes were wide with terror as she moved like an outcast and became lost in a sea of faces in the gutters of poverty.

In a slightly better place we met an English woman, who was white and as British as you come. She had been born in Calcutta during British Rule and told us of all the changes Calcutta had undergone in the last few decades. She was old and unkempt, and one could see her life had been hard. Her face was a mass of deep worried lines, her teeth were brown and her eyes had a sadness about them. Left behind by choice from the departing Brits in 1947, I felt that she was the only white person left in Calcutta waving the Union Jack as a reminder of those glorious Imperial days.

We saw two dead dogs and a squashed cat with flies buzzing around in a frenzy. Naturally the smell was awful but this was normal and we walked past without uttering a word. Again it was survival of the fittest for both man and beast.

Wanting to get to Sudder Street we got a human rickshaw. It felt degrading to be pulled along by a poor human. I felt like a rich white master sitting comfortably like a king in the old world of apartheid South Africa, while a black man sweated buckets at my expense.

People stared at us as we rode through the squalor of backstreets with people washing in gutters and looking for food like starving animals. We passed a sign on a building that read: 'Abortion, confidential, quick and easy, economical, legal, safe and reliable. Coppert, sterilization and Gynae consultation affered.' The bad spelling was one thing and the outside of the building was filthy with a barred window. Karin and I wondered how many botched abortions had taken place and how many women had died through the lack of cleanliness.

I looked at the man pulling us. He was lean and in good shape and worked with a smile. There was one good thing about us riding with him. He was now earning something to feed his family. For a 10 minute ride we gave him 15Rs which he was happy with.

Starving we found a Chinese place for lunch. For six months I had not eaten a scrap of meat because of my rampant fear of where the meat had come from, and how long it had sat around cooking in the sun.

The Blue Sky welcomed us back for dinner which we shared with four English girls. They told us how hot it was the previous night when their fan had stopped working. They couldn't sleep in the sauna like conditions and blamed it on a power failure. I looked at them puzzled for a moment as I thought back to last night when I had fumbled around for a switch to turn the lounge light on. I clearly remembered flicking a few switches on and off. I admitted it was most probably me and they cursed me with much laughter. A fan in India is a must. There had been many a night when the sweat ran off us like rain drops as if we were sitting in a steam room.

Returning to the lodge we packed our bags and went to the Sunset Bar for a few bottles of Black Label beer. We met two Dutch travellers who we had last seen and spoken with on the Pokhara to Kathmandu bus journey. They told us how they had gambled 1000 Nepalese Rupees and had won 20 000 Indian Rupees at the Kathmandu casino, which was a fair bit of cash in anyone's eyes.

On our way back we saw a man blinded by cataracts, he had no fingers and he was paralysed from the waist down. He lay on an old wooden board with trolley wheels that could barely turn. Mumbling as though he was delirious he tried to gain the attention of the throngs that rushed by. Sadly no one saw him or chose not to see him. It was as if someone had left him there for the day to beg and earn a living. His face looked hardened and empty with his glazed over eye sockets and yet he looked up trying to make eye contact, needing that ever valuable rupee.

The morning dawned and our eagerly awaited departure from India had arrived. At 5:30am we were up and ready to rock and roll out of India. At 6am we hailed a taxi. On setting a price with the driver we gave him 65 Rs and we were off to the airport in in an Ambassador taxi. The taxi was racing as if to leave behind the hardships we had seen and our struggles to cover the distances in the same way as the average Indian person would have done. After all, we ate like them, lived as cheaply as we could in the most humble abodes, travelled on their transport like them and struggled through the filth, heat and hardship just as they would.

It felt great to arrive at the airport. On passing through customs the official took a second look at my clean cut passport picture and then glanced back at me. I looked wild with a brownish red beard, necklaces and bangles and tanned face, a healthy golden brown. I looked thinner and I was. I now only weighed 73 kilograms thanks to curry and rice for months on end, with no meat at all in my diet.

At 8:30am we boarded Druk Air-Bhutan Airways, a 78 seater and unbelievably at 8:50am we took to the air precisely on time. It was a good comfortable airline with good food and friendly service with a smile.

Looking out of the window India was disappearing fast, and Thailand was coming into focus as I thought about a holiday free from travel hardship.

I couldn't help reflecting on our experience over the last three and a half months and this is what I wrote in my journal.

Where else can one see such a monument like the Taj Mahal, a huge sandy golden fort surrounded by arid desert in Jaisalmer, a rowing boat down the Ghats in the holiest of holy palces in Varanasi, ancient buildings in ancient cities in the Elora Caves. A culture ever so colourful within a beautiful ancient land with one state so different to the next, ranging from white Himalayan snow caps, to the golden desert sands of Rajasthan, the green sea of palms in Kerela and the fiery sunsets on the beaches of Goa. All this interwoven with excitement and intrigue in a nation of poverty, dead, starving and unloved animals, filth, homelessness, sickness and disability just too horrific to see on Western streets.

India will remain a part of me forever with such a contrast of culture. There are 18 different languages, 36 gods, 18 states and 4 territorial states in a country over populated with more than a billion people. One is never alone in India.

The beauty amongst the squalor and triumph over tragedy adds a unique feel and outweighs the hardship to get through one's journey and reach the destination. The time spent crossing India felt as though we just scratched the surface, but for me it was long enough and I had seen what I had set out to see.

Farewell to the disabled and the poor, the filth, the stench, the heat, the flies, the hassle, the fatigue, the No's and the Thankyou's, the buses and their endless journeys, the curries and the rice, the baksheesh and corruption.

India is like a moving picture painted in rich sunset colours. As one takes a step back and sees through the putrid filth, the continual swarms of people, the constant drum of noise, the endless line of uncared for animals, one can feel the warm rays of a rising sun reflecting hope on its people as if to give those the strength to face another day.

Thank you, *Dhanyawad* India for an unforgettable experience, an experience imprinted like a photograph in my memory.

THAILAND (1993)

It felt as though I had been in a time warp, it was six months since I had last been in Bangkok. The feeling of being in Calcutta only a few hours ago and now in Bangkok was a traveller's high.

Down Khao San Road we went passing a stream of Westerns, some looking lost, some drunk and high while others were getting their bearings. We booked in at a place we found in the Lonely Planet. It was a small wooden hut and I noticed that the wooden window openings didn't lock. With thoughts of, would we be robbed raced through my head as we made our way to the ferry. The ferry was packed but we still got a seat and headed down the Chao Phraya River. It was dirty and choppy as the waves hit the sides. Relaxing, I hung one foot over the edge, but to my anger a wave took my flip flop with it. When the ferry docked I had no choice but to walk barefoot along some god awful stinking streets. It didn't matter as we were on our way to get something to eat. Except this time it was going to be meat. A burger or two from MacDonald's the home of the Big Mac, also known as good old Rotten Ronnie's. The burgers were just brilliant; the taste of meat had my saliva almost dripping out of my mouth. Unfortunately my bowels didn't feel the same way and before I knew it I was spray painting the ceramic.

On the second day in Bangkok someone got into our hut through the window and went through our packs. I lost a walkman, a few bank notes from countries we had visited and Karin lost a hat. There was no doubt we were lucky. Our passports and money were in our money belts around our waists and our cameras were with us in our day bags. This is what they were after and we could breathe a sigh of relief. We had been on guard with our possessions right the way through India, and now that we were back in what we thought was a safer place we had let our guard down and paid the price.

'We are getting out of here!' I angrily said to Karin.

We threw our stuff together and walked out past a group of Thai men who were the owners.

'We are leaving and we are not paying. Someone from here robbed us!'

My gut said it was an inside job. They looked at me in the most threatening kind of way and said, 'You pay us!'

'No we are not!' I shot back. And then they got up and started shouting.

'Let's go!' and we walked fast past them. I was nervous as hell thinking they were going to pull out a knife or something knowing full well that I was playing with their livelihood. But they just shouted and pointed their fingers in threat. Once on the street I felt the safety of numbers as we became lost in the crowd of people, our white faces blending with the other Western backpackers.

We found a much better place that welcomed us with a sign that read: 'The use of narcotics, candles and prostitutes in the rooms is strictly prohibited. Thank-you.'

The room was safer and the windows locked.

Karin and I planned a trip to an island called Ko Chang on the opposite side of the Gulf of Thailand, a short boat trip from the Cambodian border. We caught a taxi to the main bus terminal in Bangkok and while we were walking over towards it, three Thai policemen came marching right up to us. They carried small truncheons and motioned us to take our bags off our backs. Wondering what this was about we placed our packs on the roadside as people streamed past. To my shock they started unzipping my bag and with the sternest of expressions began searching it. I was shitting bricks. They took some of my clothes out, ran their hands along the sides and in and out of pouches. I stood like a zombie and all I could think was that these corrupt policemen are going to plant some drugs on me, and then take me to jail where an expensive bribe could give my freedom back if I was lucky. I stood stock still and didn't want to appear nervous so I looked at them as if to say, have you finished, I have a bus to catch. I had a couple of necklaces round my neck and bangles around my wrists and legs, dishevelled hair and an unshaven face, all possible signs to them that I was smoking dope and possibly carrying some on me.

After what felt like an hour, which was five long haunting minutes they waved us on. I couldn't believe it, and without another word I had my pack zipped and on my back and we moved as fast as lightning to the right bus where we lost ourselves in the crowd.

I looked at Karin and with a blank face I said, 'Shit we were lucky! They could have done what they wanted!'

Once on the bus I dropped to the seat as if I had been pushed and breathed a deep sigh of relief.

After a long bus trip with numerous stops and bus changes that took us through Chantaburi and Trat we finally came to a pier where a small ferry along with other fishing boats were docked.

We were the only Westerns around and it seemed as though we were way off the beaten track. It was also the rainy season and the roads were muddy, the sky was equally depressing and we were wondering what had possessed us to come here.

After a choppy ride on the ferry we clambered on the back of a small truck and were taken to some lodging. It was drizzling and uncomfortable as we slid on the muddy roads hitting big water-filled holes and getting thrown about like cargo. It was off the tourist map with wild bush encroaching on the road, palms trees standing like lookouts with clumps of coconuts hanging like round green decorations from thin branches. After half an hour we emerged in front of rows of square grass huts all identical, with green grass all around and palm trees planted like umbrellas over each hut. It was magnificent and we were the only ones here.

Each hut had mosquito nets, an ever so important precaution against the silent killer, called malaria.

In the morning we were drawn to a crowd of screaming and crying Thai's who stood outside their huts with stunned expressions of shock. We soon learned that a young girl had wanted to take her life by eating rat poison. She was taken off the island to the mainland as we watched. Unfortunately the news came back fast that she had sadly succeeded in commiting suicide.

Karin and I took to Mekong whiskey which we purchased from a small store that carried everything from a box of matches to the strongest alcohol. A little half jack did the trick and we were staggering around like two uncoordinated twits banging into trees and tripping over coconuts.

Coconuts were lethal in Thailand, almost like hidden landmines. Falling coconuts had claimed many lives and I think we were way too drunk to worry about these falling bombs.

I had heard them fall and when they hit the ground they landed with a thud that could easily split a skull.

We welcomed getting back to Bangkok and thought about how much it had changed since we had been here over six months ago. We met a Scot who had 10 000 Baht stolen from his back pocket, which was stupid of him, but nevertheless it was theft. We saw two Thai men fighting with scissors and when a pair was thrown it only just missed a passing foreigner. A Dutch national had poured petrol over himself on Khao San Road and became a human torch. He suffered severe burns and I am not sure if he lived or died.

The 'lady men' were everywhere and prostitution was a growing business along with the sale of young girls from rural villages into the sex clubs. Some were barely ten, it was warped and very sick, and it was the Westerns that were growing the market.

Bangkok was the end of the road for us. Karin was going on to Austria to visit family. I was heading to Hong Kong and Macau to round off the last six weeks of my year long adventure in South East Asia. I had to see the last of British rule before it would be handed back to the Chinese in 1997. I also had a fascination for Macau, this old Portuguese colony that too would be back in Chinese hands by 1999.

We dressed up and decided to splash out for a memorable evening which was expensive by our standards. Our conversation ranged from the present and back to the unforgettable past with all experiences that a backpack traveller revels in.

We had been there, seen it and done it. But we had done it the hard way which had made it even more gratifying. We had done it in true backpacking style on a shoe string.

In the morning we sadly went our different ways with not a goodbye but rather a see you later.

BACK TO LONDON FROM CANADA (1994/1995)

As I was only allowed to stay six months at a time on a British passport in Canada, I returned to London to get some work.

I got a job with another cable network company and made some good money working in a hotel a stone's throw from one of Mick Jagger's houses. When this work dried up I began working with a cable installer as a two man crew. My partner was a young man who was dirty and disheveled and looked like someone from the low income Welfare Estates. Half his teeth were missing and those that were left were a yellowish black. He had a broken pelvis to make matters worse. No one liked him and they called him, 'Shit bag.'

'Stop talking shit, shit bag. Wipe your side!' some of the workers would shout out. I soon learned he had no stomach and a bag attached to his side.

'I am taking a crap,' he would blurt out while we were driving. I didn't think much of him and could only work with him a couple of weeks before I found another person to crew with.

South African politics were on the news nightly and it was unsettling to hear what looked like civil war on the horizon.

On 10 and 11 March 1994, the AWB took it on themselves to defend the dictatorial rule of Lucas Mangope in the homeland of Bophuthatswana, after a coup had threatened to oust Mangope.

About 90 AWB Afrikaners in their civilian cars arrived in convoy and began to shoot and kill at will, tossing grenades from their cars.

In Mambatho, while attempting to retreat and getting wounded in the process, a group of three hard-line Afrikaners were cornered by the Defence force.

A film crew and journalists stood by with footage rolling on two dead AWB, one on the ground and one on the backseat and the last remaining man cowering by the side of his Mercedes.

There was a black policeman who stood over him with a pistol as the Afrikaner pleaded for his life. He was executed in cold blood.

It was all over the papers and the TVs as the man's dying seconds were shockingly played out to the world.

I couldn't believe how stupid they had been to think they were in the army again and could do as they pleased.

Not even this could put a damper on the first historic multi-racial elections which took place on 27 April 1994, with black queues winding through the bushveld with each black vote ready to change South Africa's history.

Dave, Guy and I went into London and voted at a polling station in Trafalgar Square. I knew the ANC would win but we were hoping to avoid the two- thirds majority, whereby the Constitution could be changed and greatly affect the whites. There were many South African's around the polling station all with worried frowns at what life would be like with imminent change and black ruling over white.

The ANC as expected won with 62% of the votes, but thankfully not enough to change the Constitution. This paved the way for Nelson Mandela who on 10 May 1994 was inaugurated as the country's first black President.

We South African's in England were worried, there was no doubting that. After a long night talking I returned to my room on the Surbiton High Street.

I was staying in a small room in a really dirty welfare recipient's apartment that stank of dog and was a cluttered filthy mess with a kitchen covered in caked on dirt and grease, and dishes that were beyond cleaning.

Pauline, the woman I rented off was middle age, anorexically thin, a face as pale as the moon with long unkempt ginger hair that hung to her shoulders like a mop end. What teeth she had left were brown and her fingers were yellow from all the nicotine. Here was a prime example of a woman kept alive by tax payer's money.

One evening I passed her in the passageway and she had a glazed look plastered over her face and seemed a million miles away. I didn't think too much of it until I walked into the kitchen and saw a tea spoon heating over a hot plate on the stove. It had a brown liquid in it which was bubbling slowly.

I knew this was bad and she confirmed it for me when she stumbled in with a syringe in her hand, with the needle uncapped and ready to siphon up the deadly drug.

Shit this is heroin, a voice in my head shouted. I went cold at the thought that this woman was a heroin addict and was about to shoot up.

'What are you doing?' I could feel my voice rising and I couldn't control the tone.

'It's not for me,' she lied tripping and stammering on her words like a drunkard. Five minutes later I saw her slumped in a chair comatose and swirling in her high, with barely enough strength to lift her head as I entered the room.

Her eyes were glazed and her face was a mask of death. Her pale arms hung limply over the arm chair like white flags of surrender.

It was sad to see the real and chilling effects of drug addiction.

I went to sleep very fearful at what I had witnessed. It was as if I had seen someone making a bomb, it hadn't gone off yet but eventually it would explode in death, and I didn't want to witness it.

I knew I had to get out of here and with my decision to return to my homeland I began to finalize my plans.

For the first time in a long time I was missing home.

I was an African with my homeland locked in my heart, even with these political changes that had to come. I had been stamped African by the sheer beauty and mystique that my country had bred in me. Those high mountains reaching to the blue blue skies, and those oceans tumbling and crashing in a cascade of foam with the pure scent of fresh sea salt, the animals on the plains and the dusty smell of heavy rains on the dry soil, the mesmerizing sunsets ending another scorching day-the sights and the smells would linger in me forever, where ever in the world I might be. Africa was in my blood and it pumped through my veins like a cavalry charge, making me so proud to call myself South African.

I wondered, along with all these significant changes, if I would remember the country I had last seen many years ago.

MY RETURN TO MY BELOVED LAND
(1996)

After years of travelling and experiencing cultures so far removed from what I was used to, I returned home after an absence of five years. I had seen and experienced the world first hand from being robbed, living homeless, scrounging for an income, and begging for work all in my quest to see a small part of this wide world. There had been some scary and lonely times but I welcomed it like a needle to a junkie with my adrenaline racing.

Travelling had been my drug and I had loved it, the good as well as the bad, after all that is what the journey of life is all about.

I had kept to my word of doing jobs that for the most part were considered unskilled work and in South Africa would be deemed as work for blacks. I had said all my jobs will be ones without wearing a tie as I had done for the OK Bazaars. I had worked as a waiter in Holland, an apple sorter in Germany, labourer, printing logo's on T-shirts, a dustbin boy or rubbish collector and a cable television worker in England, washed dishes and worked for a gardening company in Italy, and handed out leaflets in Hong Kong. Work had been hard but it paid for my travels and humbled me no end.

I had been taught life lessons, learned about cultures and religions, seen wealth and poverty and had the value of friendship instilled in me.

The five years had changed me, I saw people differently and I certainly saw my old country differently.

Apartheid had been abolished and one could see those invisible shackles removed and replaced with freedom of choice and an acceptance of the Africans as people and not fourth class citizens.

It would take a generation to work through all the hate that was still present in many, but it was a start, a start that had taken 350 years to begin.

My friends were nervous with black majority rule, and if one had to look at the rest of Africa, an easy prediction was that South Africa was doomed with civil war in the cards. With black on black tribal differences and black and white hatred like a raging volcano set to erupt at any minute, South Africa was living on a ticking time bomb.

Miriam our old and respected servant had died and my Mum did the unselfish deed of driving into the unsafe black area to be with her family in their simple abode so far removed from our upscale white community.

She was the only white face in a sea of black and they knew who she was. She was the madam who gave food and clothing to their loved one and a job, even though she was too old to clean, and polish brass and dust the house. It was an income that she could channel back to her kids and grand kids for education and food. One white hand had helped a black hand over many decades and vice versa.

Never once did Miriam sit at our table and share a story of her life so different from ours. And never once did I enter her *khaya,* her servant's room. Apartheid ruled everywhere; it was the way we had always known.

Soon after arriving back I met up with Alain and one of my old bosses for a few drinks along the Durban beachfront. It got out of hand with many stories flowing and filling the five year gap. With many beers under my belt I staggered out and drove home. On the way I encountered a road block that had me trapped with no possible way out.

A breathalyzer was thrust into my face, and while I blew I knew it would be off the charts. I was not surprised to be ordered out of the car and then to my drunken shock I was marched into a caravan on the side of the road with a few nurses inside. Before I could work out what was going on a needle punctured my arm and vials of blood were siphoned out.

Then I was placed in the back of a police van and sat like an animal that had been drugged awaiting a long journey. After a few more unlucky white people were herded into the back, the van set off

Tim Ramsden

for the Police Station. I was asked every detail about myself and it was documented into a report which seemed to drag on for hours. I stayed in the charge office for the last hours of night and then I had to appear at the Magistrates Court at 8am. I was not only still drunk, but I had a hangover of note and hadn't slept in what felt like days. I just wanted this over so I could sleep.

A date was set when I was to appear back in court and hear the verdict of my insane action. Not only could I lose my licence but I could get a criminal record which would make my entry into Canada impossible.

When my name was read out, the judge stuttered and stammered and then went quiet before he said: 'The evidence has been misplaced. Mr. Ramsden you are free to go!'

With a smile that said it all, I walked out of court thanking my lucky stars for another chance. I had learned my lesson; I would never get behind the wheel in that condition ever again.

I felt very uneasy in this new life, it was a life I did not know anymore and one where I felt I no longer belonged.

It was a sad feeling as I loved this continent with such passion and pride but my calling was to Canada to be with my son, Shaun and my wife to be, Karin.

I had such admiration for Nelson Mandela. He served 27 years in jail to gain freedom for all blacks and then emerge as the first black leader of South Africa. He led the country without a tinge of white hate, so unlike the way Nationalist whites had treated the blacks.

'Children are the rock on which our future will be built,' he said. With white and black children growing up together, one knew that there was so much hope for this new South Africa, known as the Rainbow Nation.

It was so hard to say goodbye to a land that was connected to my soul like an umbilical cord to a baby, and here I was cutting my ties to the place I had always and so proudly called home.

I looked around Westerford, the rooms filled with priceless antiques from paintings to porcelain china and beautiful furniture in dark wood including a Grandfather clock made in 1740 by Brentnall of Sutton, in England. This clock was brought to South Africa in 1850 by my Great Great Grandfather, a journey by sea which took 112 days. It was a treasured possession that was handed down through the family and my parents entrusted it to me, to be shipped with my other possessions across the ocean again, this time on a shorter voyage and a bigger ship to Canada.

The desire and will to explore, to see, to feel, to smell and to have my heart and soul touched in some way by a country foreign to me, would always be with me. I knew my backpacking style would change as I needed to settle into a career and put down roots.

It was sad to realize I was leaving the land of my birth and upbringing. South Africa would always be with me, in my heart and in my soul, in my senses and my feeling, where ever the journey of life took me, there was no doubt of that.

The travel journey would continue on beyond boundaries, but with a little more calculated decision making.

NAMIBIA (2003)

The evening was cool and refreshing, the stars were just as plentiful and I was as nervous as hell.

Here I was back in a country that I had vowed never to return to. It was here that I had served in the South African army in 1985 and 1988 when this country was still governed by South Africa, known then as South West Africa.

I can remember branding South West Africa as the arse end of the world, thanks to all the fear and frustration that was instilled in me as a young National Serviceman and Citizen Force soldier.

Now I was back to revisit the country through a civilian's eyes and without a rifle hanging off my arm.

I had to be here to jog my memory on all those frustrations and anger that ran like a turbulent river in me. It had been a million dollar experience, an experience that I would not give a dime to do again. I had begun to write a book on my time in the army, and being here was going to help me put my reminiscences down on paper.

After a very tiring 14 hour flight from New York to Johannesburg and then a wait in transit before my flight to Windhoek, the capital of Namibia, I finally walked out of a very quiet terminal to a waiting taxi.

Looking at my Lonely Planet travel book I picked out a hostel by the name of the 'Cardboard Box,' and told the driver to take me there. Enjoying the cool evening air on my face, I sat back and looked ahead at a deserted and very dark road. The headlights bore holes through the pitch darkness as the taxi raced ahead hogging the road with no other vehicles to slow it down. With 45 kilometres behind us we arrived at the hostel and for a hefty N$ 50 I got a dorm bed. Each dorm room had a flag painted on the door and funnily enough I was assigned to the South African room with the rainbow nation flag.

I met some interesting people who were lined up at the bar drinking Castle and Windhoek lager, one a Brit who had served as a peace keeper in 1990 with the United Nations and another a South African who was looking for work as a pilot.

As always it felt odd to be in Africa again and even odder to be in the old South West Africa drinking a Castle, with all those army patrols in Owamboland swirling in my mind with each sip.

In the morning I got a good feel of the city with all the old German architecture, roads named after communist leaders, well kept government buildings and gardens very colourful with jacarandas in full purple bloom.

I visited a museum with a full section on Namibian independence and Sam Nujoma's struggles to win freedom for the South West African people through his banned party called SWAPO.

I ordered breakfast over the bar at the Cardboard Box, which was taken with a shy smile by an African woman called Tuli. Tuli was an Angolan by birth, born in the capital Luanda before moving southwards with her parents to Ombalantu in northern Owamboland in South West Africa. Her father was a SWAPO delegate and they were always on the move with danger close behind them. They were in Havana, Cuba and Lusaka, Zambia in support of Namibian independence through the South West African People's Organization known as SWAPO.

She was a short round faced woman with scars across her face as testament to her cultural upbringing. Her eyes were big and round and her teeth were as white as a fresh snowfall. Her smile was short but sweet as if hiding a dark secret. Tuli spoke with a quiet voice which seemed to gain in confidence when she heard I was South African.

'I served here in Owamboland when I was in the army,' I said trying to make conversation.

'I and my family supported SWAPO,' she struck back.

'Oh, I see. To be honest I really did not want to be in the army. For us it was mandatory,' I replied.

With tears welling up in her eyes she told me a horrific story. I had heard such stories but could never attach a living face to the ordeal.

One of her relatives were killed in front of her by the South African Security Forces and then dragged behind the vehicle for all to see.

'If you shed a tear you too will be killed!' a white uniformed soldier screamed at them.

Filled with fear and grief they watched the limp body churning up dust as the warning of the Security Forces resounded: If you support SWAPO this is what will happen.

In a separate incident she told me about a woman who had recently given birth and how she was forced to pound her newborn baby with a log as if she was pounding millet.

A pregnant woman had her stomach slit open, dropping the unborn baby to the ground.

She told me how the men would dig holes and bury themselves with a piece of corrugated tin covering them with earth and brush to further conceal their position. So when the South African soldiers arrived they would not be able to find them and also would not fall into the freshly dug trenches.

Tuli went on to tell me about the battle at Cassinga in Angola in 1978 when over 1000 people were killed. It was SWAPO's darkest day and, according to her, most of the deaths were women and children. When the South African's had finished raining down the bombs she told me the sky was red. I can imagine the ground must have been red with blood and the sky red with dust.

I felt like I was a sounding board for all her pent up anger and turmoil that her young life had been through.

With tears flowing from her eyes she told me how she was raped, the shame reflected like thick make up on her youthful face. I realized I was looking into a sad picture of Africa where poverty and human abuse go hand in hand. The tears dripped like slow rain and in between sniffles she kept on talking, as if trying to cleanse her system from a horrific past.

The stories were pouring out and I was listening with a sharp ear. An English speaking soldier warned her relatives that the 'Boers' (Afrikaans soldiers) were on their way to capture them in Ombalantu. Before the soldiers arrived, they managed to flee. Looking me in the eye she told me that whenever her relatives hear this story they shed a tear that a white man put his life on the line to save a black family that was considered the enemy.

When she turned away to continue serving I finished my now cold breakfast with my mind processing her difficult life. Again I thought how lucky I was to have been born with a white skin.

The next morning I left the Cardboard Box with Connie, the manager of a car rental company on the main street in Windhoek. After signing my life away on more papers than I cared to remember, I eventually hit the road at 9:30am bound for the Etosha Game Reserve. Eventually, after nine hours of driving over a distance of 600 kilometres I pulled into the Namutoni rest camp.

I was well rewarded for the long hot drive, for on my entry into the Etosha I was given the privilege of viewing two of the big five. I could not believe my eyes when I saw a huge male lion guarding his giraffe kill from hungry vultures and hyenas. Then a little further on I saw a herd of 15 to 20 elephants with their little calves carefully protected by their giant elders. The game then appeared out of the coolness of thorn trees and small bushes; kudu, gemsbok, hyena, jackal, wildebeest, impala, springbok, duiker, bontebok, zebra, giraffe, ostrich, and finally a lone fox. What a sight to see, this was the Africa that I loved and missed so much, animals in their own habitat roaming free across the open savannah as they had done for centuries.

The highlight of the day was definitely a lone bull elephant completely white from a sand bath in a long dried out salt pan. He looked tired, his sad face weathered with sagging lines of leathery folds as he raised his head with his small dirty brown tusks protruding and trunk curling up from the ground. His massive feet stamped authority onto the dusty road as he strolled past my car.

Getting out of the car only four metres from him and with my camera ready, I screamed at this giant, ready to snap an award-winning shot had he glanced in my direction. He was in his own world and plodded on as if I was not even there. I certainly gave little thought to a charge that could have easily come my way. One comforting thought was that I had the car running and was ready to dive back in and slam it into reverse if the need arose, lucky for me I did not have to attempt this getaway.

Back at the old white German fort now serving as a rest camp I was greeted by at least 10 mongooses in the courtyard that scurried around like rats. So tame that they almost went as far as extending a hand in friendship and welcome to this most amazing but simple rest stop inside one of Africa's most famous game sanctuaries.

After a deep sleep and a couple of Windhoek lagers I left for another camp, 75 kilometres east to the Halali Resort, spotting a lone elephant, some giraffe towering over a small thorn tree in the distance with the usual zebra and springbok moving around in small herds under the burning midday heat.

At the resort I cooled off in a large swimming pool, washing the heat and sweat from my body in an instant, rejuvenating myself with a smile of contentment. One minute scorched open dry land with teeming wildlife and the next a massive swimming pool in the middle of a game park. Wow, isn't Africa amazing, I thought to myself.

As the sun started to set I walked down to a huge waterhole where the animals would congregate as the coolness set in across the plains. It was like watching a live movie with all the sounds in place with the most magnificent backdrop to crown it all. After a few rustles through the bush a huge black rhino emerged and lumbered up to the water right in front of us. He stayed there for at least half an hour and was totally oblivious to the cameras that clicked off frames in between ooh's and aah's of pure delight. With the sun a beautiful shining orange on the horizon, two hyenas came out followed by a jackal and a warthog with his stiff legged trot and aerial tail standing erect as it cut through the long dry grass to get to the muddy water.

What a sight to witness, true Africa on my doorstep.

At 7:30 in the morning I left Halali for Namutoni, and to my disappointment I did not see much wildlife besides a massive kudu, some gemsbok and as always lots of zebra and springbok.

At the camp I filled up my rented very dirty white Hyundai and then got directions for Ondangwa. The quickest way was to head through the park to Andoni and then out of the gate at Mpingana.

With my windows down and Connie's silent voice willing me to turn the air conditioner on or have the car filled with tiny particles of fine powder that would be impossible to get rid of. Hating air conditioning I smiled and decided to take the chance with the car rental, enjoying the breeze brushing across my face with a scalding slap. Great I thought, now I can see more animals on the drive, which I did. Just before the gate I saw hundreds of animals gathered around a very deep waterhole as they milled around cautiously and on alert at all times.

Leaving the park I drove through Ondangwa and then Oshakati before filling up with petrol at Uutapi, also known as Ombalantu, where I began asking where the old South African army base was. I was met with blank stares and shrugging of shoulders, as the local Owambo's either did not understand me or cared not to.

I decided to try and find it on my own and after driving up and down the same stretch of road that I had just been on; I eventually stumbled across what looked like an old eroded wall that was once the bases perimeter. Getting closer I saw the old potato sacks layered as bricks to make bunkers and then I saw the shell of the old mess hall and shower area built from ash blocks with black netting covering the windows, now ripped and torn with gaping holes like a sail that had tried to ride through a storm. As the wind blew so did the netting, as if it was waving a black flag of surrender.

An eerie calm hung over the old deserted base. The picture perfect details of discipline and uniformity in army language had been eroded over the sands of time. In the same way that wind and rain break down walls of sand so had the mighty presence of South African control whittled away, with South Africa's withdrawal from South West Africa paving the way for independence for Namibia.

Memories of many long days and nights when we patrolled in this area as the rains lashed mercilessly down, were all too vivid in my mind. Tormenting us for hours on end the rain would prod my sanity like slow Chinese torture, all part and parcel of being a conscripted soldier on the border in the height of the rainy season. We would lie there paralyzed with helplessness wishing for an end to the madness. Sleep deprivation part and parcel of army life from the hell of basic training to the *opfok*, *rondfok* and mindfuck of the border.

Then I thought about that eight hour forced march over 25 to 30 kilometres through the pouring rain and stumbling like cripples through the shonas. It hit me as though it had happened yesterday. It was just another nightmare added to the many we as young National Service conscripts had experienced.

'Fuck how I had hated this place. Only god knew how much.'

Tim Ramsden

While I walked kicking at the dirt I thought about my two years and the mindfuck that we had been through. My mind regressed to 1 SAI and the daily slander that cut at us like lashes from a whip, rushed back like a tidal wave. One sentence of verbal abuse ran into the next and it kept going.

Roer jou gat jou dom ding. Move your arse you dumb thing!
Ek sal jou bliksem. I will hit you!
Jou lang drol. You long piece of shit!
Jou vark peel. You dumb prick!
Jy is vet deur die kak. You are really stupid!
Jou klink soos spyt poep op die asveld. You sound like diarrhoea on the tarmac!
Lag vir jou gat en bid vir jou seel. Laugh at your arse and pray for your soul!
Jou lierlike ding. You ugly thing!
Jy is n vark ding. You are a stupid thing!
Jou vark eter. You dumb fool.
Kom hier vet seun. Come here fat son!
Julle is besig om my moer te koer. You are busy getting on my nerves!
Lag vir jou ma. Laugh at your mother!
Word wakker die dag word all hoe kakker. Wake up the day is getting shitter!
Suurhol en n vyf cent stuk. Sore arse and a five cent piece.
Jy is laer as kaffer kak. You are lower than black shit.
Jy is nie betaal om te dink. You are not paid to think.
Jy is net n nommer. You are just a number.

I smiled as I thought about the harsh Afrikaans language and then laughed at the stupidity of some of those expressions. A saying came to mind: 'Sticks and stones may break my bones but words will never harm me.' These words were so true and came very close to breaking me, but I emerged as a man through it.

Wayne popped into my thoughts as I rememberd being told about the PBs. We had no idea what PB stood for and could only surmise that it stood for *Poes bek*, poes mouth. To us it made total sense with Blacks being the brunt of all white jokes, not to mention the loathing that most of us had for them.

'Look over there. A bunch of *poes beks* are sitting under a tree!' Little did we know it stood for *plaaslike bevolking*, the local population. When we found out we just killed ourselves laughing at our ignorance, that we had actually called every local a *poes bek*.

An old bomb shelter which still had a sign above the entrance 'BEV' standing for *Bevelvoeder*, or officer in charge, marking his sleeping quarters, with the difference being that local Owambos were now living in it, who had laid claim to the shelter as their home.

A huge baobab tree, at least 1000 years old, towered over the base, looking out of place with its disfigured branches haphazardly growing as it wished standing as a beacon in the base. The inside of the tree had been hollowed out and could fit at least 20 people inside, and was extremely cool. What a massive room I had just walked into, dark and secluded and a place where no one would be the wiser if captured terrorists were temporarily imprisoned in it.

Not that I ever witnessed it, but this tree had been used as an interrogation chamber for captured SWAPO terrorists.

A couple of Owambo children emerged from nowhere and I took a photograph of them in front of the entrance to capture the enormous size of this tree that stood like a giant dwarfing everything including the water tower.

Inside the mess area there was a circle of stones on the cracked concrete floor with remnants of a fire, ironically on the same floor where I had huddled shivering with cold on one of my many saturated nights under the unforgiving elements.

Inside the building there was an old army stove on wheels still equipped with a trailer hitch that would normally be towed behind a Samil troop carrier. It had been left behind and stood as a marker on its flat tyres as the telltale sign of the strong South African presence.

The water tower was still standing minus the tin tank that sat on the top, scavenged by a local for their use.

I watched a woman hanging her washing on a line hung from the BEV bunker, which was her home. A makeshift corrugated tin door had been bolted at the entrance to the bunker securing her home from intruders. I looked at her and wondered whose side she had been on during the drawn out bush war that spanned more than two decades, but it certainly did not matter anymore.

I soon realized why I had not been able to find the base having driven past it a few times. South African bases had always been built with nothing around them, with the open bush being the buffer between the enemy and the fortress. How things had changed, a cluster of huts and a few small brick buildings had sprung up right next to the old eroding sand walls.

Very glad to be leaving the base behind, I headed out in the direction of Ruacana. The scenery was the same as I had seen back in the army, makalani palms standing tall above the rock-hard anthills that stood like cones dotted over the flat as a table top dry land.

There was no colour besides the odd painted building with a wall advertising a trademark brand. The land was harsh and unforgiving and as dry as a bone as if the Gods had cursed it.

I passed an old mud walled building with Coke-Cola emblazoned on the crumbled walls symbolizing a struggle against the elements with not a soul around. It must have been a trading post of sorts in its day but now it was just a shell of mud, standing like a monument to the owner's business venture that had failed.

Listening to the radio and enjoying the breeze I saw two small kids no more than seven years of age riding tandem on a donkey. The donkey stood unmoving in the heat of the day and had to be coaxed along by the leading child and a stick.

The African sun was as hot as hell as I got out to take a really good picture of rural Africa. The two kids were as dark as the ace of spades testament to the harsh sun that beat down and sucked life from the dry earth.

The road was a one lane highway with a haze rising from the heat of the tarmac that stretched endlessly for as far as the eye could see.

Again I thought about the arse end of the world, the name we as soldiers had branded this land.

It seemed different and much less fearful to be here this third time around, this time being a civilian to do as I wished, how I wished and when I wished.

After a few hours I arrived in Ruacana and driving a little further I got an amazing view of the Calueque dam in Angola, nestled between the mountains.

Looking at the dam I thought about all those soldiers that had been killed by the Cubans in an aerial attack by a Mig 23 fighter plane and a lethal bomb that obliterated 11 South African soldiers.

The loss was a direct link to my hometown Hillcrest where Greg Scott, one of those killed was a resident and a person we all knew.

I could also never forget those 12 people who had been so barbarically slaughtered worse than any animal and left to stink and rot in pools of fly infested blood in the remains of their burned village. The smell had got into our army uniform and stayed with us on that nightmarish patrol like a curse as if to remind us of every gruesome detail we had witnessed.

I carried on driving until I came to the Namibian border post where I saw an old power station overlooking the dry Ruacana Falls, pock marked and peppered with AK 47 bullets by the SWAPO liberation forces.

The Angolan border post was a heap of rubble and unguarded. It lay in ruins as a symbol of how the country teetered on disintegration through decades of civil war.

The faded red and black Angolan flag flew behind the border post denoting the boundary, its tattered and torn condition further depicting what lay ahead in this old once very proud and wealthy Portuguese colony.

Looking at the flag I shook my head with relief. This is where we as Ratel soldiers would have entered into Angola had Pretoria given us the green light to attack the advancing column of Cuban and FAPLA (Angolan) forces.

Luckily for us we never did experience mechanized war, even though so many white soldiers wanted the opportunity to kill, but more importantly to kill a kaffir.

After all, this is what we had been trained for.

In the small town of Ruacana I tried looking for accommodation, but with no luck I decided to head south with my focus set on finding the Olukonda Village. After 10 hours of nonstop driving, I eventually found the Finnish Mission huts surrounded by a traditional Owambo kraal, where I was thankfully given a hut with a bed and a very comfortable mattress.

Here I was in Owamboland lying on a bed that I would have given anything for back in my National Service days, where the ground had been my mattress for over three months.

Walking around outside I saw the oldest structure in northern Namibia, an old church dating back to 1870 when the first Finnish missionaries arrived, along with a great museum of old and well preserved pieces of history. The walls were adorned with faded black and white photographs of people who played an important role, good and bad, in history of this region.

Just before the sun set a truck pulled in to the mission station. It was an overlander truck with a group of Westerners from Holland who had been travelling for a month with the driver, a native from Zim. He was a Shona and a proud 'When we,' a saying given to those die hard Rhodesians who always remembered their country by uttering: 'When we were Rhodesia!'

He had been born after the bush war and yet he was an Ian Smith admirer, the last white leader of the old Rhodesia.

'Many blacks want Ian Smith back!' he said. 'There was food and work, now the country is fucked thanks to Mugabe. There is no petrol or you are paying a fortune for it and the whites are leaving or being chased off their farms,' the Shona spoke with a subdued and drunken slur as if in acceptance of the depressing state of one of Africa's richest countries since gaining its independence.

I sat and ate with them as they reminisced about their adventure over the past day. I could sense the excitement that Southern Africa had stamped on their consciousness for a life time. In the same way as a passport is stamped at customs, so a life is whisked out of the hustle and bustle of the city world and placed wide eyed on the open savannah. And shortly after the first glorious African sunset, so a new soul awakens on the open plains of Africa burning like fire in their veins with a yearning for more. This is what Africa can and will do to anyone stepping on its magical soil.

I listened to one of the Dutch girls who had recently been in Luanda the capital of Angola and had travelled a dangerous route all the way south to the Namibian border. She spoke about young boys, drunk and swaying about with fully loaded AK 47s in their deadly grasp as they demanded their papers. Scared as all hell they arrived in one piece paying their way in bribes, the unwritten law of all African countries to get where you wish and as soon as you wish. There is a price for everything and foreign currency goes a long way in Africa.

Leaving Luanda she said one could visualize the past beauty of this old Portuguese city set on the ocean, even though it was now dirty, falling to pieces and in ruin like the country itself.

After a few beers and an exchange of stories I dropped into bed totally exhausted after the day's long drive. Before I extinguished the candle I watched a couple of spiders disappear into the thatch roof above my head, and then under a mosquito net I fell into a deep and very rewarding sleep.

At 8am I rose and walked out into a sandstorm. Throwing my pack into the boot of the car I headed out for Tsumeb.

On the way I discovered my camera was broken, and cooling down after some choice words to myself, I decided that I would have to buy one in Tsumeb as the only other place that I knew would sell a camera was Windhoek and that was days away.

Arriving in the small town was a sight for sore eyes. Beautifully manicured grass as green as any golf course, well kept buildings looking as German as one could ever get, all thanks to the colonial past when Namibia was once called German South West Africa.

Wandering around the quaint and very pleasant town I entered an old museum that was once an old German school and later a hospital.

It was well laid out with photos, flags, guns, ammunition and quantities of old relics many that had been recovered from the Lake Otjikoto. The most amazing were an old German cannon and ammunition wagons recovered from the murky depths of the limestone sinkhole at a depth of 55 metres.

I also visited the Grand Old Lady mineshaft which stood out like a sore thumb above the town, marking a prominent spot that many years ago attracted attention due to all the mining, even though today the mine ceases to operate.

In the evening I went to the Makalani Hotel and wandered up to the bar for a refreshing ice cold beer.

My hand wrapped around a bottle of Windhoek lager that hit the spot instantly. I began chatting to the barman and a local man from

Tim Ramsden

Tsumeb, who to my amazement were both ex South African's, one from Cape Town and the other from Durban.

The conversation did not take long before it touched on the violence in Namibia that was creeping up on the white minority.

Then a man next to us told me about a house break-in, which occurred two weeks ago in Windhoek. The father was shot in the head and died instantly and the son and daughter were in critical condition in hospital.

The barman then followed up with his story where his home was burgled and cleaned out when he went away for a few days. Luckily for him he was not in the house.

Conversation then turned to the bush war days during the border war.

The Afrikaans man told me about an incident that happened during the 1980s in Walvis Bay at the main market place.

Minding his own business he saw a briefcase standing alone amongst all the people that weaved and dodged their way through the market. Finding it really odd he pointed it out to his friend and jokingly said: 'Maybe it is a bomb!'

They then left the market and by the time they got to a traffic light 20 to 30 metres away it exploded killing, maiming and destroying many lives.

The Afrikaner went on to talk about Koevoet, a highly successful police counter insurgency unit. He told me that most of them were national service drop-outs who could not handle discipline and take orders from 19 and 20 year old corporals and lieutenants. They went on AWOL and were in and out of detention barracks constantly under the eyes of the Military and Regimental Police.

He went on to tell me that P.W.Botha (State President of South Africa) gave the order for them to be released from the army jails and in doing so created the Koevoet Unit.

These policemen had no fear and did not care about anything or anyone, let alone killing.

'They were high most of the time,' he said 'and were paid per kill.'

'All they had to do was cut the dead terrs ear off and hand in an AK47 and they would be paid for the kill.'

I myself did not know much about Koevoet, but I did know they were an extremely successful unit in stemming the cross border activity from Angola into SWA/Namibia.

I remember as a young National Servieman looking at them with immense respect as they drove past on their Casspirs, like new kid starting high school would look up to a Grade 12.

I was then told about an ex Koevoet soldier who was known as Piesang. Piesang was an ex Rhodesian who had fought in Rhodesia's bush war and then when that ended with Zimbabwe gaining independence, he chose the next war and joined Koevoet.

Unfortunately he was shot in a skirmish by one of his fellow troops. The bullet shot out a chunk of his brain and even though he lived it destroyed him.

'He charters boats up on the Zambezi, along the Caprivi Strip,' he said as if telling me that he is not as fucked up as all that, it was only a bullet to the brain.

These were the stories that were true and sad, ones of war and courage to keep going.

After the few beers I ventured outside and was surprised to see dozens of armed black soldiers in front of the hotel.

I soon found out that the Deputy Minister of Zimbabwe was in the hotel having dinner and this was his heightened security.

Leaving Tsumeb I headed in the direction of Grootfontein in search of the Hoba Meteorite, which was discovered in 1920 and is the world's largest. I could not believe the size of this rock that had fallen from space weighing a staggering 54000 kilograms and made up of 82% iron, 16% nickel, and a very small percentage of cobalt. It is dated to be over 800 000 years old.

I passed through Grootfontein with thoughts of my first day on the border, the blistering heat and all the uncertainty that this the arse end of the world held in store for me.

Leaving Grooties in the back of my mind I turned up the volume as I headed towards Rundu on the lone open flat road with tomorrow well in my sights.

On my way to Rundu I was stopped at a checkpoint and asked to produce my licence. It is called the Red Line which, along with Oshivello, is an animal disease control checkpoint where the commercial cattle ranchers of the south cannot be mixed with the communal subsistence herds of the north. It bars the north-south movement as a precaution against foot and mouth disease as well as rinderpest. Animals bred north of this line may never be sold south or exported overseas.

I looked at the soldier and his AK 47 and wondered if he thought that I had a couple of cows in the boot. With a hard look at the international licence and a glance at my face, I was waved through to continue my journey.

Speeding like a madman on this haze of paved road I got the fright of my life when a drunk African wandered into the road and I nearly plastered him all over the Hyundai with visions of the white car turning red.

I sped into Rundu and unbeknown to me I flew straight through a four way stop. Seeing a van in front of me I slammed on the brakes and my car skidded on the stones that were littered like marbles on the paved road. I watched my car slide right up to the van as I braced for impact with insurance and huge damage deep in my thoughts. To my amazement I stopped inches from the van and was greeted with some nice swear words from the white driver. Shocked I could not respond but instead raised an arm as an apologetic gesture for an accident that would certainly have taken these two vehicles off the road for quite some time.

On getting my bearings I booked in at the Ngandu Safari Lodge, which is very close to the Okavango River, bordering Angola.

Driving around the town I was amazed to see so many white people living in close knit neighbourhoods all with high and well fortified sandbagged bunkers and barbed wire spiralling on top of fences and high walls. The bunker entrance was a half circle made out of corrugated iron with rock hard sand bags layered like bricks to buffer a mortar bomb attack from the Angolan side, which had come this way during the border war.

Windows were crossed with neat pieces of iron welded down and across the break of each pane of glass as to somehow hide the barred in feeling behind each window frame. Freedom or jail I thought, as I reminisced about Canada with no burglar bars and no fences, and knowing that my house would remain safe and secure when I returned after six weeks away, the prospect of a break-in not entering my mind at all.

I drove down to the river and saw an amazing sunset over the water. As always it was a quiet and very rewarding time with thoughts and proud feelings to be on this continent to witness such a scene of peace and vibrant colour. The heat had been chased away for another day as the coolness massaged my burned skin. The river was still, except for the odd African washing or collecting water for their meals over a fire.

I met an old African who could not speak any English but was fluent in Afrikaans. I pointed to a derelict old pump house which stood right next to the water's edge, and asked what had happened to it. He told me it had been shot up by Angolan forces across the river.

Back at the Lodge Bar I met a few locals and we got talking over a few ice cold beers, the way all beers should be served in Southern Africa. It never took long before mention of the border war came up. He had also done his National Service and in spite of him being a South West African he was stationed at Upington and Walvis Bay. He was touched by the war having lost an uncle to a landmine, and in another incident an eight year old classmate who was bayoneted to death along with his grandmother on their farm.

War on both sides had been bad, as in all wars no one ever emerges unscathed.

He told me about Piesang which I thought strange as this was the Koevoet policeman and ex Rhodesian soldier that had been shot through the head and written off as dead.

'He works at the Hippo Lodge, taking people on fishing trips,' he said finishing it off with a 'You have to see the Hippo Lodge.'

And so the next morning I set off for the 524 kilometre journey to Katima Mulilo in search of this must see, Hippo Lodge.

It seemed quite deserted and on walking in I met the owner of the establishment and after a pleasant conversation she charged me N$80 for a small room.

After dropping my pack in the room I went out to the deck and got a great view of the water that was a tributary of the great Zambezi River. Just to sit and look as the sun reflected its rays off the water, was a breath-taking experience where peace and solitude were worth its weight in gold.

Tim Ramsden

In the afternoon I took a drive into Katima and visited the small town and the market area where I got a feel of rural Africa. I found a telephone exchange and rang through to Canada making that all-important connection with my son. Here I was in a place that was as third world as one could reach and yet I was talking to my son linking Africa to North America, father to son over such a great divide.

On getting back to the Hippo Lodge I felt really thirsty and so thinking nothing of it, I ran the tap and gulped hungry mouthfuls of yellowish water until my belly hurt. I woke in the middle of the night with chronic stomach pains and just managed to reach the toilet before an explosion took place.

Returning to bed I shook like a leaf, raked with chills and then burning with fever, as I tossed and turned and then curled up in pain.

I thought of malaria, as I looked up at the netting around my bed and shutting my eyes to clear the thought of the dreaded disease known as the silent killer.

To my amazement I felt a lot stronger in the morning and after a hot shower and a steaming cup of coffee on the deck I was a new man, with the pain from the night before now a memory.

Birds chirped and time seemed to stand still.

While I sipped contentedly on my coffee I met a German who told me never to drink the water. Where was he last night when I could have used this warning, I thought to myself.

'The water is full of parasites and disease, from animals, human waste and pollution,' he spoke very good English but with a noticeable German accent. Now it all made perfect sense. Rather late than never, as knowing me I would have done it again had thirst got the better of me.

Christine, a very pleasant and plain woman in her fifties was the owner of the Hippo Lodge. She told me it had been used by the South African Defence Force as a rehabilitation centre for all those messed up troops who saw action in Angola.

Then she went on to tell me about Piesang who was an ex-Koevoet policeman who had served in the border war, and worked at the Lodge taking tourists out on fishing trips.

She was speaking about the very man that had been talked about over some beers thousands of kilometers away and now here I was hearing about the same man again.

'Don't ask him questions about the war!' she snapped as if trying to spare him further pain.

'He was accidentally shot by one of his own, and left for dead with part of his head and brain shot out!'

With a deep sigh she went on: 'He can barely speak and is paralyzed on his right side.'

My attention was totally captivated by her words as I thought about all those years of bush war where blood was shed, whether it be black or white it was still shed on the same dusty soil with the same anguish and pain that went with it.

I thought about the troop who had shot him and how it must have affected his life in that split second of miscalculation.

Shortly after she finished Piesang emerged on the deck dragging his paralyzed leg like a dead weight towards the nearest chair. Slumping himself down with the aid of his well used cane he let out a deep breath as he stared out over the water and into oblivion.

Christine thrust a glass of whisky at him and with a shaking hand he took the glass with the clinking of ice the only sound. Sipping on the neat whisky it seemed to calm him as if he was taking his daily dose of medicine.

His face was round and weather beaten and his mouth was skewed with his paralysis, allowing the saliva to hang from his mouth like a string.

Gazing out at nothing he startled me as he blurted out: 'I only remember two dates, the day I was shot and my birthday.'

I looked at him and visualized a once proud Rhodesian soldier from one bush war and a Koevoet policeman in his last war, now reduced to a shell of the man he once was. Here was a man who had given his all to stem the tide of black majority rule, and when the government gave in and paved the way for independence he was left as one of the many forgotten ones who paid the price with his own blood.

'Tiger fish!' Piesang blurted out as he pointed to the rings that circled in the water of the Zambezi. His passion was fishing and he had that fisherman's read on the waters that held so many promises and hopes.

When his whisky was finished he pushed himself up with his cane and like a man that had fallen from grace he dragged himself away, with the drink having covered over his horrific war years for the night at least.

Later that day I went into town and changed some money getting the lowest US exchange rate in quite some time. I also stumbled across an internet café and sent an email to Canada, letting Shaun and his mother know where I was and that I was fine. In Katima I was 1200 kilometres from Windhoek, the furthest point from the capital while still remaining in Namibia.

I got talking to the lady that ran the café and she told me that tourism had been at an all time low since 1999 when a few rebel soldiers killed some tourists and the media got control of the story. Military convoys were once again started and ran from Kongola to Katima but this had since stopped.

Leaving the building I got into my car and before I could start it an African man waltzed up to the passenger side door with a bottle of black label beer in his hand. Slurring his Himba tongue and as drunk as a skunk he began pulling on the door. Thank god it was locked or he would have got right inside. I reversed out of the spot leaving him to sway awkwardly and unashamedly in full view of the passersby.

Namibia has a population of 1.7 million one of the lowest population densities in Africa. The Owambo population is 650 000, the Afrikaner 65 000, and the German 20 000. The country is made up of 11 ethnic groups with 75% of the population living in rural areas.

I am amazed at how many Africans speak Afrikaans, from really young children to the really old.

Back at the Hippo Lodge I went on a fishing boat along with a local and two Afrikaners from South Africa, one of whom had been a medic as a National Serviceman and so we shared a few army experiences of days never to be lived again.

One of the Afrikaners nearly caught two tiger fish, but after a bit of a fight they both managed to escape the hook and frenzied reeling in of the taut line.

We saw eight hippos a little way away from us. These monsters can crush a boat in half and make mince meat of those on board, so it was wise to stay a safe distance from these cumbersome creatures that sounded like tug boats leaving a harbour.

Birds were in abundance from herons and cranes to all the smaller more colourful ones that made a breath taking scene as we passed through their paradise.

The African driving the boat raced it full tilt across the water allowing it to skim and hop over the water with the nose of the boat rising alarmingly in the air. This thing is going to flip I thought, as it raced down the Zambezi with Zambia's river bank only a stone's throw away. There were some Zambians on the river, standing and rowing their hollowed out logs as their form of transport as they illegally crossed in to Namibia to buy food and fuel to sell on to the local population for a hefty profit.

The police are always on the lookout for these illegal's and if caught their goods are confiscated and they are sent back to Zambia empty handed.

The sunset was amazing as we raced from one inlet into another with the wind streaking through our hair and the fine spray settling very soothingly over us. The sun as always was huge and magnificent especially over water as it performed Africa's closing ceremony on another glorious day on the exciting African continent.

Back on land we went into the Hippo Lodge and placed our orders for dinner while sipping on our cold beers. The two Afrikaners had come up on business from South Africa and had driven up through Botswana before deciding to do some fishing on the Zambezi.

By the time dinner was served, a very appetizing beef schnitzel, we were in deep conversation about South Africa and the rocky political road it was on. The army days, of 'where did you serve' and 'what was your role,' came up as it always does with any of my age group who were conscripted during the turbulent years of white minority rule.

After a good evening of laughs, too many beers and an insight into the new democratic South Africa where violence was on the upswing along with the white exodus overseas, I staggered off to bed.

At 6:30am I was up and on the road in the direction of Grootfontein, an uncomfortable 800 kilometres away.

Along the Caprivi Strip while driving the Golden Highway I passed a herd of at least 20 elephant's right on the edge of the paved roadway. I stopped the car and gazed at these old prehistoric monarchs as they swayed their trunks and their bodies as they reached up into the trees for a helping of green leaves with incredible agility. Placid and undeterred by my presence they remained in a close herd with their ears working like huge fans and their trunks like protective arms as they shielded the little calves. They moved like a controlled hurricane through the overgrowth snapping and tearing away branches at will, leaving behind an aftermath of devastation. They were enormous and moved peacefully through the undergrowth offering me a quick glimpse into their world before they moved off deeper into the bush.

Back in my car I hit the road again. These roads were a constant nightmare with cows, donkeys, goats and dogs that wandered across, running the gauntlet against the stream of trucks and cars.

I remember Connie telling me to only drive between sunrise and sunset to avoid animal collisions and also never to drive below half a tank as petrol stations are extremely few and far between.

Taking my chance with animal crossings I had the pedal to the metal and at 140 kilometres an hour I hit a guinea fowl that bounced off the front of the car like a soccer ball. I stopped, first of all to access the damage and surprisingly found none. Relieved I began a search for the fowl and found it dead in the grass at least 30 metres from the car.

On arriving in Grooties I got a room in a Afrikaner woman's private house and after a nice hot bath and a cup of tea with her I headed off into town.

In town an African man ambled up to me asking for money, and being the person I am, I stopped and looked at him giving him permission to talk.

'I fought with Koevoet for many years,' he said to me as he unfolded a piece of paper.

'I want to go to America and fight with the American army,' he blurted out.

'I need money to get there and these are all the people who have given me money.' Raising the paper to my face I read a long list of names and money denominations.

Quite certain that the money was going on drink if his eyes were anything to go by, and yet sympathizing for what a void he must now have in his life, I gave him N$ 20.

Getting into my car I heard the rolling sounds of thunder and that dreadful feel in my gut that meant the rains were on their way, taking me back to those God awful nights of saturation as the elements tortured our souls to breaking point.

Back in the house it was rewarding to have the rain beat at the roof tiles instead of on my skin, while I sipped on a nice cup of steaming tea.

At 7:30am I was on the road heading in the direction of Swakopmund with a completely recovered stomach after the severe cramping in Katima thanks to one too many mouthfuls of Zambezi water.

On the drive I saw a huge female Kudu trapped on the roadway between the barricades of fencing that had been erected to keep the animals off the road. With nowhere to go it continually jumped into the fencing in a bid to escape but unfortunately to no avail. It was panicking and I knew it would be a matter of time before it crossed the road and became road kill.

It reminded me of a man I had met in Rundu that had hit a Kudu and was very lucky to tell the tale.

Stopping at a shell petrol station I met an ex SWAPO fighter from Angola who filled my tank and after a brief conversation he shook my hand, knowing full well that I was from South Africa and had served in SWA under our apartheid government.

I picked up an African on the side of the road who was thumbing a lift in the direction of Swakopmund, even before I had time to question myself at this crazy action.

It was the strangest feeling with my untrusting South African mentality, to have a black man in the car let alone riding in the front seat. He was a tall and very slender Owambo with skin as black as coal and a warm smile that lit up his face, chasing away any worries.

He was on his way to Swakopmund on business and carried a small black canvas briefcase that looked as though it had done one too many deals.

I was really taken aback when he offered to pay for petrol, but I would not accept anything as I was on my way there anyway and I knew he needed the money more than I did.

Just before Swakopmund I dropped him off and felt the soothing cool temperature and a steady wind that blew off the Atlantic Ocean and over the dunes of the famous Kalahari Desert.

What a great feeling it was to smell the salt off the ocean, inhalling lungfulls of this deep cleansing auroma. It is a smell that binds me to the coast of Africa wherever in the world I might be.

Driving into Swakopmund was like driving through Germany itself with the street names German and the buildings as colonial as one could get. Many restaurant menus were in German and so too a vast number of the inhabitants spoke the German language. This was a home away from home for many tourists from Europe and also for those German South West Africans that had been born in Africa and chose a place connecting them to their European roots.

I booked in at the Desert Sky Backpackers which was filled with travellers from many corners of the globe that were all on missions of adventure. Some were on shoe string budgets and others on drunken binges of all night partying with hangovers and long sleeps to show for their time, while others ventured out with their Lonely Planet guide book in search of their must-see places and sites.

I began the drive out of Swakopmund towards Walvis Bay but did not go very far before I stopped, parked the car and ventured out on a whim to climb a Kalahari dune.

The sun was beating down as I walked up to the mountain of sand that was perfectly formed with not a print or indentation as evidence that man had been here before. The wind had gusted across the sand like a vacuum cleaner would over a carpet presenting a clean and untouched look.

My feet in my flip flops slipped and slid as the sand cascaded over the tip of the dune as I followed its path, winding my way up to the highest point. When I eventually turned around I was rewarded with a remarkable sight. Sweating like a pig I sat down and marvelled at the beauty. Here I was sitting on top of a dune at least 30 to 40 metres high in the Kalahari Desert, watching the waves from the Atlantic Ocean crest and break, with a picture- perfect German town on my right.

Africa certainly is diverse, but Namibia must be the most diverse country on the continent with a rugged beauty that cannot be appreciated until one ventures through it.

I watched a man far below riding his bicycle on the road with a fishing rod protruding from the front and the back as he made his way to his fishing spot, where he would wait with hope and patience to catch dinner for his family.

How calm I felt looking out over this African paradise, in the same country that I had scorned so harshly and unashamedly when I was in my army uniform holding a loaded R4 rifle.

Arriving in Walvis Bay I was greeted with one of the biggest flocks of flamingoes in Southern Africa along with a few pelicans that looked so prehistoric and out of place.

The tide was out so I waded through the water towards this sea of pink and the noise that they were making, but on getting closer I sent them into flight that created a ripple effect as one flock after the next took to the air.

Wings flapped and fanned like sails in the wind leaving the sea blue again and the sky instantly a pink and white while I stood in silence and alone over 200 metres from the shore line.

Walking back my foot sank into the wet sand and when I pulled it out it was black and oily minus my flip flop. This was evidence of oil tanker spills that washed ashore polluting and devastating the bird life, all to get their cargo of black gold to the waiting markets.

Back at the Desert Sky backpackers hangout I met a lot of English travellers who were hitchhiking their way around Namibia and had been working as volunteers to help the local people.

I could not help feeling worried for their safety as hitching and riding African taxis were not the same as Europe. A white skin in Africa can be trouble as it represents money and worse colonial supremacy where the whites had raped and pillaged Africa over the last century for financial gain, whatever the cost and at the detriment of many lives.

I took a drive to Henties Bay and passed a salt refinery with a mound of salt like a mine dump that looked as fresh as snow with a beautiful clear blue ocean behind it.

Making my way to the beach I came across two separate toilets built of concrete with a roof but minus the privacy of the doors. They were in the middle of nowhere with the ocean only a stone's throw away. What a peculiar setting I thought as I looked into these abandoned porcelain kingdoms that were leaning like the tower of Pisa.

Carrying on with my journey it struck me as odd not to see any car wrecks on the side of the road that are so prevalent in Owamboland.

In northern Owamboland the shell of the car is left on the side of the road where the accident took place. Like an animal eaten by ants, it doesn't take long before it is stripped down from wiring to wheel leaving the carcass to rust on the roadside like a skeleton.

As in any third world country whatever can be used and reused will be. Tyres make great rubber footwear, the back axle of the car can be used to carry a bin with donkeys making up for the horse power, wiring to secure things, the battery to run a radio and so the list goes on.

Down on the beachfront in Swakopmund I continued writing up my daily journal, enjoying the peace and salt aroma wafting off the ocean.

It never takes very long before someone starts selling you something that you do not want. It does not matter what you say they hang around with the sad begging eyes, and the guilt trip that they are hungry.

Tired and frustrated after a lengthy battle to get rid of the sellers from my space and my comfort of the bench, I told them to ask for food and money from their own people.

Reluctantly they left me, and leaning back into the bench I was reminded of my back pain that I must have picked up on one of the uncomfortable beds on the trip not to mention the sitting and driving for miles.

Back at the Desert Sky hostel I joined a group of travellers who were sitting on sofa chairs, some gazing at the television as the Springboks played the All Blacks, while others talked and thumbed through the Lonely Planet.

It never takes long to meet people, with the usual questions of, 'where are you from' and 'how long have you been here' and 'where have you been' and 'where to next.'

Through the conversation I met a Canadian who was from Vancouver. He seemed so different from any other Canadian that I had met thus far. He was arrogant and had a chip on his shoulder and brushed me off like a fly on a wall.

'Canada is shit! The people are boring and I want to die as a grandfather in South Africa.'

Feeling proud to be Canadian, I shot back at him. 'Well at least it is safe there and there is a future, unlike here.'

'I have been here 14 years and this is my home.'

I could never dream of calling Canada shit after the life it has given me where with hard work, money can buy the goods you need with a sound night's sleep in a neighbourhood without fences.

There is no doubt that South Africa is stunningly beautiful but it becomes blurred as one stares through the burglar bars into the outside world.

Everyone has the right to their opinion but putting your country down is very low, and I felt angry with him for his arrogance and his desire to be considered a South African.

While watching the game I met a few New Zealanders who had worked in England like most backpackers and then flown to Nairobi also known as *Nairobbery*, and had travelled their way south with some good stories.

Leaving Swakopmund I decided to get the car cleaned as the white paint had been sandblasted brown.

I then hit the Kalahari Highway and began to work out when I should be handing the car back. I soon realized I had worked it out wrong and would be arriving in Windhoek one day earlier than I should have.

I made a phone call to get the date changed by a day but without 48 hours notice I was shit out of luck.

The Kalahari Highway was just a single lane paved road as straight as a ruler like most roads in Namibia. After a little way I stopped at the side of the road to stretch my legs and take a leak and then wandered over to a small roadside stall selling crystals and gem stones.

Liking some of the shapes and colours I bought a few which made the sellers day.

To my amusement I saw a phone box equipped with a phone attached to a wooden pole. I was in the middle of nowhere and here was a pay phone. It was as ludicrous as the two toilets on the beach.

I stopped at a place called Okahandja, 60 kilometres from Windhoek. As soon as I opened the door I was surrounded by a throng of Africans like a swarm of flies to a bloody piece of meat.

'Come with me. Come with me!' they shouted, pulling at my vest.

I was in a market with umpteen stalls of wooden animals, clay pots, mats and the list went on.

I followed one and it did not take long to see the most amazing elephant carved so perfectly out of a piece of iron wood. It was heavy and smooth and so meticulous in detail.

'How much?' I asked, knowing that the reply would be double what it was worth.

'One hundred Namibian dollars,' which was soon followed with N$80 and then after some haggling we settled on N$45, which I felt was an excellent deal for such workmanship.

Driving into Windhoek was a strange feeling after being away two weeks, which felt considerably longer having put on 4800 kilometres on the clock and driving the car as fast as I could.

It cost me N$1000 to hire and with around 13 kilometres to the litre, it was certainly worth every penny.

Walking back into the Cardboard Box I met some familiar faces who had not moved out and were still looking for work, while others were just chilling and planning the next adventure on the continent of Africa.

I always find it amazing how one can meet a fellow traveller, part ways and forget about them and then somehow miraculously bump into them again. In Windhoek I ran into a Frenchman and an Australian that I had met in Swakopmund two days before and of all places they were staying at the Cardboard Box, certainly a small world on this huge land mass.

Over a few chilled beers I pondered whether I should head south to see the dunes in the desert and whether I should extend my car hire to get me there.

It did not take long to decide and in the morning I extended the car rental.

While I was doing so, a local girl called Jackie who was in charge of tour organizing told me that she knew of a person that wanted to head down to the dunes at Sossusvlei.

It was always amazing how well things worked out. I bumped into this girl at the tour desk and after a brief conversation she told me she wanted to go.

Ten minutes later I met a Frenchman who was also interested in going along with his Italian travel companion.

So without a second thought we all checked out of the Cardboard Box, piled into the car with our backpacks and headed for the Sesriem campsite.

We travelled 80 kilometres southwards on the smooth tar roads, before stopping at a Spar supermarket to stock up on some food for the campsite.

While stopping for petrol at a lone petrol station in the middle of nowhere we met two Israelis, who I had last seen in Swakopmund a few days back and a good two days travel away.

On the road again we headed onto a dirt road which was very bumpy, winding, hilly and full of sharp stones.

I drove like a madman and freaked the group out with some rally style driving.

William the Frenchman rather enjoyed it from his front passenger seat as he smirked through his ginger beard. The same could not be said for Gianni from Italy and Tehela from Israel who cowered into the backseat as nervous as all hell as I slid, braked and accelerated with each blind turn.

What a feeling it was to floor the car like a rally driver, something I had always wanted to be.

Coming up to a truck I was always amazed at how courteous the drivers were. On him sighting me he immediately put his right signal on as a sign that it was safe to pass and then he pulled over as far as he could, allowing me to speed by.

There were a few cars that I had passed with the unmistakable ZA stickers standing for Zuid Afrika in Dutch and South Africa as I knew it.

After some great speed and less time than we had anticipated we arrived at the Sesriem campsite where we checked in for two nights. One night was to be spent at the emergency campsite and the other in a proper site with a fire pit and a low stone wall around it.

The African attendant warned us of hyenas and told us how someone had recently been bitten very badly by one of these scavengers in the night.

At the site I met a New Zealander and his girlfriend who I had last seen at Swakopmund. I got on really well with them and they told me they were heading for Canada in the near future.

And so like all travellers do, addresses were exchanged with time and fate being the factors if there was ever to be another meeting.

We ate like kings over the gas stove with Gianni excelling as the chef, making us amazing spaghetti with onions in a tomato sauce.

After our dinner Gianni and I went to a small makeshift bar that sold ice cold Castle Lager. Enjoying a few beers we chatted about life in general, South African politics and the world of travel.

It is always very rewarding to get a fellow travellers perspective on things especially when they have experienced very similar circumstances in countries that we both have ventured through.

Back at the tent the wind was really getting up and blew for at least an hour with the sand hitting the walls of the tent like a blizzard.

In spite of the gusts of wind, the hard ground and the small tent, I still managed a good sleep.

As planned the four of us rose at 5am and set out by car for Sossusvlei for sunrise. The roads were tarred but were battle scarred with pot hole after pot hole which became increasingly hard to navigate in pitch darkness.

We eventually got to a point where no cars were allowed any further due to the density of the thick sand that would have bogged the car down in an instant.

So with our cameras and water bottles in our day bags we walked into the desert and the sun like a light dial that was turned ever so slightly on, illuminated mounds of sand one after the next like a miracle all around us.

It was unbelievable to be in this world with nothing other than a mountain of sand heaped and windblown to perfect precision.

We continued walking for at least five kilometers climbing the dunes at will one of which was at least a 70 metre climb with a spectacular view over Dead Valley.

Dead trees were still standing like crosses in a cemetery on a dried-up salt pan with the earth a crusted white and the backdrop a massive dune of red sand.

Sitting and catching our breath while looking down over it we wallowed in the sheer beauty of it all as if we were sitting on another planet, Mars certainly coming to mind.

How I had hated South West Africa, and yet this scene was out of this world, a world that any person in their right mind would do back flips to see.

In the distance I watched a small group of gemsbok as they wandered over a flat area with their heads down and their long spiral horns sticking up like sharpened spears.

It always amazed me how animals could survive in these extremes but if there is water and some vegetation life will exist.

I also spotted an ostrich and a herd of springboks which leapt across the dried-up salt pan. It was encouraging to see movement in this dead quiet setting which broke the contrast of shadows and dunes and the odd thorn tree which looked so out of place in this enchanted world we had discovered.

Sitting with no cares in the world Gianni and I began chatting to some Belgians who were speaking Flemish, which sounded so much like Afrikaans.

With new energy we threw ourselves over the sheer drop and at a run we charged down the mountainside with sand cascading at each step as we pulled our legs out of the sand with each stride.

It felt like I was floating and getting pulled at the same time because my feet felt weighted down with each step as my shoes filled with sand.

'It looks like you are walking on the moon!' someone shouted as we ran with laughter flowing from us.

At the bottom we walked through Dead Valley, thankful for the overcast day which allowed us to stay that much longer without the heat driving us out with dehydration.

The contrast of colours was simply amazing and the beauty of sand was beyond my wildest dreams. A sea of red dunes was to me as beautiful as a clear blue ocean. It was like a lost paradise that remained hidden from package tourists, allowing those adventurous backpackers an experience that has to be seen to be fully comprehended.

After six hours of walking in the desert we wandered back to the car ready for a hot cup of coffee and a bowl of cornflakes while we admired the scenery, feeling grateful for the experience.

Content with life and a full belly we climbed into the car and headed past Dune 45, one of the highest dunes in the desert, and made our way back to Sesriem.

Once at the campsite we moved our tents from the emergency site into the proper camping place with a fire area and a stone wall surrounding it, with a thorn tree offering valuable shade.

I tried to manoeuver the car into our new campsite but to my disgust I got it stuck in the sand. I tried to go forward and then back but I just dug it in deeper.

So after a good string of swear words we cleared the sand away from behind the front wheels and filled the hole with some big stones to act as traction. Flooring and over revving it like a madman and with three pushing, I reversed out and kept it going backwards until to my horror I hit a small wooden stump that acted as a road marker.

With a 'for fucks sakes' I jumped out of the car and looked at the damage, which had sounded like lots of dollars.

I could not believe my eyes when I looked at the bumper and saw that I had taken off some white paint and dented the plastic slightly.

Relieved to see the minimal damage I let out a sigh, especially as the rental company had my MasterCard number and could do as they wished for any repairs.

It soon proved beneficial for us to have this site. At 2:30pm a really strong wind came out of nowhere and blew sand like a wintery blizzard cutting at us like rough sand paper pulled over our skin.

Seeking refuge we sheltered in the dish-washing area behind the corrugated tin, but the sandstorm still came at us from underneath and over the top, whipping and cutting menacingly at us.

It did not let up and so we decided to seek safety in the car and for the next four hours we watched as the sand like a brown cloud billowed across the car like a hurricane.

People battled to stay on their feet, while we watched and laughed critisizing and predicting their every move as they got sand blasted.

It was as though we had smoked a joint as we could not control our laughter over the smallest details before us while we passed the time.

Eventually, when it was safe to venture out we walked over to a small shack and placed an order of cheese burgers and chips.

To me it seemed like this was wishful thinking, how the hell could a kitchen in the middle of the bush churn out a few cheese burgers and chips.

At 6:30pm we went back to the kitchen and lo and behold there were our cheese burgers and chips for only N$23.

Smiling like small kids at play in a sandpit, we munched on our food that had been cooked up in the middle of the Namib Desert.

We savoured each bite with enjoyment that I had never experienced before in civilian life.

After our meal we found a nice place to watch the sunset but unfortunately the dust had destroyed the final setting for us. It did not come close to the previous night as the fiery red radiated over the dunes and thorn trees, making a perfect picture to end the day.

Gianni and I went on the hunt for some dry wood which we carried and dragged back to the fire pit. On the way back we saw a springbok and then in the camp we saw a gemsbok which had walked right into the camp.

Brave and stupid it stood still, and was lucky that no one shot it and made a big desert braai.

The fire we made was huge as we kept heaping wood on it along with some creosote poles which stank to high heaven as the tar melted off them.

The flames flickered and licked around the logs as crackles and pops erupted from the fire under a sky filled with bright stars with a segment of moon adding to the magic of a beautiful evening in the African bush.

Each with a Castle in our hands we laughed and joked as we learned more about each other's countries in our little United Nations group, with representation from Italy, France, Israel and South Africa/Canada.

'To Soussusvlei!' I said as we raised our beers to a mind blowing day in the Namib Desert.

After an enjoyable evening around the fire we retired to our tents, mine was so small I had to sleep diagonally, but still managed a good deep sleep.

At 5am we awoke to the annoying sound of the alarm clock. Still under darkness in the very cool morning air we tore down the tents and packed the car, and an hour later we were on the road again bound for the Naukluft Reserve.

We arrived at 8am and immediately set about heating water over the stove for a coffee along with a bowl of cornflakes.

After some discussion we decided to leave the park and head back to Windhoek.

To our delight we saw a herd of kudu, and turning the engine off we observed their movements as they grazed right in front of us, flicking their ears and curling their tongues around the thorn trees as they ate the leaves off the branches. The males looked so prominent with their elegant curved horns as they stared curiously at us.

Africa certainly has a way of working magic when you least expect it, and this was no different as we watched the herd with keen interest.

With William navigating our course on the spread open and very well used map we made our way out on some smooth dirt roads.

While driving I remembered the rule in South West Africa, never to allow the petrol tank to go below half full. Watching the gauge I realized it was time to fill up as the needle sat slightly below half a tank.

I had two choices, I could go a few kilometers in the opposite direction and fill up or we could continue forward and wait for the next petrol station to appear.

With just a quarter tank left we pulled into a one horse town and gratefully drove up to the pump.

To our horror we were told that they had no petrol but it would be here tonight. So with no choice we had 125 kilometres to drive before we hit the next major town.

Coasting down all the hills to save each precious drop we carried on with tension in the car.

To run out of petrol here would be like trying to walk our way out of a desert. To our dismay the reserve light flickered on and we still had a way to go. Holding thumbs and literally willing the car on we drove into a main petrol station on fumes alone and smiles of sheer relief.

With a full tank, some drinks for the road and a wash of the car by a poor local man we were off again for the last 85 kilometres to Windhoek and the Cardboard Box.

It was good to be back in Windhoek which meant that I could hand the car back and not be liable for any damage to this rental.

Unloading the gear and my fellow travellers I headed off to find Connie and the car rental company.

After a lot of difficulty I eventually found it and walked into the main office which was beautifully cool with the air conditioner working overtime.

Connie sauntered out and proceeded to do an inspection as though he was a sergeant major inspecting a troop.

'I told you to use the air conditioner!' he said as he pointed to all the fine dust that had settled over the seats and as I looked closer, into every crack and opening in the car.

I hated air conditioning and that is why the windows were down, I said to myself.

To my surprise that was all he could find. He had missed the marks of the guinea fowl and the wooden pole, the bird I had hit and two large gashes in the tyre thanks to the roads with razor sharp rocks.

Considering I had driven 5800 kilometres in 15 days across some pretty rough terrain I had got off lightly and was very relieved to sign it back.

I got a lift back to the Box and then had lunch and a beer or two with Gianni, William and Tehila.

In the afternoon I went to town to see if I could change my flight back to Johannesburg and arrive three days earlier than originally planned, but was told to call on Monday.

In the evening Gianni, William and I walked into town and had dinner at the Kentucky Fried Chicken which was good value but that was all.

Back at the Cardboard Box we had a few beers at the bar and watched a movie called 'Rock' before retiring to bed in the six bed dorm room which at times stank of sweat and old socks.

In the morning we said our goodbyes as William and Gianni caught a bus to Swakopmund.

I was astounded at how many of the same faces were still at the Cardboard Box without the slightest desire to move on in the way I had forced myself on as an avid backpacker.

Some were looking for work, how hard they were looking was another question, while others were chilling and working their way through their travel guides in a quest to conquer another country.

While I had breakfast at the bar I was told about a German, who was working as a travel guide having R19 000 stolen from his bag in the tent. The police were called in but nothing was gained by it. It certainly sounded like another traveller which was sad, but when the need to survive is paramount there is no stopping someone's temptation. Not even a fellow traveller could be trusted when it was survival of the fittest in a foreign land.

It had happened to me in Holland and twice in Thailand and it was a fact that the longer one travelled the higher the chances of being robbed and losing vital items needed for one's survival.

I never forgot the emotional turmoil that this sent through me with the language barrier standing like a wall between me and the police to a degree that I felt as though I had robbed myself.

Feeling bad for the German I lay on my soft mattress which was like a bed made in paradise compared to the gritty and hard Namib Desert.

In the morning I took a walk into town to the local grocery store to stock up on a few supplies for the days meals and then I watched the Springboks play the Samoans, which was a crucial game in the World Cup. To our delight the Boks came through, which was cheered on with a few too many beers.

Walking back into town I met some locals from whom I had bought some curios that I wanted to take back to Canada with me.

They were amazed that I was South African, and when I told them that I was in the army they were even more amazed.

'You were a soldier!' they said, looking me over for some detail that would in fact identify me as a soldier.

They had no idea that all white South African's were conscripted to join the South African Defence Force and be moulded into white soldiers.

I told them that if we did not serve we would be put in jail and as far as serving on the border with SWA and Angola we really did not want to be here but it was our government who drafted us up here to serve.

They looked at me and I could genuinely see that there were no hard feelings. And yet 18 years earlier I would have branded them as black bastards hating them for supporting our enemy, but who in hindsight only wanted independence and liberation from South African control.

In Windhoek the class difference was as clear as day as the rich mainly white well dressed people walked with an air of supremacy and a cell phone glued to their ear. In contrast the poor Africans sat on the roadside with a canvas sheet spread over the tar as they tried to sell their curios to the tourists for a hefty price to cover their licence and R100 a month for a space in which to sell.

Life could not be harder for them but again this was Africa, where it is and always has been the survival of the toughest.

Walking the streets I had seen a lot of broken bottles and sharp shards of glass littering the city, as well as many empty beer and coke bottles all worth a deposit.

Here is money just waiting to be picked up by the hungry poor African and yet there does not seem to be much begging and hassling which seems so ironic with the number of people who have little to nothing.

Traffic was crazy and I was surprised that I had not witnessed a death on a road crossing yet. People drove like Philistines with no regard for zebra crossings and light signals. I felt that drivers here had more chance of striking a pedestrian than other places in the world because people walked where they liked and drivers most definitely drove as if they were the rightful owners of the tarmac.

The hooter, like most African countries works very well, and from the pedestrians point of view so does his middle finger.

Not only was the driving crazy but so was the drinking, smoking and gun control which all went hand in hand with the tense lifestyle.

Tim Ramsden

Houses were fenced in with high brick walls and circles of barbed wire, and electrified fences linked to high tech security alarm systems. Windows were barred as thick as a jail cell; huge dogs roamed the gardens, barking ferociously at passersby, all to keep those jailed-in white people safe from the outside world.

In Tsumeb I remember seeing a church with mesh coverings over the beautiful stained glass windows to prevent a break-in or vandalism. It really hit me hard that not even a church, a place of the Lord which was open to one and all, was safe from the poverty and robbery of the African underprivileged in Namibia.

Also in Swakopmund I remember noticing that every shop had a metal barred gate that the shop owner had to buzz open for every patron before one could pull it open and enter the store.

I also saw this very nice new house that had just been built and while I was admiring it I was disgusted to see the walls with shards of glass set into the cement, standing like razor sharp triangles as a warning to all intruders who might think of scaling the walls.

At the Cardboard Box cars are never left on the street, but are rather driven into the property behind a huge gate on runners with barbed wire adorning the top of it, and a chain and a massive padlock to secure it.

At the bar I had a few beers with a young Englishman who had travelled alone from Cairo to East Africa and then around Southern Africa. He raved about Uganda and how beautiful it was, and listening to his stories I realized what little I had seen of Africa.

One day in the near future I promised myself that I would see more.

Back in the dorm room I fell fast asleep on one of the bunk beds and in the middle of the night I was awoken by a thundering crash. A comatose body had rolled off the top bunk and had landed on the hard floor and after a few mumbled and jumbled words he climbed back up onto his bed and lapsed back into sleep.

In the morning I met a Canadian girl from Toronto, of Chinese descent who was travelling alone for a planned one year trip. I admired her courage to travel through wild Africa where anything can go horribly wrong.

Walking down Independence Ave in Windhoek I decided to stop for a decent meal and went into the Spur Restaurant, which had a great balcony overlooking the street and the life that passed below.

It was Sunday so the shops were closed, there was less traffic on the road and fewer people walking the pavements to and from work.

It was nice to see the city in this light as I enjoyed my burger and chips, a far cry from the camping food we had eaten in the desert.

I thought about the African family that I had bought some curios off, and I remembered asking them why they spoke Afrikaans.

'The South African's colonized South West Africa and Afrikaans was taught to us in school!' she had replied.

To me it always seemed odd to see an African speak Afrikaans and she told me that they did not view it as the language of the oppressor.

While eating my burger I looked over the street and watched a few Africans turn on a water main that immediately had water gushing everywhere like a fountain.

The free flow of water attracted more Africans as honey would to bees. Some washed their heads and feet, while others danced around gleefully. One man washed the jeans he was wearing as he scrubbed them down with them tight on his legs.

This circus was viewed by us as we sat like royalty looking down over the poor as they made what they could out of the moment.

'We will be paying for this on the next water bill!' an Afrikaner joked at the table next to me.

The price of food here was just crazy, making Canadian food prices look so exceptionally cheap. It was more expensive to live meal by meal out of a supermarket than eating out. The supermarkets were plain, the fruit and vegetables were few and far between and the food offering minimal compared to North America where one can buy the best of everything for a reasonable price.

Many of the backpackers at the Box would buy their food from the supermarket and then in labeled and tied up bags store the perishables in the fridge and the non perishables in a pantry, with the owner's name clearly marking the product as theirs.

The communal kitchen was shared by anyone who wished to use the amenities to concoct a recipe as a stomach lining for the vast quantities of alcohol that would be washed down soon afterwards.

Tim Ramsden

Today I was looking forward to a few cups of coffee and tinned guava and peaches for breakfast, but it had vanished into a thieving backpacker's bag leaving me high and dry.

I still had some cheese and a couple of rolls that filled me up and then I borrowed a few spoons of coffee to add to my mug, then I was set for the day.

I met a few travellers from England, Holland, a couple of South African's and a local Namibian and we sat talking and laughing over a few Tafel lager beers.

One of the English guys had arrived in South Africa for the Rugby World Cup in 1995 and had never returned home. He had been in Namibia for the past six years working as a tour guide, taking tourists up to Damaraland in the most north western part of Namibia.

He was a funny man and according to him, was revered as some sort of God by the tourists as he guided them across and through the most rural areas, presenting them with a picture of Africa that they could only have dreamed about in the luxury of their expensive homes, oceans away.

There were many travellers staying at the Box who worked in Windhoek, and there were others who were tour guides. Some had been there for months and others years, making a fair wage to keep their adventure of travel alive.

And then I thought of the locals who were earning N$600 to N$800 a month, which at N$5.40 to the Canadian dollar equated to a measly $111 to $148 a month.

How they survived on this was beyond me, but again we were in Africa and as difficult as life might be, the Africans march on in a struggle that they know better than any white person.

As a backpacker I had been told that this was one of the most expensive countries in Africa to travel, and so far with car rental, accommodation and food I definitely agreed. The cheapest dorm bed cost N$50, 1 litre of petrol N$3.80, a loaf of bread N$4.50, a can of coke N$5.00, a tin of canned fruit N$8.00 and worth mentioning two nights in the Etosha Game park clost a staggering N$600.00, which targets the elite travellers. For the down to earth backpacker these prices would eat up the shoestring that most of us lived on in an effort to gain an extra day in the paradise of world travel.

All to live another day in a new land and take with us a tale to be remembered and revered.

Speaking to some English people that were working at the Cardboard Box I was amazed at how it got its name. The name was acquired from London where there are so many homeless people living in makeshift shelters made mostly from cardboard boxes, for protection from the wind and cold.

When I was in London I had witnessed this, and at the time I felt no sympathy for those hundreds hiding themselves under dirty cardboard as they lived out their life with absolutely nothing.

India had also been the same with bodies lying homeless in the streets, and again I felt less than nothing to see them this way. Our blacks are better off than them I thought as I stepped over some of the sleeping bodies.

The word Cardboard Box meant so much more to me now as my mind raced back to all the homeless I had seen as I travelled through my list of 35 countries.

It was time for me to leave Namibia and head to Johannesburg in South Africa, but I needed to get my flight changed by a couple of days.

I went into the South African Airways office in Windhoek and after a long line up I was told to pay US$75 to make the change.

This is too hefty I thought and the lady behind the counter suggested that I go to the airport and see what I could do there, which made sense.

Morgan, the lady working the reception at the Cardboard Box, arranged for a taxi to pick me up and take me the 45 kilometre journey to the airport for a cost of N$100.

Loading my heavy pack into the boot we were on our way. The driver was a friendly African man who drove with caution and sensible speed unlike many taxi drivers.

On the way I spotted a troop of baboons numbering at least 30 as they crossed the road, some with little babies hanging from underneath them. Once on the roadside they sat and watched the cars race by while they picked and scratched each other and frowned curiously as if they were deep in thought.

Tim Ramsden

Glad to be at the airport I scanned the row of faces at the check-in counter and chose a white lady as my hope to get on the flight without having to fork out a very unnecessary US$75.

I explained my story of needing to get back to South Africa a couple of days earlier and that I was to arrive at the airport and it would not be a problem.

'It will cost you $75!' she said.

'No that is not what I was told!' I shot back lying through my teeth with a straight face.

'Who did you speak to?' she retaliated.

'I have spoken to a few different people, and they all said it wouldn't be a problem!' I challenged with a voice of authority, which did the trick.

My ticket was processed and my bag was checked, and then after a pleasant chat to the lady I walked jubilantly through customs.

I still felt stiff from the desert walk and sore from all the driving. My neck ached like it would just crack off and hurt like hell and so did my back, with just less than 6000 kilometres travelled in 18 days.

It seemed like a whirlwind journey across this magnificent country. What I saw and experienced wiped away my army memories and gave me a rich and rewarding feeling to be savoured for years to come.

The slate had been wiped clean and on it had been inscribed a land to be experienced.

This was not the arse end of the world any more, but it was a land of such contrasts. Open desert and sand dunes, rock solid anthills some as high as trees, a Game Park rivalling the best in Africa where wild animals roam the flat plains, rivers with African sunsets shimmering off the peaceful waters, German buildings and Owambo huts, and a nation of people white and black living without war in a growing economy.

Namibia is certainly a success story on the African map, where there are approximately 1.7 million people, which translates to two people per square kilometre, making it one of Africa's lowest population densities.

One knows one is in a third world country when one has to walk onto the runway and board the plane.

The sun beat down with such venom almost as a farewell from this harsh climate as I climbed the stairs onto the plane, took my seat and looked out of the window.

I had done what I set out to do and more. I had wanted and needed to see this land and experience all those same conditions that were meted out to me as a young National Serviceman, many many years ago.

Now I would be able to write my army story with more passion and feeling and with constructive views, views that were definitely not in my apartheid- driven and angry teenage brain.

The engines roared to life and casting a look at my watch the plane was leaving on time.

Taking to the air I was on my way to Johannesburg, the place of my birth before I would be heading to Durban, my hometown before I chose Canada as my new home.

Leaning back in the seat I had done something I vowed never ever to do, and that was to return to this God awful country.

I am glad I was privileged to travel through it again and see for myself a land and a nation blessed with beauty and free speech.

In 18 days I had erased 150 days for hatred to a land and its people that had festered in me for nearly two decades.

South West Africa with my closed and corrupted mind was no more, and thankfully Namibia is now a gem that I am so grateful to have rediscovered.

Tim Ramsden

MOZAMBIQUE (2005)

It was a strange feeling to be standing next to Wayne at the Durban airport as we watched Laurence clear through customs.

It had been 19 years ago since I had last seen Laurence, and although he had packed on a few pounds, he was still recognizable as the Laurence we knew as part of 23Alpha section in our Platoon 3 army unit.

With smiles and handshakes we reconnected in a split second, with that army bond ever present.

It seemed like yesterday that the three of us were in uniform bonded in our steadfast platoon, a platoon that weathered whatever was thrown at us and emerged stronger and more enmeshed each time.

The last three months of our service were marred by the capture of three of our Alpha section as they crossed for a swim in Mozambique. We had all done it but the unlucky three were our section leader Paul, our LMG gunner

Sandor and the LMG number two Laurence.

Unfortunately Paul had been killed in a car accident some years later, and all I knew of his story was through his daughter.

This is what she told me: He was in that underground prison. Mom says he had nightmares every night and she had to wake him up...they told him they had killed his two friends, in fact they dragged a body past his cell...they tortured him and right to the very end of his life you couldn't touch his fingernails and if you brought a syringe with a needle anywhere near him he would pass out...he couldn't talk about these terrible things that happened to him...he carried a lot of pain inside of him and he started having counseling a month before his death, but got so upset and couldn't stop crying with mom one whole night...mom never saw him cry before, even when his dad died...so he stopped going.

I along with many who knew Paul were very saddened by his untimely death, he was not only a great person but a great leader.

Sandor, according to Laurence was living up in Port Nolloth in Namaqualand close to Namibia, where his line of work was connected with diamonds. I had not heard from him since December 1985.

All three had languished for three months in Mozambique as captured soldiers. Laurence had spent two long months in the high security prison called Machava in Maputo.

I later found out that methods of interrogation and torture from East Germany were exported to third world countries belonging to the Soviet bloc. Mozambique's Marxist ruling party, FRELIMO, had used Stasi (East German Secret Police)-like methods in its political prison at Machava.

Laurence had been confined to a tiny cell and deprived of sunlight to break him down, just as the East Germans had done to their prisoners during the Cold War.

With my writing the book on our time as National Servicemen, Laurence was here to tell us his story in person and to take us back to the place where his mind and spirits were tortured to the very core.

We did not waste any time, drinking beer after beer as we caught up on 19 years of laughs and the rekindling of memories that we shared so vividly together.

Wayne and I had kept in contact ever since the day we were handed our clear out papers to end our mandatory two year military call up. He had not changed, besides some streaks of grey in his black hair and a few wise suntanned lines on his smiling face.

Bottles clanged against each other as we held our arms outstretched with smiles locking the moment, everything else forgotten while we reconnected, as we had done so many times in our past.

Beers flowed and so did the laughs until we crashed into bed in the early hours of the morning.

It wasn't long before the alarm clock rudely forced us out of bed, and walking around like zombies we dressed and were packed and ready to move at the ungodly time of 5:30am.

With a coffee mug in hand we climbed into Wayne's truck and settled in for the drive with Wayne at the wheel.

The time on the road went fast as we talked and laughed with excitement while we sped up the north coast towards Swaziland with the adventure beckoning us.

After clearing customs at the Swazi border post and having the truck inspected we clambered aboard and headed through Swaziland in the direction of Mozambique.

Under a light drizzle we arrived at the Mozambique border where we had to first of all get a visa stamped into our passports.

Any government run organization worldwide is a test of patience where time drags at a snail's pace and one is ushered around from one counter to another, totally at the official's mercy.

But in Africa it is ten times worse as there is a total lack of organization in a go-slow environment.

I wanted to shout out at the African gentleman to move his arse, especially as we were the only three being seen to.

After an hour we were set to go from his room, having paid for the visa in South African Rand, and into the next for another check of the passport and a stamp that gave us permission to head to the border gate.

At the gate a uniformed soldier looked over our documents and then miraculously waved us through.

Following a winding potholed road we were now in Mozambique and it wasn't long before a cluster of old Portuguese houses presented themselves.

One of the structures looked like the shell of a once proud home now reduced to ruin, standing like a statue to the present condition of the country, a country having endured two decades of civil war.

Only the brick remained as the bush encroached on the dwelling. We had entered one of the poorest countries in the world and it certainly showed.

Once in Maputo, the capital of Mozambique, we found a Bank to exchange our Rands into the Mozambican currency of the Meticais, and literally overnight we became millionaires with Joaquim Chisssano's face gracing a very worn 10 000 Meticais bill.

With our wallets bulging we headed back to the truck and then we began searching for the Ibis Hotel. We drove by it at least five times on the very busy main street called Avenue September 25, until we asked someone and then we found it easily.

We quickly booked in and then walked over to the Continental Café where we sat at tables on the wide sidewalk and ordered some local beer. With three Laurentina's firmly in our grasp we banged our glass bottles together and then took a gulp of this Mozambican beer brewed since 1932 and which actually tasted very good. The country may be in total ruin but the beer is still good, I thought, as I lowered the quart bottle to the dirty table top.

Smiling, we enjoyed the moment as we watched the Third World life amble by amongst the ruin and disrepair where ever we seemed to gaze.

Walls were dirty with flaking paint; litter blew in the wind as people drifted hopelessly by, some begging while others walked with urgency as if they were trying to catch a bus at the next stop.

It was here that I felt so rich with my job and new Canadian life while these people had almost nothing as they eked out a miserable existence from one day to the next.

One only had to look at the political strife with the FRELIMO government and its war with RENAMO to understand the predicament of the people in a once very prosperous country.

The waiter looked after us well, and before the bottles were empty another round was quickly served. Miguel was a small man with a shy smile and looked no older than a teenage schoolboy. His head was shaved giving him a wise look and his skin was lighter than most Africans. He stood over us and asked questions in relatively good English, with Portuguese being his mother tongue.

After a few more beers I looked up to Miguel and asked: 'Do you know where Machava is?'

He looked at us for a few seconds and then replied.

'Yes I know where it is and I can take you there.'

'We are looking for the Machava Prison!' I blurted out.

'Yes I can take you there tomorrow,' he replied very casually.

So at 11am we arranged to meet Miguel at the Continental Café and he would direct us to the prison and the nightmare that Laurence was about to open up.

As the beers flowed so I began to ask Laurence more leading questions on his capture and imprisonment.

I could see the strain on his face as he tried to find the words to describe his experiences in his broken English that was way better than how I would be replying in Afrikaans.

Laurence asked Miguel for a box of matches and some cigarettes and so Miguel went inside and returned a few minutes later.

He lit up and then he looked down at the matches and cigarettes and shouted to us.

'Look at my arms. Do you see the goosebumps!' Laurence coughed out.

'This is a Palmer cigarette and these are Pala Pala matches. I tasted this smoke 20 years ago and these are the same matches that lit it!' he exclaimed as if he had just witnessed a revelation.

I looked at Laurence and could see and feel his mind racing back 20 years into the depths of a secluded cell.

I stared at the buck on the front of the box of matches and then looked back at Laurence. I knew this was confirmation and I too felt a chill race through my body.

We were indeed in the country where his life was tortured at the hands of his FRELIMO captors.

He tilted his head back and blew out cigarette smoke above our heads and then reached for his beer with his arms still beaded with bumps.

It was not only a privilege, but the rekindling of a bond from our army service as we sat and listened to jumbled pieces from Laurence's life at the hands of FRELIMO inside Machava.

It was like watching a curtain being opened ever so slowly in the middle, revealing a new world never seen before.

After at least three beers each we headed in search of the Costa Del Sol, famous many years ago for its colossal and delicious grilled king prawns.

It wasn't difficult to find, but the open verandah was packed abuzz with conversation as the waiters weaved between the tables to serve the hungry customers.

A young African who we nicknamed James Bond offered to watch Wayne's green Colt *bakkie* for a small fee, which we agreed to.

The smell of prawns was in the air as soon as we set foot on the verandah, and like a fish on a hook we were reeled to a table.

Before we had time to think we had three beers plonked down in front of us and after a quick cheers we were drinking again.

Behind us I noticed a table of at least 15 people all talking Russian, confirming the communist presence since 1975, which certainly made me feel slightly uneasy.

They looked like a combination of young soldiers and businessmen discussing deals in this poor land that had been raped and pillaged by war, and where corruption continues to cause conflict.

I had heard of stories regarding food that was harvested in Mozambique by the starving poor being sold to Russia for arms and ammunition to continue Marxist rule.

It seemed crazy, but war is cold and uncaring, protecting the lifestyle of the elite linked to the ruling government, all at the expense of the people trying to steer their families away from it, who in the end are caught up so selfishly in the middle.

When the prawns arrived we could not believe what we saw. There were a dozen prawns at least five inches thick swimming in a pool of garlic butter with a huge plate of chips on the side.

We were in heaven as we sucked and chewed on these massive prawns famous in this place once called Lourenco Marques, before the Portuguese were forced to flee. With the Portuguese relinquishing their power the country was handed over to FRELIMO, who wasted no time in renaming the capital Maputo.

After a late night, a full belly and a head dazed with beer and whisky we returned to the Ibis Hotel and crashed in our room, absolutely dead to the quiet outside world of Maputo.

With hangovers of note we drove to the Holiday Inn and had a few coffees and then nearly vomited at the bill. Coffee was a ridiculous price of $3.50 a cup which was daylight robbery in Africa.

Missing out on breakfast we rushed to the Continental Café which was once an old Portuguese pastry shop with ceramic tiles and old paintings adorning its walls, and there we found an anxious Miguel waiting for us.

As soon as Miguel stepped into the truck and sat next to Laurence in the back, I had no choice but to blurt out: 'Gee it is really hot in here!' and then wasting no time I wound down the window.

The smell that he gave off was too offensive for words, with wood smoke and stale sweat giving off a pungent odour that hit our nostrils with a disgusting slap.

With Miguel as the backseat navigator we set off in search of the Machava maximum security prison.

'Wake up!' Miguel shouted as he pointed to a car that came too close to us and then again 'Wake up!' as Wayne nearly hit a pedestrian. It did not take us too long to realize that he should have been saying: 'Watch out!' but we pissed ourselves laughing as the 'Wake ups' were being thrown around.

'Wayne wake up!' Laurence and I shouted as Miguel smiled back as if to say yes he should.

After a very bumpy drive through a city that looked as though it had been bombed out and then left to slowly disintegrate through neglect into a dirty worthless ruin, we finally took a right turn.

We followed a straight dirt road towards a set of double battleship-grey steel gates, which were firmly shut.

Getting out we stretched our legs and looked up at the walls that were close to five metres high and extremely thick and unwelcoming.

Laurence still did not know where he was and continually looked for anything to jog his memory and confirm that this was indeed the Machava Prison.

'Look!' he shouted as he pointed to a sewer pipe that ran under the wall.

'I just saw one of those fuckin huge rats! The same as the ones that came into the cells every night,' he spoke out with a shudder to his voice.

'This is Machava!' he said with such conviction that there was no doubt in either of our minds.

I turned and only saw a small dead rat, not the rat that was as big as a cat that had scurried through their cellblocks daily in search of rice scraps.

The prison stood like a fortress walling those inside to never get out and also walling those outside to never get in.

Looking around I saw a circular concrete island about 10 metres from the gate with a tall pole in the middle which had once flown a flag. The concrete was cracked and the flag pole stood like an abandoned post, which most probably last flew a flag when the Portuguese were in power.

Walking up to the gate we were surprised to see it slightly ajar. We noticed faded writing in black paint written in Portuguese, but what it meant we had no idea.

The greyish cream walls seemed to tower over me with peeling paint in the same neglectful way as the rest of the capital. Maputo and Machava for that matter certainly needed a good touch of paint to freshen the appearance and wipe away decades of abandonment.

We poked our heads through the gates and saw a holding area where vehicles would be enclosed on either side by two sets of grey gates, before it could enter or exit the prison.

Suddenly a guard wandered out with a face as solemn as if a family member had just died, and at his side a stern looking soldier dressed in a camouflaged uniform and a green beret walked towards us.

'Can we have a look inside?' Miguel asked in Portuguese.

'Why?' the solemn faced man shot back.

'We look at prisons from all around the world!' I challenged while Miguel translated to them in Portuguese.

He thought about it for a long while and after some deep and careful consideration he shook his head.

I had some American money and wanted to bribe him so that I could see what this place was all about. It was said that this notorious prison could kill a person in six months, and judging by the outside I could certainly believe it.

There were guard towers cut into the walls leaving a curved slit as wide as half a face to peer out from, like a hijab over a face allowing only the eyes to see through the opening.

Overhead lights curved over the wall with bulbs either shattered or missing, standing like scarecrows in a field.

I asked Miguel to ask him again to see if he would change his mind, but again after some sighing and weighing of the pros and cons, his head shook from side to side.

I now really wanted to hand over some hard currency but thought that this could be viewed in the wrong light and have me imprisoned for corruption and bribery.

Thanking him for nothing we ambled back to the *bakkie* and waited for Miguel who was still talking to the solemn faced man.

When we drove away Laurence suddenly shouted: 'This is it, I remember the water tower. This is Machava.'

We looked over the wall and saw a water tower next to some palm trees with the rectangular structure standing as the symbol to Laurence's recollection of one of the precious few things he ever saw on the outside of his cellblock.

With this in mind we were determined to see more, and so we drove around the prison to another entrance where Wayne and I got out and walked towards the main gate. At the gate there was another set of slits in the wall and I noticed two sets of eyes staring like snipers at us.

I looked at the walls and saw a concrete block with the words 'Central' along with another Portuguese word etched into the stone.

To me it just confirmed that this was indeed the Machava Central Prison.

Then all of a sudden an African in plain clothes came rushing out of the gate flanked by two uniformed soldiers waving their hands and shouting with menacing faces that looked as though they could kill in a second.

Thrown off guard we stopped in our tracks.

'What do you want!' the man in the plain clothes screamed out as if he already knew we had tried to get into the prison from the other side.

Miguel immediately began talking Portuguese, trying to calm this tense situation while Laurence sat frozen in the back of the 4X4 truck.

'Let's get out of here!' Laurence said with definite fear in his voice.

Nodding agreement we all climbed back in and waited for Miguel to smooth things over.

I could sense the panic in Laurence as he looked at this hell hole, clearly not wanting to get an inch closer to reopening his nightmare.

'I would rather kill myself than go back in there!' Laurence said as he looked at the walls and soldiers with a pale face filled with horror at what he had lived through two decades ago.

'Let's go!' I said with hidden fear, my gut feeling that the situation we were in could turn ugly in an instant.

We drove away in silence all very spooked at how fast things had moved and for all we knew they could have assumed we were three white mercenaries trying to get a prisoner out. Things could have turned ugly on us with poor communication, third world African mentality and the possible threat we presented as we lurked around the prison.

Back at the road that led down to the main prison gate we stopped, and I got out and quickly snapped a picture. The walls looked sinster and overpowering surrounding the misery within. Inside the prison, palm trees gave off an air of beauty while the guard towers with bricks missing and a huge square concrete pylon that looked as though it had once carried electricity stood like sinister markers. The water tower and the corrugated iron tank on top reflected the sun's rays like a warning symbol to all those that might be unlucky enough to be incarcerated here.

Local Africans wandered by as I snapped a shot, feeling as if I had just committed the sin of all sins, with all African eyes on me.

'No photos!' an African man shouted as he waved his hands madly, as if trying to erase the frame I had just taken.

Not a moment too soon we were on our way.

I looked at Laurence and he sat as rigid as a corpse. His head was pounding and he looked as though he had seen a ghost.

'I would rather die than go back in there again!' he mumbled like a man stoned out of his mind.

The tension in the *bakkie* was unbelievable as we smiled to ourselves, putting distance between us and the prison.

Not even three minutes from the prison we rode up to a police roadblock with policemen milling around and randomly pulling cars over.

My thoughts were racing as a big policeman strolled up to our vehicle and pointed to Wayne to park it on the side of the road.

Had he been tipped off about our effort to gain entry into the Machava Prison, and was he here to extort something out of us through blackmail?

'Licence!' he said looking at Wayne as we all sat and stared.

Laurence sat still and stiff as his mind raced a million miles an hour with spine-chilling nightmares of Machava resurfacing.

'I left my licence at the hotel!' Wayne responded to the policeman.

Laurence then reached over and handed his licence to the stern faced African man, who took it and thumbed through his Identity Document.

'Miguel, start translating!' we told him as the cop held on to the licence with the same care as if he was holding a large wad of money.

We looked at him in horror as he held his bargaining chip with bribe written all over his face and yet he did not say anything.

'We have no money!' we lied trying to squash his thought of an easy bribe.

Before we left South Africa we had been told that under no circumstance should we part with any of our documents as once they had it in their hands the only way to get it back was by handing over some cash.

Laurence's headache was now pounding as we sat like pawns in a chess game, while he stood over us like a threatening king cornering us in checkmate.

We did not back down and continually pushed Miguel to get the document back, which after 20 minutes we finally did, but only in exchange for Miguel's papers.

The cop told Miguel he was charging us 50 000 Meticus or in our terms, five big red ones.

The policeman wanted Wayne to stay behind and Laurence to drive back to the hotel to get the money, which we refused.

Eventually we all returned to the hotel gave Miguel the five big red ones, which were five 10 000 Meticus notes, and told him to return to the waiting policeman.

When Miguel left we wondered if he had struck up a deal with the cop as we would have been none the wiser as to what was said in Portuguese.

With Miguel and the cop out of our thoughts we all went to Nandos for lunch and a couple of very necessary Castle beers which sent the jolts of Machava and the roadblock out of our minds.

In the afternoon we drove along the coastline where little fishing boats were bobbing on the ocean like corks as African bodies worked the nets for their incomes.

Africans on the shore stood by their flimsy boats weighing and sorting their days catch like bankers counting money. If one could read their smiles it was as if they were saying we have food tonight and some money in our pocket.

These people were poor, their clothing said it all and yet they seemed to smile through it like sun breaking through a cloud. Crowds gathered around each boat out of inquisitiveness and boredom as they looked into the paper thin hull that had sailed the seas once too often.

We stopped at a market outside Costa Del Sol and looked at a few beautiful wood carvings made by poor Africans eking out a living by hoping to attract tourists who in their eyes were like walking money bags.

In the dying hours of daylight we made it to the Continental Café for a few drinks, where we met Miguel who had managed to get his identity papers back after handing over the cash.

Laurence puffed away on his Palmer cigarettes that continued to raise goosebumps on his arms every now and then as the taste took him back to captivity in his pitch black cellblock.

While we watched life amble by on the dark street named after the month and day (Ave September 25th) that Mozambique gained its independence from its colonial overseas master, we were approached by an African salesman.

Drunk and without any intention of parting with our money we beckoned him over and looked at his works of art.

He had three massive wood carvings that he set down on our table. We all eyed them and like three kids in a candy store we selected what we liked. I grabbed the rhino, a beautiful rusty red 'white' rhino with its square jaw a perfect replica of the real animal. Wayne selected a nice smooth redwood hippo and Laurence cradled a fish eagle with a wing span to be remembered. After a little bit of drunken bargaining we

Tim Ramsden

were R470 poorer and very happy, the salesman considerably richer and a lot lighter.

With our trophies clutched in our hands we walked back to the Ibis Hotel and went straight to the bar where we met an African woman from Beira, and in my dazed state I mistook her name to be Vicious.

'Vicious please can you take a photo of us?' I asked as we lined up behind the bar with our mascots as memories of Mozambique.

It was a great picture and a great moment as we stood as civilians with that link back to our teenage army days as part of Section Two Three Alpha.

I continued calling the African woman Vicious for most of the evening until Wayne came up to me and told me that her name was in fact Precious.

Wow I thought, Vicious and Precious, I could not have picked more of an opposite name, but she had not said a single word to correct me.

She rested against the bar in an elegant way with make-up on, which enhanced a perfect white smile that would have made any toothpaste company proud. She was tall and slim and well dressed, and we could not help thinking that she was a prostitute waiting for a pick up from a hotel guest.

One by one we went up to the room for a shower and when we were all ready we decided to head out for a T-bone steak at the Spur restaurant which was run by a South African.

First things first, we ordered a round of beers and said a quick 'cheers' before taking a gulp and smiling the smile of contentment that an ice cold beer can give in the heat of Africa.

After a short wait we each had a big steak in front of us with a beer on the side to go with it.

Enjoying the moment and getting a little plastered I was amazed to see all the African waiters converge on our table.

Then with beautiful voices and rhythmic clapping they proceeded to sing happy birthday to me.

I looked at Laurence with a 'what the hell' look. He looked back and laughed, having put me on the spot for a two month earlier than expected celebration.

What a feeling it gave me to see these people giving their all with such harmony and joy, all for me at the supposed day of my birth. Little did they know that we had gained a free ice-cream in a tall glass with a dashing sparkler flickering and hissing in the darkened room. Enjoying the moment we were in fits of hysterical laughter and it certainly marked a night to remember.

Drunk and staggering out we drove to Coconuts for some very loud music in a local club filled with young people dancing and enjoying the night. Here we were in a country where the capital looked more like war torn Lebanon, with the infrastructure in a shambles and some of the people dirt poor. And yet in the club it was as though this was not the same country where these people had hope and enjoyed life with a bright future.

At 3am we arrived back at the hotel and passed out.

Blurry eyed and dying of thirst I awoke to find that my money belt had vanished, either stolen or lost on the previous night's beer run.

I hunted through my bag and then went down to Wayne's Colt *bakkie* where I continued my search to no avail.

Tired and dispirited I lay on my bed resigned to the fact that it had gone. With my hands under my head as I lay back staring at the ceiling, I wondered how I would get out of the country with no passport. Moving my hand under the pillow I felt this lump which I grabbed at and miraculously pulled out my money belt.

'Okay, I just bullshitted. Here it is!' I said which had Wayne laughing.

Now richer by nine red big ones I agreed to treat all of us to a breakfast at Steers. The greasy eggs, bacon and toast and bottomless coffee did wonders for our hangovers.

At noon we headed out along the coast to a resort run by a Portuguese South African and another fellow from Pietermaritzburg.

We got talking to them about the state of Mozambique and then the conversation turned to prisons.

'Stay well clear of prisons, especially the notorious Machava,' they instructed us and then added, 'Machava can break a person in three months.'

I looked at them and then back at Laurence, without uttering a word about Laurence's hell that broke him in the very place they had just mentioned.

With Wayne and Laurence hitting back the beers I stuck with Fanta's as I nursed my severe hangover that seemed to worsen with the heat. Sitting on the concrete ledge we overlooked the beach which seemed very odd and open with the tide far out.

African salesmen continually came up to us and bugged the hell out of us as they showed off their works of art from wooden carvings to paintings, and sunglasses to CD's hoping to make a sale for a few Rands or Meticus.

It did not take long to say 'Foekoff' which they seemed to understand as a verbal signal to literally fuckoff.

Sipping my Fanta I watched a gang of sweating fishermen in a tug of war with their nets as they pulled their catch ashore arm over arm. Unfortunately it produced more seaweed than fish much to everyone's disappointment.

In the late afternoon we took a drive along the coast enjoying the rustic beauty of a colonial city abandoned decades ago by its Portuguese colonists. I could visualize how magical it must have been when it was still called Lourenzo Marques, with the same palm trees lining a beautiful coastline. We stopped to look at a tree standing a metre off the ground with its roots totally eroded of all soil and looking every bit as though the roots were uprooting the tree from the earth.

We decided to stop in at the famous Polana Hotel which was built in 1922 and which had been totally restored to its former glory. It offered a spectacular view over the ocean and with the view, the grounds and the elegance of such a place we all realized we would never be able to afford a night here. Again, the contrast of Africa came into play with this out of reach getaway in paradise compared with a tin hut with a smouldering fire and a family literally living on scraps of food.

On the way back to the Hotel Ibis we watched the sun sinking through a line of palm trees marking another splash of beauty in this dysfunctional part of majestic Africa.

At the hotel we made straight for the bar and had a cold one each before taking it in turns to run up to the room for a shower and a change, with another beer served to the fresher looking man while the next left for a cleanup.

Sitting at the bar we reminisced about the day's events and those of the past days which quickly turned to those of yesteryear back in the army, which seemed like only yesterday.

Our laughter wiped away all anger and hatred as we delved into a life that no sane man would volunteer for. The conversation touched on stupid accidents and really close calls that could so easily have claimed a few lives, and thanks to our intense training and discipline we had side stepped a few negative statistics.

After a few more beers at the bar with the 'Laurintina's' flowing, we met a coloured man from Cape Town who was an aide to Nelson Mandela. After some great stories we heard that 'Madiba' was actually in Mozambique with his wife Grace, the former wife of Samora Machel, who had died very mysteriously in a plane crash on South African soil in 1986.

Hungry, we left for the same bar that we had hung out for the day and ordered three plates of LM prawns, which unfortunately proved no match for those at Costa Del Sol.

We ate in the upper story of the wooden bar watching a Portuguese game of soccer on the big screen. After dinner we returned to the lower deck and enjoyed a few more beers while watching a big rat running back and forth along the side of the low wall scavenging for food. It was a restaurant and yet none of the paying patrons complained about the lack of hygiene. This was Africa and one had to always expect the unexpected.

We were suddenly ripped from our relaxed positions as two shots from an AK-47 splintered the calm.

Looking outside we saw all the commotion and ventured closer towards a group who were crowded around a security guard and a policeman. After a heated discussion the group dispersed, climbing into their cars and speeding away.

Totally at ease as if we had just got a breath of fresh air we returned to finish off our beers, and then headed back to the hotel.

Wayne parked in the reserve parking, as the security guard moved the stand up metal markers reserving the parking spots for the hotel guests. Once we had parked we were told to move around the corner

which worried us, with the threat of theft a hundred times greater. I spotted a parking place close to the traffic light and stood there marking it, but to my surprise another *bakkie*
pulled in and snatched it from right under my nose.

I tried to reason with the parking thief, but to no avail, forcing Wayne to drive round the corner and park in a darkened row totally out of sight from our normal car guards.

'Who's this poesie that stole my parking?' Wayne shouted out in anger. The culprit immediately heard the comment and retaliated: 'Who's calling me a poesie?' he challenged as he stared Wayne down.

I noticed the African man was wearing a T-shirt with a Zimbabwean flag, which signified that he was not a local. Laurence came to the rescue with some quick thinking.

'He said, who's pushing in, not poesie!' as he tried to simmer down the anger that was reaching boiling point.

It continued to heat up as we entered the reception area while we both tried to calm the two down. It was not going to subside unless one walked away, and so Wayne and myself took the lift to our room and left Laurence behind as the peacemaker.

Finally at 2:30am Laurence stumbled into the room after an excessive drinking night with the African man who had stolen the parking space. He in fact was not Zimbabwean but Angolan, and was here for business and pleasure.

On Sunday in the late morning we picked Miguel up and drove to where he lived, taking along two bags containing shirts, pens and paper and little odds and ends that I had brought from Canada.

His home was as I expected it, a picture of Africa with poverty etched into the abode and the rural neighbourhood with a mix of faces looking on inquisitively.

The hollow eyes reflected resignation and despair and yet a light of hope burned like a candle as they stared across the dusty road at us, three white men and Miguel the African.

We walked down a pathway towards his home passing pieces of corrugated iron standing as fences, along with branches speared into the ground. Twisted strands of wire held the pieces together from blowing down in the wind. After a minute walk we stepped through an opening in the fence and into a grassless patch of earth and before us stood

Miguel's home. It was a one roomed house built with rectangular ash blocks of all shapes and sizes with cement plastered at will wherever the builder thought it necessary. There was a window opening crisscrossed with bars with not a single pane of glass. The corrugated iron roof was held down by rocks, bricks and the odd rubber tyre. All the house needed was a heavy wind and it would fold like a pack of cards.

He was proud and showed us around, pointing to two plastic chairs and an old wooden one that made up the living room, and then a small table and a cooking pot that was the kitchen. The bed was a few blankets on the concrete floor. The toilet was outside, barricaded by a bamboo screen and was a hole in the ground with a rubber tyre circling it, which was the toilet seat. The scene was depressing and worse than any of our servants quarters back home in South Africa. Miguel had lost his parents at a young age and was the breadwinner at 15 years old and a parent to his younger brother. Again it was survival of the fittest where misery was inflicted on the poorest of the poor. If the war hadn't got them, sickness and Aids would.

Back at the truck we started to throw shirts to people who snatched them up like no tomorrow. It was a fight to see who got one, rather than smiles of joy at what these three white men were doing. When it was time to throw pens and pencils to the wind all hell broke loose. Pens were ripped from our hands, and Africans were knocked to the ground as they charged off to retrieve a pen lying unclaimed in the soil. It was gratifying and yet so sad to see people deprived of the basics needed for an education. It was a pleasure to watch a grubby little girl's face light up as she watched Spider Man ascend a tall building as I flicked with speed through a small booklet of sequences.

Once the turmoil had subsided those with treasures guarded them like vultures with their carrion. It was no wonder as there was not a single toy in this community.

In their eyes we were Father Christmas, and Christmas for them had come eight months early.

Miguel got a call on his cell phone and then relayed the message to us. It was his neighbour asking if we had any more shirts, but unfortunately they were gone and already proudly worn with the logo of Presidents Choice advertising in red and blue for the third world of Mozambique to see.

After some painstaking organization we managed to round up 15 people for a photo, all clad with their new shirts. It was shocking to see the contrast, a brand new shirt above the waist and a torn dress, or ripped pants and dirty dusty feet on the lower half.

In the photo group there was an albino woman, glaring with her sensitive eyes as she shielded her blistered pinkish white skin. How she survived this harsh unrelenting heat was a mystery to me.

In South Africa I remembered a saying that I had learned during the structured world of apartheid.

'Do you know why God created an albino? To show the blacks how ugly they would look if they were white.'

Sadly it always got a huge racist laugh and yet today I find it mind-boggling how such a comment could be uttered without thinking twice about its obscenity.

I also knew that albinos were not well received amongst their own people, branded by most as evil. Most of them were ostracized or worse, killed at birth for their odd skin colour.

In Tanzania they are hunted down and killed for their organs and bones, which are ground down into powder and given out as potion by witch-doctors to ward off evil and bring good luck to other blacks.

I wondered on what scale of fear she lived day to day on top of the filth and poverty that greeted her with each sunrise.

At least our small handout had brought a smile and a story to temporarily cover the hardship.

The next morning we were rudely awoken by Miguel who had entered the hotel and got the reception to call us down. Shortly after 9 am Wayne and I met Miguel in the lobby and headed out on our prearranged second trip to the prison. Laurence had told us that there was no way he was ever going back there, even if it was to look at the sinister place from a distance.

The guard towers of Machava loomed like lighthouses towering above the walls with slits and broken windows from which the guard was meant to watch the outside world. Rows of lighting ran along the length of the wall evenly spaced like scarecrows with burned out and broken bulbs along with a spiderweb of matted wires. One could clearly see that light had not shone from these tall fixtures in many a long year. The walls looked overpowering and very cold and grey.

Bricks were missing from the guard towers and lookout windows were broken leaving shards of glass as a further unwelcoming sign to this neglected and evil prison. It was every bit like an old Portuguese fort, except that the pristine look that the colonists had brought to this country had long vanished into squalid ruin like all the architecture in Maputo. The palm trees standing like giant criminals behind the walls were the only beauty in this most depressing scene.

Having been as close as we could ever get to Laurence's hellish nightmare, we headed back to the hotel imagining what it must have been like for him, trapped and caged in darkness beyond those walls. Soon they became lost from view and another row of rundown buildings and shacks captured our vision.

We did not see a single dog, cat or even a bird for they had all been hunted out and killed for food as the people did what they had to do, to survive in Africa's poorest land.

Back at the hotel we collected Laurence and went to a Bank so that Wayne could withdraw money. In the meantime Laurence and I wandered over to a very well kept Portuguese fort with a treasure trove of relics, from cannons protruding from the red walls to wagons and inscriptions in Portuguese.

Laurence was delighted to see one of his Afrikaner forefathers riding a bronze horse, forever in history as part of the Great Trek as the wagons made their way north to this Portuguese enclave.

After a nice walk around the old fort we made our way across the road and met Wayne as he exited the bank with a bulging wallet of Meticas. Comfortably in the truck we navigated our way through the potholed and crowded streets with cars coming at us from all directions. We squinted our eyes for a sign that read Xai-Xai and when we spotted it Wayne swerved and cut through a slow line of traffic so that we could stay on course to get to a place called Bilene along the beautiful Mozambican coast.

The roads were good with little transport activity besides a burned-out land rover and a car that had been wrapped around a tree.

Time went quickly and we passed the turnoff to Bilene, not realizing that we should have been looking for a town called Marcia. After a few kilometres of back-tracking we followed a road that led us to the most stunning white sandy beach that I had ever seen with an ocean

Tim Ramsden

a brilliant turquoise. It was again so hard to believe that such beauty could excist in a country as filthy and decrepit as Mozambique.

I watched a few fishermen push their boats out to sea with their nets layered in the hull as they hoped to earn a meal and money.

We sat outside a small restaurant under an umbrella made of thatch resting on a pole that shielded us from the blow-torch of heat from the sun. With a beer in hand we chatted and laughed and enjoyed the peace without a care in the world. The only bother were a few locals who saw our white skins as money and pestered us no end to buy a few curios. Laurence caved in and bought a couple of things to take back to loved ones.

I took a walk along the beach towards the sea and had to side step past some sharp shards of glass that littered the glistening white sand. It was a pity that the beauty was tarnished but it was just another indication of what the country was see sawing through.

After a good lunch consisting of another round of beer and a burger and chips we began the trip back to Maputo. We passed numerous police checkpoints who randomly signalled drivers to pull over, but luckily this time it was not us. For sure we were all over the limit as far as alcohol intake was concerned.

We got the fright of our lives as a truck hurtled past us on this single lane road and then cut back in front of us, nearly creating a head on collision with a car in the opposite lane. It was a close call and just showed the third world driving skill that used these potholed roads.

We hit Maputo at 6pm and lined up in the traffic in gridlock with frustration playing through the hooter. While we idled along we passed a Russian troop carrier loaded with soldiers and even though we did not comment, this had been us on all too many occasions as we sat like sardines packed tight in a tin can.

Once back at the Ibis we washed and decided on the Spur for dinner, and with a rack of ribs in our minds we quickly set off. Beers and ribs, we tucked in and ate like kings, paying for the first rack and then eating for free. With three racks behind us and umpteen beers we settled the bill and returned to the hotel for an early night.

On entering the reception area Laurence was quick to point out a white man that looked the spitting image of Engelbrecht, a person from Durban who had been in our company in 1 SAI. He was considered by us to be a total waste of white skin and an oxygen thief. We all immediately saw the resemblance and laughed as we connected back to that time in our lives that had such a hold over us.

Packing our belongings we got ready for an early departure, and an unusually early night.

In the morning we paid the bill along with an unexpected bar tab that had somehow avoided us until now. Our gear was loaded into the *bakkie* and we were ready to hit the road. The security guards who had watched the truck for the last few days were there to wave a farewell to us and in thanks we gave them a combination of Rands and Meticas adding up to around R50. They held their hands out graciously as we filled their worn palms and were rewarded with wide open ivory-white smiles that said it all. One thing was for sure, they would be celebrating tonight with weeks of wages paid to them in one day.

We found our way out of Maputo easily passing the likes of Karl Marx and Lenin Avenues, stopping one last time for petrol before we journeyed to Swaziland. After a few hours of interesting driving we drove through the Mozambique border post at Boanne, half expecting to be searched and pay duty on our curios. After our passports were stamped we were cleared into Swaziland and after another round of frustrating customs duties we were permitted into Swaziland, but not before I was ordered to pay R5 car entry fee.

It was amazing how the roads could be so vastly different over a border crossing where one African land was running a better economy than another and also where one country had just ended decades of civil war. Swaziland was so much cleaner and free of the hardship that the Mozambicans were toiling with daily.

We saw animals on the side of the road and immediately we were struck by the fact that we had not seen a single cow, goat, donkey or bird in Mozambique, besides a few wild looking stray dogs. It was a fact that what walked or flew was eaten.

After getting a little lost in a small town, we were thankfully pointed in the right direction by following the car in front of us. We soon found ourselves at Golela after taking the slightly longer route. We had arrived at the border post where we exited from Swaziland into South Africa. After a normal quick search and a stamp of the passport we were free to drive on the best roads in Africa and back into the land of our births. It always makes me proud to step back on South African soil and be in this magical land again.

At Mkuze we stopped for a well deserved Wimpy breakfast, sitting on wooden benches outside the small restaurant. Coffee was hot and very rewarding and the breakfast definitely did the trick before we clambered back in the truck, filled up with petrol and set our sights on Richards Bay. After a shorter drive we arrived at Laurence's sister's house and after a quick hello to his sister and a firm handshake from Wayne and me, we said our goodbyes to Laurence.

In the late afternoon we arrived at Umhlanga, Wayne's hometown where we said our see you laters, as we would be seeing each other again before I flew back to Canada.

The time together had been amazing as we reconnected and laughed in the present about the past and we spoke of what we had done, seen and learned since those old army days.

We had all grown up and matured with life's challenges and it was clearly evident that Laurence had struggled with his experience in Machava.

Laurence had allowed me to write his story into my book on our National Service and I thank him for that, because it not only told his story but it paved the way for our little reunion in Mozambique.

LOOKING BACK

S itting on the plane on my way back to Canada my mind drifted into the past, back to my years when I was an avid and hardcore backpacker. I smiled thankfully at the experience I had carved out for myself.

I had crossed many borders by foot, in vehicles and on trains and had travelled beyond the normal places on the average tourist's to do list. I had seen the people, lived like the people, eaten with the people and trusted them when I entered their homes. I had smelt the smells, seen the colours and contrasts, and heard the noise that each culture is enveloped in, and tasted the food and drank the beer of each country I passed through. I had experienced the good times and some very difficult bad times in my quest to backpack beyond the realm of safe organized travel. There was no internet, lap-top computers, cell phones, Blackberrys and instant messaging; my Lonely Planet was my map and resource guide to get me through my travels with pay phones and gut instinct directing me to accommodation.

Backpacking had taught me tolerance whereby I had come to an understanding and for the most part a deep trust of all these cultures and their plights that crossed my path.

I had exposed myself to the hardships with limited funds and I had encountered language barriers all too often. My life was on my back, an old beaten up blue backpack, torn, straps knotted and zips held together with wire to keep them working. The old South African flag proudly sewn onto it to show my allegiance to my country, which no one that I came across had ever seen. Years later I got hold of a new flag and replaced the old one linked to apartheid with the new colourful Rainbow Nations. Throughout my travels I was immensely proud of my country in spite of the horrific apartheid past which should not be forgotten but definitely forgiven. I am proud that I never once lied where I was from, even though we got a bad rap by many countries and their citizens.

I had been a narrow minded South African with pent up anger, thanks to my two and a half years in the SADF, when I left the shores of Durban for an adventure overseas. But today I am a man filled with respect and compassion with a tolerance for others who cross my path from all walks of life. Religion, culture, race make this world a melting pot of intrigue and interest and if we took the time to understand people better there would be far less trouble and wars in this world.

Someone in Canada once told me: 'Every leader of a country should be a woman. A mother would never send her sons to war!'

The world is beautiful and ugly with greed and corruption, selfless and selfish acts mixed in each society touching the rich and poor, overweight and starving, the sick and the dying and the happy and sad. To see this I had backpacked beyond the borders and had pushed the boundaries, travelling into remote areas off the beaten track, hard to find on a map, in my quest to see the real picture of a country through the eyes of the people and the lens of my cheap camera. I hoped to trap the moment to one day write about it with the help of my journals and bring back to life those wonderful memories.

I am thankful I had the courage to leave my job and step fearfully into the unknown and allow myself to be taken with the wind across parts of the world that one might be lucky to only dream about.

Backpacking and travel had most definitely added perspective to my life, a time in my youth that I hold and cherish firmly in my heart. The backpacking days are over but I am ready for that next travel experience that will always be knocking on my door.

In Canada the president of my company made a speech at a work conference and it had a profound effect on me.

'The future has a strange way of appearing unannounced,' and never in a million years did I think that I would be living in Canada after my backpacking days of trekking through 35 very different countries.

My future had most definitely appeared unannounced.